POEMS AND POETRY

Elisabeth W. Schneider   TEMPLE UNIVERSITY

American Book Company   NEW YORK

Copyright © 1964 by American Book Company
Schneider: *Poems and Poetry.* Manufactured in the United States of America. All rights reserved. No part of this book protected by the copyright hereon may be reprinted in any form without written permission of the publisher.

1 3 5 7 9 EP 10 8 6 4 2

Acknowledgments

Grateful acknowledgment is made to the following publishers and individuals for permission to reprint material which is in copyright or of which they are the authorized publishers:

THE BELKNAP PRESS OF HARVARD UNIVERSITY PRESS: For "The Soul selects her own Society" and "Finding is the first Act," reprinted by permission of the publishers and the Trustees of Amherst College from Thomas H. Johnson, Editor, *The Poems of Emily Dickinson,* Cambridge, Mass.: The Belknap Press of Harvard University Press, Copyright, 1951, '55, by The President and Fellows of Harvard College.

THE BODLEY HEAD LTD.: For "George III" from *Clerihews Complete* by Edmund Clerihew Bentley. Further acknowledgment to T. Werner Laurie, associate company, as publishers.

THE CLARENDON PRESS, OXFORD: For "In der Fremde," "Narcissus," and "Low Barometer" from *Poetical Works* by Robert Bridges.

ABBIE HUSTON EVANS: For "Under Cover" from *Outcrop,* copyright 1928 by Abbie Huston Evans, renewed 1955.

GROVE PRESS, INC.: For "Lethe" from *Selected Poems* by H. D. Published by Grove Press, Inc., copyright © 1957 by Norman Holmes Pearson.

HARCOURT, BRACE & WORLD, INC.: For "Euroclydon," copyright, 1952, by Abbie Huston Evans, and "Fact of Crystal," © 1960 by Abbie Huston Evans, reprinted from her volume *Fact of Crystal* by permission of Harcourt, Brace & World, Inc. For "The Embankment" and "Conversion" from *Speculations* by T. E. Hulme, reprinted by permission of Harcourt, Brace & World, Inc. "nobody loses all the time," copyright, 1926, by Horace Liveright, renewed 1954, by E. E. Cummings, reprinted from *Poems 1923-1954* by E. E. Cummings by permission of Harcourt, Brace & World, Inc. For "The Love Song of J. Alfred Prufrock," "Rannoch, by Glencoe," "Journey of the Magi," "Burnt Norton," and "Marina" from *Collected Poems of T. S. Eliot,* copyright, 1936, by Harcourt, Brace & World, Inc. and reprinted with their permission.

HARVARD UNIVERSITY PRESS: For "Of Jeoffry, His Cat" from *Jubilate Agno* by Christopher Smart. Reprinted by permission of the publishers, Cambridge, Mass.: Harvard University Press, 1954. Re-edited from the Original Manuscript by W. H. Bond.

HOLT, RINEHART AND WINSTON, INC.: For "Dust of Snow," "After Apple-Picking," "Fire and Ice," "Nothing Gold Can Stay," "Stopping by Woods on a Snowy Evening," and "Desert Places" from *Complete Poems of Robert Frost.* Copyright 1923, 1930, 1939 by Holt, Rinehart and Winston, Inc. Copyright 1936 by Robert Frost. Copyright renewed 1951 by Robert Frost. Reprinted by permission of Holt, Rinehart and Winston, Inc. For "We'll to the woods no more," "Lancer," "The rain, it streams on stone and hillock" and "Easter Hymn" from *Complete Poems* by A. E. Housman. Copyright 1922 by Holt, Rinehart and Winston, Inc. Copyright 1936 by Barclays Bank Ltd. Copyright renewed 1950 by Barclays Bank Ltd. Reprinted by permission of Holt, Rinehart and Winston, Inc. For "To an Athlete Dying Young," "When smoke stood up from Ludlow," and "Bredon Hill" from "A Shropshire Lad"—Authorized Edition—from *Complete Poems* by A. E. Housman. Copyright © 1959 by Holt, Rinehart and Winston, Inc. Reprinted by permission of Holt, Rinehart and Winston, Inc.

HOUGHTON MIFFLIN COMPANY: For "You Andrew Marvel" from *Collected Poems of Archibald Macleish.*

ALFRED A. KNOPF, INC.: For "The Death of a Soldier," "Domination of Black," "Sunday Morning," "Disillusionment of Ten O'Clock," and "The Snow Man," copyright, 1923, 1951 by Wallace Stevens. For "Autumn Refrain" and "The Idea of Order at Key West," copyright, 1936 by Wallace Stevens. For "Asides on the Oboe" and "The Candle a Saint," copyright, 1942 by Wallace Stevens. For "The Motive for Metaphor," copyright, 1947 by Wallace Stevens. All the preceding reprinted from *The Collected Poems of Wallace Stevens* by permission of Alfred A. Knopf, Inc.

LITTLE, BROWN AND COMPANY: For "After great pain a formal feeling comes," copyright 1929, © 1957 by Mary L. Hampson, from *The Complete Poems of Emily Dickinson,* by permission of Little, Brown and Co.

THE MACMILLAN COMPANY: For "Waiting Both," reprinted with permission of the publisher from *Collected Poems* by Thomas Hardy, copyright 1925 by The Macmillan Company, renewed 1953 by Lloyds Bank Ltd. For "No Second Troy," "The Cold Heaven," and "That the Night Come," copyright 1912 by The Macmillan Company, renewed 1940 by Bertha Georgie Yeats. For "The Three Beggars" and "The Magi," copyright 1916 by The

Macmillan Company, renewed 1944 by Bertha Georgie Yeats. For "The Wild Swans at Coole," "The Balloon of the Mind," "Under the Round Tower," and "The Hawk," copyright 1919 by The Macmillan Company, renewed 1946 by Bertha Georgie Yeats. For "The Second Coming," copyright 1924 by The Macmillan Company, renewed 1952 by Bertha Georgie Yeats. For "Sailing to Byzantium," "Leda and the Swan," and "Among School Children," copyright 1928 by The Macmillan Company, renewed 1956 by Bertha Georgie Yeats. For "Byzantium," copyright 1933 by The Macmillan Company, renewed 1961 by Bertha Georgie Yeats. For "Meru," copyright 1935 by The Macmillan Company. For "The Great Day" and "The Circus Animals' Desertion," copyright 1940 by Georgie Yeats. For "Cuchulain's Fight with the Sea," "The Lake Isle of Innisfree," and "The Host of the Air," copyright 1906 by The Macmillan Company, renewed 1934 by William Butler Yeats. All the preceding reprinted with permission of the publishers from *Collected Poems* by W. B. Yeats. For "England," "To a Steam Roller," and "The Fish," reprinted with permission of The Macmillan Company from *Collected Poems* by Marianne Moore, copyright 1935 by Marianne Moore. For "Mr. Flood's Party," reprinted with permission of The Macmillan Company from *Collected Poems* by E. A. Robinson, copyright 1921 by Edwin Arlington Robinson, renewed 1949 by Ruth Nivison.

NEW DIRECTIONS: For "Ancient Music," "The Lake Isle," "The River-Merchant's Wife: A Letter," "Lament of the Frontier Guard," and "Salutation the Second" from *Personae: The Collected Poems of Ezra Pound*, copyright 1926, 1954 by Ezra Pound, reprinted by permission by New Directions, Publishers. For "After the Funeral" and "Fern Hill" from *The Collected Poems of Dylan Thomas*, copyright 1939, © 1957 by New Directions, reprinted by permission of New Directions, Publishers.

RICHARD O'CONNELL: For "Sea Turtle" from *Four New Poets* (Contemporary Poetry XVII).

OXFORD UNIVERSITY PRESS, INC.: For "Museums," "Sunday Morning," and "Bagpipe Music" from *Eighty-Five Poems* by Louis MacNeice, © 1959 by Louis MacNeice, reprinted by permission of Oxford University Press, Inc.

OXFORD UNIVERSITY PRESS, LONDON: For "The Sea and the Skylark," "The Windhover," "Pied Beauty," "Felix Randal," "No worst, there is none," "I wake and feel the fell of dark," "My own heart let me more have pity on," "That Nature Is a Heraclitean Fire," "Thou art indeed just, Lord," "To R. B.," "Heaven-Haven," and the fragment "Strike, churl" from *Poems of Gerard Manley Hopkins*. Also for twelve lines from Hopkins's *Notebooks* (1937 ed.).

RANDOM HOUSE, INC.: For Part I of "In Memory of W. B. Yeats," copyright 1940 by W. H. Auden; for "Look, stranger, on this island now," copyright 1937 by W. H. Auden; for "Pur," copyright 1934 and renewed 1961 by W. H. Auden; for "Musée des Beaux Arts," copyright 1940 by W. H. Auden. All the preceding reprinted from *The Collected Poetry of W. H. Auden*, by permission of Random House, Inc. For "What I expected," and "I hear the cries of," copyright 1934 and renewed 1961 by Stephen Spender, reprinted from *Collected Poems 1928-1953*, by Stephen Spender, by permission of Random House, Inc. For "The Inquisitors," copyright 1948 by Robinson Jeffers, reprinted from *The Double Axe and Other Poems*, by Robinson Jeffers, by permission of Random House, Inc.

CHARLES SCRIBNER'S SONS: For "Miniver Cheevy" (Copyright 1907 Charles Scribner's Sons; renewal copyright 1935,) reprinted with the permission of Charles Scribner's Sons from *The Town Down the River* by Edwin Arlington Robinson. For "Question," reprinted with the permission of Charles Scribner's Sons from *Another Animal: Poems* by May Swenson, copyright 1954 May Swenson (*Poets of Today* I).

HARRISON SMITH: For "The Hermit" from *Collected Poems* by W. H. Davies published by Cape & Smith.

THE SOCIETY OF AUTHORS: For "The Listeners," "The Ghost," "The Old Men," "Old Shellover," "At the Keyhole," "The Mocking Fairy," "Peak and Puke," and "The Song of Finis" from *Collected Poems 1901-1918* by Walter de la Mare. For "Maerchen" and "The House" from *Poems 1919 to 1934* by Walter de la Mare. Permission granted by The Literary Trustees of Walter de la Mare and The Society of Authors as their representative.

MRS. HELEN THOMAS: For "Gallows," "Out in the Dark," and "The New House," by Edward Thomas.

VANGUARD PRESS, INC.: For "Said King Pompey" copyright 1954; "Dark Song" and "The Little Ghost Who Died for Love" copyright 1949, 1954; and "Heart and Mind" copyright 1946, 1954, reprinted by permission of the publisher from *The Collected Poems of Edith Sitwell*.

Prefatory Note

The arrangement of this book rests upon two convictions, the first a belief that it is both desirable and possible to employ a critical and largely inductive approach to poetry without losing sight of chronology altogether, the second a conviction that while ultimately the object of attention is the individual poem as a self-contained work of art, much is to be gained from seeing the poem in relation to other poems written by the same author. As with a one-man exhibition of paintings, the separate work becomes both more intelligible and more memorable through the presence of others wrought in the same idiom. For this reason the long final chapter is devoted to groups of poems by a number of writers whose special idioms render this kind of treatment particularly advantageous. The representation is unequal, Donne and Yeats, for example—and in an earlier chapter the sonnets of Shakespeare—being more fully represented than others that may be thought comparable. The justification is—or so one hopes—that the interested reader, seeing how much a few writers gain from a moderately generous sampling, may go on to explore the work of these and other poets for himself.

The Text and Notes

I have followed the texts of standard editions, some of which do and others of which do not modernize spelling and punctuation; and I have not altered these for the sake of consistency within this volume. To tamper with standard texts without in all cases consulting the early printings and manuscript versions is to court at least an occasional gross error. The reader will therefore find here some sixteenth-century poems in modern dress and some not. In a few of the older poems only, where the best text reproduces spelling so archaic as to hinder smooth reading, I have modernized the spelling.

Brief notes explaining unfamiliar words and allusions are printed at the foot of the page, extended notes and discussions at the end of the volume. Many of the latter are integral parts of the chapters to which they refer and are applicable to other poems besides the single one to which they are attached; but even so it has been thought best to subordinate them to the poetry by retiring them rather than to risk printing a volume in which the poems float in a sea of pedagogical prose.

No notes are provided for words and names that are adequately explained in standard collegiate dictionaries. On the other hand, believing that a volume of this kind does not further the reader's interest in poetry by being made an exercise in library reference work, I have tried throughout to provide necessary information not readily available in the average reader's own library.

The critical notes vary in dimension, some poems being treated rather fully, others briefly, with hints for further study. Some poems are left for the reader to explore independently. It has seemed best to furnish detailed discussions throughout the volume wherever particular poems seemed to call for them or where special points called for illustration. After careful consideration, this course has appeared preferable to an arrangement by which the reader receives close guidance in the first part of the book and none at all later.

Acknowledgments

This book and its author owe a debt of gratitude to friends and colleagues whose advice and expert knowledge have been freely and most profitably drawn upon. I have imposed perhaps most of all upon the kindness of Abbie Huston Evans, Mabel P. Worthington, and Charles Irwin Griggs; scarcely less upon others equally generous. I am also greatly indebted to the staff of the Sullivan Memorial Library for their unfailingly skillful and courteous assistance.

E.W.S.

Contents

ACKNOWLEDGMENTS ii

PREFATORY NOTE v

INTRODUCTION, including   1

SIR JOHN SUCKLING	*Why so pale and wan, fond lover?*	12
SIR PHILIP SIDNEY	*With how sad steps, O Moon, thou climb'st the skies*	15
WILLIAM SHAKESPEARE	*Sonnet No. 64*	17
WALTER DE LA MARE	*The House*	27

I   CHARACTERS AND NARRATIVES   33

RUDYARD KIPLING	*Tommy*	34
	The Vampire	36
EDWIN ARLINGTON ROBINSON	*Mr. Flood's Party*	37
	Miniver Cheevy	39
E. E. CUMMINGS	*nobody loses all the time*	40
THOMAS HOOD	*Sonnet, On Mistress Nicely, a Pattern for Housekeepers*	42
CHRISTOPHER SMART	*Of Jeoffry, His Cat*	42
ROBERT BROWNING	*My Last Duchess*	46
	The Bishop Orders His Tomb at Saint Praxed's Church	47
	Soliloquy of the Spanish Cloister	51
ANON.	*Bonny Barbara Allan*	53
ANON.	*Marie Hamilton*	55
ANON.	*The Three Ravens*	57
ANON.	*The Twa Corbies*	58
ANON.	*Sir Patrick Spence*	59
ANON.	*Thomas Rymer*	61
ANON.	*The Cherry-Tree Carol*	63
SIR WALTER SCOTT	*Proud Maisie*	65
WILLIAM COWPER	*The Castaway*	66
SAMUEL TAYLOR COLERIDGE	*The Rime of the Ancient Mariner*	68

viii CONTENTS

WILLIAM BUTLER YEATS *The Host of the Air* 88
  The Three Beggars 90

II METRICAL FORMS 92

ANON. *The Bellman's Song* 95
WILLIAM WORDSWORTH *She dwelt among the untrodden ways* 101
  A slumber did my spirit seal 101
WILLIAM SHAKESPEARE *Fear no more* 102
  Full fathom five 102
ROBERT FROST *Dust of Snow* 103
PERCY BYSSHE SHELLEY *Fragment: A Wanderer* 103
ISAAC WATTS *The Sluggard* 103
WILLIAM BLAKE *The Chimney Sweeper* 104
PERCY BYSSHE SHELLEY *Lines: When the lamp is shattered* 105
A. E. HOUSMAN *Lancer* 106
WALTER DE LA MARE *The Listeners* 107
ANON. *A Lament for Our Lady's Shrine at Walsingham* 108
ROBERT HERRICK *Upon Julia's Clothes* 110
THOMAS HARDY *Birds at Winter Nightfall* 110
WALT WHITMAN *From* Song of Myself 110
  When I peruse the conquer'd fame 111

III PATTERN AND IMAGERY 112

ROBERT BRIDGES *Triolet* 114
ANON. *A Lyke-Wake Dirge* 118
JOHN LYLY *Cupid and my Campaspe played* 119
THOMAS CAMPION *Follow thy fair sun* 120
  Rose-cheekt Laura, come 121
ECCLESIASTES *From Chapter 12* 121
ROBERT HERRICK *Corinna's Going a-Maying* 122
SAMUEL TAYLOR COLERIDGE *Kubla Khan* 124
GERARD MANLEY HOPKINS *Fragment (Strike, churl)* 126
A. E. HOUSMAN *To an Athlete Dying Young* 126
  We'll to the woods no more 127
  Easter Hymn 128
WILLIAM BUTLER YEATS *The Balloon of the Mind* 128
T. E. HULME *The Embankment* 128
  Conversion 129
H. D. *Lethe* 129
MAY SWENSON *Question* 130
DYLAN THOMAS *Fern Hill* 131

IV THE LYRIC 133

ANON.	Sumer is icumen in	134
ANON.	Westron winde, when will thou blow	135
ANON.	Back and side go bare, go bare	135
SIR THOMAS WYATT	To a Lady to Answer Directly with Yea or Nay	139 137
	The Lover Showeth How He is Forsaken of Such as He Sometime Enjoyed	137
THOMAS HOWELL	Who would have thought that face of thine	138
ANON.	Brown is my love	139
CHRISTOPHER MARLOWE	The Passionate Shepherd to His Love	139
(?) SIR WALTER RALEGH	The Nymph's Reply to the Shepherd	140
GEORGE PEELE	Song (Whenas the rye reach to the chin)	141
THOMAS NASHE	Song (Adieu, farewell earth's bliss)	141
WILLIAM SHAKESPEARE	Songs from the plays	
	Spring	141
	Winter	143
	Tell me where is fancy bred	144
	Take, O take those lips away	145
	Come away, come away, death	145
BEN JONSON	Still to be neat, still to be drest	146
GEORGE WITHER	Shall I, wasting in despair	146
SIR JOHN SUCKLING	Out upon it! I have lov'd	148
RICHARD LOVELACE	To Lucasta, on Going to the Wars	148
ROBERT HERRICK	To the Virgins, to Make Much of Time	149
	To Daffodils	149
JOHN MILTON	On Time	150
ANDREW MARVELL	To His Coy Mistress	151
	The Mower to the Glo-Worms	152
	The Mower against Gardens	153
LORD BYRON	Stanzas for Music	154
EMILY DICKINSON	The Soul selects her own Society	155
	After great pain, a formal feeling comes	155
	Finding is the first Act	156
THOMAS HARDY	The Convergence of the Twain	156
	Waiting Both	158
A. E. HOUSMAN	When smoke stood up from Ludlow	158
	Bredon Hill	159
	The rain, it streams on stone and hillock	160
W. H. DAVIES	The Hermit	161
EDWARD THOMAS	The Gallows	162
	The New House	163
	Out in the Dark	163
WALTER DE LA MARE	At the Keyhole	164
	Old Shellover	165
	The Mocking Fairy	165

x CONTENTS

	Peak and Puke	166
	The Old Men	166
	The Ghost	167
	Maerchen	168
EZRA POUND	The River-Merchant's Wife: A Letter	169
	Lament of the Frontier Guard	170
ABBIE HUSTON EVANS	Euroclydon	171
	Fact of Crystal	171
ARCHIBALD MACLEISH	You, Andrew Marvell	173
MARIANNE MOORE	The Fish	174
	To a Steam Roller	175
	England	176
W. H. AUDEN	Look, stranger, on this island now	177
	Pur	178
STEPHEN SPENDER	I hear the cries of evening	179
	What I expected	180
RICHARD O'CONNELL	Sea Turtle	181

V THE SONNET 182

SIR THOMAS WYATT	A Renouncing of Love	183
	The Lover Compareth His State to a Ship in Perilous Storm Tossed on the Sea	184
SIR PHILIP SIDNEY	Leave me, O love, which reachest but to dust	185
MICHAEL DRAYTON	Since there's no help, come let us kiss and part	185
EDMUND SPENSER	From Amoretti	
	34 Lyke as a ship that through the Ocean wyde	186
	75 One day I wrote her name upon the strand	186
WILLIAM SHAKESPEARE	Sonnet 17 Who will believe my verse in time to come	187
	18 Shall I compare thee to a summer's day	187
	19 Devouring Time, blunt thou the lion's paws	188
	29 When in disgrace with fortune and men's eyes	188
	30 When to the sessions of sweet silent thought	189
	33 Full many a glorious morning have I seen	189
	55 Not marble, nor the gilded monuments	190
	57 Being your slave, what should I do but tend	190

60	Like as the waves make towards the pebbled shore	191
62	Sin of self-love possesseth all mine eye	191
65	Since brass, nor stone, nor earth, nor boundless sea	192
71	No longer mourn for me when I am dead	192
73	That time of year thou mayst in me behold	193
86	Was it the proud full sail of his great verse	193
87	Farewell! thou art too dear for my possessing	193
90	Then hate me when thou wilt; if ever, now	194
97	How like a winter hath my absence been	194
98	From you have I been absent in the spring	195
106	When in the chronicle of wasted time	195
116	Let me not to the marriage of true minds	196
121	'Tis better to be vile than vile esteemed	196
129	Th' expense of spirit in a waste of shame	197
130	My mistress' eyes are nothing like the sun	197
138	When my love swears that she is made of truth	198
146	Poor soul, the centre of my sinful earth	198
147	My love is as a fever, longing still	199

JOHN MILTON On the Late Massacre in Piedmont 199
When I consider how my light is spent 200
On His Deceased Wife 200
WILLIAM WORDSWORTH Nuns fret not at their convent's narrow room 201
Composed upon Westminster Bridge, September 3, 1802 201
The World is too much with us 202
Where lies the Land 203

	With Ships the sea was sprinkled	203
	Mutability	204
PERCY BYSSHE SHELLEY	Ozymandias	204
JOHN KEATS	Kean, fitful gusts are whisp'ring here and there	205
	On First Looking into Chapman's Homer	205
	On the Grasshopper and Cricket	206
	On the Sea	206
	When I have fears that I may cease to be	207
	If by dull rhymes our English must be chain'd	207
GEORGE MEREDITH	Lucifer in Starlight	208
ROBERT BRIDGES	Sonnet No. 23	208
ABBIE HUSTON EVANS	Under Cover	209
LOUIS MACNEICE	Sunday Morning	209

VI IRONICAL MODES AND THE GROTESQUE 210

ALEXANDER POPE	The Rape of the Lock	213
	Engraved on the Collar of a Dog, Which I gave to His Highness [Epigram]	237
SIR JOHN HARINGTON	Of Treason [Epigram]	237
JOHN WILMOT, SECOND EARL OF ROCHESTER	Epitaph on King Charles II	238
WILLIAM BLAKE	[Epigram]	238
	Imitation of Pope: A Compliment to the Ladies	238
ROBERT BURNS	Tam O'Shanter	239
WILLIAM SHAKESPEARE	From Macbeth	246
ANON.	Tom O'Bedlam's Song	249
JOHN WEBSTER	The Madman's Song	251
WALTER SAVAGE LANDOR	Alas, how soon	252
LORD BYRON	[Epigram] The World is a bundle of hay	252
	Who killed John Keats?	252
	Darkness	253
WALTER DE LA MARE	The Song of Finis	255
WILLIAM BUTLER YEATS	The Great Day	256
EDMUND CLERIHEW BENTLEY	George III	256
ROBERT SOUTHEY	The Old Man's Comforts	256
"LEWIS CARROLL"	Father William	257
EZRA POUND	Ancient Music	258
	Salutation the Second	259
	The Lake Isle	260
ROBINSON JEFFERS	The Inquisitors	261
LOUIS MACNEICE	Museums	263
	Bagpipe Music	263

VII ELEGIES, ODES, AND OTHER REFLECTIVE POEMS 266

JOHN MILTON	*Lycidas*	267
WILLIAM WORDSWORTH	*Lines Composed a Few Miles Above Tintern Abbey, on Revisiting the Banks of the Wye* . . .	273
	Ode: Intimations of Immortality from Recollections of Early Childhood	278
SAMUEL TAYLOR COLERIDGE	*Dejection: An Ode*	284
PERCY BYSSHE SHELLEY	*Ode to the West Wind*	288
ALFRED, LORD TENNYSON	*Ulysses*	291
	The Lotos-Eaters	293
MATTHEW ARNOLD	*Dover Beach*	299
	Philomela	300
WALT WHITMAN	*When lilacs last in the dooryard bloom'd*	301
W. H. AUDEN	*Musée des Beaux Arts*	309
	In Memory of W. B. Yeats, Part I	310
DYLAN THOMAS	*After the Funeral*	311

VIII INDIVIDUAL POETS 313

JOHN DONNE	*Song (Go and catch a falling star)*	314
	The Indifferent	315
	The Bait	316
	The Flea	317
	The Triple Fool	318
	The Ecstasy	318
	The Good-Morrow	321
	The Sun Rising	322
	The Anniversary	323
	The Canonization	324
	A Valediction: Forbidding Mourning	325
	The Funeral	327
	The Blossom	327
	Twickenham Garden	329
	A Nocturnal upon St. Lucy's Day; being the Shortest Day	330
	At the round earth's imagin'd corners	331
	If poisonous minerals	332
	Death, be not proud	332
GEORGE HERBERT	*The Collar*	333
	The Pulley	334
	Denial	335
	Peace	336

WILLIAM BLAKE	To the Muses	337
	Mad Song	338
	The Tyger	339
	A Poison Tree	339
	The Sick Rose	340
	Ah Sun-flower!	340
	The Garden of Love	341
	London	341
	The Human Abstract	342
	from Auguries of Innocence	342
	from Milton	343
	Mock on, Mock on, Voltaire, Rousseau	343
	To the Accuser who is The God of This World	344
JOHN KEATS	La Belle Dame sans Merci	344
	Ode to a Nightingale	346
	Ode on a Grecian Urn	348
	To Autumn	350
	Ode on Melancholy	351
GERARD MANLEY HOPKINS	Heaven-Haven	352
	I must hunt down the prize	352
	The Sea and the Skylark	353
	Pied Beauty	354
	The Windhover	354
	Felix Randal	355
	No worst, there is none	355
	I wake and feel the fell of dark	356
	My own heart let me more have pity on	356
	That Nature Is a Heraclitean Fire and of the Comfort of the Resurrection	357
	Thou art indeed just, Lord	358
	To R. B.	359
ROBERT BRIDGES	A Passer-By	359
	London Snow	360
	Nightingales	361
	November	362
	In der Fremde	363
	Narcissus	364
	Low Barometer	365
WILLIAM BUTLER YEATS	The Lake Isle of Innisfree	366
	Cuchulain's Fight With the Sea	366
	No Second Troy	369
	That the Night Come	370
	The Cold Heaven	370
	The Magi	370
	The Hawk	371
	The Wild Swans at Coole	371
	Under the Round Tower	372

	The Second Coming	373
	Leda and the Swan	374
	Among School Children	375
	Sailing to Byzantium	377
	Byzantium	378
	Meru	380
	The Circus Animals' Desertion	380
ROBERT FROST	After Apple-Picking	382
	Fire and Ice	383
	Nothing Gold Can Stay	383
	Stopping by Woods on a Snowy Evening	383
	Desert Places	384
WALLACE STEVENS	Domination of Black	385
	The Snow Man	386
	Disillusionment of Ten O'Clock	386
	Sunday Morning	387
	The Death of a Soldier	390
	The Idea of Order at Key West	391
	Autumn Refrain	393
	The Candle a Saint	393
	Asides on the Oboe	394
	The Motive for Metaphor	395
EDITH SITWELL	Said King Pompey	396
	Dark Song	396
	The Little Ghost Who Died for Love	397
	Heart and Mind	398
T. S. ELIOT	The Love Song of J. Alfred Prufrock	399
	Rannoch, by Glencoe (From "Landscapes")	404
	Journey of the Magi	404
	Marina	405
	Burnt Norton	407

NOTES   413

GLOSSARY OF TERMS COMMONLY EMPLOYED IN VERSIFICATION   500

INDEX OF AUTHORS AND TITLES   505

Introduction

Written language is commonly classified as either prose or verse. Most of it is prose. When words are combined in such a way as to produce a noticeable rhythm, they become verse, either "free" or metrical. This may also be poetry, or it may not, for the term "poetry" implies a judgment of value about verse, an implication that the words are not only rhythmically arranged but have become in some degree a work of art. Beyond this point it is probably best to abandon definition, because the terms "art" and "value" lead into problems of aesthetics and philosophy upon which men have always differed, as they do about religion, the "meaning of life," and other fundamental questions.

Many of the most famous "definitions" of poetry have been in fact not so much definitions as assertions of value or interesting, often enlightening, descriptions of the poet's experience in creating his work. To say that poetry is "the breath and finer spirit of all knowledge," as Wordsworth did, or "the best words in the best order," as Coleridge did, is to assert its superiority rather than to define it. Wordsworth also said, "Poetry is the spontaneous overflow of powerful feelings: it takes its origin from emotion recollected in tranquillity: the emotion is contemplated till, by a species of reaction, the tranquillity gradually disappears, and an emotion, kindred to that which was before the subject of contemplation, is gradually produced, and does itself actually exist in the mind. In this mood successful composition generally begins, and in a mood similar to this it is carried on. . . ." This is a description, derived from introspection, of the way in which Wordsworth's own poems were produced and which he believed to be other poets' creative process as well. Some, but not all, poets have agreed with him.

It may be possible to construct a definition that could be agreed upon as accurate—"a work of art consisting of language arranged in verse form" might do—but this would not tell us anything we did not already know, and it could therefore be of little use. Here it will be more profitable to assume a rough everyday understanding of general terms and to attempt rather to describe what goes into the making of poetry and so perhaps arrive at a more precise working idea of what it is.

Subject and Meaning

Poetry has no subject matter distinct from that of prose. Within even the limited range of this volume there are poems dealing with religion, philosophy, war, death, murder, astronomy, athletics, history; with love, flirtation, happiness, character, success, and failure; with flower, snail, ant, house, machinery. Conceivably, anything of interest to man may be the subject of a poem. Love or sex inspires statistics in Kinsey, fiction in D. H. Lawrence, sonnets in Shakespeare. The distinction lies not in the subject but in the attitude of the writer, in his intention and feeling and, ultimately, in what he does with his subject.

When we decide to read an article or almost any book that is not fiction, we do so primarily to find out what it says. It may contain factual information that we require or find interesting; it may convey opinions which persuade or fail to persuade us. In any case, *what it says*—its substance or direct meaning—is usually what we are after. This is not true, or it is true only in a radically modified way, of poetry. Nearly all, perhaps all, good poems have a meaning. But a "good" meaning does not make a good poem, nor does a "true" meaning, for the poet is not trying to teach the reader facts he did not know or persuade him to support a cause the poet believes in; rather, he is creating something with words that he himself wishes to create, something that did not exist before and that provides men with an extension and deepening of their experience or adds a new dimension to it. A religious reader therefore may quite properly like and approve a gloomy, atheistic poem by Housman, in the first place because it is a good poem, and in the second place because it makes one aware in a vivid, living way of what it is really like to live in a world without hope; and a profoundly skeptical reader may appreciate, without in the least being persuaded by, a poem by Hopkins that is founded on Roman Catholic doctrine.

For most people, the unforgettable moments of life are as incommunicable as they are unforgettable. The very words someone spoke, the tone, the room, may be imprinted with utmost vividness in one's memory, along with the feeling that made the occasion unforgettable. The moment of pride and excitement of the athlete carrying the ball for his greatest achievement may be relived in his memory, sensation for sensation. But rarely can he transfer this experience whole and alive into the mind, emotions, and sensations of another person. As Yeats once observed, a man may work the conversation around till he can casually introduce the name of the woman he loves in order to say it and to hear others talk of her; but the result disappoints him: his companion merely looks abstracted, "as if another name ran in his head." The poet, however, through his power over language, succeeds in communicating the otherwise incommunicable. He does more, for he makes the ever-transitory moments of life permanent—at least for the duration of the language. The passing experience that he has "immortalized" becomes an experience shared with others, with men present and future, illuminating their own experience. It is there on record, to be recaptured, revisited at will.

This is one function of poetry—communication, as we say nowadays, "in depth." Its second and perhaps greatest function, which has to do with form, can best be considered after some account has been given of the primary formal element of verse: rhythm.

Rhythm and Tune

When we open a book at random, the first thing we know about it is that it is prose or that it is verse. The spaced printing tells us this before we have read a word. Though the expensive arrangement on the page is no more than a convention and a convenience, it exists as a sign that the reader may expect something different from ordinary writing and something that must be read differently. It points to two primary elements of verse: first, to rhythm and its necessary concomitant, pause; and second, to the prominence of the individual words and groups of words of which verse is composed. Rhythm, because from earliest times it has been the chief distinguishing mark of verse, should be understood first of all.

Defined simply, it consists of a more or less regular recurrence of something—an event, a movement, a sound. At least two elements or some kind of alternation is required to produce it, for simple continuity cannot be rhythmical. There must be discontinuity or change, sound alternating with silence, motion with immobility, a loud with a softer sound. Innumerable kinds of rhythm occur throughout the world of matter. The reader scarcely needs to be reminded of such large-scale rhythms as the alternation of day and night or the changing seasons. In man also, rhythm is fundamental and instinctive. Most unconscious and half-conscious life processes are rhythmical. We walk and breathe rhythmically. Though with effort we can do both otherwise, the moment we relax our attention, the rhythm returns.

A simple and mechanically regular rhythm, however, quickly becomes intolerable if we pay conscious attention to it. Alone in a room with a loudly ticking clock, we find ourselves unconsciously varying the sound by thinking we hear "tick-tock," though the actual sound is "tick-tick." But this imaginary variation "tick-tock" is still too simple, and soon, to avoid unbearable monotony, we have to stop listening or muffle the clock. Natural as rhythm is and much as we like it, a perfectly regular beat that is forced on our attention bores us and, worse, if we cannot shut it out gets on our nerves, seems to ride or tyrannize over us. We endure it only if we can take control by manipulating it somehow to suit our own will. Thus people in a railroad train, if their mind is otherwise unoccupied, will hear or hum a tune or imagine a series of words to vary the simple meter of the train's noises and to impose on them a more elaborate and less mechanical pattern.

Rhythm is more than a mere habit, however; it is an expressive power as well. Since the rhythms of ordinary speech and written prose are extremely irregular (if they are to be called rhythms at all), any alteration of common language in the direction of increased regularity draws attention. The oratorical spellbinder knows this very well. So, instinctively, does the child in a tantrum. "I — hate — you! — I — hate — you!" he will scream in evenly measured beats, knowing by instinct that loudness alone is not strong enough; he needs rhythm also to express the full force of his hate with satisfaction to himself and sufficient devastation to his mother. It is on this basic but ambivalent human feeling for rhythm that verse is founded. In good poetry, rhythm will be present but will be flexible and varied; it cannot be mechanical or simple.

Individuals differ a good deal in their natural response to rhythm and in their gifts for making use of it, as most people will have noticed in connection with dancing, which in certain respects is analogous to poetry. Nearly everyone has encountered different degrees of skill in social dancing. There is the person with no rhythmic sense at all, who has learned the steps but seems not to hear the music and can do no better than shuffle along, with his steps conforming to the music only now and then by chance. There is the dancer who hears the beat of the music and keeps time with it at every step conscientiously and slavishly; his dancing may be acceptable and correct but is sure to be somewhat dull. Then there is the good dancer, who never loses his sense of the musical rhythm but deals with it creatively and adventurously. He anticipates, delays, syncopates; he plays variations upon it, departs from it for two or three measures for a whirl, returning to pick up the beat again precisely on the dot. This is mastery, and when we see it we like it.

Writers of verse might be classified in the same way, for they range from contributors to local newspapers who sometimes cannot keep time at all, to the great poets, who handle rhythms with utmost mastery. Similarly, readers approach poetry with varying degrees of sensitivity. The inexperienced person may be temporarily pleased by a regular rhythm that will become intolerable to him after a while. He finds it at first "catchy," for it is perceptible without effort.

> I like to look at little John,
> I find him fat and clean.
> I hate to see his sister Jane,
> She looks so thin and mean.

These flat lines are about as regular as verse can be. Every even-numbered syllable is accented, every odd one not. Human speech, it is true, is so varied that scarcely any series of words or syllables, spoken naturally, will produce an exactly mechanical rhythm, and so even in this doggerel there is variation: "John" is more heavily stressed than the preceding stressed syllable, "lit-," and "hate" receives more emphasis than "see." Still, the lines are intolerably mechanical. At the opposite extreme, one may take the familiar line of Shakespeare in which Hamlet is half-contemplating suicide, "To be, or not to be: that is the question." No words, individually, could be more flat. What saves them (in addition to their context) is the rhythmical flexibility that brings out the thought. The first six words are extremely regular, but the strong accent on the key small words makes them emphatic, as the meaning requires: "To bé, or nót to bé." In the next two words the accent is sharply reversed: not, as it might have been written, "To bé,/or nót/to bé:/I múst/decíde/," but "To bé,/or nót/

to bé:/THÁT is/the qués/tion." Special emphasis is placed on "that" by the reversed accent, and afterwards, with the extra light syllable at the end, the line trails off as if in indecision. Shakespeare does not lose the beat in the long run, but he says what he wishes to say, with the emphasis required by the thought, and so he masters the rhythm instead of letting it master him. The result is an expressive line, in spite of a complete absence of intrinsically interesting or vivid words.

Conventional rules of versification, along with imitation and practice, have produced many writers of singsong, pedestrian verse. The rhythm and music of good poetry, however, are as far beyond this in gracefulness, expressiveness, and variety as the fine dancer is beyond the clodhopper who can do no more than keep time. Good poetry, in short, like good dancing, is a satisfying expression of freedom within the bounds of a convention or a form.

The overriding importance of rhythm and other effects of sound, among the fused elements that make up a poem, may be observed in a common nursery rhyme. Few people who have once known it ever forget the old rhyme about "Pease porridge hot,/Pease porridge cold." Yet it seems strange that a grown man should remember these verses when he has forgotten a thousand more interesting, more personal, and more important things that he knew as a child. Frequent repetition is only part of the answer, for he has forgotten many things that he has heard or repeated much oftener. The attraction cannot be in the meaning, for that is so slight as to be almost nonexistent. Though a man may remember the lines for seventy years, he probably does not even know what pease porridge is (perhaps a near relation of split pea soup); and he certainly does not care whether it is hot or cold, since he does not expect to eat it. This is a surprising phenomenon, the almost universal memory, surviving through a lifetime out of the welter of things once known and forgotten, of a trivial statement about an uninteresting and unidentified food.

The explanation is simply that it is good poetry, of a small sort and on its own level. It satisfies, for one thing, the natural liking for a rhythm that is both strongly marked and varied. Though comparatively simple, the rhythm of "Pease Porridge" has surprising variety: no two lines of the stanza are exactly alike. The sounds, moreover, are appropriate, for they are inextricably interwoven with what little meaning there is. The key words "hot" and "cold" are emphasized by pauses and rhyme, "Hot" is a light, quick word, whose sounds cannot be prolonged (try prolonging a *t* sound or even a short *o* sound); it easily coalesces with its meaning: we drop the word as quickly as we would a hot object. "Cold," in contrast, is a long slow syllable, and solid—one might almost say, like congealed porridge. A diagram may be unpoetical but will show something of what is meant.

The accents and timing (the natural reading corresponds to a series of four-bar musical phrases, counting the pauses):

Péase/pórridge/hót/ [—]

Péase/pórridge/cóld/ [—]

Péase/pórridge/ĭn the/pót

Níne/dáys/óld. [—]

The tune: a rising inflection in lines 1 and 3 with staccato endings; a falling in lines 2 and 4 with prolonged endings:

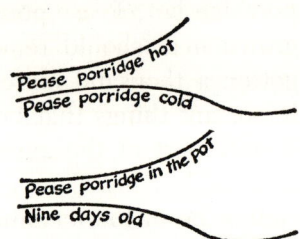

There are larger and smaller units of rhythm in a poem, and there are other elements having to do with sound that play an important, often subtle, part in the effect of the whole. In "Pease Porridge" the smallest units, those indicated with a slant line as feet, each with its single accent, are less important than the rhythmic relation to each other of the lines taken as a whole. These are quite exactly timed. A still larger rhythmic unit is created and made dominant by the presence of another element altogether—the inflection of the sentence, which corresponds roughly in poetry to melody or tune in music. Here an upward inflection of the first and third lines alternating with the downward of the second and fourth creates this larger two-line rhythm. The sound pattern of the opening line is not complete till the fourth line ends, and here again the nursery rhyme illustrates a principle of poetic structure. What goes up, it is said, must come down; and though this may not be strictly true in space, we usually expect it in poetry. Hence the use of stanzas in many poems. The close of the stanza brings to rest a movement of tune, rhythm, and thought that began four lines earlier. Finally, if we add the second stanza to the poem ("Some like it hot . . ."), we shall find the four-line rhythmic unit repeated. This is a very simple poem, yet it has four different rhythms going at once, all fitted within each other like a nest of boxes, and all perceptibly related to each other.

In poetry, rhythm and tune are usually reinforced, as here, by other effects of sound. The poet may employ rhyme to mark the ends of lines, and he nearly always makes use of other kinds of repetition, such as assonance and alliteration. Like rhythm itself, these are a natural development of man's apparently instinctive liking for repetitive echoes. Any child would prefer "Ring a round a Rosy" to "Make a ring about Violet." When Housman writes

> Look into the pewter pot
> To see the world as the world's not,

his rhyme, besides producing a pleasant matching of sounds, emphasizes the meaning. The placing of the negative word last, with an accent and a rhyme, sharpens the epigrammatic turn of thought. In other lines from the same poem,

> And malt does more than Milton can
> To justify God's ways to man,

Housman obviously preferred "malt" to "ale" because its alliteration sharpens the absurd contrast between ale and Milton (who announced in *Paradise Lost* that his purpose was "to justify the ways of God to men"). In these lines rhyme, meter, and alliteration combine to heighten the writer's cynical statement that only when a man is drunk can he think well of the universe. In good verse the texture is enriched by an often intricate linking of these interwoven sound patterns.

Form and Content

Poetry is often said to be more intense than prose, and undoubtedly it is, but not always in the obvious sense. Milton, it is true, condensed into fourteen lines the events of a religious massacre, his own indignation, and his deeply felt prayer that the evil might be turned to good (the sonnet "On the Late Massacre in Piedmont"). On the other hand, Robert Frost wrote with cool detachment about a colt in a field frightened by its first snowstorm. It was not his colt, and he probably did not care enough about it to go and see it again; yet the moment of interest in its fright and the visual image of it running wildly in the snow were enough to make a poem ("The Runaway"). His interest had become so sharply focused that he was able to crystallize his subject, to sharpen and condense it by giving it the point, pith, and emphasis of verse form. The poet Suckling (in "Out upon it," p. 148), who boasts ironically of his faithfulness—he has been in love for three whole days, he says, and if the lady is accommodating he may continue in love for three more—probably does not feel very intensely about his lady. In fact, a moderately good prose thriller will tie its reader into more "intense" knots than most poems will, even if the reader is one who likes poetry better than thrillers.

T. S. Eliot explained that it is not a matter of greatness or intensity in the raw material from which the poem is made but of intensity in "the artistic process, the pressure . . . under which fusion takes place." A very different earlier critic, Hazlitt, wrote that the poetic impulse arises when an experience "takes such a hold of the mind as to make us dwell upon it," when the mind "seeks to prolong and repeat the emotion, to bring all other objects into accord with it, and to give the same movement of harmony . . . to the sounds that express it." Earlier still, Francis Bacon said that poetry "doth raise the mind, by submitting the shows of things [material phenomena] to the desires of the mind; whereas reason doth buckle and bow the mind unto the nature of things." These statements from different points of view all have to do with fusion, harmony, intelligible order—that is, ultimately, with form.

We mentioned to begin with two major functions of poetry, of which the first is communication (of a particular sort, not simply any communication). The second function, more important though dependent on the first and more exclusively a function of the arts, is that of creating order out of chaotic experience by subjecting the materials of life to poetic form. In life, we never know the whole of anything and rarely the end of any story; rarely do we have a sense of completeness in any experience. Life is full of loose ends, blurred issues, irrelevant impulses and crosscurrents; and only rarely do we have a satisfying moment of vision in which all the loose ends for a moment fall into place and we seem to be aware of something, for once, perfectly formed and whole. This is the experience the poet provides. The main function of form in any art is to bestow this kind of completeness upon some aspect of reality and thereby to create a new, ordered reality. This gives pleasure and a sense of illumination also, even when the experience that is brought to order is not one's own—for if it is human it is potentially every man's—and even when the order has been created out of rather trifling experience, where the satisfaction may lie in the ordering more than in what is ordered.

Everyone has experienced the occasional pleasure and pride of having something perfectly shipshape: rows of extra-straight, fine-growing corn in a field; a workbench with tools all in order, bright and sharp; a desk or bureau drawer reorganized so that its former chaos is transformed into perfect and intelligible order; or a muddy and confused situation suddenly seen whole, with vividness and clarity. One dwells upon such things a little longer and more intently and warmly than the practical value alone warrants. A man likes to go out and look at such a field, though looking will not increase its yield or bring him in more money. This dwelling upon something, this pleasure in its perfect fitness or this glimpse of its whole meaning is a brief experience that one would like to preserve and prolong just as it is, with its full flavor and unique quality; one would like if one could to represent or recreate it in a communicable form with every bit of its reality and of one's pleasure in it fully transferable to others. In a good poem this is accomplished. By his mastery over language the poet does it, through the rhythm, the sounds, the images, the completeness and intensity bestowed by poetic form. The experience relished or dwelt upon may be pleasant or unpleasant, great or small, personal or impersonal, actual or imaginary; only it must have been realized to the full. The poet's awareness of it must have been so vivid and his formalizing power so great that the images, sounds, and meaning all become fused.

How light the experience to be ordered may be, as well as what, in part, turns it into a poem, may be illustrated by some verses written by Sir John Suckling in the seventeenth century. They are still read for pleasure, and in fact no poem in English since then has succeeded so well in saying just what this one says. It is the equivalent in words of a cynical, worldly shrug of the shoulders at romantic love—a single highly polished, flippant gesture. What is to be examined now as specifically as possible is the precise relation between the form and the content of this poem.

> Why so pale and wan, fond lover?
>   Prithee, why so pale?
> Will, when looking well can't move her,
>   Looking ill prevail?
>   Prithee, why so pale?

> Why so dull and mute, young sinner?
> Prithee, why so mute?
> Will, when speaking well can't win her,
> Saying nothing do't?
> Prithee, why so mute?
>
> Quit, quit, for shame, this will not move:
> This cannot take her.
> If of herself she will not love,
> Nothing can make her:
> The devil take her!

The poem is constructed from simple elements, and its meaning is perfectly clear at a glance. It contains no figurative language, not one comparison, not even a single image, and only the simplest everyday words. But the effect of the whole is by no means simple. The poet uses two contrasting, indeed half-conflicting, elements of style and form, and almost nothing else, to create the poem. The first element is a casual, conversational tone with inflections and intonations of colloquial speech leading to what amounts to slang in the last line. Not "Why are you so pale?" but more casually, "Why so pale?"; not "cannot" but "can't" and "do't", with its comic imperfect rhyme, "mute"; and finally, "The devil take her!" Other imperfect rhymes —"lover . . . move her" and "sinner . . . win her"—are casual, too. Less easily shown on paper but clearly heard in the poem are the colloquial and casual up-and-down inflections of the sentences, as natural as if they were not in meter at all.

On the other hand, in structure the poem is the opposite of casual; it is artificial and symmetrical. The first two stanzas are identical in rhythm and almost mechanically alike in rhyme and even in grammar. In both, the first and third lines end with feminine (two-syllable) imperfect rhymes; the other three lines in both stanzas have masculine (one-syllable) rhyme. In the third stanza this is reversed, so that the poem begins and ends with double, rather flip, rhymes. The syntax is even more precisely duplicated in the first two stanzas. The first line in each asks a question, with the vocative noun at the end; the second line repeats the question with the end removed and "prithee" inserted at the beginning. The third and fourth lines together ask another question through an identical, artificial formula: "Will," the author begins, but interrupts his syntax immediately at an unnatural point: "Will, when x—— won't do, y—— do?" The fifth line repeats the second exactly. The second stanza, then, is artificially constructed to match the first in almost every particular, so that, as in "Pease Porridge," there is symmetry within symmetry. The third is constructed differently for climax, contrast, and sense. It answers the questions instead of asking another, yet it is tied into the unified form of the whole because some of the preceding structure is retained. The second line again repeats the thought of the first; the third and fourth, as before, are hung up on the suspended grammar of a periodic sentence; and the unfinished, upturned inflections of the preceding stanzas are brought down in the final cadence. By these means the larger units of rhythm and form are related in all three stanzas.

Well, what is the result of this union of opposites, the extremely casual and the extremely artificial? The result is that Suckling has perfectly conveyed the polite shrug of the experienced man of the world, so sure of himself that the most controlled and elaborate pattern of speech comes from him in an offhand, half-contemptuous tone. The easy mastery in his manner, quite as much as the advice he offers, is in ironic contrast with the frustration of the helpless young lover who is in control of nothing. The poem is light, yet it perfectly conveys its gesture. Besides being a momentary comment on a particular young man's dilemma, it dramatizes a more general attitude, that of the realist toward the romantic, the man who would cut his wishes to fit his chances commenting on the man who would not or cannot.

Had the poem been written from the point of view of the lover, its form and tone must have been quite different. The lover's poem might have been, in fact, not unlike the sonnet Sir Philip Sidney addressed to the moon in the century before

INTRODUCTION 15

Suckling wrote. "Is constant love in heaven deemed merely lack of wit?" Sidney asked the moon; and Suckling's man-of-the-world reply would have been "yes." But Sidney is on the lover's side.

> With how sad steps, O Moon, thou climb'st the skies,
> How silently, and with how wan a face!
> What, may it be that even in heav'nly place
> That busy archer his sharp arrows tries?
> Sure, if that long-with-love-acquainted eyes
> Can judge of love, thou feel'st a lover's case;
> I read it in thy looks; thy languisht grace,
> To me that feel the like, thy state descries.
> Then, ev'n of fellowship, O Moon, tell me,
> Is constant love deem'd there but want of wit?
> Are beauties there as proud as here they be?
> Do they above love to be lov'd, and yet
> Those lovers scorn whom that love doth possess?
> Do they call Virtue there ungratefulness?

The poet sets the tempo of the lover's mood with a first line so full of long slow sounds that a slow, heavy rhythm is established at once. He is dwelling upon a mood of sadness colored by resentment, lingering over his unhappiness as if to get used to it without trying to escape. Words and thoughts are bound to each other by the pattern of echoes. Besides the set end-rhyme, which keeps eight lines rhyming with either "skies" or "face" (the Italian sonnet form), alliteration ("*s*ad *s*teps") and assonance ("*cli*mb'st the *sky*") not only bind adjoining words but carry from line to line: "*how sad* ...*cli*mb ... *sky* .../*How silent*ly"; "*Do* they *above love* ... *lov'd* ... *lovers* ... *love doth*." One line begins, "To *me*, that *feel*" and the next, "Then *ev*'n of *fell*owship." To dwell upon something is to cling, return, circle about it; and even the grammar may express the mood of this circling by parallel construction, sometimes with repeated words at the beginning (anaphora): "how sad ... how silently"; "Is ... ? Are ... ?" "Do they ... ? Do they ... ?" All this pattern of sound is brought to bear upon the single unifying image of a lover addressing the moon with a fanciful suggestion of parallel love affairs above and below.

Organic form is the broad term often used to describe such attributes of a poem as we have been discussing. The poem with organic form creates the illusion of having grown inevitably as it is, with the meaning influencing the form and the form the meaning, not as if the meaning were poured into a set, ready-made vessel. Even when the poet employs a fixed form, as Sidney does in his sonnet, this comes to seem as if it were created almost as much from the inside as from the outside; and in the rigid grammatical symmetry of Suckling's poem, form is completely merged with content.

Movement is related to organic form but involves something more, something subtle and difficult, not perhaps to define but certainly to demonstrate. Only gradually do we learn how often its presence is the source of a particularly fine effect or its absence the source of vaguely recognized failure. For a poem to have movement the parts must be related to each other in such a way as to create a sense of progression or suspense. The poem must not die at the end of each line and be started over again with the next. Often a run-on line provides movement by ending at a point of the sentence where there is no pause in the sense. The mind and voice cannot drop or relax but are impelled onward. Certain effects of timing also carry us on: a little time stolen and later paid back, like a *rubato* in music, for the completion of which the mind or ear waits; or a pattern that begins to sound symmetrical and therefore to require completion.

Here again "Pease Porridge" provides an illustration. Its stanza is so written as to make the last line, or some such last line, inevitable, not primarily because of the sense—there being so little of that to begin with—but because the tune and pattern create an expectation of the fourth line and without it the stanza will not do. Having had one rhyme ("hot" and "pot"), the ear expects another; and, the inflection having turned upward twice, one expects it to turn downward a second time and waits unsatisfied till it does. Here it is the form chiefly that produces the movement of suspense. In run-on lines it is the sense that does so. Often it is the grammar, which of course involves the meaning. In the following sonnet by Shakespeare the two units illustrate three kinds of movement. The first sentence is held in grammatical incompleteness and therefore suspense till the end of the twelfth line. The final two lines also form an unbreakable unit, for where the sentence might end (with "death"), the line, and therefore the rhythm, are incomplete, and where the line ends, the sentence runs on.

> When I have seen by Time's fell hand defaced
> The rich proud cost of outworn buried age,
> When sometime lofty towers I see down rased,
> And brass eternal slave to mortal rage;
> When I have seen the hungry ocean gain
> Advantage on the kingdom of the shore,
> And the firm soil win of the wat'ry main,
> Increasing store with loss and loss with store;
> When I have seen such interchange of state,
> Or state itself confounded to decay,
> Ruin hath taught me thus to ruminate
> That Time will come and take my love away.
>   This thought is as a death, which cannot choose
>   But weep to have that which it fears to lose.

A small poem of Housman's (not one of his best) illustrates a slightly different kind of grammatical suspense employed where the subject demands an exaggeration of this kind of movement. It consists of two short stanzas about a youth in a country town who is about to be hanged. He has listened to the town clock striking the quarter hours preceding his hour:

> He stood and counted them and cursed his luck;
> And then the clock collected in the tower
>   Its strength, and struck.

The hard c and ck sounds suggest the preliminary click that clocks make, leaving a second or two of suspense before they strike (*c*ounted, *c*ursed, lu*ck*, *c*lock, *c*olle*c*ted, stru*ck*). The sentence itself is interrupted at an artificial place and so produces suspense till it is completed: "the clock collected"—but a clock does not collect strength; it has it. This first verb is interrupted, waiting till the next line for its object, and it is itself, besides, only a delaying verb. So we are held off by a delay within a delay till the last word. This is all very inconspicuously done, as it must be; if the technique is obvious, the effect is lost. For a far greater poem that secures part of its effect through a similar use of grammatical interruption and delay, the reader should turn to Yeats's "The Magi," p. 370.

It has been impossible to discuss rhythm and other elements of form without speaking of content, and equally impossible to discuss meaning without reference to form. The reason is plain. A poem, even an apparently simple one such as Suckling's, is a complex structure in which meaning and form, sound and sense are woven together inextricably.

The Poet's Language

When language is arranged metrically, words and phrases acquire an individual prominence that they do not receive in ordinary prose. The meter itself calls attention to the words; and pauses, which are more frequent and more marked in verse, draw still further attention, for the reader's mind during a pause rolls back for an instant over the word or phrase just past. This means that the words must be worth the prominence they receive if they are not to seem dull or foolish. In good prose the words accurately represent the writer's meaning. They may be more than just literally accurate, but they are not required to be more. In poetry accuracy is essential but is not enough; it is little more than the beginning, in fact. "When he called me on the telephone" is quite all right in prose if it is what one means. But if a song writer should write, as one did (approximately if not exactly),

When he called me-e-e
On the telephone,

he needs a very good tune to cover up the flatness of the words that have been made conspicuous, syllable for syllable, by rhythm and pause.

Connotation It is not that the poet's language need be unusual in any obvious sense. His words are nearly always familiar. He does not use a medium invented and reserved, like musical tones and musical instruments, specifically for an artistic purpose; he uses language, the common function of which is communication of the practically useful. Everybody employs language, but only now and then is it put together for a poetic purpose.

In their everyday use, words are subject to two somewhat contrary processes. They become freighted with innumerable associations of all sorts, which means that they become rich in power of suggestion. One may write that a man "fell to the earth," "fell to the ground," or "fell in the dirt," and all three expressions may be equally true for the same event. The literal meaning or denotation of "earth," "ground," and "dirt" in this context is the same. Their associations and suggestions, or connotations, however, are different: earth is relatively soft and clean, ground is harder and dirtier, and dirt is dirtiest. "He" fell down, in any case, but of the three words the writer may choose the one that best suggests a particular attitude toward the man and his fall, or the impression the fall is intended to make. And so it is with all except mere connective words, some highly abstract scientific terms, and a few others that are too new or too rare to have gathered many associations.

Everyday speech and writing, however, deface the language almost as much as they enrich it. Words become dull, their distinguishing features rubbed flat by careless, half-accurate everyday use. The poet is almost by definition a man who likes language; and what he does through his fresh awareness of it is to bring out its inherited load of richness and at the same time clear away the incrustations of careless use, so that his words have the value of both fresh bright newness and old rich association.

For example, the expression "glamorous eyes" one would think pretty stale; it has long been a sentimental cliché fit only for a Hollywood magazine, if that. But the poet de la Mare uses it. He precedes it, however, by "stare," a hard unsentimental word, avoiding the more conventional "gaze"; and he employs it to describe not a woman but a moth hovering about a candle: the moth "stares from her glamorous eyes." The worn-out coin "glamorous eyes" is here new-minted, with its stale, cheap associations dusted off by "stares" and by the reader's memory of bug eyes, yet with its original powerful associations remaining. Even if the subject were a woman instead of a moth, the word "stare" would have some power to alter and re-create "glamorous." In general, the context controls the implications of a word, and part of any poet's excellence lies in his power both to enrich the connotations of his words and to screen out unwanted connotations. A second example of real yet scarcely noticeable originality in the use of language occurs in another poet's use of the word "pick" (in the sense of picking flowers or leaves). Instead of an elaborate description of late, cold autumn, W. H. Davies wrote a simple phrase, "the cold, leaf-picking winds of autumn." His originality consisted of nothing more than making winds instead of human beings the picker; yet by this means he conveys a sense of the season with physical, tactual vividness, for the word "picking" directs us, though we are scarcely conscious of the fact, to the very joint at which the leaf will break from the twig. These are typical examples, all the more typical because so small and so far from spectacular, of the poet's language. They may help to show how alert the reader must be to catch the full force of what the poet writes. For in good poetry the words and phrases are chosen with almost uncanny precision and are packed, often with layers and layers of meaning.

Sometimes the words may be suggestive just because they are so spare or so astonishingly simplified. Housman, who had a genius for the use of apparently simple language, frequently wrote about soldiers, who always go off to war and never return. At the end of one poem they march away accompanied by fife and drum, and so

> With dying note and swelling
> Walk the resounding way
> To the still dwelling.

Here turmoil of war is reduced to one attribute, noise; and death to one, silence. Neither "resounding" nor "still" would say much alone; it is the extreme understatement and the combination of them that transform the commonplace into something more—with the aid, also, of an extreme though smoothly executed irregularity in the meter of the last line, where two accents are banked together.

Image, Metaphor, and Symbol The concentration and force of poetry are achieved in great measure through concrete and figurative language. Concrete words almost always affect us more powerfully than abstract or general words. The statement "I want to travel and see the world" leaves the mind of the reader unimpressed by comparison with "I want to see London, the pyramids, Tahiti," a sentence that fills the mind with remembered or imagined images. The word "motherhood" is likely to pass through the mind without leaving a stir, whereas "my mother in the kitchen" will stir up numerous memories, pictures, and feelings. Even in ordinary conversation, metaphorical language provides a kind of emphatic shorthand. One man, we say, is "down to earth"; another "has his head in the clouds." The expressions are stale, yet even so they tell us more, and tell it more forcefully, than if we said literally that the men were practical and impractical. To supplement "impractical" with the further implications of "head in the clouds" without using figurative language would require several sentences at least; and the long literal statement would still lack the force and vividness of the figurative one (though it is now too stale to be used in serious discourse). This is an elementary truth applicable to prose as well as to verse; however, because a poem must make us experience something fully as well as think it clearly, the poet generally uses even more imagery than the prose writer does.

Imagery is said to be composed of "vestigial representatives of sensation" or, more simply, of "mental pictures," if we can extend the meaning of "picture" to images deriving from other senses besides that of sight—to taste, odor, sound, and tactile or kinesthetic sensation. The term "imagery" is also used to refer to the language that creates such pictures for the mind's eye or ear. Imagery may be simply descriptive, as in Davies' "leaf-picking winds"; and this description may consist of anything from a phrase to an elaborately wrought scene. Or it may be metaphorical, in either a broad or a narrow sense (the term "metaphorical" being used in two ways, as a general name for all language that is not literal and as the name of one specific figure of speech). If a man is referred to as rabbit, fox, or pig, the zoological image is introduced not for its own sake but to make vivid by means of metaphor (in the narrower sense—"that old fox") something about the man. In such a metaphor, both terms are concrete, but something more abstract also is implied: the fox and the man who is called a fox are concrete, but wiliness, the quality that brings the two together, is abstract. Here the metaphor is a kind of equation with three terms, one in the background, unnamed, uniting the other two.

> Now is the winter of our discontent
> Made glorious summer by this sun of York;
> And all the clouds . . .

So runs the opening of Shakespeare's *Richard III*. Here we have an extended metaphor in which seasons in the natural world are used to describe the political condition of England. Again an unnamed, very general middle term unites "winter" and national "discontent."

In the broad sense of the term, metaphor includes language that is symbolic. In a symbol, however, as the term is commonly used in literature, there seems to be no middle term;

the relation subsists directly between one thing, usually concrete, and some more important, often general or abstract one which it represents. When the fox, for example, is a symbol, he corresponds to no particular man but to abstract wiliness, of which he is the concrete representative.

These definitions are not as exact as they sound. For one thing, the terms "metaphor" and "symbol" have been variously defined and variously applied through many centuries. And for another, even when a definition is agreed on, imagery, suggestive or connotative language, metaphor, and symbol shade so imperceptibly into each other that it is impossible in practice and perhaps in theory to draw precise and invariable distinctions between them. When a metaphor is treated in certain ways, particularly when it is extended or recurs systematically, or when an important meaning seems to overshadow the concrete image, we are apt to think of it as a symbol; but no defined amount of intensification, recurrence, or extension marks the change from one to the other. Yeats, for example, often referred to Helen of Troy when he was writing of Maud Gonne, with whom he was in love. This use of Helen corresponds to the definition of metaphor in the narrow sense, but scarcely to that of symbol, yet it is always thought of as a symbol, partly no doubt because in his poems the real woman seems to symbolize for Yeats all that is supreme, beautiful, and unconsciously destructive in universal woman, but also because to all of us Helen of Troy is herself a symbol of these things more than she is an individual character in a legend.

Symbols are sometimes distinguished as natural, traditional, and arbitrary. Because one can see and know less of one's surroundings at night than by daylight, it is natural to associate night and darkness with mystery or ignorance, and light with knowledge. This is a simple kind of natural symbolism in which the connection between image and idea is so universal as to have become an actual part of the language. To speak of "the light of knowledge" or of "throwing light" on a subject seems no more than a literal way of speaking. Helen of Troy, the Christian cross, and the crown of royalty are familiar examples of the traditional symbol; they have been known for centuries and are widely understood though they are not a part of nature. Blake's use of Jerusalem, on the other hand, and Yeats's of Byzantium are arbitrary because they were invented by the poet for reasons of his own and are not founded on the nature of things or on an accepted, already existing tradition.

Symbolism in literature is not confined, of course, to imagery. A situation, an event, or a story with its train of events may be symbolic. In the myths, religion, and literature of many cultures certain themes appear over and over in symbolic form, and their power to move us seems to derive from their affinity with universal feelings and preoccupations that lie half-buried under our conscious everyday life. The theme of rebirth, which plays an important role in the modern poetry of T. S. Eliot, is one such ancient universal theme. Whatever else "rebirth" may mean, either universally or within a particular cultural frame, it can be a symbolic means of taking care of—by in a sense denying—the universally unwelcome event of death. Imagery, event, situation, all bound together in what is often called an "archetypal" pattern, may carry some such symbolic meaning as this.

A few specific instances will illustrate the poetic use of concrete language in image, metaphor, and symbol. Housman's "To an Athlete Dying Young" offers an interesting example of a set of images used twice in succession, first as simple imagery and immediately afterwards as metaphor.

> The time you won your town the race
> We chaired you through the market-place;
> Man and boy stood cheering by,
> And home we brought you shoulder-high.
>
> To-day, the road all runners come,
> Shoulder-high we bring you home,
> And set you at your threshold down,
> Townsman of a stiller town.

The first stanza describes an event literally, by means of a few key images which stand for nothing beyond what they actually say. The statement and the imagery of the second stanza are nearly identical with this—town, runner, home, being carried on others' shoulders—except that here it is the road "all" runners travel and the town is "stiller," the "cheering" gone. These changes are slight, but the transformation wrought by them is complete. The funeral is described through the transformation of metaphor in imagery belonging to a triumph, and death itself is not even mentioned. The peak of life and its extinction are thus presented through images that, with only the slightest alteration, seem perfectly appropriate to both. The result of this patterned use of images is that the reader for a moment sees both death and victory in a single ironic view. Though the effect is more complex than that of an ordinary metaphor, this second stanza is thought of as metaphorical rather than symbolic. To decide on the name, however, is less important than to recognize the nonliteral effect.

Metaphorical or symbolic language is sometimes so bold that the inexperienced reader has difficulty in making out the literal meaning of a poem. This is in part because the poet will not weaken the impact of what he writes by inserting explanations that have too little interest in themselves to deserve the prominence of rhythm and that would sound unpleasantly flat in verse. He may therefore leave his meaning for the reader to figure out. With a little practice the reader becomes mentally agile enough to do this most of the time without much trouble. His reward lies in finding the poem a packed piece, with inessentials and dullness left out. A celebrated and rather extreme instance of such a gap occurs in T. S. Eliot's "The Love Song of J. Alfred Prufrock," when Prufrock interrupts his inner soliloquy. Should he, he has been asking himself, propose marriage (or possibly an affair) to a woman? As he wonders what he might say to her, he breaks off abruptly with the thought:

> I should have been a pair of ragged claws
> Scuttling across the floors of silent seas.

The reader is left to understand from this image that, brought face to face with the thought of actually proposing to a woman, Prufrock recognizes that his nature is solitary and that he is incapable of "coming out of his *shell*" (an everyday version of the poet's "ragged claws" image). By comparison with most men, Prufrock might have explained, he is like a lobster, which is a cold-blooded creature living a lonely life at the bottom of the sea and which, as every elementary student of biology knows, wears its skeleton on the outside as protective covering. The metaphor is true to feeling though doubly false to fact, for we do not suppose Prufrock literally wished to be a lobster, and, besides, claws do not scuttle by themselves without a body (see "synecdoche" in the Glossary). Instead of explaining all this at length, the poet assumes that his reader has a mind sufficiently agile to make the leap, such a leap as everyone makes in musing. By presenting it without explanation, Eliot gains realism as well as dramatic effect, at the same time avoiding dull exposition.

Symbol and Statement   Sometimes it is difficult to decide whether, within the complex structure of a given poem, a symbolic or metaphorical meaning is present or whether the words are to be taken simply at face value. "Night" in a poem, for instance, is not always a symbol of mystery; it is often only an indication of time. In reading poetry, it is probably best not to ride the horse of symbolism too hard, for language is frequently suggestive or connotative without becoming quite symbolic, though the difference may be only a matter of emphasis. The sentence "He looked out upon the empty sea and the sky" merely states a fact, but the images chosen do also suggest loneliness and wide, unoccupied space. They might help create a mood, but they are not symbols. They may become symbolic—of eternity, for example—if the writer places them in such a context and develops them in such a way that eternity is felt to be the real subject and sea and sky less real. The difference lies in where the center of gravity is felt to be, whether in the literal statement enriched with broader suggestions or in the broad abstract subject, with the literal particular statement only a vehicle for presenting that.

Though it cannot be expected that even experienced readers will invariably agree, in such a subtle matter, on where this center of gravity is, they do so more often than not. Suckling's "Why so pale," for example, is not to be read as a symbolic poem. The situation of the particular lover receiving advice from his worldly friend is enriched and made more meaningful by the universal implication of a realist's comment on romantic values, but the central purpose of the poem is not to make this philosophical generalization, nor are the details of the one-sided conversation invented primarily as an illustration of a philosophical position. In poems of this kind it seems more precise to call the relation between the particular and the general suggestive rather than symbolic. On the other hand, de la Mare's little poem "The House" is clearly symbolic. The "narrow" and "lonely" house is the grave, as we know from these epithets, from the "ghost" that speaks, and from the repetitive and incantatory pattern of the whole. The real subject is death, not a house:

"Mother, it's such a lonely house,"
The child cried; and the wind sighed.
"A narrow but a lovely house,"
The mother replied.

"Child, it is such a narrow house,"
The ghost cried; and the wind sighed.
"A narrow and a lonely house,"
The withering grass replied.

In the very deepest sense, all poetry by virtue of its formal elements is symbolic, and always symbolic of the same thing—order. When Suckling had finished his poem he probably had not altered the situation on which it was founded, assuming for convenience that he had an actual lover in mind. Presumably there still remained an unhappy young man in love, an unco-operative young woman, and an unromantic friend, all of them mixed up with other extraneous affairs in a disorderly world—and all of them now long dead if they ever lived. But there have been many more such trios since, in a still disorderly world, and only once has their confusion been reduced to order in this particular way. By the formalizing power of his imagination, the poet created the ordered whole which we now have as the work of art. A poem may have, but does not have to have, any other symbolism than this, which belongs to all art.

It is this fact that explains what has puzzled some people, why good and durable poems can be written on relatively unimportant themes and why we can take continued pleasure in them just as they are, without having to read other symbols into them. A poem may employ images of spring as symbols of rebirth or describe a dim evening in a way that makes it symbolic of death. On the other hand, Herrick can write about May Day without our having to suppose that his subject is rebirth, and Frost can write of a snowy evening without our having to believe—though the mood of the poem is influenced by solitude and approaching darkness—that he is really writing about death. The reason is that poetic form itself is a symbol of something much desired by man: order; and to see any part of life, great or small, reduced by form to order is itself a satisfying and valuable experience.

Theories of Function

In the ancient debate concerning the function of poetry, some writers maintained that poetry exists to give pleasure, others that its proper aim is moral improvement. The poet Horace's dictum, which offered a choice—poetry is either to delight or to be useful, or to combine the two ("pleasure with profit")—became for many centuries the leading view, though under the successive influences of Plato, mediaeval Christianity, and Puritanism, Horace's "or" was usually forgotten and the poet was expected to justify his existence by "teaching delightfully," a function that could, and sometimes did, deteriorate into the purveying of sugar-coated moral pills.

The thought of Aristotle, though often distorted by later interpreters, led in a somewhat different direction. In the *Metaphysics*, he wrote briefly of the development of the arts: "As more arts were invented, and some were directed to the necessities of life, *others to its recreation,* the inventors of the latter were naturally always regarded as wiser than the inventors of the former, because their branches of knowledge did not aim at utility." Today, both the sugar-coated pill and "art for art's sake" are in disrepute. Both are superficial formulations of their points of view, but the second may be closer to the truth than the first. A wife-beater may love good poetry or write it and continue to beat his wife. Didactic poetry is rarely, if ever, good poetry; and good poetry, one may suspect, never cured a vice or reformed a scoundrel. But Aristotle's view of a kind of greatness of spirit is relevant, of "higher" pleasures beyond the simple satisfaction of animal needs—beyond, in more modern terms, the Darwinian struggle for existence and industrial man's equivalent of this struggle, his competitive pursuit of material gain.

Like all the arts, poetry speaks with vivid intensity, not to the senses exclusively, or to the emotions or the intellect alone, but to all three combined and reconciled. A poem may be about unresolved conflict, as some of Shakespeare's sonnets are when they represent the conflict between passion and reason; but the poem itself, through the fusion of form and the poet's momentarily achieved "aesthetic distance," transcends conflict. It is this harmonizing, this fusion of often conflicting elements of the human psyche that constitutes the primary value of poetry. Whether we think of it as pleasure or utility scarcely matters; it occurs at a level of experience where the two are scarcely distinguishable.

The foregoing account of poetry has placed a pretty heavy weight of significance on "Pease Porridge" and, not quite so disproportionately, on "Why so pale and wan, fond lover." Obviously, most good poetry deals with larger subjects than porridge or shrugged shoulders. For the consideration of poetic principles, however, the greatest themes and the superlative lines can be distracting, and the principles may often be illustrated with greater clarity in poems whose subjects are less overwhelming. Good but minor poems have therefore been cited frequently in the preceding pages. Major poems dealing directly with the heights and depths of human experience have for the most part been reserved for later chapters.

The Art of Reading

Reading as a subject taught in school is only the beginning of real reading, for this is a skill that continues to develop throughout one's lifetime unless it is allowed to wither away from disuse. So a reader approaching poetry seriously for the first time has no reason to be discouraged when he finds that by himself he perceives only part of what is there. To appreciate a good poem fully involves holding together within a single span of attention a structure of thought, form, image, feeling, attitude or tone, and sound, all woven together into an intricate, unified whole. There is no single best way to approach a poem, but a reader who likes a systematic method might wish to try the following "how-to" recipe or some variation of it.

1. Read the poem first, hearing it mentally, with full attention but without any purpose other than to enjoy its effect (if possible), as if you were eating a new kind of peach. Just see how it strikes you as a whole.

2. Read it through next to see, as far as possible, what it says on the surface. If this is not clear, try to locate particular words or passages that seem difficult. If there are unfamiliar words, look them up. If, and this occurs more often than might be supposed, there seems to be an odd use of a familiar word, look this up before you try to wrench a meaning you know into an ill-fitting context. The word "fell," for example (see the poem on p. 356), besides being the past tense of "fall," means to cut down, or to sew a special kind of seam; it means fierce or deadly; it means a moor, and a furry hide of an animal. These are all common meanings, though you may not have known them all. Search, then, before you wrench or let your reading become vague.

INTRODUCTION

See also if a central thought seems to run through the poem, and see how it is developed and how the parts fit. This will give you the intellectual structure of the poem.

3. Ask yourself what the mood, the tone, and the poet's attitude toward his subject seem to be, and ask what in the poem conveys these things.

4. Consider whether the poem suggests more than it says on the surface. If so, ask what it is, what makes you think it is there, and how it affects the poem as a whole.

5. Read the poem aloud or, perhaps even better, not aloud but hearing it with your mind's ear—your auditory imagination—which may give you a better performance than your voice does. Do this more than once, trying to get a sense of the sound patterns in relation to the meaning, the mood, the structure, and everything else you have noticed in previous readings.

6. Finally, simply read it as you did the first time, hearing it mentally, and with full attention. This must be done at leisure. You cannot dance in a hurry—cannot, that is, enjoy the movements of a dance if your muscles are tightened for a contrary kind of movement by the urgent thought that you must catch a train. Neither can you read poetry in a hurry.

It is not expected, or even literally recommended, that a poem be read quite as many times in close succession as this outline suggests; the procedure has been exaggerated in order to dramatize a number of truths about the reading of poetry which the reader will easily recognize.

In all that has been said hitherto, we have not answered one of the questions most likely to be raised by a reader who is not yet at ease with poetry, the question of taste and standards. He finds himself sometimes liking a piece of verse that the experts say is inferior, and indifferent to one they recommend. He asks, reasonably enough, for criteria that will enable him to distinguish the good from the mediocre; the expert can give him no simple or absolute criteria; and he then concludes, understandably, that there are no standards, that all judgment is subjective, and that what he likes is as good, since he likes it, as what anybody else likes. His argument is reasonable, but he is wrong. The experts may even differ slightly among themselves, and still he will be wrong. An analogy will illustrate the point most easily.

In essence, football is an extremely simple form of human activity—by comparison, that is, with poetry. The object of the game is merely to place a particular kind of ball at a particular place in conformity with particular, known rules. Nothing could be much simpler, in definition. In actual fact, as everyone knows, the game is so complicated that even experts sometimes disagree on the relative excellence of good players or the value of a particular play. No known formula can prove that x degree of quick judgment and speed of reaction is more or less valuable than y degree of running speed or z degree of strength. Since weather and twenty-two or more human beings are involved, the game contains so many variables that neither a player nor a play can be tested with scientific accuracy. Twenty-two men's individual weight; their strength of arm, back, and legs; their speed of thought, movement, and muscular reaction; their will power, intelligence, steadiness, stamina; not to mention their momentary condition of freshness or exhaustion, their moods, and the momentary position of each on the field—these are but a few of the variables that prevent the use of simple criteria to reach absolute judgments. Knowing this, we still know that games, players, and plays can be good or poor and can be good in varying ways and degrees. No one can give the football tyro wisdom in a capsule. If we imagine multiplying this complexity a few hundred times —a ball, a field, and four goalposts compared with subject matter that can include almost anything in life—it will be plain why capsule criteria for poetry have not yet been invented and why one comes to understand this complex art only through time, interest, attention, discussion, and occasional help from the experts.

~ I ~

Characters and Narratives

("I don't care much for poetry, but I like Kipling.")

The poems in this chapter are of several kinds, but most of them have this in common, that they are relatively unpoetical in the popular, if not always accurate, sense of that term. Some of them are first-rate poems, but their immediate appeal lies in their subject matter or, as with Kipling, in a certain liveliness and an elementary, rather catchy rhythm. The characters are sometimes superficially sketched; the stories are simple. The poems do not employ elaborate language, and they do not usually express emotion directly, though several have a strong emotional undercurrent. In some the writing is cool and objective; the author may use verse form only to give what he says a neat, crisp outline, to point up a few key words or thoughts, or to make each thing that is said stand out with emphasis. A few transcend the outward simplicity of their form to become complex poems, particularly those, toward the end of the chapter, in which later poets employed the old ballad style for sophisticated poetic effects.

The "character" or character sketch in prose dates back to the Greeks. In verse, however, it is a relatively modern development, not often found before the middle of the nineteenth century. Of the few printed here, most portray a type rather than a particular individual. All were written by poets who judged for themselves; hence they are free from the "stock response." The longest and perhaps most vivid of them is not a character of a human being at all but of an animal.

Of narratives, the simplest type is the folk or popular ballad, originally a "song that tells a story" composed by an unknown author and transmitted orally. Its story is usually violent or tragic. As a rule it is presented not through consecutive narrative but in a simple dramatic scene or a series of detached scenes without connecting links and without explanation of motives or direct expression of emotions. The listener's imagination and, when the ballad is sung, the melody must supply what the words leave unsaid. Refrains are common, as are other kinds of repetition; sometimes the story is told entirely through a repetitive question-and-answer formula. During the last two centuries poets have found much to admire in these old ballads and have written literary ballads not meant for actual song, in which some of the old simplicity and immediacy are revived. Both kinds are represented here, along with a few other poems that bear some resemblance to them.

Tommy

RUDYARD KIPLING

I went into a public-'ouse to get a pint o' beer,
The publican 'e up an' sez, "We serve no red-coats here."
The girls be'ind the bar they laughed an' giggled fit to die,
I outs into the street again an' to myself sez I:
    O it's Tommy this, an' Tommy that, an' "Tommy, go away";
    But it's "Thank you, Mister Atkins," when the band begins to play—
    The band begins to play, my boys, the band begins to play,
    O it's "Thank you, Mister Atkins," when the band begins to play.

I went into a theatre as sober as could be,
    They gave a drunk civilian room, but 'adn't none for me; 10

They sent me to the gallery or round the music-'alls,
But when it comes to fightin', Lord! they'll shove me in
  the stalls!
  For it's Tommy this, an' Tommy that, an' 'Tommy,
    wait outside';
  But it's "Special train for Atkins" when the trooper's on
    the tide—
  The troopship's on the tide, my boys, the troopship's
    on the tide,
  O it's "Special train for Atkins" when the trooper's on
    the tide.

Yes, makin' mock o' uniforms that guard you while you
  sleep
Is cheaper than them uniforms, an' they're starvation
  cheap;
An' hustlin' drunken soldiers when they're goin' large a
  bit
Is five times better business than paradin' in full kit.
  Then it's Tommy this, an' Tommy that, an' "Tommy,
    'ow's yer soul?"
  But it's "Thin red line of 'eroes" when the drums begin
    to roll—
  The drums begin to roll, my boys, the drums begin to
    roll,
  O it's "Thin red line of 'eroes" when the drums begin
    to roll.

We aren't no thin red 'eroes, nor we aren't no blackguards
  too,
But single men in barricks, most remarkable like you;
An' if sometimes our conduck isn't all your fancy paints,
Why, single men in barricks don't grow into plaster
  saints;
  While it's Tommy this, an' Tommy that, an' "Tommy,
    fall be'ind,"
  But it's "Please to walk in front, sir," when there's
    trouble in the wind,

12 stalls: seats in the front part of the orchestra in a theater.

There's trouble in the wind, my boys, there's trouble
    in the wind,
  O it's "Please to walk in front, sir," when there's
    trouble in the wind.

You talk o' better food for us, an' schools, an' fires, an' all:
We'll wait for extry rations if you treat us rational.
Don't mess about the cook-room slops, but prove it to our
    face
The Widow's Uniform is not the soldier-man's disgrace.
  For it's Tommy this, an' Tommy that, an' "Chuck him
    out, the brute!"
  But it's "Saviour of 'is country" when the guns begin to
    shoot;
  An' it's Tommy this, an' Tommy that, an' anything you
    please;
  An' Tommy ain't a bloomin' fool—you bet that Tommy
    sees!   40

36 Widow's: Queen Victoria's.

The Vampire

RUDYARD KIPLING

A fool there was and he made his prayer
(Even as you and I!)
To a rag and a bone and a hank of hair
(We called her the woman who did not care)
But the fool he called her his lady fair—
(Even as you and I!)

Oh, the years we waste and the tears we waste
And the work of our head and hand
Belong to the woman who did not know
(And now we know that she never could know)   10
And did not understand!

A fool there was and his goods he spent
(Even as you and I!)
Honour and faith and a sure intent
(And it wasn't the least what the lady meant)
But a fool must follow his natural bent
(Even as you and I!)

Oh, the toil we lost and the spoil we lost
And the excellent things we planned
Belong to the woman who didn't know why   20
(And now we know that she never knew why)
And did not understand!

The fool was stripped to his foolish hide
(Even as you and I!)
Which she might have seen when she threw
    him aside—
(But it isn't on record the lady tried)
So some of him lived but the most of him died—
(Even as you and I!)

And it isn't the shame and it isn't the blame
That stings like a white-hot brand—   30
It's coming to know that she never knew why
(Seeing, at last, she could never know why)
And never could understand!

Mr. Flood's Party

EDWIN ARLINGTON ROBINSON

Old Eben Flood, climbing alone one night
Over the hill between the town below
And the forsaken upland hermitage
That held as much as he should ever know
On earth again of home, paused warily.
The road was his with not a native near;
And Eben, having leisure, said aloud,
For no man else in Tilbury Town to hear:

"Well, Mr. Flood, we have the harvest moon
Again, and we may not have many more; 10
The bird is on the wing, the poet says,
And you and I have said it here before.
Drink to the bird." He raised up to the light
The jug that he had gone so far to fill,
And answered huskily: "Well, Mr. Flood,
Since you propose it, I believe I will."

Alone, as if enduring to the end
A valiant armor of scarred hopes outworn,
He stood there in the middle of the road
Like Roland's ghost winding a silent horn. 20
Below him, in the town among the trees,
Where friends of other days had honored him,
A phantom salutation of the dead
Rang thinly till old Eben's eyes were dim.

Then, as a mother lays her sleeping child
Down tenderly, fearing it may awake,
He set the jug down slowly at his feet
With trembling care, knowing that most things break;
And only when assured that on firm earth
It stood, as the uncertain lives of men 30
Assuredly did not, he paced away,
And with his hand extended paused again:

"Well, Mr. Flood, we have not met like this
In a long time; and many a change has come
To both of us, I fear, since last it was
We had a drop together. Welcome home!"
Convivially returning with himself,
Again he raised the jug up to the light;
And with an acquiescent quaver said:
"Well, Mr. Flood, if you insist, I might. 40

"Only a very little, Mr. Flood—
For auld lang syne. No more, sir; that will do."

20 Roland's ghost: When treacherously attacked, Roland, a hero of French medieval legend, refused to blow his horn to summon aid till he lay dying.

So, for the time, apparently it did,
And Eben evidently thought so too;
For soon amid the silver loneliness
Of night he lifted up his voice and sang,
Secure, with only two moons listening,
Until the whole harmonious landscape rang—

"For auld lang syne." The weary throat gave out,
The last word wavered; and the song being done,   50
He raised again the jug regretfully
And shook his head, and was again alone.
There was not much that was ahead of him,
And there was nothing in the town below—
Where strangers would have shut the many doors
That many friends had opened long ago.

Miniver Cheevy

EDWIN ARLINGTON ROBINSON

Miniver Cheevy, child of scorn,
   Grew lean while he assailed the seasons;
He wept that he was ever born,
   And he had reasons.

Miniver loved the days of old
   When swords were bright and steeds were prancing;
The vision of a warrior bold
   Would set him dancing.

Miniver sighed for what was not,
   And dreamed, and rested from his labors;   10
He dreamed of Thebes and Camelot,
   And Priam's neighbors.

Miniver mourned the ripe renown
   That made so many a name so fragrant;

11–12 Thebes, Camelot, and Priam's neighbors refer to the legends of Oedipus, King Arthur, and the Trojan war.

He mourned Romance, now on the town,
　And Art, a vagrant.

Miniver loved the Medici,
　Albeit he had never seen one;
He would have sinned incessantly
　Could he have been one.   20

Miniver cursed the commonplace
　And eyed a khaki suit with loathing;
He missed the mediæval grace
　Of iron clothing.

Miniver scorned the gold he sought,
　But sore annoyed was he without it;
Miniver thought, and thought, and thought,
　And thought about it.

Miniver Cheevy, born too late,
　Scratched his head and kept on thinking;   30
Miniver coughed, and called it fate,
　And kept on drinking.

15 on the town: on relief.

nobody loses all the time

e. e. cummings

nobody loses all the time

i had an uncle named
Sol who was a born failure and
nearly everybody said he should have gone
into vaudeville perhaps because my Uncle Sol could
sing McCann He Was A Diver on Xmas Eve like Hell Itself which
may or may not account for the fact that my Uncle

Sol indulged in that possibly most inexcusable
of all to use a highfalootin phrase
luxuries that is or to
wit farming and be
it needlessly
added

my Uncle Sol's farm
failed because the chickens
ate the vegetables so
my Uncle Sol had a
chicken farm till the
skunks ate the chickens when

my Uncle Sol
had a skunk farm but
the skunks caught cold and
died and so
my Uncle Sol imitated the
skunks in a subtle manner

or by drowning himself in the watertank
but somebody who'd given my Uncle Sol a Victor
Victrola and records while he lived presented to
him upon the auspicious occasion of his decease a
scrumptious not to mention splendiferous funeral with
tall boys in black gloves and flowers and everything and

i remember we all cried like the Missouri
when my Uncle Sol's coffin lurched because
somebody pressed a button
(and down went
my Uncle
Sol

and started a worm farm)

Sonnet
On Mistress Nicely, a Pattern for Housekeepers

THOMAS HOOD

She was a woman peerless in her station,
  With household virtues wedded to her name;
  Spotless in linen, grass-bleach'd in her fame,
And pure and clear-starch'd in her conversation;
Thence in my Castle of Imagination
  She dwells for evermore, the dainty dame,
  To keep all airy draperies from shame,
And all dream furnitures in preservation:
  There walketh she with keys quite silver bright,
In perfect hose, and shoes of seemly black,   10
  Apron and stomacher of lily-white,
And decent order follows in her track:
  The burnish'd plate grows lustrous in her sight,
And polish'd floors and tables shine her back.

3 grass-bleach'd: Good housewives used to bleach their white linens by spreading them on sunny grass to dry.   12 decent: suitable and pleasing.

Of Jeoffry, His Cat
From *Jubilate Agno*

CHRISTOPHER SMART

For I will consider my Cat Jeoffry.
For he is the servant of the Living God duly and daily serving him.
For at the first glance of the glory of God in the East he worships in his way.
For is this done by wreathing his body seven times round with elegant quickness.

For then he leaps up to catch the musk, which is the blessing of God upon his prayer.
For he rolls upon prank to work it in.
For having done duty and received blessing he begins to consider himself.
For this he performs in ten degrees.
For first he looks upon his fore-paws to see if they are clean.
For secondly he kicks up behind to clear away there.
For thirdly he works it upon stretch with the fore paws extended.
For fourthly he sharpens his paws by wood.
For fifthly he washes himself.
For Sixthly he rolls upon wash.
For Seventhly he fleas himself, that he may not be interrupted upon the beat.
For Eighthly he rubs himself against a post.
For Ninthly he looks up for his instructions.
For Tenthly he goes in quest of food.
For having consider'd God and himself he will consider his neighbour.
For if he meets another cat he will kiss her in kindness.
For when he takes his prey he plays with it to give it chance.
For one mouse in seven escapes by his dallying.
For when his day's work is done his business more properly begins.
For [he] keeps the Lord's watch in the night against the adversary.
For he counteracts the powers of darkness by his electrical skin & glaring eyes.
For he counteracts the Devil, who is death, by brisking about the life.
For in his morning orisons he loves the sun and the sun loves him.

---

6 prank: frolicsome movement of an animal.   15 upon the beat: on the course habitually traveled (as said of a constable or policeman).   26 brisking about: enlivening.

For he is of the tribe of Tiger.
For the Cherub Cat is a term of the Angel Tiger.
For he has the subtlety and hissing of a serpent, which in goodness he suppresses. 30
For he will not do destruction, if he is well-fed, neither will he spit without provocation.
For he purrs in thankfulness, when God tells him he's a good Cat.
For he is an instrument for the children to learn benevolence upon.
For every house is incompleat without him & a blessing is lacking in the spirit.
For the Lord commanded Moses concerning the cats at the departure of the Children of Israel from Egypt.
For every family had one cat at least in the bag.
For the English Cats are the best in Europe.
For he is the cleanest in the use of his fore-paws of any quadrupede.
For the dexterity of his defence is an instance of the love of God to him exceedingly.
For he is the quickest to his mark of any creature. 40
For he is tenacious of his point.
For he is a mixture of gravity and waggery.
For he knows that God is his Saviour.
For there is nothing sweeter than his peace when at rest.
For there is nothing brisker than his life when in motion.
For he is of the Lord's poor and so indeed is he called by benevolence perpetually—Poor Jeoffry! poor Jeoffry! the rat has bit thy throat.
For I bless the name of the Lord Jesus that Jeoffry is better.
For the divine spirit comes about his body to sustain it in compleat cat.
For his tongue is exceeding pure so that it has in purity what it wants in musick.
For he is docile and can learn certain things. 50

29 Cherub . . . Angel: the Cherubim are closer to God than the Angels, but both are members of the celestial hierarchy.

For he can set up with gravity which is patience upon
   approbation.
For he can fetch and carry, which is patience in
   employment.
For he can jump over a stick which is patience upon
   proof positive.
For he can spraggle upon waggle at the word of
   command.
For he can jump from an eminence into his master's
   bosom.
For he can catch the cork and toss it again.
For he is hated by the hypocrite and miser.
For the former is affraid of detection.
For the latter refuses the charge.
For he camels his back to bear the first notion of
   business.   60
For he is good to think on, if a man would express
   himself neatly.
For he made a great figure in Egypt for his signal
   services.
For he killed the Icneumon-rat very pernicious by land.
For his ears are so acute that they sting again.
For from this proceeds the passing quickness of his
   attention.
For by stroaking of him I have found out electricity.
For I perceived God's light about him both wax and fire.
For the Electrical fire is the spiritual substance, which
   God sends from heaven to sustain the bodies both
   of man and beast.
For God has blessed him in the variety of his movements.
For, tho he cannot fly, he is an excellent clamberer.   70
For his motions upon the face of the earth are more than
   any other quadrupede.
For he can tread to all the measures upon the musick.
For he can swim for life.
For he can creep.

---

51 set: sit.   63 Icneumon-rat: an animal related to the mongoose, resembling
a weasel, sometimes called Pharaoh's rat.   65 passing: surpassing.

My Last Duchess

ROBERT BROWNING

Ferrara

That's my last Duchess painted on the wall,
Looking as if she were alive. I call
That piece a wonder, now: Frà Pandolf's hands
Worked busily a day, and there she stands,
Will't please you sit and look at her? I said
"Frà Pandolf" by design, for never read
Strangers like you that pictured countenance,
The depth and passion of its earnest glance,
But to myself they turned (since none puts by
The curtain I have drawn for you, but I)   10
And seemed as they would ask me, if they durst,
How such a glance came there; so, not the first
Are you to turn and ask thus. Sir, 'twas not
Her husband's presence only, called that spot
Of joy into the Duchess' cheek: perhaps
Frà Pandolf chanced to say "Her mantle laps
Over my lady's wrist too much," or "Paint
Must never hope to reproduce the faint
Half-flush that dies along her throat:" such stuff
Was courtesy, she thought, and cause enough   20
For calling up that spot of joy. She had
A heart—how shall I say?—too soon made glad,
Too easily impressed; she liked whate'er
She looked on, and her looks went everywhere.
Sir, 'twas all one! My favour at her breast,
The dropping of the daylight in the West,
The bough of cherries some officious fool
Broke in the orchard for her, the white mule
She rode with round the terrace—all and each
Would draw from her alike the approving speech,   30
Or blush, at least. She thanked men,—good! but thanked
Somehow—I know not how—as if she ranked
My gift of a nine-hundred-years-old name

With anybody's gift. Who'd stoop to blame
This sort of trifling? Even had you skill
In speech—(which I have not)—to make your will
Quite clear to such an one, and say, "Just this
Or that in you disgusts me; here you miss,
Or there exceed the mark"—and if she let
Herself be lessoned so, nor plainly set   40
Her wits to yours, forsooth, and made excuse,
—E'en then would be some stooping; and I choose
Never to stoop. Oh sir, she smiled, no doubt,
Whene'er I passed her; but who passed without
Much the same smile? This grew; I gave commands;
Then all smiles stopped together. There she stands
As if alive. Will 't please you rise? We'll meet
The company below, then. I repeat,
The Count your master's known munificence
Is ample warrant that no just pretense   50
Of mine for dowry will be disallowed;
Though his fair daughter's self, as I avowed
At starting, is my object. Nay, we'll go
Together down, sir. Notice Neptune, though,
Taming a sea-horse, thought a rarity,
Which Claus of Innsbruck cast in bronze for me!

The Bishop Orders His Tomb at Saint Praxed's Church

ROBERT BROWNING

Rome, 15—

Vanity, saith the preacher, vanity!
Draw round my bed: is Anselm keeping back?
Nephews—sons mine . . . ah God, I know not! Well—
She, men would have to be your mother once,
Old Gandolf envied me, so fair she was!
What's done is done, and she is dead beside,
Dead long ago, and I am Bishop since,
And as she died so must we die ourselves,

And thence ye may perceive the world's a dream.
Life, how and what is it? As here I lie
In this state-chamber, dying by degrees,
Hours and long hours in the dead night, I ask
"Do I live, am I dead?" Peace, peace seems all.
Saint Praxed's ever was the church for peace;
And so, about this tomb of mine. I fought
With tooth and nail to save my niche, ye know:
—Old Gandolf cozened me, despite my care;
Shrewd was that snatch from out the corner South
He graced his carrion with, God curse the same!
Yet still my niche is not so cramped but thence
One sees the pulpit o' the epistle-side,
And somewhat of the choir, those silent seats,
And up into the aery dome where live
The angels, and a sunbeam's sure to lurk:
And I shall fill my slab of basalt there,
And 'neath my tabernacle take my rest,
With those nine columns round me, two and two,
The odd one at my feet where Anselm stands:
Peach-blossom marble all, the rare, the ripe
As fresh-poured red wine of a mighty pulse.
—Old Gandolf with his paltry onion-stone,
Put me where I may look at him! True peach,
Rosy and flawless: how I earned the prize!
Draw close: that conflagration of my church
—What then? So much was saved if aught were missed!
My sons, ye would not be my death? Go dig
The white-grape vineyard where the oil-press stood,
Drop water gently till the surface sink,
And if ye find . . . Ah God, I know not, I! . . .
Bedded in store of rotten fig-leaves soft,
And corded up in a tight olive-frail,
Some lump, ah God, of *lapis lazuli*,
Big as a Jew's head cut off at the nape,
Blue as a vein o'er the Madonna's breast . . .
Sons, all have I bequeathed you, villas, all,

41 frail: a basket.

That brave Frascati villa with its bath,
So, let the blue lump poise between my knees,
Like God the Father's globe on both his hands
Ye worship in the Jesu Church so gay,
For Gandolf shall not choose but see and burst!   50
Swift as a weaver's shuttle fleet our years:
Man goeth to the grave, and where is he?
Did I say basalt for my slab, sons? Black—
'Twas ever antique-black I meant! How else
Shall ye contrast my frieze to come beneath?
The bas-relief in bronze ye promised me,
Those Pans and Nymphs ye wot of, and perchance
Some tripod, thyrsus, with a vase or so,
The Saviour at his sermon on the mount,
Saint Praxed in a glory, and one Pan   60
Ready to twitch the Nymph's last garment off,
And Moses with the tables . . . but I know
Ye mark me not! What do they whisper thee,
Child of my bowels, Anselm? Ah, ye hope
To revel down my villas while I gasp
Bricked o'er with beggar's mouldy travertine
Which Gandolf from his tomb-top chuckles at!
Nay, boys, ye love me—all of jasper, then!
'Tis jasper ye stand pledged to, lest I grieve
My bath must needs be left behind, alas!   70
One block, pure green as a pistachio-nut,
There's plenty jasper somewhere in the world—
And have I not Saint Praxed's ear to pray
Horses for ye, and brown Greek manuscripts,
And mistresses with great smooth marbly limbs?
—That's if ye carve my epitaph aright,
Choice Latin, picked phrase, Tully's every word,
No gaudy ware like Gandolf's second line—
Tully, my masters? Ulpian serves his need!
And then how I shall lie through centuries,   80
And hear the blessed mutter of the mass,

46 Frascati: a resort near Rome.   77–79 Tully's . . . Ulpian: The classical
Latin of Cicero (Tully) is contrasted with the inferior Latin of a later writer.

And see God made and eaten all day long,
And feel the steady candle-flame, and taste
Good strong thick stupefying incense-smoke!
For as I lie here, hours of the dead night,
Dying in state and by such slow degrees,
I fold my arms as if they clasped a crook,
And stretch my feet forth straight as stone can point,
And let the bedclothes, for a mortcloth, drop
Into great laps and folds of sculptor's-work: 90
And as yon tapers dwindle, and strange thoughts
Grow, with a certain humming in my ears,
About the life before I lived this life,
And this life too, popes, cardinals and priests,
Saint Praxed at his sermon on the mount,
Your tall pale mother with her talking eyes,
And new-found agate urns as fresh as day,
And marble's language, Latin pure, discreet,
—Aha, ELUCESCEBAT quoth our friend?
No Tully, said I, Ulpian at the best!   100
Evil and brief hath been my pilgrimage.
All *lapis*, all, sons! Else I give the Pope
My villas! Will ye ever eat my heart?
Ever your eyes were as a lizard's quick,
They glitter like your mother's for my soul,
Or ye would heighten my impoverished frieze,
Piece out its starved design, and fill my vase
With grapes, and add a visor and a Term,
And to the tripod ye would tie a lynx
That in his struggle throws the thyrsus down,   110
To comfort me on my entablature
Whereon I am to lie till I must ask
"Do I live, am I dead?" There, leave me, there!
For ye have stabbed me with ingratitude
To death—ye wish it—God, ye wish it! Stone—
Gritstone, a-crumble! Clammy squares which sweat

87 crook: a bishop's staff.   89 mortcloth: death or funeral cloth.
99 ELUCESCEBAT: he shone. The Bishop is still contemptuous of Gandolph's unclassical Latin. The classical form is *elucebat*.   103 ever eat: always be eating.   108 Term: end post decorated with a head.

CHARACTERS AND NARRATIVES   51

   As if the corpse they keep were oozing through—
   And no more *lapis* to delight the world!
   Well go! I bless ye. Fewer tapers there,
   But in a row: and, going, turn your backs   120
   —Ay, like departing altar-ministrants,
   And leave me in my church, the church for peace,
   That I may watch at leisure if he leers—
   Old Gandolf, at me, from his onion-stone,
   As still he envied me, so fair she was!

Soliloquy of the Spanish Cloister
ROBERT BROWNING

   Gr-r-r—there go, my heart's abhorrence!
     Water your damned flower-pots, do!
   If hate killed men, Brother Lawrence,
     God's blood, would not mine kill you!
   What? your myrtle-bush wants trimming?
     Oh, that rose has prior claims—
   Needs its leaden vase filled brimming?
     Hell dry you up with its flames!

   At the meal we sit together:
     Salve tibi! I must hear   10
   Wise talk of the kind of weather,
     Sort of season, time of year:
   Not a plenteous cork-crop: scarcely
     Dare we hope oak-galls, I doubt:
   What's the Latin name for "parsley"?
     What's the Greek name for Swine's Snout?

   Whew! We'll have our platter burnished,
     Laid with care on our own shelf!
   With a fire-new spoon we're furnished,
     And a goblet for ourself,   20

10 *Salve tibi!*: Hail to thee!

      Rinsed like something sacrificial
    Ere 'tis fit to touch our chaps—
Marked with L for our initial!
   (He-he! There his lily snaps!)

Saint, forsooth! While brown Dolores
    Squats outside the Convent bank
With Sanchicha, telling stories,
    Steeping tresses in the tank,
Blue-black, lustrous, thick like horsehairs,
   —Can't I see his dead eye glow,   30
Bright as 'twere a Barbary corsair's?
   (That is, if he'd let it show!)

When he finishes reflection,
   Knife and fork he never lays
Cross-wise, to my recollection,
   As do I, in Jesu's praise.
I the Trinity illustrate,
   Drinking watered orange-pulp—
In three sips the Arian frustrate;
   While he drains his at one gulp.   40

Oh, those melons! If he's able
   We're to have a feast! so nice!
One goes to the Abbot's table,
   All of us get each a slice.
How go on your flowers? None double?
   Not one fruit-sort can you spy?
Strange!—And I, too, at such trouble,
   Keep them close-nipped on the sly!

There's a great text in Galatians,
   Once you trip on it, entails   50
Twenty-nine distinct damnations,

37–39 The Arian heresy maintained that Christ is inferior to God in opposition to the Trinitarian doctrine of the equality of the Three Persons of the Trinity.   46 fruit-sort: pistillate, i.e., flowers from which fruit will be developed, as opposed to staminate flowers, which produce the pollen.

One sure, if another fails:
If I trip him just a-dying,
  Sure of heaven as sure can be,
Spin him round and send him flying
  Off to hell, a Manichee?

Or, my scrofulous French novel
  On grey paper with blunt type!
Simply glance at it, you grovel
  Hand and foot in Belial's gripe: 60
If I double down its pages
  At the woeful sixteenth print,
When he gathers his greengages,
  Ope a sieve and slip it in't?

Or, there's Satan!—one might venture
  Pledge one's soul to him, yet leave
Such a flaw in the indenture
  As he'd miss till, past retrieve,
Blasted lay that rose-acacia
  We're so proud of! Hy, Zy, Hine . . .   70
'St, there's Vespers! Plena gratia,
  Ave, Virgo! Gr-r-r—you swine!

64 sieve: a kind of basket used for produce.   70 Hy, Zy, Hine: words still unexplained; possibly the beginning of a spell invoking Satan.   71–72 Plena gratia, Ave, Virgo!: Hail, Virgin, full of grace!

Bonny Barbara Allan

ANON.

It was in and about the Martinmas time,
  When the green leaves were a falling,
That Sir John Græme, in the West Country,
  Fell in love with Barbara Allan.

1 Martinmas: November 11.

He sent his man down through the town,
    To the place where she was dwelling:
"O haste and come to my master dear,
    Gin ye be Barbara Allan."

O hooly, hooly rose she up,
    To the place where he was lying,   10
And when she drew the curtain by,
    "Young man, I think you're dying."

"O it's I'm sick, and very, very sick,
    And 't is a' for Barbara Allan:"
"O the better for me ye's never be,
    Tho your heart's blood were a spilling.

"O dinna ye mind, young man," said she,
    "When ye was in the tavern a drinking,
That ye made the healths gae round and round,
    And slighted Barbara Allan?"   20

He turned his face unto the wall,
    And death was with him dealing:
"Adieu, adieu, my dear friends all,
    And be kind to Barbara Allan."

And slowly, slowly raise she up,
    And slowly, slowly left him,
And sighing said, she coud not stay,
    Since death of life had reft him.

She had not gane a mile but twa,
    When she heard the dead-bell ringing,   30
And every jow that the dead-bell geid,
    It cry'd, Woe to Barbara Allan!

"O Mother, mother, make my bed!
    O make it saft and narrow!
Since my love died for me to-day,
    I'll die for him to-morrow."

8 gin: if.   9 hooly: slowly.   31 jow: stroke. geid: gave.

Marie Hamilton

ANON.

Word's gane to the kitchen,
   And word's gane to the ha,
That Marie Hamilton gangs wi bairn
   To the hichest Stewart of a'.

He's courted her in the kitchen,
   He's courted her in the ha,
He's courted her in the laigh cellar,
   And that was warst of a'.

She's tyed it in her apron
   And she's thrown it in the sea;   10
Says, "Sink ye, swim ye, bonny wee babe!
   You'l neer get mair o me."

Down then cam the auld queen,
   Goud tassels tying her hair:
"O Marie, where's the bonny wee babe
   That I heard greet sae sair?"

"There was never a babe intill my room,
   As little designs to be;
It was but a touch o my sair side,
   Come oer my fair bodie."   20

"O Marie, put on your robes o black,
   Or else your robes o brown,
For ye maun gang wi me the night,
   To see fair Edinbro town."

"I winna put on my robes o black,
   Nor yet my robes o brown;

---

3 gangs wi bairn: is pregnant.   4 The Stewarts were the royal family of Scotland. hichest: highest, i.e., the king.   7 laigh: low.   14 goud: gold. 16 greet: weep.

But I'll put on my robes o white,
   To shine through Edinbro town."

When she gaed up the Cannogate,
   She laughd loud laughters three;   30
But whan she cam down the Cannogate
   The tear blinded her ee.

When she gaed up the Parliament stair,
   The heel cam aff her shee;
And lang or she cam down again
   She was condemnd to dee.

When she cam down the Cannogate,
   The Cannogate sae free,
Many a ladie lookd oer her window,
   Weeping for this ladie.   40

"Ye need nae weep for me," she says,
   "Ye need nae weep for me;
For had I not slain mine own sweet babe,
   This death I wadna dee.

"Bring me a bottle of wine," she says,
   "The best that eer ye hae,
That I may drink to my weil-wishers,
   And they may drink to me.

"Here's a health to the jolly sailors,
   That sail upon the main;   50
Let them never let on to my father and mother
   But what I'm coming hame.

"Here's a health to the jolly sailors,
   That sail upon the sea;
Let them never let on to my father and mother
   That I cam here to dee.

---

29 Cannogate: street leading from the palace to the Parliament House.

"Oh little did my mother think,
   The day she cradled me,
What lands I was to travel through,
   What death I was to dee.   60

"Oh little did my father think,
   The day he held up me,
What lands I was to travel through,
   What death I was to dee.

"Last night I washd the queens feet,
   And gently laid her down;
And a' the thanks I've gotten the nicht
   To be hangd in Edinbro town!

"Last nicht there was four Maries,
   The nicht there'l be but three;   70
There was Marie Seton, and Marie Beton,
   And Marie Carmichael, and me."

69 Maries: The name is accented as in the alternate spelling "Mary."

The Three Ravens

ANON.

There were three ravens sat on a tree,
   Downe a downe, hay downe, hay downe
There were three ravens sat on a tree,
   With a downe
There were three ravens sat on a tree,
They were as black as they might be.
   With a downe derrie, derrie, derrie,
      downe, downe.

The one of them said to his mate,
"Where shall we our breakfast take?"

"Downe in yonder greene field, 10
There lies a knight slain under his shield.

"His hounds they lie downe at his feete,
So well they can their master keepe.

"His haukes they flie so eagerly,
There's no fowle dare him come nie."

Downe there comes a fallow doe,
As great with yong as she might goe.

She lift up his bloudy hed,
And kist his wounds that were so red.

She got him up upon her backe, 20
And carried him to earthen lake.

She buried him before the prime,
She was dead herself ere even-song time.

God send every gentleman,
Such haukes, such hounds, and such a leman.

21 earthen lake: ?pit (actual meaning unknown).   22 prime: first hour of the day.

The Twa Corbies

ANON.

As I was walking all alane,
I herd twa corbies making a mane;
The tane unto the t' other say,
"Where sall we gang and dine to-day?"

2 corbies: ravens or crows.   mane: moan, lament.

"In behint yon auld fail dyke,
I wot there lies a new slain knight;
And naebody kens that he lies there,
But his hawk, his hound, and lady fair.

"His hound is to the hunting gane,
His hawk to fetch the wild-fowl hame,   10
His lady's ta'en another mate,
So we may mak our dinner sweet.

"Ye'll sit on his white hause-bane,
And I'll pike out his bonny blue een;
Wi ae lock o his gowden hair
We'll theek our nest when it grows bare.

"Mony a one for him makes mane,
But nane sall ken where he is gane;
Oer his white banes when they are bare,
The wind sall blaw for evermair."   20

5 fail: turf.   7 kens: knows.   13 hause-bane: neck bone.   16 theek: thatch.

Sir Patrick Spence

ANON.

The king sits in Dumferling toune,
  Drinking the blude-reid wine:
"O whar will I get guid sailor,
  To sail this schip of mine?"

Up and spak an eldern knicht,
  Sat at the kings richt kne:
"Sir Patrick Spence is the best sailor,
  That sails upon the se."

POEMS AND POETRY

The king has written a braid letter,
    And signd it wi his hand,   10
And sent it to Sir Patrick Spence,
    Was walking on the sand.

The first line that Sir Patrick red,
    A loud lauch lauched he;
The next line that Sir Patrick red,
    The teir blinded his ee.

"O wha is this has don this deid,
    This ill deid don to me,
To send me out this time o' the yeir,
    To sail upon the se!   20

"Mak hast, mak haste, my mirry men all,
    Our guid schip sails the morne:"
"O say na sae, my master deir,
    For I feir a deadlie storme.

"Late late yestreen I saw the new moone,
    Wi the auld moone in hir arme,
And I feir, I feir, my deir master,
    That we will cum to harme."

O our Scots nobles wer richt laith
    To weet their cork-heild schoone;   30
Bot lang owre a' the play wer playd,
    Their hats they swam aboone.

O lang, lang may their ladies sit,
    Wi thair fans into their hand,
Or eir they se Sir Patrick Spence
    Cum sailing to the land.

O lang, lang may the ladies stand,
    Wi thair gold kems in their hair,

9 braid: broad.   14 lauch: laugh.   29 laith: loath.   32 aboone: above.

Waiting for thar ain deir lords,
   For they 'll se thame na mair.   40

Haf owre, haf owre to Aberdour,
   It's fiftie fadom deip,
And thair lies guid Sir Patrick Spence,
   Wi the Scots lords at his feit.

Thomas Rymer

ANON.

True Thomas lay oer yond grassy bank,
   And he beheld a ladie gay,
A ladie that was brisk and bold,
   Come riding oer the fernie brae.

Her skirt was of the grass-green silk,
   Her mantle of the velvet fine,
At ilka tett of her horse's mane
   Hung fifty silver bells and nine.

True Thomas he took off his hat,
   And bowed him low down till his knee: 10
"All hail, thou mighty Queen of Heaven!
   For your peer on earth I never did see."

"O no, O no, True Thomas," she says,
   "That name does not belong to me;
I am but the queen of fair Elfland,
   And I'm come here for to visit thee.

. . . .

"But ye maun go wi me now, Thomas,
   True Thomas, ye maun go wi me,

4 brae: hillside.   *7* ilka tett: each lock.   *17* maun: must.

For ye maun serve me seven years,
    Thro weel or wae as may chance to be." 20

She turned about her milk-white steed,
    And took True Thomas up behind;
And aye wheneer her bridle rang,
    The steed flew swifter than the wind.

For forty days and forty nights
    He wade thro red blude to the knee,
And he saw neither sun nor moon,
    But heard the roaring of the sea.

O they rade on, and further on,
    Until they came to a garden green: 30
"Light down, light down, ye ladie free;
    Some of that fruit let me pull to thee."

"O no, O no, True Thomas," she says,
    "That fruit maun not be touched by thee,
For a' the plagues that are in hell
    Light on the fruit of this countrie.

"But I have a loaf here in my lap,
    Likewise a bottle of claret wine,
And now ere we go farther on,
    We'll rest a while, and ye may dine." 40

When he had eaten and drunk his fill,
    "Lay down your head upon my knee,"
The lady sayd, "ere we climb yon hill,
    And I will show you fairlies three.

"O see not ye yon narrow road,
    So thick beset wi thorns and briers?
That is the path of righteousness,
    Tho after it but few enquires.

44 fairlies: wonders.

"And see not ye that braid, braid road,
    That lies across yon lillie leven?
That is the path of wickedness,
    Tho some call it the road to heaven.

"And see not ye that bonny road,
    Which winds about the fernie brae?
That is the road to fair Elfland,
    Where you and I this night maun gae.

"But Thomas, ye maun hold your tongue,
    Whatever you may hear or see,
For gin ae word you should chance to speak,
    You will neer get back to your ain countrie."

He has gotten a coat of the even cloth,
    And a pair of shoes of velvet green,
And till seven years were past and gone
    True Thomas on earth was never seen.

50 lillie leven: probably lovely lawn, but the meaning of "lillie" is not certain.

The Cherry-Tree Carol

ANON.

Joseph was an old man,
    and an old man was he,
When he wedded Mary,
    in the land of Galilee.

Joseph and Mary walked
    through an orchard good,
Where was cherries and berries,
    so red as any blood.

Joseph and Mary walked
    through an orchard green,

Where was berries and cherries,
    as thick as might be seen.

O then bespoke Mary,
    so meek and so mild:
"Pluck me one cherry, Joseph,
    for I am with child."

O then bespoke Joseph,
    with words most unkind:
"Let him pluck thee a cherry
    that brought thee with child."   20

O then bespoke the babe,
    within his mother's womb:
"Bow down then the tallest tree,
    for my mother to have some."

Then bowed down the highest tree
    unto his mother's hand;
Then she cried, "See, Joseph,
    I have cherries at command."

O then bespake Joseph:
    "I have done Mary wrong;   30
But cheer up, my dearest,
    and be not cast down."

Then Mary plucked a cherry,
    as red as the blood,
then Mary went home
    with her heavy load.

Then Mary took her babe,
    and sat him on her knee,
Saying, "My dear son, tell me
    what this world will be."   40

"O I shall be as dead, mother,
  as the stones in the wall;
O the stones in the streets, mother,
  shall mourn for me all.

"Upon Easter-day, mother,
  my uprising shall be;
O the sun and the moon, mother,
  shall both rise with me."

Proud Maisie

From *The Heart of Midlothian*

SIR WALTER SCOTT

Proud Maisie is in the wood,
  Walking so early;
Sweet Robin sits on the bush,
  Singing so rarely.

"Tell me, thou bonny bird,
  When shall I marry me?"—
"When six braw gentlemen
  Kirkward shall carry ye."

"Who makes the bridal bed,
  Birdie, say truly?"—   10
"The grey-headed sexton
  That delves the grave duly.

"The glow-worm o'er grave and stone
  Shall light thee steady.
The owl from the steeple sing,
  'Welcome, proud lady.'"

---

7 braw: fine.

The Castaway

WILLIAM COWPER

Obscurest night involv'd the sky,
    Th' Atlantic billows roar'd,
When such a destin'd wretch as I,
    Wash'd headlong from on board,
Of friends, of hope, of all bereft,
His floating home for ever left.

No braver chief could Albion boast
    Than he with whom he went,
Nor ever ship left Albion's coast,
    With warmer wishes sent.
He lov'd them both, but both in vain,
Nor him beheld, nor her again.

Not long beneath the whelming brine,
    Expert to swim, he lay;
Nor soon he felt his strength decline,
    Or courage die away;
But wag'd with death a lasting strife,
Supported by despair of life.

He shouted: nor his friends had failed
    To check the vessel's course,
But so the furious blast prevail'd,
    That, pitiless perforce,
They left their outcast mate behind,
And scudded still before the wind.

Some succour yet they could afford;
    And, such as storms allow,
The cask, the coop, the floated cord,
    Delay'd not to bestow.

But he (they knew) nor ship, nor shore,
Whate'er they gave, should visit more.   30

Nor, cruel as it seem'd, could he
    Their haste himself condemn,
Aware that flight, in such a sea,
    Alone could rescue them;
Yet bitter felt it still to die
Deserted, and his friends so nigh.

He long survives, who lives an hour
    In ocean, self-upheld;
And so long he, with unspent pow'r,
    His destiny repell'd;   40
And ever, as the minutes flew,
Entreated help, or cried—Adieu!

At length, his transient respite past,
    His comrades, who before
Had heard his voice in ev'ry blast,
    Could catch the sound no more.
For then, by toil subdued, he drank
The stifling wave, and then he sank.

No poet wept him: but the page
    Of narrative sincere,   50
That tells his name, his worth, his age,
    Is wet with Anson's tear.
And tears by bards or heroes shed
Alike immortalize the dead.

I therefore purpose not, or dream,
    Descanting on his fate,
To give the melancholy theme
    A more enduring date:
But misery still delights to trace
Its 'semblance in another's case.   60

No voice divine the storm allay'd,
    No light propitious shone;

When, snatch'd from all effectual aid,
We perish'd, each alone:
But I beneath a rougher sea,
And whelm'd in deeper gulphs than he.

The Rime of the Ancient Mariner

SAMUEL TAYLOR COLERIDGE
Argument

How a Ship, having first sailed to the Equator, was driven by Storms to the cold Country towards the South Pole; how the Ancient Mariner cruelly and in contempt of the laws of hospitality killed a Seabird and how he was followed by many and strange Judgements: and in what manner he came back to his own Country.

PART I

An ancient Mariner meeteth three Gallants bidden to a wedding-feast, and detaineth one.

It is an ancient Mariner,
And he stoppeth one of three.
"By thy long grey beard and glittering eye,
Now wherefore stopp'st thou me?

The Bridegroom's doors are opened wide,
And I am next of kin;
The guests are met, the feast is set:
May'st hear the merry din."

He holds him with his skinny hand,
"There was a ship," quoth he.
"Hold off! Unhand me, gray-beard loon!"
Eftsoons his hand dropt he.

The Wedding-Guest is spellbound by the eye of the old seafaring man, and constrained to hear his tale.

He holds him with his glittering eye—
The Wedding-Guest stood still,
And listens like a three years' child:
The Mariner hath his will.

The Wedding-Guest sat on a stone:
He cannot choose but hear;
And thus spake on that ancient man,
The bright-eyed Mariner.   20

"The ship was cheered, the harbour cleared,
Merrily did we drop
Below the kirk, below the hill,
Below the lighthouse top.

<small>The Mariner tells how the ship sailed southward with a good wind and fair weather, till it reached the Line.</small>

The sun came up upon the left,
Out of the sea came he!
And he shone bright, and on the right
Went down into the sea.

Higher and higher every day,
Till over the mast at noon—"   30
The Wedding-Guest here beat his breast,
For he heard the loud bassoon.

<small>The Wedding-Guest heareth the bridal music; but the Mariner continueth his tale.</small>

The bride hath paced into the hall,
Red as a rose is she;
Nodding their heads before her goes
The merry minstrelsy.

The Wedding-Guest he beat his breast,
Yet he cannot choose but hear;
And thus spake on that ancient man,
The bright-eyed Mariner.   40

<small>The ship driven by a storm toward the south pole.</small>

"And now the STORM-BLAST came, and he
Was tyrannous and strong:
He struck with his o'ertaking wings,
And chased us south along.

With sloping masts and dipping prow,
As who pursued with yell and blow
Still treads the shadow of his foe,
And forward bends his head,

27 (gloss). Line: the Equator.

The ship drove fast, loud roared the blast,
And southward aye we fled.   50

And now there came both mist and snow,
And it grew wondrous cold:
And ice, mast-high, came floating by,
As green as emerald.

<small>The land of ice, and of fearful sounds where no living thing was to be seen.</small>

And through the drifts the snowy clifts
Did send a dismal sheen:
Nor shapes of men nor beasts we ken—
The ice was all between.

The ice was here, the ice was there,
The ice was all around: 60
It cracked and growled, and roared and howled,
Like noises in a swound!

<small>Till a great sea-bird, called the Albatross, came through the snow-fog, and was received with great joy and hospitality.</small>

At length did cross an Albatross,
Thorough the fog it came;
As if it had been a Christian soul,
We hailed it in God's name.

It ate the food it ne'er had eat,
And round and round it flew.
The ice did split with a thunder-fit;
The helmsman steered us through!   70

<small>And lo! the Albatross proveth a bird of good omen, and followeth the ship as it returned northward through fog and floating ice.</small>

And a good south wind sprung up behind;
The Albatross did follow,
And every day, for food or play,
Came to the mariners' hollo!

In mist or cloud, on mast or shroud,
It perched for vespers nine;
Whiles all the night, through fog-smoke white,
Glimmered the white moon-shine."

55 clifts: cliffs.

> "God save thee, ancient Mariner!
> From the fiends, that plague thee thus!—
> Why look'st thou so?"—"With my crossbow
> I shot the ALBATROSS." 80

The ancient Mariner inhospitably killeth the pious bird of good omen.

PART II

> "The Sun now rose upon the right:
> Out of the sea came he,
> Still hid in mist, and on the left
> Went down into the sea.
>
> And the good south wind still blew behind,
> But no sweet bird did follow,
> Nor any day for food or play
> Came to the mariners' hollo! 90
>
> And I had done a hellish thing,
> And it would work 'em woe:
> For all averred, I had killed the bird
> That made the breeze to blow.
> Ah wretch! said they, the bird to slay,
> That made the breeze to blow!

His shipmates cry out against the ancient Mariner, for killing the bird of good luck.

> Nor dim nor red, like God's own head,
> The glorious Sun uprist:
> Then all averred, I had killed the bird
> That brought the fog and mist. 100
> 'Twas right, said they, such birds to slay,
> That bring the fog and mist.

But when the fog cleared off, they justify the same, and thus make themselves accomplices in the crime.

> The fair breeze blew, the white foam flew,
> The furrow followed free;
> We were the first that ever burst
> Into that silent sea.

The fair breeze continues; the ship enters the Pacific Ocean, and sails northward, even till it reaches the Line.

> Down dropt the breeze, the sails **dropt** down,
> 'Twas sad as sad could be;

The ship hath been suddenly becalmed.

And we did speak only to break
The silence of the sea! 110

All in a hot and copper sky,
The bloody Sun, at noon,
Right up above the mast did stand,
No bigger than the Moon.

Day after day, day after day,
We stuck, nor breath nor motion;
As idle as a painted ship
Upon a painted ocean.

And the Albatross begins to be avenged.

Water, water, every where,
And all the boards did shrink; 120
Water, water, every where,
Nor any drop to drink.

The very deep did rot: O Christ!
That ever this should be!
Yea, slimy things did crawl with legs
Upon the slimy sea.

About, about, in reel and rout
The death-fires danced at night;
The water, like a witch's oils,
Burnt green, and blue and white. 130

A Spirit had followed them; one of the invisible inhabitants of this planet, neither departed souls nor angels; concerning whom the learned Jew, Josephus, and the Platonic Constantinopolitan, Michael Psellus, may be consulted. They are very numerous, and there is no climate or element without one or more.

And some in dreams assurèd were
Of the Spirit that plagued us so;
Nine fathom deep he had followed us
From the land of mist and snow.

And every tongue, through utter drought,
Was withered at the root;

125–126 slimy things . . . with legs: Coleridge had alligators or crocodiles in mind, as his notebooks show. *127–30* (also later, ll. 270–81). A somewhat heightened description of phosphorescence in tropical waters.

> We could not speak, no more than if
> We had been choked with soot.

The ship-mates, in their sore distress, would fain throw the whole guilt on the ancient Mariner: in sign whereof they hang the dead sea-bird round his neck.

> Ah! well a-day! what evil looks
> Had I from old and young!   140
> Instead of the cross, the Albatross
> About my neck was hung.

PART III

The ancient Mariner beholdeth a sign in the element afar off.

> There passed a weary time. Each throat
> Was parched, and glazed each eye.
> A weary time! a weary time!
> How glazed each weary eye,
> When looking westward, I beheld
> A something in the sky.
>
> At first it seemed a little speck,
> And then it seemed a mist;   150
> It moved and moved, and took at last
> A certain shape, I wist.
>
> A speck, a mist, a shape, I wist!
> And still it neared and neared:
> As if it dodged a water-sprite,
> It plunged and tacked and veered.

At its nearer approach, it seemeth him to be a ship; and at a dear ransom he freeth his speech from the bonds of thirst.

> With throats unslaked, with black lips baked,
> We could nor laugh nor wail;
> Through utter drought all dumb we stood!
> I bit my arm, I sucked the blood,   160
> And cried, A sail! a sail!

A flash of joy;

> With throats unslaked, with black lips baked,
> Agape they heard me call:
> Gramercy! they for joy did grin,
> And all at once their breath drew in,
> As they were drinking all.

74 POEMS AND POETRY

<small>And horror follows. For can it be a ship that comes onward without wind or tide?</small>

See! see! (I cried) she tacks no more!
Hither to work us weal;
Without a breeze, without a tide,
She steadies with upright keel! 170

The western wave was all aflame,
The day was well nigh done!
Almost upon the western wave
Rested the broad bright Sun;
When that strange shape drove suddenly
Betwixt us and the Sun.

<small>It seemeth him but the skeleton of a ship.</small>

And straight the Sun was flecked with bars,
(Heaven's Mother send us grace!)
As if through a dungeon-grate he peered
With broad and burning face. 180

Alas! (thought I, and my heart beat loud)
How fast she nears and nears!
Are those her sails that glance in the Sun,
Like restless gossameres?

<small>And its ribs are seen as bars on the face of the setting Sun. The Spectre-Woman and her Death-mate, and no other on board the skeleton ship.</small>

Are those her ribs through which the Sun
Did peer, as through a grate?
And is that Woman all her crew?
Is that a DEATH? and are there two?
Is DEATH that woman's mate?

<small>Like vessel, like crew!</small>

Her lips were red, her looks were free, 190
Her locks were yellow as gold:
Her skin was as white as leprosy,
The Nightmare LIFE-IN-DEATH was she,
Who thicks man's blood with cold.

<small>Death and Life-in-Death have diced for the ship's crew, and she (the latter) winneth the ancient Mariner.</small>

The naked hulk alongside came,
And the twain were casting dice;
'The game is done! I've won! I've won!'
Quoth she, and whistles thrice.

No twilight within the courts of the Sun.	The Sun's rim dips; the stars rush out: At one stride comes the dark; 200 With far-heard whisper, o'er the sea, Off shot the spectre-bark.
At the rising of the Moon,	We listened and looked sideways up! Fear at my heart, as at a cup, My life-blood seemed to sip! The stars were dim, and thick the night, The steersman's face by his lamp gleamed white; From the sails the dew did drip— Till clomb above the eastern bar The hornèd Moon, with one bright star 210 Within the nether tip.
One after another,	One after one, by the star-dogged Moon, Too quick for groan or sigh, Each turned his face with a ghastly pang, And cursed me with his eye.
His ship-mates drop down dead.	Four times fifty living men (And I heard nor sigh nor groan) With heavy thump, a lifeless lump, They dropped down one by one.
But Life-in-Death begins her work on the ancient Mariner.	The souls did from their bodies fly— 220 They fled to bliss or woe! And every soul, it passed me by, Like the whizz of my cross-bow!"

PART IV

The Wedding-Guest feareth that a Spirit is talking to him;	"I fear thee, ancient Mariner! I fear thy skinny hand! And thou art long, and lank, and brown, As is the ribbed sea-sand.
	"I fear thee and thy glittering eye, And thy skinny hand, so brown."—

But the ancient Mariner assureth him of his bodily life, and proceedeth to relate his horrible penance.

"Fear not, fear not, thou Wedding-Guest! 230
This body dropt not down.

Alone, alone, all, all alone,
Alone on a wide wide sea!
And never a saint took pity on
My soul in agony.

He despiseth the creatures of the calm,

The many men, so beautiful!
And they all dead did lie:
And a thousand thousand slimy things
Lived on; and so did I.

And envieth that they should live, and so many lie dead.

I looked upon the rotting sea, 240
And drew my eyes away;
I looked upon the rotting deck,
And there the dead men lay.

I looked to heaven, and tried to pray;
But or ever a prayer had gusht,
A wicked whisper came, and made
My heart as dry as dust.

I closed my lids, and kept them close,
And the balls like pulses beat;
For the sky and the sea, and the sea and
    the sky, 250
Lay like a load on my weary eye,
And the dead were at my feet.

But the curse liveth for him in the eye of the dead men.

The cold sweat melted from their limbs,
Nor rot nor reek did they:
The look with which they looked on me
Had never passed away.

An orphan's curse would drag to hell
A spirit from on high;
But oh! more horrible than that
Is the curse in a dead man's eye! 260

Seven days, seven nights, I saw that curse,
And yet I could not die.

In his loneliness and fixedness he yearneth towards the journeying Moon, and the stars that still sojourn, yet still move onward; and every where the blue sky belongs to them, and is their appointed rest, and their native country and their own natural homes, which they enter unannounced, as lords that are certainly expected and yet there is a silent joy at their arrival.

The moving Moon went up the sky,
And nowhere did abide:
Softly she was going up,
And a star or two beside—

Her beams bemocked the sultry main,
Like April hoar-frost spread;
But where the ship's huge shadow lay,
The charmèd water burnt alway   270
A still and awful red.

By the light of the Moon he beholdeth God's creatures of the great calm.

Beyond the shadow of the ship,
I watched the water-snakes:
They moved in tracks of shining white,
And when they reared, the elfish light
Fell off in hoary flakes.

Within the shadow of the ship
I watched their rich attire:
Blue, glossy green, and velvet black,
They coiled and swam; and every track   280
Was a flash of golden fire.

Their beauty and their happiness.

O happy living things! no tongue
Their beauty might declare:
A spring of love gushed from my heart,

He blesseth them in his heart.

And I blessed them unaware:
Sure my kind saint took pity on me,
And I blessed them unaware.

The spell begins to break.

The selfsame moment I could pray;
And from my neck so free
The Albatross fell off, and sank   290
Like lead into the sea.

PART V

"Oh, sleep! it is a gentle thing,
Beloved from pole to pole!
To Mary Queen the praise be given!
She sent the gentle sleep from Heaven,
That slid into my soul.

By grace of the holy Mother, the ancient Mariner is refreshed with rain.

The silly buckets on the deck,
That had so long remained,
I dreamt that they were filled with dew;
And when I awoke, it rained.   300

My lips were wet, my throat was cold,
My garments all were dank;
Sure I had drunken in my dreams,
And still my body drank.

I moved, and could not feel my limbs:
I was so light—almost
I thought that I had died in sleep,
And was a blessèd ghost.

He heareth sounds and seeth strange sights and commotions in the sky and the element.

And soon I heard a roaring wind:
It did not come anear;   310
But with its sound it shook the sails,
That were so thin and sere.

The upper air burst into life!
And a hundred fire-flags sheen,
To and fro they were hurried about!
And to and fro, and in and out,
The wan stars danced between.

And the coming wind did roar more loud,
And the sails did sigh like sedge;
And the rain poured down from one
    black cloud;   320
The Moon was at its edge.

The thick black cloud was cleft, and still
The Moon was at its side:
Like waters shot from some high crag,
The lightning fell with never a jag,
A river steep and wide.

The bodies of the ship's crew are inspired, and the ship moves on;

The loud wind never reached the ship,
Yet now the ship moved on!
Beneath the lightning and the Moon
The dead men gave a groan.   330

They groaned, they stirred, they all uprose,
Nor spake, nor moved their eyes;
It had been strange, even in a dream,
To have seen those dead men rise.

The helmsman steered, the ship moved on;
Yet never a breeze up-blew;
The mariners all 'gan work the ropes,
Where they were wont to do;
They raised their limbs like lifeless tools—
We were a ghastly crew.   340

The body of my brother's son
Stood by me, knee to knee:
The body and I pulled at one rope,
But he said nought to me."

"I fear thee, ancient Mariner!"
"Be calm, thou Wedding-Guest!

But not by the souls of the men, nor by demons of earth or middle air, but by a blessed troop of angelic spirits, sent down by the invocation of the guardian saint.

'Twas not those souls that fled in pain,
Which to their corses came again,
But a troop of spirits blest:

For when it dawned—they dropped
    their arms,   350
And clustered round the mast;
Sweet sounds rose slowly through their mouths,
And from their bodies passed.

Around, around, flew each sweet sound,
Then darted to the Sun;
Slowly the sounds came back again,
Now mixed, now one by one.

Sometimes a-dropping from the sky
I heard the sky-lark sing;
Sometimes all little birds that are,   360
How they seemed to fill the sea and air
With their sweet jargoning!

And now 'twas like all instruments,
Now like a lonely flute;
And now it is an angel's song,
That makes the heavens be mute.

It ceased; yet still the sails made on
A pleasant noise till noon,
A noise like of a hidden brook
In the leafy month of June,   370
That to the sleeping woods all night
Singeth a quiet tune.

Till noon we quietly sailed on,
Yet never a breeze did breathe:
Slowly and smoothly went the ship,
Moved onward from beneath.

The lonesome Spirit from the south-pole carries on the ship as far as the Line, in obedience to the angelic troop, but still requireth vengeance.

Under the keel nine fathom deep,
From the land of mist and snow,
The spirit slid: and it was he
That made the ship to go.   380
The sails at noon left off their tune,
And the ship stood still also.

The Sun, right up above the mast,
Had fixed her to the ocean:
But in a minute she 'gan stir,
With a short uneasy motion—

CHARACTERS AND NARRATIVES

Backwards and forwards half her length,
With a short uneasy motion.

Then like a pawing horse let go,
She made a sudden bound: 390
It flung the blood into my head,
And I fell down in a swound.

The Polar Spirit's fellow-dæmons, the invisible inhabitants of the element, take part in his wrong; and two of them relate, one to the other, that penance long and heavy for the ancient Mariner hath been accorded to the Polar Spirit, who returneth southward.

How long in that same fit I lay,
I have not to declare;
But ere my living life returned,
I heard, and in my soul discerned
Two voices in the air.

'Is it he?' quoth one, 'Is this the man?
By him who died on cross,
With his cruel bow he laid full low   400
The harmless Albatross.

The spirit who bideth by himself
In the land of mist and snow,
He loved the bird that loved the man
Who shot him with his bow.'

The other was a softer voice,
As soft as honey-dew:
Quoth he, 'The man hath penance done,
And penance more will do.'

PART VI

First Voice

'But tell me, tell me! speak again   140
Thy soft response renewing—
What makes that ship drive on so fast?
What is the ocean doing?'

Second Voice

'Still as a slave before his lord,
The ocean hath no blast;

His great bright eye most silently
Up to the Moon is cast—

If he may know which way to go;
For she guides him smooth or grim.
See, brother, see! how graciously   420
She looketh down on him.'

The Mariner hath been cast into a trance; for the angelic power causeth the vessel to drive northward faster than human life could endure.

First Voice

'But why drives on that ship so fast,
Without or wave or wind?'

Second Voice

'The air is cut away before,
And closes from behind.

Fly, brother, fly! more high, more high!
Or we shall be belated:
For slow and slow that ship will go,
When the Mariner's trance is abated.'

The supernatural motion is retarded; the Mariner awakes, and his penance begins anew.

I woke, and we were sailing on   430
As in a gentle weather:
'Twas night, calm night, the moon was high;
The dead men stood together.

All stood together on the deck,
For a charnel-dungeon fitter:
All fixed on me their stony eyes,
That in the Moon did glitter.

The pang, the curse, with which they died,
Had never passed away:
I could not draw my eyes from theirs,   440
Nor turn them up to pray.

The curse is finally expiated.

And now this spell was snapt: once more
I viewed the ocean green,
And looked far forth, yet little saw
Of what had else been seen—

Like one, that on a lonesome road
Doth walk in fear and dread,
And having once turned round walks on,
And turns no more his head;
Because he knows, a frightful fiend   450
Doth close behind him tread.

But soon there breathed a wind on me,
Nor sound nor motion made:
Its path was not upon the sea,
In ripple or in shade.

It raised my hair, it fanned my cheek
Like a meadow-gale of spring—
It mingled strangely with my fears,
Yet it felt like a welcoming.

Swiftly, swiftly flew the ship,   460
Yet she sailed softly too:
Sweetly, sweetly blew the breeze—
On me alone it blew.

And the ancient Mariner beholdeth his native country.

Oh! dream of joy! is this indeed
The light-house top I see?
Is this the hill? is this the kirk?
Is this mine own countree?

We drifted o'er the harbour-bar,
And I with sobs did pray—
O let me be awake, my God!   470
Or let me sleep alway.

The harbour-bay was clear as glass,
So smoothly it was strewn!
And on the bay the moonlight lay,
And the shadow of the Moon.

The rock shone bright, the kirk no less,
That stands above the rock:

The moonlight steeped in silentness
The steady weathercock.

And the bay was white with silent light,   480
Till rising from the same,
Full many shapes, that shadows were,
In crimson colors came.

The angelic spirits leave the dead bodies,

And appear in their own forms of light.

A little distance from the prow
Those crimson shadows were:
I turned my eyes upon the deck—
Oh, Christ! what saw I there!

Each corse lay flat, lifeless and flat,
And, by the holy rood!
A man all light, a seraph-man,   490
On every corse there stood.

This seraph-band, each waved his hand:
It was a heavenly sight!
They stood as signals to the land,
Each one a lovely light;

This seraph-band, each waved his hand,
No voice did they impart—
No voice; but oh! the silence sank
Like music on my heart.

But soon I heard the dash of oars,   500
I heard the Pilot's cheer;
My head was turned perforce away,
And I saw a boat appear.

The Pilot and the Pilot's boy,
I heard them coming fast:
Dear Lord in Heaven! it was a joy
The dead men could not blast.

I saw a third—I heard his voice:
It is the Hermit good!

>   He singeth loud his godly hymns   510
>   That he makes in the wood.
>   He'll shrieve my soul, he'll wash away
>   The Albatross's blood.

PART VII

The Hermit of the Wood,

>   This Hermit good lives in that wood
>   Which slopes down to the sea.
>   How loudly his sweet voice he rears!
>   He loves to talk with marineres
>   That come from a far countree.
>
>   He kneels at morn, and noon, and eve—
>   He hath a cushion plump: 520
>   It is the moss that wholly hides
>   The rotted old oak-stump.
>
>   The skiff-boat neared: I heard them talk,
>   'Why, this is strange, I trow!
>   Where are those lights so many and fair,
>   That signal made but now?'

Approacheth the ship with wonder.

>   'Strange, by my faith!' the Hermit said—
>   'And they answered not our cheer!
>   The planks looked warped! and see those sails,
>   How thin they are and sere!   530
>   I never saw aught like to them,
>   Unless perchance it were
>
>   Brown skeletons of leaves that lag
>   My forest-brook along;
>   When the ivy-tod is heavy with snow,
>   And the owlet whoops to the wolf below,
>   That eats the she-wolf's young.'
>
>   'Dear Lord! it hath a fiendish look—
>   (The Pilot made reply)
>   I am a-feared'—'Push on, push on!'   540
>   Said the Hermit cheerily.

The boat came closer to the ship,
But I nor spake nor stirred;
The boat came close beneath the ship,
And straight a sound was heard.

The ship suddenly sinketh.

Under the water it rumbled on,
Still louder and more dread:
It reached the ship, it split the bay;
The ship went down like lead.

The ancient Mariner is saved in the Pilot's boat.

Stunned by that loud and dreadful sound,   550
Which sky and ocean smote,
Like one that hath been seven days drowned,
My body lay afloat;
But swift as dreams, myself I found
Within the Pilot's boat.

Upon the whirl, where sank the ship,
The boat spun round and round;
And all was still, save that the hill
Was telling of the sound.

I moved my lips—the Pilot shrieked,   560
And fell down in a fit;
The holy Hermit raised his eyes,
And prayed where he did sit.

I took the oars: the Pilot's boy,
Who now doth crazy go,
Laughed loud and long, and all the while
His eyes went to and fro.
'Ha! ha!' quoth he, 'full plain I see,
The Devil knows how to row.'

And now, all in my own countree,   570
I stood on the firm land!
The Hermit stepped forth from the boat,
And scarcely he could stand.

CHARACTERS AND NARRATIVES

_{The ancient Mariner earnestly entreateth the Hermit to shrieve him; and the penance of life falls on him.}

'O shrieve me, shrieve me, holy man!'
The Hermit crossed his brow,
'Say quick,' quoth he, 'I bid thee say—
What manner of man art thou?'

Forthwith this frame of mine was wrenched
With a woeful agony,
Which forced me to begin my tale;   580
And then it left me free.

_{And ever and anon throughout his future life an agony constraineth him to travel from land to land;}

Since then, at an uncertain hour,
That agony returns;
And till my ghastly tale is told,
This heart within me burns.

I pass, like night, from land to land;
I have strange power of speech;
That moment that his face I see,
I know the man that must hear me:
To him my tale I teach.   590

What loud uproar bursts from that door!
The wedding-guests are there;
But in the garden-bower the bride
And bride-maids singing are:
And hark the little vesper bell,
Which biddeth me to prayer!

O Wedding-Guest! this soul hath been
Alone on a wide wide sea:
So lonely 'twas, that God himself
Scarce seemèd there to be.   600

O sweeter than the marriage-feast,
'Tis sweeter far to me,
To walk together to the kirk
With a goodly company!—

To walk together to the kirk,
And all together pray,

While each to his great Father bends,
Old men, and babes, and loving friends
And youths and maidens gay!

<small>And to teach, by his own example, love and reverence to all things that God made and loveth.</small>

Farewell, farewell! but this I tell   610
To thee, thou Wedding-Guest!
He prayeth well, who loveth well
Both man and bird and beast.

He prayeth best, who loveth best
All things both great and small;
For the dear God who loveth us,
He made and loveth all."

The Mariner, whose eye is bright,
Whose beard with age is hoar,
Is gone: and now the Wedding-Guest   620
Turned from the bridegroom's door.

He went like one that hath been stunned,
And is of sense forlorn:
A sadder and a wiser man,
He rose the morrow morn.

The Host of the Air

WILLIAM BUTLER YEATS

O'Driscoll drove with a song
The wild duck and the drake
From the tall and the tufted reeds
Of the drear Hart Lake.

And he saw how the reeds grew dark
At the coming of night-tide,
And dreamed of the long dim hair
Of Bridget his bride.

He heard while he sang and dreamed
A piper piping away,   10

And never was piping so sad,
And never was piping so gay.

And he saw young men and young girls
Who danced on a level place,
And Bridget his bride among them,
With a sad and a gay face.

The dancers crowded about him,
And many a sweet thing said,
And a young man brought him red wine
And a young girl white bread.   20

But Bridget drew him by the sleeve,
Away from the merry bands,
To old men playing at cards
With a twinkling of ancient hands.

The bread and the wine had a doom,
For these were the host of the air;
He sat and played in a dream
Of her long dim hair.

He played with the merry old men
And thought not of evil chance,   30
Until one bore Bridget his bride
Away from the merry dance.

He bore her away in his arms,
The handsomest young man there,
And his neck and his breast and his arms
Were drowned in her long dim hair.

O'Driscoll scattered the cards
And out of his dream awoke:
Old men and young men and young girls
Were gone like a drifting smoke;   40

But he heard high up in the air
A piper piping away,
And never was piping so sad,
And never was piping so gay.

The Three Beggars

WILLIAM BUTLER YEATS

"Though to my feathers in the wet,
I have stood here from break of day,
I have not found a thing to eat,
For only rubbish comes my way.
Am I to live on lebeen-lone?"
Muttered the old crane of Gort.
"For all my pains on lebeen-lone?"

King Guaire walked amid his court
The palace-yard and river-side
And there to three old beggars said, 10
"You that have wandered far and wide
Can ravel out what's in my head.
Do men who least desire get most,
Or get the most who most desire?"
A beggar said, "They get the most
Whom man or devil cannot tire,
And what could make their muscles taut
Unless desire had made them so?"
But Guaire laughed with secret thought,
"If that be true as it seems true, 20
One of you three is a rich man,
For he shall have a thousand pounds
Who is first asleep, if but he can
Sleep before the third noon sounds."
And thereon, merry as a bird
With his old thoughts, King Guaire went
From river-side and palace-yard
And left them to their argument.
"And if I win," one beggar said,
"Though I am old I shall persuade 30
A pretty girl to share my bed";

5 lebeen: minnows.   6 Gort: an Irish place name.

The second: "I shall learn a trade";
The third: "I'll hurry to the course
Among the other gentlemen,
And lay it all upon a horse";
The second: "I have thought again:
A farmer has more dignity."
One to another sighed and cried:
The exorbitant dreams of beggary,
That idleness had borne to pride,   40
Sang through their teeth from noon to noon;
And when the second twilight brought
The frenzy of the beggars' moon
None closed his blood-shot eyes but sought
To keep his fellows from their sleep;
All shouted till their anger grew
And they were whirling in a heap.

They mauled and bit the whole night through;
They mauled and bit till the day shone;
They mauled and bit through all that day   50
And till another night had gone,
Or if they made a moment's stay
They sat upon their heels to rail,
And when old Guaire came and stood
Before the three to end this tale,
They were commingling lice and blood.
"Time's up," he cried, and all the three
With blood-shot eyes upon him stared.
"Time's up," he cried, and all the three
Fell down upon the dust and snored.   60

"*Maybe I shall be lucky yet,
Now they are silent*," said the crane.
"*Though to my feathers in the wet
I've stood as I were made of stone
And seen the rubbish run about,
It's certain there are trout somewhere
And maybe I shall take a trout
If but I do not seem to care.*"

~ II ~

Metrical Forms

Many elements contribute to the form of a poem. Some a poet inherits from his predecessors, and it is with the most obvious of these that the present chapter is concerned: meter, rhyme, and stanza forms. English versification is an extremely complicated as well as controversial subject. Conflicting theories are held, for example, about whether accent or duration is the "real" basis of its poetic rhythm. But in spite of disagreement, an accepted terminology exists which is useful in describing the fixed, traditional verse forms, and of which the educated reader is expected to know the main outlines. Later, if he is curious, he may explore conflicting scientific (or pseudoscientific), historical, and aesthetic theories. The terms given here consist merely of those most commonly employed, and they are defined in the commonest way. In studying meter, however, even at a relatively simple level, it should always be remembered that the poet's ear is his final guide and that the established verse forms in English are full of variations in actual practice.

The unit of conventional English verse is the foot, which ordinarily consists of either two or three syllables. The iambic foot, by far the most common, has two syllables with stress on the second (betráy; he laughed); the trochaic, two syllables with stress on the first (wícket; beát it). The anapest consists of three syllables, with stress on the last (interfére; in a stéw), and the dactyl of three, with stress on the first (Flórida). Ordinarily, one or another of these feet will predominate in a poem and the meter of the poem will be named accordingly: iambic pentameter, for example, if the standard foot is iambic and there are five feet to a line; or iambic hexameter if six to a line; tetrameter if four; trimeter if three; and so on.

Two other feet are common: the spondee, a foot made up of two stressed or "long" syllables; and the pyrrhic, a foot of two unstressed syllables. These are used, not as the meter for a whole poem, but as frequent variations from one of the standard meters. The standard ones themselves are to some extent interchangeable: a poem whose basic meter is iambic will nearly always contain feet in which the stress is inverted and which are therefore trochaic, most commonly at the beginning of a line or after a pause; it may also contain an occasional anapestic foot, as well as spondees and pyrrhics.

The distinction between stressed and unstressed syllables is not a hard-and-fast one. In actual speech, syllables run the gamut from the syllabically almost nonexistent "-tle" in "little" to a strong and long one such as "prowled." Intermediate syllables may be treated as either accented or not, depending on their metrical position or the sense. Poetry should be read with these varied shadings in mind and not in rigid categories of stressed and unstressed. A mechanical reading of the following lines of Wordsworth would give

A slum/ber did / my spir/it seal;

I had / no hu/man fears.

But such a reading kills the meaning. The lines should rather be read (with ˘ representing an intermediate degree of stress):

A slum/ber did / my spir/it seal;

I had / no hu/man fears.

or perhaps

I had / no hu/man fears.

Even this grossly oversimplifies what should be the real reading. For in the first line, "my," though unaccented, and "did," which stands where an accent is expected, have a great deal more weight than the opening syllable "A" or the "-it" of "spirit." Every syllable in the line, in fact, has a slightly different degree of stress and pitch (varying as the voice is louder or softer, higher or lower) and a different duration. The same thing is true of the second line: the two light syllables of the opening pyrrhic foot, for example, differ slightly. "No" and "hu-" differ more. Some authorities, indeed, maintain that there can be no spondees in English, because the adjoining stresses will always differ. However, since in this line and very commonly elsewhere both syllables are noticeably stronger than either syllable in the preceding foot, it seems more accurately descriptive of the line as a whole (and of the way it should be read) to call such feet spondees rather than iambics, recognizing, of course, that all these terms, which come down to us from the Greek, involve somewhat different elements in English.

The general functions of rhythm were discussed in the "Introduction." It may be added here that meter affects the underlying texture of what we read by alternately, almost imperceptibly, creating and then satisfying "expectancy," as the poet Robert Bridges called it, or by an almost imperceptible alternation of suspense and the resolution of suspense. If the meter is too regular, our suspense or expectancy lapses out of boredom. One of the marks of excellence, therefore, in poetry composed in traditional meters is the maintaining of a fine balance between the regularity of the pattern and the variety dictated by individual words and meaning or, as T. S. Eliot described it, the constant "unperceived evasion of monotony, which is the very life of verse." Hence, in general, meter is properly studied not in isolation but along with the poem as a whole, and therefore in this chapter only a few supplementary poems are presented to illustrate certain meters, metrical effects, and forms.

Most of the poems in Chapter I are written in iambic verse and will serve there for study, in addition to the first two selections here.

There is little consistently trochaic verse in English. A song of Shakespeare from *The Tempest* is one of the few examples, but since it is not among his best songs, a few lines will suffice:

> Honour, / riches, / marriage/, blessing,
> Long con/tinuance, / and in/creasing,
> Hourly / joys be / still up/on you!
> Juno /sings her /blessings /on you.

A good deal of trochaic verse exists, however, in which the light final syllable is omitted in half or more than half of the lines, as in Suckling's "Why so pale and wan, fond lover" and "Fear no more." Many other poems, which at first puzzle the reader who wishes to determine their meter, hover between iambic and trochaic, often with one or the other seeming to predominate but with either the initial or the final light syllable regularly omitted. This may produce a sturdy, downright movement in which the lines begin and end with a small thump, as in this early seventeenth-century anonymous "Bellman's Song":

> Maids to bed and cover coal;
> Let the mouse out of her hole;
> Cricket in the chimney sing
> Whilst the little bell doth ring:
> If fast asleep, who can tell
> When the clapper hits the bell.[1]

[1] Some writers explain such four-stress verse with markedly strong accents as a descendant of Anglo-Saxon verse, which normally had four stresses irregularly placed and a varying number of unstressed syllables. There is certainly a good deal of verse, especially nursery rhymes and songs written for already existing music, in which the meter is one of strictly timed beat regardless of the number of syllables ("Tom, Tom, the piper's son," etc.). "The Bellman's Song," however, has seven syllables in each line.

In such poems as this, the phrasal units may be predominantly ⌣´/⌣´ or´⌣ /´⌣ or may shift back and forth between the two. The reader need not be disturbed by the absence of a name or set of rules covering all such verse if he simply recognizes how clear and natural its rhythm is.

Anapestic meter is conspicuous and catchy, often too catchy for serious poetry. Its high proportion of light, quickly moving syllables produces an effect of driving acceleration that, if uncontrolled, sends a poem galloping off the page. It is therefore sparingly used and is nearly always interspersed freely with iambics. The rhythm of unadulterated anapests does in fact resemble the sound of a horse galloping, as addicts of cowboy programs on television will easily recognize and as writers of verse have long known. Hence Byron's "The Assyrian came down like a wolf on the fold,/ And his cohorts were gleaming in purple and gold," and Browning's "I sprang to the stirrup, and Joris, and he;/ I galloped, Dirck galloped, we galloped all three;/ 'Good speed!' cried the watch, as the gate-bolts undrew;/ 'Speed!' echoed the wall to us galloping through." Modified anapests are capable of more subtle effects, as several poems in this chapter will show.

There is little successful dactylic verse in English, though it has been tried many times, usually in the hope of producing something that will sound like Virgil in Latin or Homer in Greek. No examples are given in this volume. Perhaps the most celebrated attempt is that of Longfellow's dactylic hexameters in "Evangeline":

This is the / forest pri/meval. The / murmuring / pines and

the / hemlocks,

Bearded with / moss, and in / garments / green, indis/tinct

in the / twilight.

Nearly all English verse except blank and free verse employs

rhyme in which the ends of lines are matched, one with another, by identical (or sometimes, for variety, merely similar) sounds. Like meter, rhyme is a structural component serving to bind together the verse, to mark off the line as a unit of rhythm or thought or both, and to organize groups of lines into various stanzaic units. Like meter, rhyme heightens the tension of language by alternately arousing and satisfying expectancy. When skilfully used, its matching yet varied chime is pleasant to hear; and it serves also for special effects of emphasis or linking now and then, as was pointed out earlier in the example of Housman's lines

> Look into the pewter pot
> To see the world as the world's not.

Rhyme, like meter, has its conventions; it has been systematized in more or less fixed ways which a poet inherits from his predecessors, though he will also vary them or invent new systems if he chooses. Standard rhyme requires the matching of sounds beginning with an accented vowel and including all following sounds. Most rhyme is masculine, or one-syllable rhyme: "match-patch," "throw-below." The consonants preceding the accented vowel are different: thus, "made" and "played" are accepted masculine rhyme but "played" and "displayed" are not, because the consonants preceding the vowel, "pl-," are the same (this "identical rhyme," or *rime riche*, is nevertheless occasionally used). A two-syllable or feminine rhyme—"slipper-dipper," "daisy-mazy"—occurs when the next to the last syllable of the line is accented, as in regular trochaic verse and fairly often in iambic, where an extra unaccented syllable may soften the end of the line without affecting the basic rhythm. Triple rhyme, often included under the term "feminine," applies the same principle to lines in which the third from the last syllable is accented, as in "dimity-sublimity," "vanity-insanity." Because it is so conspicuous, triple rhyme is almost exclusively confined to comic verse where an absurd effect is wanted, as in the examples just given, taken from Byron's *Don Juan*. Even two-syllable rhyme can be too much of a good thing, for the constant double echo is apt to jingle unless it is used sparingly. This is no doubt one reason why pure trochaic verse, which requires double (if any) rhyme is uncommon.

Many poets depart from standard rhyme occasionally. The folk ballads contain inexact rhymes of various kinds. In the work of poets who are conscious craftsmen we find "weak rhyme," in which only unaccented or faintly accented syllables correspond ("revelry"-"fairily" in Keats, "astonishment"-"monument" in Milton, where, however, the weak rhyme is preceded by other similarities of sound), or an unaccented syllable rhymes with an accented one ("tell"-"citadel" in Keats), or there is mere spelling or "eye rhyme" ("victory"-"sky" in Shelley, "love"-"prove" in Shakespeare and often elsewhere. (This last, however, in older pronunciation was a true rhyme). Modern poets have explored other kinds of partial rhyme.

Related to rhyme, in the sense of being repetition used as a fixed structural element, are refrain and chorus. The first is a line or part of a line (occasionally two lines) recurring at regular intervals, often at the end, sometimes in the middle, of each stanza (see "The Three Ravens," p. 57). The chorus everyone knows as a stanza that is repeated, usually after each other stanza (see "Back and side," p. 135).

End-rhyme, refrain, and chorus, then, constitute the repetitive sound patterns other than meter that are governed by firmly established convention which the poet does not have to invent afresh for each poem but which he inherits. Free forms of repetition, in some respects even more important, are dealt with in the next chapter.

Of English stanza forms the most familiar is the so-called ballad stanza, in which some, but not all, of the popular ballads are composed; it is a quatrain in iambic verse made up of alternating four- and three-stressed lines with the second and fourth (sometimes also the first and third) rhyming. "Sir

Patrick Spence" and "Bonny Barbara Allan" in Chapter I are typical examples. The ballad stanza is also one of the commonest forms for lyric poems and for hymns, in which it is known as "common meter."

Blank verse—unrhymed iambic pentameter—is of course best known for its use in longer works such as Shakespeare's plays and Milton's *Paradise Lost*. Ordinarily it is written with paragraph divisions rather than in stanzas.

The heroic couplet is represented by Pope's *The Rape of the Lock* in Chapter VI and is explained in the notes to that poem; the sonnet is discussed separately in Chapter V; the Spenserian and other special stanzas are noted where they occur. Besides the named stanzas, there are many unnamed ones, such as the famous eight-line stanzas of Keats's odes and the frequently used octosyllabic couplet (see Burns's "Tam O'Shanter"). Conventional meters are in fact employed in a wide variety of stanza forms with many different rhyme schemes.

A number of elaborate, highly artificial verse forms exist, most of them derived from medieval French lyric poetry. The triolet, one of the most rigid and artificial of all, furnishes a good example of this kind of writing. As in the use of any fixed form, success requires that the poet create the illusion of freedom: he must seem to say precisely what he chooses to say in the way he chooses to say it, yet he must do so without breaking the boundaries of the form, however rigid this may be. In the triolet the technical difficulty is great because the actual freedom is very small. The poem must consist of eight lines with only two rhymes. The entire first line is repeated as the fourth and again as the seventh, and the second line is repeated as the eighth. Once the poet has composed his first two lines, therefore, he has very little liberty, since only three are left to his choice and even in these the rhyme is fixed. Yet he must not seem encumbered by the obligation to repeat and to rhyme so monotonously; and his poem must somehow progress, not stand still. The triolet by Hardy in this chapter shows the strain of the technical difficulty but illustrates the form perhaps all the better for that reason. A much better one by Bridges appears in Chapter III.

At the opposite pole from the triolet and other strict forms stands *free verse (vers libre)*. Some writers have succeeded in producing poetic rhythms without employing any of the traditional metrical and rhyme schemes. Since the norm of speech and written prose is rhythmically irregular, even a distant approach to regularity of beat becomes noticeable as rhythm, particularly when parallel grammatical constructions are used or when major pauses occur at more or less regular intervals. Occasionally what appears to the eye as verse differs from prose only typographically and may properly be ignored in any study of poetry. On the other hand, much free verse seems to have a half-regular ground-rhythm underlying its freedom, as in many passages of the King James translation of the Bible. It is especially noticeable in some of the Psalms:

> The heavens declare the glory of God: and the firmament showeth his handywork.
> Day unto day uttereth speech, and night unto night showeth knowledge.
> There is no speech nor language, where their voice is not heard.
> Their line is gone out through all the earth, and their words to the end of the world (Psalm 19).

The first sentence scans quite conventionally as anapestic verse with the usual sprinkling of iambics. The rest is not quite so regular, but there is still a tendency toward a rhythmical beat, reinforced by the balanced parallelism of the phrasal units. In free verse, however, since by definition it follows no established rule, the form of each poem has to be considered independently. A good example of free verse that is barely this side of prose and that considerably antedates the term now used to describe it, is Smart's description of his cat Jeoffrey in Chapter I. In the present chapter are printed two examples of Whitman's verse in which other formalizing elements are used to compensate for the absence of meter. These should be compared with the much finer example of free verse from Ecclesiastes in Chapter III.

She dwelt among the untrodden ways

WILLIAM WORDSWORTH

She dwelt among the untrodden ways
    Beside the springs of Dove,
A Maid whom there were none to praise
    And very few to love:

A violet by a mossy stone
    Half hidden from the eye!
—Fair as a star, when only one
    Is shining in the sky.

She lived unknown, and few could know
    When Lucy ceased to be;
But she is in her grave, and, oh,
    The difference to me!

A slumber did my spirit seal

WILLIAM WORDSWORTH

A slumber did my spirit seal;
    I had no human fears:
She seemed a thing that could not feel
    The touch of earthly years.

No motion has she now, no force;
    She neither hears nor sees;
Rolled round in earth's diurnal course,
    With rocks, and stones, and trees.

Fear no more

WILLIAM SHAKESPEARE

Fear no more the heat o' th' sun,
   Nor the furious winter's rages;
Thou thy worldly task hast done,
   Home art gone, and ta'en thy wages:
Golden lads and girls all must,
As chimney-sweepers, come to dust.

Fear no more the frown o' th' great;
   Thou art past the tyrant's stroke;
Care no more to clothe and eat;
   To thee the reed is as the oak: 10
The sceptre, learning, physic, must
All follow this, and come to dust.

Fear no more the lightning-flash,
   Nor th' all-dreaded thunder-stone;
Fear not slander, censure rash;
   Thou hast finish'd joy and moan:
All lovers young, all lovers must
Consign to thee, and come to dust.

No exorciser harm thee!
   Nor no witchcraft charm thee!   20
Ghost unlaid forbear thee!
   Nothing ill come near thee!
Quiet consummation have;
And renowned be thy grave!

Full fathom five

WILLIAM SHAKESPEARE

Full fathom five thy father lies;
   Of his bones are coral made;
Those are pearls that were his eyes;
   Nothing of him that doth fade

But doth suffer a sea change
Into something rich and strange.
Sea-nymphs hourly ring his knell:
                    Ding-dong!
Hark! now I hear them,—Ding-dong, bell!

Dust of Snow

ROBERT FROST

The way a crow
Shook down on me
The dust of snow
From a hemlock tree

Has given my heart
A change of mood
And saved some part
Of a day I had rued.

Fragment: A Wanderer

PERCY BYSSHE SHELLEY

He wanders, like a day-appearing dream,
  Through the dim wildernesses of the mind;
Through desert woods and tracts, which seem
  Like ocean, homeless, boundless, unconfined.

The Sluggard

ISAAC WATTS

'Tis the voice of the Sluggard; I hear him complain,
"You have waked me too soon; I must slumber again."
As the door on its hinges, so he on his bed,
Turns his sides, and his shoulders, and his heavy head.

"A little more sleep, and a little more slumber,"
Thus he wastes half his days, and his hours without number:
And when he gets up, he sits folding his hands,
Or walks about saunt'ring, or trifling he stands.

I pass'd by his garden, and saw the wild brier,
The thorn and the thistle grow broader and higher; 10
The clothes that hang on him are turning to rags;
And his money still wastes, till he starves, or he begs.

I made him a visit, still hoping to find
He had took better care for improving his mind:
He told me his dreams, talk'd of eating and drinking;
But he scarce reads his Bible, and never loves thinking.

Said I then to my heart, "Here's a lesson for me,
That man's but a picture of what I might be.
But thanks to my friends for their care in my breeding,
Who taught me betimes to love working and reading." 20

The Chimney Sweeper

WILLIAM BLAKE

From Songs of Innocence

When my mother died I was very young,
And my father sold me while yet my tongue
Could scarcely cry " 'weep! 'weep! 'weep! 'weep!"
So your chimneys I sweep & in soot I sleep.

There's little Tom Dacre, who cried when his head,
That curl'd like a lamb's back, was shav'd: so I said,
"Hush, Tom! never mind it, for when your head's bare
You know that the soot cannot spoil your white hair."

And so he was quiet, & that very night,
As Tom was a-sleeping, he had such a sight! 10
That thousands of sweepers, Dick, Joe, Ned & Jack,
Were all of them lock'd up in coffins of black.

And by came an Angel who had a bright key,
And he open'd the coffins & set them all free;
Then down a green plain leaping, laughing, they run,
And wash in a river, and shine in the Sun.

Then naked & white, all their bags left behind,
They rise upon clouds, and sport in the wind;
And the Angel told Tom, if he'd be a good boy,
He'd have God for his father, & never want joy. 20

And so Tom awoke; and we rose in the dark,
And got with our bags & our brushes to work,
Tho' the morning was cold, Tom was happy & warm;
So if all do their duty they need not fear harm.

Lines
When the lamp is shattered

PERCY BYSSHE SHELLEY

I

When the lamp is shattered
The light in the dust lies dead—
When the cloud is scattered
The rainbow's glory is shed.
When the lute is broken,
Sweet tones are remembered not;
When the lips have spoken,
Loved accents are soon forgot.

II

As music and splendour
Survive not the lamp and the lute, 10
The heart's echoes render
No song when the spirit is mute:—
No song but sad dirges,
Like the wind through a ruined cell,

  Or the mournful surges
That ring the dead seaman's knell.

III

  When hearts have once mingled
Love first leaves the well-built nest,
  The weak one is singled
To endure what it once possessed.   20
  O Love! who bewailest
The frailty of all things here,
  Why choose you the frailest
For your cradle, your home, and your bier?

IV

  Its passions will rock thee
As the storms rock the ravens on high:
  Bright reason will mock thee,
Like the sun from a wintry sky.
  From thy nest every rafter
Will rot, and thine eagle home   30
  Leave thee naked to laughter,
When leaves fall and cold winds come.

Lancer

A. E. HOUSMAN

I 'listed at home for a lancer,
 Oh who would not sleep with the brave?
I 'listed at home for a lancer
 To ride on a horse to my grave.

And over the seas we were bidden
 A country to take and to keep;
And far with the brave I have ridden,
 And now with the brave I shall sleep.

For round me the men will be lying
 That learned me the way to behave,   10

And showed me my business of dying:
   Oh who would not sleep with the brave?

They ask and there is not an answer;
Says I, I will 'list for a lancer,
   Oh who would not sleep with the brave?

And I with the brave shall be sleeping
   At ease on my mattress of loam,
When back from their taking and keeping
   The squadron is riding at home.

The wind with the plumes will be playing,
   The girls will stand watching them wave,
And eyeing my comrades and saying
   Oh who would not sleep with the brave?

They ask and there is not an answer;
Says you, I will 'list for a lancer,
   Oh who would not sleep with the brave?

The Listeners

WALTER DE LA MARE

"Is there anybody there?" said the Traveller,
   Knocking on the moonlit door;
And his horse in the silence champed the grasses
   Of the forest's ferny floor:
And a bird flew up out of the turret,
   Above the Traveller's head:
And he smote upon the door again a second time;
   "Is there anybody there?" he said.
But no one descended to the Traveller;
   No head from the leaf-fringed sill
Leaned over and looked into his gray eyes,
   Where he stood perplexed and still.
But only a host of phantom listeners
   That dwelt in the lone house then

Stood listening in the quiet of the moonlight
    To that voice from the world of men:
Stood thronging the faint moonbeams on the dark stair,
    That goes down to the empty hall,
Hearkening in an air stirred and shaken
    By the lonely Traveller's call.   20
And he felt in his heart their strangeness,
    Their stillness answering his cry,
While his horse moved, cropping the dark turf,
    'Neath the starred and leafy sky;
For he suddenly smote on the door, even
    Louder, and lifted his head:—
"Tell them I came, and no one answered,
    That I kept my word," he said.
Never the least stir made the listeners,
    Though every word he spake   30
Fell echoing through the shadowiness of the still house
    From the one man left awake:
Ay, they heard his foot upon the stirrup,
    And the sound of iron on stone,
And how the silence surged softly backward,
    When the plunging hoofs were gone.

A Lament for Our Lady's Shrine at Walsingham

ANON.

In the wrackes of Walsingham
    Whom should I chuse,
But the Queene of Walsingham
    To be guide to my muse.
Then thou Prince of Walsingham,

Title: The priory at Walsingham, destroyed after the Reformation, had contained a famous image of the Virgin, to which pilgrims had come from all parts of Europe.   5 Prince: Christ.

Graunt me to frame,
Bitter plaints to rue thy wronge,
    Bitter woe for thy name.
Bitter was it soe to see
    The seely sheepe
Murdred by the raveninge wolves
    While the sheephardes did sleep;
Bitter was it oh to view
    The sacred vine,
Whiles the gardiners plaied all close,
    Rooted up by the swine;
Bitter, bitter, oh to behould,
    The grasse to growe
Where the walles of Walsingham
    So stately did shewe:
Such were the workes of Walsingham,
    While shee did stand;
Such are the wrackes as now do shewe
    Of that holy land.
Levell, Levell with the ground,
    The towres doe lye,
Which with their golden glitteringe tops
    Pierced once to the skye;
Wher were gates no gates are nowe,
    The waies unknowen
Wher the presse of peers did passe
    While her fame far was blowen.
Owls do scrike wher the sweetest hymns
    Lately were songe;
Toades and serpentes hold ther dennes,
    Wher the Palmers did thronge.
Weepe, Weepe, o Walsingham,
    Whose dayes are nightes,
Blessinges turned to blasphemies,
    Holy deedes to despites!
Sinne is wher our Ladie sate,
    Heaven turned is to Hell;
Sathan sittes wher our Lord did swaye:
    Walsingham, oh farewell!

Upon Julia's Clothes

ROBERT HERRICK

When as in silks my Julia goes,
Then, then (me thinks) how sweetly flowes
That liquefaction of her clothes.

Next, when I cast mine eyes and see
That brave Vibration each way free;
O how that glittering taketh me!

Birds at Winter Nightfall
Triolet

THOMAS HARDY

Around the house the flakes fly faster,
And all the berries now are gone
From holly and cotonea-aster
Around the house. The flakes fly!—faster
Shutting indoors that crumb-outcaster
We used to see upon the lawn
Around the house. The flakes fly faster,
And all the berries now are gone!

From *Song of Myself*

WALT WHITMAN
Section 32

I think I could turn and live with animals, they are so
    placid and self-contain'd,
I stand and look at them long and long.

They do not sweat and whine about their condition,
They do not lie awake in the dark and weep for their sins,
They do not make me sick discussing their duty to God,
Not one is dissatisfied, not one is demented with the mania
   of owning things,
Not one kneels to another, nor to his kind that lived thousands
   of years ago,
Not one is respectable or unhappy over the whole earth. . . .

When I peruse the conquer'd fame

WALT WHITMAN

When I peruse the conquer'd fame of heroes and the victories of
   mighty generals, I do not envy the generals,
Nor the President in his Presidency, nor the rich in his great house,
But when I hear of the brotherhood of lovers, how it was with them,
How together through life, through dangers, odium, unchanging,
   long and long,
Through youth and through middle and old age, how unfaltering,
   how affectionate and faithful they were,
Then I am pensive—I hastily walk away fill'd with the bitterest envy.

~ III ~

Pattern and Imagery

The most obvious effect of imagery and of repetitive patterns of sound other than meter, rhyme, and stanza is enrichment. Alliteration and assonance[1] are mildly pleasant in themselves; they appeal naturally to the ear at every level of sophistication; they are employed in advertising slogans as often as by Shakespeare. Imagery appeals to the senses no less strongly though more indirectly, for what pleases in it, since the concrete object is not present, is the mental image of sensuous experience created by memory and imagination at the suggestion of the poet's words. Such images give force and life to a poem. Sometimes this enrichment is the only or the chief function of an image or a pattern of sound: the poet may use it once, then drop it and go on to another, producing an effect of freshness and variety. Often, however, both images and patterns of sound serve a further and possibly even more important purpose by becoming essential elements in the formal structure of a poem.

As we have seen, meter, rhyme, and stanza forms are relatively fixed, predetermined structural elements. Both poet and reader know them beforehand as patterns that, though they will be varied somewhat within the poem, will remain essentially unbroken till the end. Much more than this is needed

---

[1] The term "assonance" is employed in a variety of senses. By many writers it is used to designate all repetition of verbal sounds, both vowel and consonant, that are not commonly included under the terms "rhyme" or "alliteration." That is its meaning here.

to make a poetic whole. The principle of "unity with variety," or "the unification of the various"—which is one way of describing a principle by which the artist creates order out of chaos—antedates Aristotle and has been recognized by poets in all ages. Theme and progression of thought are major structural elements that in practically all poems serve this unifying purpose. So also, very often, are assonance, alliteration, grammatical symmetry, and imagery, from all of which the poet may create designs afresh with each new poem, and which often directly serve to unite thought, feeling, and form. Subtle and elaborately patterned echoes of sound may produce an extraordinarily rich texture. Take, for example, the remarkable opening line of Shakespeare's poem quoted in Chapter II:

Full fathom five thy father lies.

Most conspicuous is the alliteration of four "f's" in only six words, which in an ordinary poem might well be too much of a good thing, too obvious. In this line, however, obviousness is avoided through the interweaving of other patterns. Of the four words having primary stresses, two-syllable and one-syllable words alternate with the grouping "fathom"-"five"-"father"-"lies"; and the first words of the pairs are bound together by consonants, "th"[2] as well as "f," and the second words by the long "i" vowels, so that "fathom" and "father" alternate with "five" and "lies." The two remaining words are also bound into the pattern, "full" by its alliterating "f" and its final "ll" foreshadowing "lies," and "thy" with the "th" of "father" and the long "i" of "five" and "lies." This is an example of what is meant by closely woven texture. In this particular line, moreover, the general softness of the consonants establishes the vocal tone and to some extent the mood for the rest of the poem.

[2] Since the earliest edition of *The Tempest* uses an alternate spelling of "fathom" ("fadom"), we cannot be certain about the "th" sound in this word. However, in most plays of the period the spelling is as likely to be the printer's as the author's; and it seems most likely that Shakespeare heard the medial consonants as similar in "fathom" and "father."

A pattern of sound is sometimes even more important, as in the triolet below by Robert Bridges, a remarkable poem technically as well as poetically, for it is made out of almost nothing except a structure of sound. It is entirely without imagery; it contains no concrete or figurative language at all; and it makes only a single apparently simple statement, without comment or reflection. The words are common, by themselves colorless, and individually not even particularly attractive in sound. Words could scarcely be less impressive than the monosyllables of the first line, yet this with the repetition required for a triolet[3] constitutes more than a third of the poem—"When first we met we did not guess"—in which the short "e's" furnish a hint of pattern but lack resonance. One might say that Bridges first deprived himself of nearly every resource the poet usually depends on—including, by adoption of the triolet form, even freedom—and then proceeded to write a small masterpiece with the almost nonexistent resources remaining.

> When first we met we did not guess
> That Love would prove so hard a master;
> Of more than common friendliness
> When first we met we did not guess.
> Who could foretell this sore distress,
> This irretrievable disaster
> When first we met—We did not guess
> That Love would prove so hard a master.

The chief resource is the structural use of sound. After the first two lines the short "e's" recur in other words, accompanied by increasingly sonorous and longer words whose meanings are progressively stronger and more intense, though the words are still common—"hard". . ."master" (with the British pronunciation of the "a"), and words with the sequence of sounds "ôr". . ."ĭ". . ."ĕ" repeated—"môre". . ."frĭĕndlĭnĕss," "fôrĕtĕll" . . ."sôre dĭstrĕss"—till the climax is reached in the five-syllabled

---

[3] For the triolet form, see p. 99.

"irretrievable"—whose main vowel, the accented long "e," has not been heard before and therefore stands out strongly—followed by "disaster." The two words occupy nearly a whole line, "irretrievable" alone carrying the weight of three of the line's four metrical stresses, and the words are absolutes or ultimates in meaning, though undefined by any concrete circumstances. After this, the poem subsides quietly to its close, the violent "disaster" flowing naturally and smoothly again into the words of the first line, "when first we met." Offhand, one would have said it would be impossible to create—not merely state but create—"irretrievable disaster" out of such colorless material in so short a space and so artificial a form, even though we read "disaster" as only the personal discovery that love is not easy. The thought is as unsentimental as the words, for the theme, evidently, is not unrequited or lost love, but the immitigible realities of what when superficially regarded presents no difficulties, mutual love. Bridges makes the discovery real and impressive in these lines by pure structure, without any of the obvious adornments of verse, without even any development of thought except what is conveyed by the series of increasingly strong and long synonyms: "hard master," "sore distress," "irretrievable disaster."

Some poets—Swinburne and Hopkins more than any others—are noted for their conspicuous, sometimes extravagant use of alliteration. But nearly all good poets use more of it than at first reading one might suppose, and a great deal more assonance also. Both help, for example, to create the tone of a sonnet in which Shakespeare writes, "And with old woes new wail my dear time's waste" and the very different, ironic tone in Housman's line, quoted before, "And malt does more than Milton can," where we have not only the conspicuous alliteration in the two dominant and contrasting words but also supporting alliteration or assonance in almost every other word: *malt-more-Milt-*, *And-than-can*.

Here, however, a warning is due. In cultivating an awareness of sound patterns, the reader must beware of overdoing matters by indiscriminately indulging in the sport of letter-hunting. There are, after all, only twenty-six letters in the alphabet; and even though many of them represent several sounds each, still, chance and necessity alone—the monkey at the typewriter—will produce a certain amount of recurrence of sound. It is significant recurrence only that concerns us.

The construction of sentences is an often neglected yet profoundly important element in the form of a poem. The value of parallel construction was observed in the discussion of Suckling's "Why so pale" (pp. 12–14) and in the brief remarks on free verse. Parallelism can easily be overdone, however, as many people feel Whitman overdoes it. Parallelism is most noticeable when it employs anaphora (that is, when successive clauses or phrases open with the same word or words); and its effect can be extremely good or extremely bad, depending on how good everything else about the poem is and whether the anaphora itself is used with restraint and at the right moment. "Day unto day uttereth speech, and night unto night showeth knowledge" (Psalm 19) has parallelism without anaphora; "To err is human, to forgive, divine" repeats only the word "to," a scarcely noticeable anaphora; Whitman's

> I will know if I am to be . . .
> I will see if I am not . . .
> I will see if I am not . . .
> I will see if I am to be . . .
> I will see if I have . . . —

which are the opening words of successive lines in "By Blue Ontario's Shore," is so conspicuous that it obliterates everything near it. Yet Eliot repeats "Those who . . . Those who . . ." a number of times, successfully, in *Marina* (p. 405). Poetry makes frequent use of grammatical structure for the purpose of balancing cadences, creating suspense when it is wanted, producing an effect of simplicity—genuine or ironic—or fitting thought and stanza form together in such a way that the stanzaic limits become a positive aid to expression and not a straitjacket. Examples of these and other significant uses of grammatical structure will be found in poems in this chapter and elsewhere.

Imagery also may be used in structural ways, and the tendency to use it so has increased markedly among modern poets. There are plenty of older examples, too, of course. Though earlier poets often delighted in a rich profusion of imagery held together only loosely by subject or theme, the imagery of some of Shakespeare's sonnets is as highly and no doubt as consciously organized as that of any modern work; and the same is very often true of Donne and other seventeenth-century poets. The poet may mark the climax or the conclusion of a poem by a sudden shift from imagery to abstraction, or vice versa. He may weave a pattern by a series of different but related images or may explore the ramifications of a single image or group of images throughout a poem till the imagery itself almost becomes the main theme. "How all's to one thing wrought!" Gerard Manley Hopkins exclaims in one of his poems, and his words might stand almost as a motto for modern poems. Several modern poems are printed in this chapter, with discussions in the notes, to illustrate this structural use of imagery. One of them, Housman's "We'll to the woods no more," combines repetitive imagery with a structural pattern of sound much like that of Bridges' "Triolet" in a way that in the end gives new vitality to stale material.

At about the time of World War I, a group of writers (Ezra Pound, Amy Lowell, H. D., and others) affirmed the overriding importance of the image and called themselves "Imagists." Poetry, they said, "should render particulars exactly," should avoid even fine-sounding generalities, should be "hard and clear, never blurred or indefinite." Few great poems have been purely "imagist" in the sense of having avoided all abstractions and all words expressing emotion, but the Imagist movement materially influenced modern readers' tastes. Several of the short poems in this section are imagist poems based on, and securing unity from, the exploitation of a single image. In

118   POEMS AND POETRY

this respect they are reminiscent of certain sixteenth- and seventeenth-century poems that also consisted in the elaboration of a single "conceit"—that is, of a striking, often farfetched metaphor, comparison, or image. The poem by Lyly in this chapter and Donne's "The Bait" in Chapter VIII are examples of these.

The poems in this chapter have been arranged chronologically rather than in groups for separate study of sound pattern, grammatical structure, and imagery, because most are notable for more than one of these things and the study of them should not be too much fragmented. Some of the selections are also of interest metrically and therefore supplement those in Chapter II; some in Chapter II illustrate principles discussed here. In "Fear no more," for example, and "The Listeners," some of the poetic effect derives from the structural use of imagery or of assonance, alliteration, or grammatical patterns.

A Lyke-Wake Dirge

ANON.

This ae nighte, this ae nighte,
   —*Every nighte and alle,*
Fire and fleet and candle-lighte,
   And Christe receive thy saule.

When thou from hence away art past,
   —*Every nighte and alle,*
To Whinny-muir thou com'st at last:
   And Christe receive thy saule.

If ever thou gavest hosen and shoon,
   —*Every nighte and alle,*   10

Title. Lyke: body.   *1* ae: one.   *7* Whinny-muir: a moor covered with whin (gorse, furze), a shrub in which sharp spines take the place of leaves. *9* hosen and shoon: hose and shoes.

Sit thee down and put them on:
And Christe receive thy saule.

If hosen and shoon thou ne'er gav'st nane
  —*Every nighte and alle,*
The whinnes sall prick thee to the bare bane;
And Christe receive thy saule.

From Brig o' Dread when thou may'st pass,
  —*Every nighte and alle,*
To Purgatory fire thou com'st at last;
And Christe receive thy saule.   20

If ever thou gavest meat or drink,
  —*Every nighte and alle,*
The fire sall never make thee shrink;
And Christe receive thy saule.

If meat or drink thou ne'er gav'st nane,
  —*Every nighte and alle,*
The fire will burn thee to the bare bane;
And Christe receive thy saule.

This ae nighte, this ae nighte,
  —*Every nighte and alle,*   30
Fire and fleet and candle-lighte,
And Christe receive thy saule.

13 nane: none.   15 bane: bone.   17 Brig: bridge.

Cupid and my Campaspe played

JOHN LYLY

Cupid and my Campaspe played
At cards for kisses; Cupid paid.
He stakes his quiver, bow, and arrows,
His mother's doves and team of sparrows,

Loses them too; then down he throws
The coral of his lip, the rose
Growing on's cheek (but none knows how),
With these the crystal of his brow,
And then the dimple of his chin:
All these did my Campaspe win. 10
At last he set her both his eyes;
She won, and Cupid blind did rise.
  O Love! has she done this to thee?
  What shall, alas, become of me?

Follow thy fair sun

THOMAS CAMPION

Follow thy fair sun, unhappy shadow,
Though thou be black as night,
And she made all of light,
Yet follow thy fair sun, unhappy shadow.

Follow her whose light thy light depriveth,
Though here thou liv'st disgrac'd,
And she in heaven is plac'd,
Yet follow her whose light the world reviveth.

Follow those pure beams whose beauty burneth,
That so have scorched thee, 10
As thou still black must be,
Till her kind beams thy black to brightness turneth.

Follow her while yet her glory shineth:
There comes a luckless night,
That will dim all her light;
And this the black unhappy shade divineth.

Follow still since so thy fates ordainèd;
The Sun must have his shade,
Till both at once do fade,
The Sun still proud, the shadow still disdainèd. 20

Rose-cheekt Laura, come

THOMAS CAMPION

 Rose-cheekt Laura, come
Sing thou smoothly with thy beauty's
Silent music, either other
  Sweetly gracing.

 Lovely forms do flow
From consent divinely framed;
Heav'n is music, and thy beauty's
  Birth is heavenly.

 These dull notes we sing
Discords need for helps to grace them; 10
Only beauty purely loving
  Knows no discord,

 But still moves delight,
Like clear springs renew'd by flowing,
Ever perfet, ever in them-
  selves eternal.

Ecclesiastes

From Chapter 12

Remember now thy Creator in the days of thy youth, while the evil days come not, nor the years draw nigh, when thou shalt say, I have no pleasure in them;
 2 While the sun, or the light, or the moon, or the stars, be not darkened, nor the clouds return after the rain:
 3 In the day when the keepers of the house shall tremble, and the strong men shall bow themselves, and the grinders cease because they are few, and those that look out of the windows be darkened,
 4 And the doors shall be shut in the streets, when the sound of

the grinding is low, and he shall rise up at the voice of the bird, and all the daughters of musick shall be brought low;

5 Also when they shall be afraid of that which is high, and fears shall be in the way, and the almond tree shall flourish, and the grasshopper shall be a burden, and desire shall fail: because man goeth to his long home, and the mourners go about the streets:

6 Or ever the silver cord be loosed, or the golden bowl be broken, or the pitcher be broken at the fountain, or the wheel broken at the cistern.

7 Then shall the dust return to the earth as it was: and the spirit shall return unto God who gave it.

8 Vanity of vanities, saith the preacher; all is vanity.

Corinna's Going a-Maying

ROBERT HERRICK

Get up, get up for shame, the blooming morn
Upon her wings presents the god unshorn.
  See how Aurora throws her fair
  Fresh-quilted colours through the air;
  Get up, sweet slug-a-bed, and see
  The dew bespangling herb and tree.
Each flower has wept and bowed toward the east
Above an hour since; yet you not dressed,
  Nay! not so much as out of bed?
  When all the birds have matins said,   10
  And sung their thankful hymns, 'tis sin,
  Nay, profanation to keep in,
Whenas a thousand virgins on this day
Spring, sooner than the lark, to fetch in May.

Rise and put on your foliage, and be seen
To come forth, like the springtime, fresh and green,
  And sweet as Flora. Take no care

---

2 god: Apollo, god of the sun.   14 May: common name for white-thorn or hawthorn.

For jewels for your gown or hair;
Fear not, the leaves will strew
Gems in abundance upon you;   20
Besides, the childhood of the day has kept,
Against you come, some orient pearls unwept;
Come, and receive them while the light
Hangs on the dew-locks of the night,
And Titan on the eastern hill
Retires himself, or else stands still
Till you come forth. Wash, dress, be brief in praying:
Few beads are best, when once we go a-maying.

Come, my Corinna, come; and coming, mark
How each field turns a street, each street a park   30
Made green, and trimmed with trees; see how
Devotion gives each house a bough
Or branch; each porch, each door, ere this,
An ark, a tabernacle is,
Made up of white-thorn neatly enterwove,
As if here were those cooler shades of love.
Can such delights be in the street
And open fields, and we not see't?
Come, we'll abroad, and let's obey
The proclamation made for May,   40
And sin no more, as we have done, by staying;
But, my Corinna, come, let's go a-maying.

There's not a budding boy or girl this day
But is got up, and gone to bring in May.
A deal of youth, ere this, is come
Back, and with white-thorn laden, home.
Some have despatched their cakes and cream
Before that we have left to dream;
And some have wept, and wooed, and plighted troth,
And chose their priest, ere we can cast off sloth;   50
Many a green-gown has been given,

22 orient: lustrous.   25 Titan: sun-god.   51 green-gown . . . given:
i.e., grass-stained from lying in the grass.

  Many a kiss, both odd and even,
  Many a glance too has been sent
  From out the eye, love's firmament,
Many a jest told of the key's betraying
This night, and locks picked, yet we're not a-maying.

Come, let us go while we are in our prime,
And take the harmless folly of the time.
  We shall grow old apace, and die
  Before we know our liberty.   60
  Our life is short, and our days run
  As fast away as does the sun;
And as a vapour, or a drop of rain
Once lost, can ne'er be found again,
  So when or you or I are made
  A fable, song, or fleeting shade,
  All love, all liking, all delight
  Lies drowned with us in endless night.
Then while time serves, and we are but decaying,
Come, my Corinna, come, let's go a-maying. 70

Kubla Khan

SAMUEL TAYLOR COLERIDGE

In Xanadu did Kubla Khan
A stately pleasure-dome decree:
Where Alph, the sacred river, ran
 Through caverns measureless to man
 Down to a sunless sea.
So twice five miles of fertile ground
With walls and towers were girdled round:
And there were gardens bright with sinuous rills,
Where blossomed many an incense-bearing tree;
And here were forests ancient as the hills, 10
Enfolding sunny spots of greenery.

But oh! that deep romantic chasm which slanted
Down the green hill athwart a cedarn cover!
A savage place! as holy and enchanted
As e'er beneath a waning moon was haunted
By woman wailing for her demon-lover!
And from this chasm, with ceaseless turmoil seething,
As if this earth in fast thick pants were breathing,
A mighty fountain momently was forced:
Amid whose swift half-intermitted burst   20
Huge fragments vaulted like rebounding hail,
Or chaffy grain beneath the thresher's flail:
And 'mid these dancing rocks at once and ever
It flung up momently the sacred river.
Five miles meandering with a mazy motion
Through wood and dale the sacred river ran,
Then reached the caverns measureless to man,
And sank in tumult to a lifeless ocean:
And 'mid this tumult Kubla heard from far
Ancestral voices prophesying war!   30
   The shadow of the dome of pleasure
   Floated midway on the waves;
   Where was heard the mingled measure
   From the fountain and the caves.
It was a miracle of rare device,
A sunny pleasure-dome with caves of ice!

   A damsel with a dulcimer
   In a vision once I saw:
   It was an Abyssinian maid,
   And on her dulcimer she played,   40
   Singing of Mount Abora.
   Could I revive within me
   Her symphony and song,
   To such a deep delight 'twould win me,
That with music loud and long,
I would build that dome in air,
That sunny dome! those caves of ice!
And all who heard should see them there,
And all should cry, Beware! Beware!
His flashing eyes, his floating hair!   50

Weave a circle round him thrice,
And close your eyes with holy dread,
For he on honey-dew hath fed,
And drunk the milk of Paradise.

[Fragment]

GERARD MANLEY HOPKINS

Strike, churl; hurl, cheerless wind, then; heltering hail
May's beauty massacre and wispèd wild clouds grow
Out on the giant air; tell Summer No,
Bid joy back, have at the harvest, keep Hope pale.

To An Athlete Dying Young

A. E. HOUSMAN

The time you won your town the race
We chaired you through the market-place;
Man and boy stood cheering by,
And home we brought you shoulder-high.

Today, the road all runners come,
Shoulder-high we bring you home,
And set you at your threshold down,
Townsman of a stiller town.

Smart lad, to slip betimes away
From fields where glory does not stay
And early though the laurel grows
It withers quicker than the rose.

Eyes the shady night has shut
Cannot see the record cut,

And silence sounds no worse than cheers
After earth has stopped the ears:

Now you will not swell the rout
Of lads that wore their honors out,
Runners whom renown outran
And the name died before the man.   20

So set, before its echoes fade,
The fleet foot on the sill of shade,
And hold to the low lintel up
The still-defended challenge-cup.

And round that early-laureled head
Will flock to gaze the strengthless dead,
And find unwithered on its curls
The garland briefer than a girl's.

We'll to the woods no more

A. E. HOUSMAN

We'll to the woods no more,
The laurels all are cut,
The bowers are bare of bay
That once the Muses wore;
The year draws in the day
And soon will evening shut:
The laurels all are cut,
We'll to the woods no more.
Oh we'll no more, no more
To the leafy woods away,   10
To the high wild woods of laurel
And the bowers of bay no more.

Easter Hymn
A. E. HOUSMAN

If in that Syrian garden, ages slain,
You sleep, and know not you are dead in vain,
Nor even in dreams behold how dark and bright
Ascends in smoke and fire by day and night
The hate you died to quench and could but fan,
Sleep well and see no morning, son of man.

But if, the grave rent and the stone rolled by,
At the right hand of majesty on high
You sit, and sitting so remember yet
Your tears, your agony and bloody sweat,   10
Your cross and passion and the life you gave,
Bow hither out of heaven and see and save.

The Balloon of the Mind
WILLIAM BUTLER YEATS

Hands, do what you're bid:
Bring the balloon of the mind
That bellies and drags in the wind
Into its narrow shed.

The Embankment
*(The fantasia of a fallen gentleman
on a cold, bitter night.)*
T. E. HULME

Once, in finesse of fiddles found I ecstasy,
In a flash of gold heels on the hard pavement.
Now see I

Title. The embankment along the River Thames in London.

That warmth's the very stuff of poesy.
Oh, God, make small
The old star-eaten blanket of the sky,
That I may fold it round me and in comfort lie.

Conversion

T. E. HULME

Light-hearted I walked into the valley wood
In the time of hyacinths,
Till beauty like a scented cloth
Cast over, stifled me. I was bound
Motionless and faint of breath
By loveliness that is her own eunuch.

Now pass I to the final river
Ignominiously, in a sack, without sound,
As any peeping Turk to the Bosphorus.

Lethe

H. D. (HILDA DOOLITTLE ALDINGTON)

Nor skin nor hide nor fleece
   Shall cover you,
Nor curtain of crimson nor fine
Shelter of cedar-wood be over you,
   Nor the fir-tree
   Nor the pine.

Nor sight of whin nor gorse
   Nor river-yew,
Nor fragrance of flowering bush,
Nor wailing of reed-bird to waken you,

Nor of linnet,
Nor of thrush.

Nor word nor touch nor sight
Of lover, you
Shall long through the night but for this:
The roll of the full tide to cover you
   Without question,
   Without kiss.

Question

MAY SWENSON

Body my house
my horse my hound
what will I do
when you are fallen

Where will I sleep
How will I ride
What will I hunt

Where can I go
without my mount
all eager and quick   10
How will I know

in thicket ahead
is danger or treasure
when Body my good
bright dog is dead

How will it be
To lie in the sky
without roof or door
and wind for an eye

With cloud for shift   20
How will I hide?

Fern Hill

DYLAN THOMAS

Now as I was young and easy under the apple boughs
About the lilting house and happy as the grass was green,
   The night above the dingle starry,
     Time let me hail and climb
  Golden in the heydays of his eyes,
And honoured among wagons I was prince of the apple towns
And once below a time I lordly had the trees and leaves
     Trail with daisies and barley
  Down the rivers of the windfall light.

And as I was green and carefree, famous among the barns   10
About the happy yard and singing as the farm was home,
   In the sun that is young once only,
     Time let me play and be
  Golden in the mercy of his means,
And green and golden I was huntsman and herdsman, the calves
Sang to my horn, the foxes on the hills barked clear and cold,
     And the sabbath rang slowly
  In the pebbles of the holy streams.

All the sun long it was running, it was lovely, the hay
Fields high as the house, the tunes from the chimneys, it was air   20
   And playing, lovely and watery
     And fire green as grass.
  And nightly under the simple stars
As I rode to sleep the owls were bearing the farm away,
All the moon long I heard, blessed among stables, the nightjars
     Flying with the ricks, and the horses
     Flashing into the dark.

And then to awake, and the farm, like a wanderer white
With the dew, come back, the cock on his shoulder: it was all

25 nightjars: birds related to the whippoorwills.

       Shining, it was Adam and maiden,   30
          The sky gathered again
      And the sun grew round that very day.
So it must have been after the birth of the simple light
In the first, spinning place, the spellbound horses walking warm
       Out of the whinnying green stable
          On to the fields of praise.

And honoured among foxes and pheasants by the gay house
Under the new made clouds and happy as the heart was long,
     In the sun born over and over,
        I ran my heedless ways,   40
    My wishes raced through the house high hay
And nothing I cared, at my sky blue trades, that time allows
In all his tuneful turning so few and such morning songs
      Before the children green and golden
         Follow him out of grace,

Nothing I cared, in the lamb white days, that time would take me
Up to the swallow thronged loft by the shadow of my hand,
     In the moon that is always rising,
        Nor that riding to sleep
    I should hear him fly with the high fields   50
And wake to the farm forever fled from the childless land.
Oh as I was young and easy in the mercy of his means,
   Time held me green and dying
 Though I sang in my chains like the sea.

IV

The Lyric

In its broadest sense, so broad as to be of little use, the term "lyric" includes most of the poetry in this volume, for it can signify any poem of short or moderate length that is not narrative. In its original narrowest sense it would include very few of the present selections—only those short poems other than ballads that were written to be sung to the accompaniment of the lyre or lute. Most commonly the term is used in a not very well defined sense, between these extremes, to signify songlike or at least musical poems that are not long and that often are personal or subjective. In content they run the gamut from simple childlike observation or exclamation to the complex symbolic poem with several levels of meaning. In this chapter are grouped a representative selection including songs, reflective lyrics, and other short poems in a variety of forms and on various subjects, including perhaps the commonest of all lyric themes, love, its illusions and disillusions.

The twentieth century, however, has seen a good deal of discussion of a modern question: why should poets continue to write so much more about nature than about towns and machinery, when so many people now live in an urban and industrial environment? Are poets, it is sometimes asked, simply refusing to face modern life as it is, or is there a sound and natural reason in human nature for their choice of subjects and imagery? We raise the question here but will not attempt to answer it categorically. Some have said that the mechanical things which man himself can make he can understand and deal with in equations or by strict reasoning, and that he does not need much imagination to deal with them once they are invented. His factories, however, cannot yet manufacture human beings, nature, or the forces and laws behind the world. These all-important and familiar, yet half-unknown things he must deal with partly by imagination. Whether or not this is the reason, the fact is that in modern as well as older poetry we see a great deal more of nature than we do of machines.

In the lyric, mood and tone are of paramount importance; so also may be distinction of form and pattern such as has been discussed in the preceding chapter.

Many additional lyrics will be found in the selections from individual poets in Chapter VIII.

Sumer is icumen in

ANON.

Sumer is icumen in,
  Lhude sing cuccu!
Groweth sed and bloweth med
  And springth the wode nu.
    Sing cuccu!
Awe bleteth after lomb,
  Lhouth after calve cu
Bulluc sterteth, bucke verteth.
  Murie sing cuccu!
    Cuccu, cuccu,   10
Wel singes thu, cuccu
Ne swik thu naver nu!
Sing cuccu nu, Sing cuccu!
Sing cuccu, Sing cuccu nu!

2 **Lhude**: loud.   3 **sed**: seed.   **bloweth med**: blossoms [the] meadow.   4 **wode**: wood.   **nu**: now.   6 **Awe**: ewe.   7 **Lhouth**: loweth or lows.   **cu**: cow.   8 **sterteth**: leaps.   **verteth**: probably veers or starts.   9 **murie**: merrily.   12 **swik**: cease.

Westron winde, when will thou blow

ANON.

Westron winde, when will thou blow,
The smalle raine downe can raine?
Crist, if my love wer in my armis,
And I in my bed againe.

1 Westron: Western.

Back and side go bare, go bare
From *Gammer Gurton's Needle*

ANON.

Back and side go bare, go bare,
  Both foot and hand go cold;
But, belly, God send thee good ale enough,
  Whether it be new or old.

I cannot eat but little meat,
  My stomach is not good;
But sure I think that I can drink
  With him that wears a hood.
Though I go bare, take ye no care,
  I am nothing a-cold;   10
I stuff my skin so full within
  Of jolly good ale and old.

    Back and side go bare, go bare, etc.

8 him that wears a hood: a friar.

I love no roast but a nutbrown toast,
    And a crab laid in the fire;
A little bread shall do me stead,
    Much bread I not desire.
No frost nor snow, no wind, I trow,
    Can hurt me if I would,
I am so wrapt, and throughly lapt   20
    Of jolly good ale and old.

Back and side go bare, go bare, etc.

And Tib my wife, that as her life
    Loveth well good ale to seek,
Full oft drinks she, till ye may see
    The tears run down her cheek.
Then doth she troll to me the bowl,
    Even as a maltworm should;
And saith, "Sweetheart, I took my part
    Of this jolly good ale and old."   30

Back and side go bare, go bare, etc.

Now let them drink, till they nod and wink,
    Even as good fellows should do;
They shall not miss to have the bliss
    Good ale doth bring men to.
And all poor souls that have scourèd bowls,
    Or have them lustily trolled,
God save the lives of them and their wives,
    Whether they be young or old.

Back and side go bare, go bare, etc.   40

---

14 nutbrown toast: toast soaked in ale.   15 crab: crab apple.   27 troll: pass around.   28 maltworm: toper.   36 scourèd: emptied.

To a Lady to Answer Directly with Yea or Nay

SIR THOMAS WYATT

Madame, withouten many words,
  Once, I am sure, ye will or no:
And if ye will, then leave your bourds
  And use your wit and show it so;

And with a beck ye shall me call.
  And if of one that burneth alway,
Ye have any pity at all,
  Answer him fair with yea or nay.

If it be yea, I shall be fain;
  If it be nay, friends as before;   10
Ye shall another man obtain,
  And I mine own and yours no more.

3 bourds: jest, mockery.

The Lover Showeth How He Is Forsaken of Such as He Sometime Enjoyed

SIR THOMAS WYATT

They flee from me that sometime did me seek,
  With naked foot stalking in my chamber.
I have seen them gentle, tame and meek
  That now are wild and do not remember
  That sometime they put themselves in danger
To take bread at my hand; and now they range
Busily seeking with a continual change.

1 sometime: formerly.

      Thankt be fortune, it hath been otherwise
        Twenty times better; but once, in special,
      In thin array, after a pleasant guise,   10
        When her loose gown from her shoulders did fall,
        And she me caught in her arms long and small,
      Therewith all sweetly did me kiss,
      And softly said: "Dear heart, how like you this?"

      It was no dream: I lay broad waking:
        But all is turned thorough my gentleness
      Into a strange fashion of forsaking;
        And I have leave to go of her goodness:
        And she also to use new-fangleness.
      But since that I so kindely am served,   20
      I would fain know what she hath deserved.

16 thorough: through.   *20* so kindely: in such a way (from "kind," meaning "sort"), or else perhaps ironic, like "goodness" in line *18*.

Who would have thought that face of thine

THOMAS HOWELL

      Who would have thought that face of thine
        Had been so full of doubleness?
      Or else within those crystal eyne
        Had rest so much unstableness?
      Thy face so fair, thy look so strange,
      Who would have thought so full of change?

3 eyne: eyes.

Brown is my Love
ANON.

Brown is my Love, but graceful:
And each renownèd whiteness
Matched with thy lovely brown loseth its brightness.

Fair is my Love, but scornful:
Yet have I seen despisèd
Dainty white lilies, and sad flowers well prizèd.

6 sad: dark, somber.

The Passionate Shepherd to His Love
CHRISTOPHER MARLOWE

Come live with me and be my Love,
And we will all the pleasures prove
That valleys, groves, hills, and fields,
Woods, or steepy mountains yields.

And we will sit upon the rocks
Seeing the shepherds feed their flocks,
By shallow rivers, to whose falls
Melodious birds sing madrigals.

And I will make thee beds of roses,
And a thousand fragrant posies,   10
A cap of flowers, and a kirtle
Embroidered all with leaves of myrtle;

A gown made of the finest wool,
Which from our pretty lambs we pull;
Fair linèd slippers for the cold,
With buckles of the purest gold;

                A belt of straw and ivy buds
                With coral clasps and amber studs:
                And if these pleasures may thee move,
                Come live with me, and be my Love.   20

                The shepherd swains shall dance and sing
                For thy delight each May morning:
                If these delights thy mind may move,
                Then live with me and be my Love.

11 kirtle: gown.

The Nymph's Reply to the Shepherd

? SIR WALTER RALEGH

                If all the world and love were young,
                And truth in every shepherd's tongue,
                These pretty pleasures might me move
                To live with thee and be thy Love.

                Time drives the flocks from field to fold,
                When rivers rage and rocks grow cold;
                And Philomel becometh dumb;
                The rest complains of cares to come.

                The flowers do fade, and wanton fields
                To wayward winter reckoning yields: 10
                A honey tongue, a heart of gall,
                Is fancy's spring, but sorrow's fall.

                Thy gowns, thy shoes, thy beds of roses,
                Thy cap, thy kirtle, and thy posies
                Soon break, soon wither, soon forgotten,
                In folly ripe, in reason rotten.

7 Philomel: the nightingale.

Thy belt of straw and ivy buds,
Thy coral clasps and amber studs,
All these in me no means can move
To come to thee and be thy Love.   20

But could youth last, and love still breed,
Had joys no date, nor age no need,
Then these delights my mind might move
To live with thee and be thy Love.

21 still: always, constantly.   22 date: terminal date, termination.

Song

GEORGE PEELE

Whenas the rye reach to the chin,
And chopcherry, chopcherry ripe within,
Strawberries swimming in the cream,
And schoolboys playing in the stream;
Then oh, then oh, then oh, my true Love said,
Till that time come again
She could not live a maid.

2 chopcherry: a game in which players tried to catch a hanging cherry with their teeth; here, more generally, the season for cherries.

Song

THOMAS NASHE

Adieu, farewell earth's bliss,
This world uncertain is;
Fond are life's lustful joys,
Death proves them all but toys.
None from his darts can fly.
I am sick, I must die.
  Lord, have mercy on us!

Rich men, trust not in wealth,
Gold cannot buy you health;
Physic himself must fade;   10
All things to end are made;
The plague full swift goes by.
I am sick, I must die.
        Lord, have mercy on us!

Beauty is but a flower,
Which wrinkles will devour;
Brightness falls from the air;
Queens have died young and fair;
Dust hath closed Helen's eye.
I am sick, I must die.   20
        Lord, have mercy on us!

Strength stoops unto the grave;
Worms feed on Hector brave;
Swords may not fight with fate;
Earth still holds ope her gate;
Come! come! the bells do cry.
I am sick, I must die.
        Lord, have mercy on us!

Wit with his wantonness
Tasteth death's bitterness;   30
Hell's executioner
Hath no ears for to hear
What vain art can reply.
I am sick, I must die.
        Lord, have mercy on us!

Haste therefore each degree,
To welcome destiny.
Heaven is our heritage,
Earth but a player's stage;
Mount we unto the sky.   40
I am sick, I must die.
        Lord, have mercy on us!

10 Physic: medical science; here, by extension, its practitioner.

Spring

WILLIAM SHAKESPEARE

When daisies pied and violets blue
And lady-smocks all silver-white
And cuckoo-buds of yellow hue
   Do paint the meadows with delight,
The cuckoo then, on every tree,
Mocks married men; for thus sings he,
       Cuckoo,
Cuckoo, cuckoo! O word of fear,
Unpleasing to a married ear!

When shepherds pipe on oaten straws,   10
   And merry larks are ploughmen's clocks,
When turtles tread, and rooks, and daws,
   And maidens bleach their summer smocks,
The cuckoo then, on every tree,
Mocks married men; for thus sings he,
       Cuckoo,
Cuckoo, cuckoo! O word of fear,
Unpleasing to a married ear!

2 lady-smocks: a white-flowered plant of the cress family.   3 The name "cuckoo-flower" was applied to several different species of plant.   12 turtles: turtle-doves. tread: mate.

Winter

WILLIAM SHAKESPEARE

When icicles hang by the wall,
   And Dick the shepherd blows his nail,
And Tom bears logs into the hall,
   And milk comes frozen home in pail,

2 blows his nail: a familiar expression meaning "waits idly, with nothing to do."

When blood is nipp'd, and ways be foul,
  Then nightly sings the staring owl,
    Tu-whit, to-who,
    A merry note,
While greasy Joan doth keel the pot.

When all aloud the wind doth blow,   10
  And coughing drowns the parson's saw,
And birds sit brooding in the snow,
  And Marian's nose looks red and raw,
When roasted crabs hiss in the bowl,
  Then nightly sings the staring owl,
    Tu-whit, to-who,
    A merry note,
While greasy Joan doth keel the pot.

9 keel: cool.   14 crabs: crab apples, used to flavor a bowl of ale.

Tell me where is fancy bred

WILLIAM SHAKESPEARE

Tell me where is fancy bred,
Or in the heart or in the head?
How begot, how nourishèd?
  Reply, reply.

It is engender'd in the eyes,
With gazing fed; and fancy dies
In the cradle where it lies.
  Let us all ring fancy's knell:
  I'll begin it—Ding, dong, bell.
  Ding, dong, bell.   10

1 fancy: love.

Take, O take those lips away

WILLIAM SHAKESPEARE

Take, O take those lips away,
   That so sweetly were forsworn;
And those eyes, the break of day,
   Lights that do mislead the morn:
But my kisses bring again,
     Bring again,
Seals of love, but seal'd in vain,
     Seal'd in vain.

Come away, come away, death

WILLIAM SHAKESPEARE

Come away, come away, death,
   And in sad cypress let me be laid;
Fly away, fly away, breath;
   I am slain by a fair cruel maid.
My shroud of white, stuck all with yew,
     O, prepare it:
My part of death, no one so true
     Did share it.

Not a flower, not a flower sweet,
   On my black coffin let there be strown;   10
Not a friend, not a friend greet
   My poor corpse, where my bones shall be thrown.
A thousand thousand sighs to save,
     Lay me, O where
Sad true lover never find my grave,
     To weep there.

Still to be neat, still to be drest

BEN JONSON

Still to be neat, still to be drest,
As you were going to a feast;
Still to be powd'red, still perfum'd:
Lady, it is to be presum'd,
Though art's hid causes are not found,
All is not sweet, all is not sound.

Give me a look, give me a face,
That makes simplicity a grace;
Robes loosely flowing, hair as free:
Such sweet neglect more taketh me,   10
Than all th' adulteries of art.
They strike mine eye, but not my heart.

1 Still: always, ever.

Shall I, wasting in despair

GEORGE WITHER

Shall I, wasting in despair,
Die, because a woman's fair?
Or make pale my cheeks with care,
'Cause another's rosy are?
Be she fairer than the day,
Or the flowery meads in May!
  If she be not so to me,
  What care I how fair she be?

Should my heart be griev'd or pin'd,
'Cause I see a woman kind?   10

Or a well disposèd nature
Joinèd with a lovely feature?
Be she meeker, kinder than
Turtle dove, or pelican!
   If she be not so to me,
   What care I how kind she be?

Shall a woman's virtues move
Me to perish for her love?
Or, her well deserving known,
Make me quite forget mine own?   20
Be she with that goodness blest,
Which may gain her, name of best!
   If she be not such to me,
   What care I how good she be?

'Cause her fortune seems too high,
Shall I play the fool, and die?
Those that bear a noble mind,
Where they want of riches find,
Think "What, with them, they would do,
That, without them, dare to woo!"   30
   And unless that mind I see,
   What care I though great she be?

Great, or good, or kind, or fair,
I will ne'er the more despair!
If she love me (this believe!)
I will die, ere she shall grieve!
If she slight me, when I woo,
I can scorn, and let her go!
   For if she be not for me,
   What care I for whom she be?   40

13–14 The female pelican was once believed to feed her young with her own blood.

Out upon it! I have lov'd

SIR JOHN SUCKLING

Out upon it! I have lov'd
    Three whole days together;
And am like to love three more,
    If it prove fair weather.

Time shall moult away his wings,
    Ere he shall discover
In the whole wide world again
    Such a constant lover.

But the spite on 't is, no praise
    Is due at all to me: 10
Love with me had made no stays,
    Had it any been but she.

Had it any been but she,
    And that very face,
There had been at least ere this
    A dozen dozen in her place.

1 Out upon it: exclamation of impatience, often used lightly.

To Lucasta, on Going to the Wars

RICHARD LOVELACE

Tell me not, Sweet, I am unkind,
    That from the Nunnery
Of thy chaste breast, and quiet mind,
    To War and Arms I fly.

True; a new Mistress now I chase,
    The first Foe in the Field;
And with a stronger Faith embrace
    A Sword, a Horse, a Shield.

Yet this Inconstancy is such,
    As you too shall adore;   10
I could not love thee, Dear, so much,
    Lov'd I not Honour more.

To the Virgins, to Make Much of Time

ROBERT HERRICK

Gather ye Rose-buds while ye may,
    Old Time is still a flying:
And this same flower that smiles to day,
    To morrow will be dying.

The glorious Lamp of Heaven, the Sun,
    The higher he's a getting;
The sooner will his Race be run,
    And neerer he's to Setting.

That Age is best, which is the first,
    When Youth and Blood are warmer;   10
But being spent, the worse, and worst
    Times, still succeed the former.

Then be not coy, but use your time;
    And while ye may, goe marry:
For having lost but once your prime,
    You may for ever tarry.

To Daffodils

ROBERT HERRICK

Fair daffodils, we weep to see
    You haste away so soon:
As yet the early-rising sun
    Has not attain'd his noon.

  Stay, stay,
 Until the hasting day
  Has run
 But to the Even-song;
And, having pray'd together, we
 Will go with you along.   10

We have short time to stay, as you,
 We have as short a spring;
As quick a growth to meet decay,
 As you, or any thing.
  We die,
As your hours do, and dry
  Away,
Like to the summer's rain;
Or as the pearls of morning's dew
 Ne'er to be found again.   20

On Time

JOHN MILTON

Fly envious *Time*, till thou run out thy race,
Call on the lazy leaden-stepping hours,
Whose speed is but the heavy Plummet's pace;
And glut thy self with what thy womb devours,
Which is no more than what is false and vain,
And merely mortal dross;
So little is our loss,
So little is thy gain.
For when as each thing bad thou hast entomb'd,
And last of all, thy greedy self consum'd, 10
Then long Eternity shall greet our bliss
With an individual kiss;
And Joy shall overtake us as a flood,
When every thing that is sincerely good
And perfectly divine,
With Truth, and Peace, and Love shall ever shine

About the supreme Throne
Of him, t' whose happy-making sight alone,
When once our heav'nly-guided soul shall climb,
Then all this Earthy grossness quit,   20
Attir'd with Stars, we shall for ever sit,
  Triumphing over Death, and Chance, and thee O Time.

To His Coy Mistress

ANDREW MARVELL

Had we but World enough, and Time,
This coyness Lady were no crime.
We would sit down, and think which way
To walk, and pass our long Loves Day.
Thou by the *Indian Ganges* side
Should'st Rubies find: I by the Tide
Of *Humber* would complain. I would
Love you ten years before the Flood:
And you should if you please refuse
Till the Conversion of the *Jews*.   10
My vegetable Love should grow
Vaster than Empires, and more slow.
An hundred years should go to praise
Thine Eyes, and on thy Forehead Gaze.
Two hundred to adore each Breast:
But thirty thousand to the rest.
An Age at least to every part,
And the last Age should show your Heart.
For Lady you deserve this State;
Nor would I love at lower rate.   20
  But at my back I alwaies hear
Times wingèd Chariot hurrying near:
And yonder all before us lye
Desarts of vast Eternity.
Thy Beauty shall no more be found,
Nor, in thy marble Vault, shall sound
My echoing Song: then Worms shall **try**

That long preserv'd Virginity:
And your quaint Honour turn to dust;
And into ashes all my Lust. 30
The Grave's a fine and private place,
But none I think do there embrace.
   Now therefore, while the youthful hew
Sits on thy skin like morning dew,
And while thy willing Soul transpires
At every pore with instant Fires,
Now let us sport us while we may;
And now, like am'rous birds of prey,
Rather at once our Time devour,
Than languish in his slow-chapt pow'r. 40
Let us roll all our Strength, and all
Our Sweetness, up into one Ball;
And tear our Pleasures with rough strife,
Thorough the Iron gates of Life.
Thus, though we cannot make our Sun
Stand still, yet we will make him run.

35 transpires: breathes forth. 39–40 –chapt: from "chap," meaning "jaw." "Let us devour time before he slowly devours us."

The Mower to the Glo-Worms

ANDREW MARVELL

Ye living Lamps, by whose dear light
The Nightingale does sit so late,
And studying all the Summer-night,
Her matchless Songs does meditate;

Ye Country Comets, that portend
No War, nor Prince's funeral,

Title: Glo-Worm (Glowworm), name given to various luminescent beetles, some of which are also known as fireflies. 5–8 Comets were formerly regarded as portents of great, usually unfortunate events.

Shining unto no higher end
Then to presage the Grasses fall;

Ye Glo-worms, whose officious Flame
To wand'ring Mowers shows the way,   10
That in the Night have lost their aim,
And after foolish Fires do stray;

Your courteous Lights in vain you waste,
Since *Juliana* here is come,
For she my mind hath so displac'd
That I shall never find my home.

The Mower against Gardens
ANDREW MARVELL

Luxurious Man, to bring his Vice in use,
   Did after him the World seduce:
And from the fields the Flow'rs and Plants allure,
   Where Nature was most plain and pure.
He first enclos'd within the Gardens square
   A dead and standing pool of Air;
And a more luscious Earth for them did knead,
   Which stupifi'd them while it fed.
The Pink grew then as double as his Mind;
   The nutriment did change the kind.   10
With strange perfumes he did the Roses taint.
   And Flow'rs themselves were taught to paint.
The Tulip, white, did for complexion seek,
   And learn'd to interline its cheek;
Its Onion root they then so high did hold,
   That one was for a Meadow sold.
Another World was search'd, through Oceans new,
   To find the *Marvel of Peru.*
And yet these Rarities might be allow'd,
   To Man, that sov'raign thing and proud,   20
Had he not dealt between the Bark and Tree,
   Forbidden mixtures there to see.

No Plant now knew the Stock from which it came;
  He grafts upon the Wild the Tame:
That the uncertain and adult'rate fruit
  Might put the Palate in dispute.
His green *Seraglio* has its Eunuchs too,
  Lest any Tyrant him out-doe.
And in the Cherry he does Nature vex,
  To procreate without a sex.   30
'Tis all enforc'd, the Fountain and the Grot;
  While the sweet Fields do lye forgot:
Where willing Nature does to all dispence
  A wild and fragrant Innocence;
And *Fauns* and *Faryes* do the Meadows till,
  More by their presence then their skill.
Their Statues polish'd by some ancient hand,
  May to adorn the Gardens stand:
But howso'ere the Figures do excel,
  The *Gods* themselves with us do dwell.   40

Stanzas for Music

LORD BYRON

There be none of Beauty's daughters
  With a magic like thee;
And like music on the waters
  Is thy sweet voice to me:
When, as if its sound were causing
The charmèd ocean's pausing,
The waves lie still and gleaming
And the lull'd winds seem dreaming:

And the midnight moon is weaving
  Her bright chain o'er the deep;   10
Whose breast is gently heaving,
  As an infant's asleep:
So the spirit bows before thee,
To listen and adore thee;
With a full but soft emotion,
Like the swell of Summer's ocean.

The Soul selects her own Society

EMILY DICKINSON

The Soul selects her own Society—
Then—shuts the Door—
To her divine Majority—
Present no more—

Unmoved—she notes the Chariots—pausing—
At her low Gate—
Unmoved—an Emperor be kneeling
Upon her Mat—

I've known her—from an ample nation—
Choose One—   10
Then—close the Valves of her attention—
Like Stone—

After great pain, a formal feeling comes

EMILY DICKINSON

After great pain, a formal feeling comes—
The Nerves sit ceremonious, like Tombs—
The stiff Heart questions was it He, that bore,
And Yesterday, or Centuries before?

The Feet, mechanical, go round—
Of Ground, or Air, or Ought—
A Wooden way
Regardless grown,
A Quartz contentment, like a stone—

This is the Hour of Lead—   10
Remembered, if outlived,
As Freezing persons, recollect the Snow—
First—Chill—then Stupor—then the letting go—

Finding is the first Act

EMILY DICKINSON

Finding is the first Act
The second, loss,
Third, Expedition for
the "Golden Fleece"

Fourth, no Discovery—
Fifth, no Crew—
Finally, no Golden Fleece—
Jason—sham—too.

The Convergence of the Twain
(Lines on the loss of the "Titanic")

THOMAS HARDY

I

In a solitude of the sea
Deep from human vanity,
And the Pride of Life that planned her, stilly
couches she.

II

Steel chambers, late the pyres
Of her salamandrine fires,
Cold currents thrid, and turn to rhythmic
tidal lyres.

III

Over the mirrors meant
To glass the opulent
The sea-worm crawls—grotesque, slimed, dumb,
indifferent.

6 thrid: thread.

IV

Jewels in joy designed
To ravish the sensuous mind
Lie lightless, all their sparkles bleared and
   black and blind.

V

Dim moon-eyed fishes near
Gaze at the gilded gear
And query: "What does this vaingloriousness
   down here?". . .

VI

Well: while was fashioning
This creature of cleaving wing,
The Immanent Will that stirs and urges everything

VII

Prepared a sinister mate
For her—so gaily great—
A Shape of Ice, for the time far and dissociate.

VIII

And as the smart ship grew
In stature, grace, and hue,
In shadowy silent distance grew the Iceberg too.

IX

Alien they seemed to be:
No mortal eye could see
The intimate welding of their later history,

X

Or sign that they were bent
By paths coincident
On being anon twin halves of one august event,

XI

Till the Spinner of the Years
Said "Now!" And each one hears,
And consummation comes, and jars two hemispheres.

Waiting Both

THOMAS HARDY

A star looks down at me,
And says: "Here I and you
Stand, each in our degree.
What do you mean to do,—
    Mean to do?"

I say: "For all I know,
Wait, and let Time go by,
Till my change come,"—"Just so."
The star says: "So mean I:—
    So mean I."   10

When smoke stood up from Ludlow

A. E. HOUSMAN

When smoke stood up from Ludlow,
    And mist blew off from Teme,
And blithe afield to plowing
    Against the morning beam
    I strode beside my team,

The blackbird in the coppice
    Looked out to see me stride,
And hearkened as I whistled
    The trampling team beside,
    And fluted and replied: 10

"Lie down, lie down, young yeoman;
    What use to rise and rise?
Rise man a thousand mornings
    Yet down at last he lies,
    And then the man is wise."

I heard the tune he sang me,
   And spied his yellow bill;
I picked a stone and aimed it
   And threw it with a will:
   Then the bird was still.   20

Then my soul within me
   Took up the blackbird's strain,
And still beside the horses
   Along the dewy lane
   It sang the song again:

"Lie down, lie down, young yeoman:
   The sun moves always west;
The road one treads to labour
   Will lead one home to rest,
   And that will be the best."   30

Bredon Hill

A. E. HOUSMAN

In summertime on Bredon
   The bells they sound so clear;
Round both the shires they ring them
   In steeples far and near,
   A happy noise to hear.

Here of a Sunday morning
   My love and I would lie,
And see the coloured counties,
   And hear the larks so high
   About us in the sky.   10

The bells would ring to call her
   In valleys miles away:
"Come all to church, good people;
   Good people, come and pray."
   But here my love would stay.

  And I would turn and answer
   Among the springing thyme,
  "Oh, peal upon our wedding,
   And we will hear the chime,
   And come to church in time."   20

  But when the snows at Christmas
   On Bredon top were strown,
  My love rose up so early
   And stole out unbeknown
   And went to church alone.

  They tolled the one bell only,
   Groom there was none to see,
  The mourners followed after,
   And so to church went she,
   And would not wait for me.   30

  The bells they sound on Bredon,
   And still the steeples hum.
  "Come all to church, good people,"—
   Oh, noisy bells, be dumb;
   I hear you, I will come.

The rain, it streams on stone and hillock

A. E. HOUSMAN

  The rain, it streams on stone and hillock,
   The boot clings to the clay.
  Since all is done that's due and right
  Let's home; and now, my lad, good-night,
   For I must turn away.

  Good-night, my lad, for nought's eternal;
   No league of ours, for sure.
  To-morrow I shall miss you less,
  And ache of heart and heaviness
   Are things that time should cure.   10

Over the hill the highway marches
  And what's beyond is wide:
Oh soon enough will pine to nought
Remembrance and the faithful thought
  That sits the grave beside.

The skies, they are not always raining
  Nor grey the twelvemonth through;
And I shall meet good days and mirth,
And range the lovely lands of earth
  With friends no worse than you.　　　　20

But oh, my man, the house is fallen
  That none can build again;
My man, how full of joy and woe
Your mother bore you years ago
  To-night to lie in the rain.

The Hermit

WILLIAM H. DAVIES

What moves that lonely man is not the boom
  Of waves that break against the cliff so strong;
Nor roar of thunder, when that traveling voice
  Is caught by rocks that carry far along.

'Tis not the groan of oak tree in its prime,
  When lightning strikes its solid heart to dust;
Nor frozen pond when, melted by the sun,
  It suddenly doth break its sparkling crust.

What moves that man is when the blind bat taps
  His window when he sits alone at night;　　　　10
Or when the small bird sounds like some great beast
  Among the dead, dry leaves so frail and light.

Or when the moths on his night-pillow beat
  Such heavy blows he fears they'll break his bones;
Or when a mouse inside the papered walls,
  Comes like a tiger crunching through the stones.

The Gallows

EDWARD THOMAS

There was a weasel lived in the sun
With all his family,
Till a keeper shot him with his gun
And hung him up on a tree,
Where he swings in the wind and rain
In the sun and in the snow,
Without pleasure, without pain,
On the dead oak tree bough.

There was a crow who was no sleeper,
But a thief and a murderer
Till a very late hour; and this keeper
Made him one of the things that were,
To hang and flap in rain and wind
In the sun and in the snow.
There are no more sins to be sinned
On the dead oak tree bough.

There was a magpie, too,
Had a long tongue and a long tail;
He could both talk and do—
But what did that avail?
He, too, flaps in the wind and rain
Alongside weasel and crow,
Without pleasure, without pain,
On the dead oak tree bough.

And many other beasts
And birds, skin, bone, and feather,
Have been taken from their feasts
And hung up there together.
To swing and have endless leisure
In the sun and in the snow,
Without pain, without pleasure,
On the dead oak tree bough.

The New House

EDWARD THOMAS

Now first, as I shut the door,
    I was alone
In the new house; and the wind
    Began to moan.

Old at once was the house,
    And I was old;
My ears were teased with the dread
    Of what was foretold,

Nights of storm, days of mist, without end;
    Sad days when the sun 10
Shone in vain: old griefs and griefs
    Not yet begun.

All was foretold me; naught
    Could I foresee;
But I learned how the wind would sound
    After these things should be.

Out in the dark

EDWARD THOMAS

Out in the dark over the snow
The fallow fawns invisible go
With the fallow doe;
And the winds blow
Fast as the stars are slow.

Stealthily the dark haunts round
And, when the lamp goes, without sound

---

2 The fallow deer is a small pale-yellow European deer.

>At a swifter bound
>Than the swiftest hound,
>Arrives, and all else is drowned;   10
>
>And I and star and wind and deer,
>Are in the dark together,—near,
>Yet far,—and fear
>Drums on my ear
>In that sage company drear.
>
>How weak and little is the light,
>All the universe of sight,
>Love and delight,
>Before the might,
>If you love it not, of night.   20

At the Keyhole

WALTER DE LA MARE

>"Grill me some bones," said the Cobbler,
>   "Some bones, my pretty Sue;
>I'm tired of my lonesome with heels and soles,
>Springsides and uppers too;
>A mouse in the wainscot is nibbling;
>A wind in the keyhole drones;
>And a sheet webbed over my candle, Susie,
>   Grill me some bones!"
>
>"Grill me some bones," said the Cobbler,
>   "I sat at my tic-tac-to;   10
>And a footstep came to my door and stopped,
>And a hand groped to and fro;
>And I peered up over my boot and last;
>And my feet went cold as stones:—
>I saw an eye at the keyhole, Susie!—
>   Grill me some bones!"

7 sheet: vapor or mist.

Old Shellover

WALTER DE LA MARE

"Come!" said Old Shellover.
"What?" says Creep.
"The horny old Gardener's fast asleep;
The fat cock Thrush
To his nest has gone,
And the dew shines bright
In the rising Moon;
Old Sallie Worm from her hole doth peep;
Come!" said Old Shellover.
"Ay!" said Creep.   10

1–2 Shellover . . . Creep: the snail and its cousin the slug.

The Mocking Fairy

WALTER DE LA MARE

"Won't you look out of your window, Mrs. Gill?"
  Quoth the Fairy, nidding, nodding in the garden;
"Can't you look out of your window, Mrs. Gill?"
  Quoth the Fairy, laughing softly in the garden;
But the air was still, the cherry boughs were still,
And the ivy-tod 'neath the empty sill,
And never from her window looked out Mrs. Gill
  On the Fairy shrilly mocking in the garden.

"What have they done with you, you poor Mrs. Gill?"
  Quoth the Fairy brightly glancing in the garden;   10
"Where have they hidden you, you poor old Mrs. Gill?"
  Quoth the Fairy dancing lightly in the garden;
But night's faint veil now wrapped the hill,

2 "Nidding" is not an actual word, but "niddle-noddle" means "to nod the head unsteadily to and fro."

Stark 'neath the stars stood the dead-still Mill,
And out of her cold cottage never answered Mrs. Gill
The Fairy mimbling mambling in the garden.

16 "Mimbling" is not a word; mamble is a dialect word for "stammer," "mutter" or "mumble."

Peak and Puke

WALTER DE LA MARE

From his cradle in the glamourie
They have stolen my wee brother,
Roused a changeling in his swaddlings
For to fret mine own poor mother.
Pules it in the candle light
Wi' a cheek so lean and white,
Chinkling up its eyne so wee,
Wailing shrill at her an' me.
It we'll neither rock nor tend
Till the Silent Silent send,   10
Lapping in their waesome arms
Him they stole with spells and charms,
Till they take this changeling creature
Back to its own fairy nature—
Cry! Cry! as long as may be,
Ye shall ne'er be woman's baby!

Title: Peak: droop or waste away in health or spirits.   1 glamourie: magic.
11 waesome: woeful.

The Old Men

WALTER DE LA MARE

Old and alone, sit we,
  Caged, riddle-rid men;
Lost to Earth's "Listen!" and "See!"
  Thought's "Wherefore?" and "When?"

Only far memories stray
   Of a past once lovely, but now
Wasted and faded away,
   Like green leaves from the bough.

Vast broods the silence of night,
   The ruinous moon
Lifts on our faces her light,
   Whence all dreaming is gone.

We speak not; trembles each head;
   In their sockets our eyes are still;
Desire as cold as the dead;
   Without wonder or will.
And One, with a lanthorn, draws near,
   At clash with the moon in our eyes:
"Where art thou?" he asks: "I am here,"
   One by one we arise.

And none lifts a hand to withhold
   A friend from the touch of that foe:
Heart cries unto heart, "Thou art old!"
   Yet, reluctant, we go.

The Ghost

WALTER DE LA MARE

"Who knocks?" "I, who was beautiful,
Beyond all dreams to restore,
I, from the roots of the dark thorn am hither,
And knock on the door."

"Who speaks?" "I—once was my speech
Sweet as the bird's on the air,
When echo lurks by the waters to heed;
'Tis I speak thee fair."

"Dark is the hour!" "Ay, and cold."
"Lone is my house." "Ah, but mine?" 10
"Sight, touch, lips, eyes yearned in vain."
"Long dead these to thine . . ."

Silence. Still faint on the porch
Brake the flames of the stars.
In gloom groped a hope-wearied hand
Over keys, bolts, and bars.

A face peered. All the grey night
  In chaos of vacancy shone;
Nought but vast sorrow was there—
  The sweet cheat gone. 20

Maerchen

WALTER DE LA MARE

Soundless the moth-flit, crisp the deathwatch tick;
Crazed in her shaken arbour bird did sing;
Slow wreathed the grease adown from soot-clogged wick:
  The Cat looked long and softly at the King.

Mouse frisked and scampered, leapt, gnawed, squeaked;
Small at the window looped cowled bat a-wing;
The dim-lit rafters with the night-mist reeked:
  The Cat looked long and softly at the King.

O wondrous robe enstarred, in night dyed deep:
O air scarce-stirred with the Court's far junketing: 10
O stagnant Royalty—A-swoon? Asleep?
  The Cat looked long and softly at the King.

Title: German for fairy tale, legend. 1 deathwatch: an insect that makes a ticking sound which was formerly supposed to be an omen of death.

The River-Merchant's Wife: A Letter

EZRA POUND

While my hair was still cut straight across my forehead
Played I about the front gate, pulling flowers.
You came by on bamboo stilts, playing horse,
You walked about my seat, playing with blue plums.
And we went on living in the village of Chokan:
Two small people, without dislike or suspicion.

At fourteen I married My Lord you.
I never laughed, being bashful.
Lowering my head, I looked at the wall.
Called to, a thousand times, I never looked back.   10

At fifteen I stopped scowling,
I desired my dust to be mingled with yours
Forever and forever and forever.
Why should I climb the look out?

At sixteen you departed,
You went into far Ku-to-yen, by the river of swirling eddies,
And you have been gone five months.
The monkeys make sorrowful noise overhead.
You dragged your feet when you went out.
By the gate now, the moss is grown, the different mosses,   20
Too deep to clear them away!
The leaves fall early this autumn, in wind.
The paired butterflies are already yellow with August
Over the grass in the West garden;
They hurt me. I grow older.
If you are coming down through the narrows of the
    river Kiang,
Please let me know beforehand,
And I will come out to meet you
              As far as Cho-fu-Sa,
                   —*By Rihaku*

Lament of the Frontier Guard

EZRA POUND

By the North Gate, the wind blows full of sand,
Lonely from the beginning of time until now!
Trees fall, the grass goes yellow with autumn.
I climb the towers and towers
    to watch out the barbarous land:
Desolate castle, the sky, the wide desert.
There is no wall left to this village.
Bones white with a thousand frosts,
High heaps, covered with trees and grass;
Who brought this to pass?
Who has brought the flaming imperial anger?
Who has brought the army with drums and with
    kettle-drums?
Barbarous kings.
A gracious spring, turned to blood-ravenous
    autumn,
A turmoil of wars-men, spread over the middle
    kingdom,
Three hundred and sixty thousand,
And sorrow, sorrow like rain.
Sorrow to go, and sorrow, sorrow returning.
Desolate, desolate fields,
And no children of warfare upon them,
      No longer the men for offence and defence.
Ah, how shall you know the dreary sorrow at the
    North Gate
With Rihoku's name forgotten,
And we guardsmen fed to the tigers.

                                  —By Rihaku

Euroclydon

ABBIE HUSTON EVANS

The east-northeaster pounds the coast tonight,
Thudding and grinding at the knees of islands;
It sets the bell-buoys clanging and calls out
The gruff storm-warnings up and down the coast.
—So this, none else, was Paul's Euroclydon,
That old tempestuous wind that leaped from Crete
And heaped the seas up till they broke the ship,
But not the man.—Pull out the Book again:
"When the south wind blew softly—" (O sweet words,
The spring is in them. Hark!)—"we loosed from Crete."   10
I sit and listen while Euroclydon,
That old storm-wind that had a name of its own
Two thousand years before I yet had mine,
Pelts on my pane with blizzard snow like grit,
Shrieks down my chimney, grips my house foursquare,
And pants against my door.
                        Old tiger, hail!

Title: Traditional name of a stormy northeast wind of the Mediterranean.
5–10 For the shipwreck of the Apostle Paul, see Acts 27.

Fact of Crystal

ABBIE HUSTON EVANS

Who shall say that the rock feels not at all
In its obscure, slumbrous, geologic way
The pinprick of incipient demolition;
Or sensed not once the dream-faint, unremitting,
Electric stir of the crystal rising in its side—
The next-to-nothing gnat-sting, the dim prickle
Of flowering not-life making try at growth,

Prefiguring afar the flying fire
That runs in the veins of men, through coils of time
Bringing prodigious newness out of earth?

Motion, that far-off whisper—it was there
In quartz, in beryl, in the mica sheath.
In crystal-building and in fusion flash
The poles of speed declare themselves, and what
Is cataclysmic, loosed in a splintered second,
Innocuous creeps down its millionth year.

Locked in dragging ages black as Tophet,
Crammed into corners in split seams of the earth,
Down deep in torpor's dungeon lodged forgotten,
Accepting off-slant cramping of the facets
As incidental and of no importance,
These mounting shapes from formlessness arriving
Were not unmindful of their glorious axes
In at the center fixed, ordaining true
The ancient inmost pivots of pure selfhood.

Behold the beauteous sluggards and their work—
The slothful quartz, the lazing tourmaline,
And their great tardy dazzle. Envy rock's glory.
This that hung once thinner than breath in space,
Wraith of a wraith, earth's uncreated dust,
Now signals with the flung-down fact of crystal,
Its stern-decreed geometry achieved,
Its pattern worked out to a T, its tip atom in place.

Where current rode the illimitable streaming
Too slow for any swirl to break the surface,
At that old, creeping, archetypal snail pace,
With none to note it, chaos inched back, worsted.
How landfall-like august form stands delivered!
Here's most diffuse most pointed, peaked, compacted,
Here's most amorphous grappled into jewel.

You, Andrew Marvell

ARCHIBALD MacLEISH

And here face down beneath the sun
And here upon earth's noonward height
To feel the always coming on
The always rising of the night

To feel creep up the curving east
The earthy chill of dusk and slow
Upon those under lands the vast
And everclimbing shadow grow

And strange at Ecbatan the trees   10
Take leaf by leaf the evening strange
The flooding dark about their knees
The mountains over Persia change

And now at Kermanshah the gate
Dark empty and the withered grass
And through the twilight now the late
Few travelers in the westward pass

And Baghdad darken and the bridge
Across the silent river gone
And through Arabia the edge
Of evening widen and steal on   20

And deepen on Palmyra's street
The wheel rut in the ruined stone
And Lebanon fade out and Crete
High through the clouds and overblown

9 Ecbatan: ancient name of the Persian city of Hamadan.   13 Kermanshah: Persian city west of Hamadan.   16 westward pass: the Zagros Gate, a pass west of Kermanshah.   21 Palmyra: ancient caravan center, with ruins of various past epochs.

And over Sicily the air
Still flashing with the landward gulls
And loom and slowly disappear
The sails above the shadowy hulls

And Spain go under and the shore
Of Africa the gilded sand   30
And evening vanish and no more
The low pale light across that land

Nor now the long light on the sea

And here face downward in the sun
To feel how swift how secretly
The shadow of the night comes on . . .

MARIANNE MOORE[1]

The Fish

wade
through black jade.
   Of the crow-blue mussel-shells, one keeps
  adjusting the ash-heaps;
     opening and shutting itself like

an
injured fan.
   The barnacles which encrust the side
  of the wave, cannot hide
     there for the submerged shafts of the   10

sun,
split like spun

---

[1] Marianne Moore often incorporates her title into the first sentence of the poem. In order to preserve the continuity of her sentence, the order of the heading here has been changed from that followed elsewhere in this volume.

glass, move themselves with spotlight swiftness
into the crevices—
   in and out, illuminating
the
turquoise sea
   of bodies. The water drives a wedge
   of iron through the iron edge
      of the cliff; whereupon the stars,   20
pink
rice-grains, ink-
   bespattered jelly-fish, crabs like green
   lilies, and submarine
      toadstools, slide each on the other.
All
external
   marks of abuse are present on this
   defiant edifice—
      all the physical features of   30
ac-
cident—lack
   of cornice, dynamite grooves, burns, and
   hatchet strokes, these things stand
      out on it; the chasm-side is
dead.
Repeated
   evidence has proved that it can live
   on what cannot revive
      its youth. The sea grows old in it.   40

To a Steam Roller
MARIANNE MOORE

The illustration
is nothing to you without the application.
   You lack half wit. You crush all the particles down
      into close conformity, and then walk back and forth on them.

Sparkling chips of rock
are crushed down to the level of the parent block.
    Were not "impersonal judgment in esthetic
      matters, a metaphysical impossibility," you
might fairly achieve
it. As for butterflies, I can hardly conceive   10
    of one's attending upon you, but to question
      the congruence of the complement is vain, if it exists.

MARIANNE MOORE

England

with its baby rivers and little towns, each with its abbey or its
    cathedral;
with voices—one voice perhaps, echoing through the transept—the
criterion of suitability and convenience; and Italy with its equal
shores—contriving an epicureanism from which the grossness has
    been

extracted: and Greece with its goats and its gourds, the nest of
    modified illusions:
and France, the "chrysalis of the nocturnal butterfly," in
whose products mystery of construction diverts one from what was
    originally one's
object—substance at the core: and the East with its snails, its
    emotional

shorthand and jade cockroaches, its rock crystal and its
    imperturbability,
all of museum quality: and America where there   10
is the little old ramshackle victoria in the south, where cigars are
    smoked on the
street in the north; where there are no proof-readers, no silk-worms,
    no digressions;

the wild man's land; grassless, linksless, languageless country in
    which letters are written

not in Spanish, not in Greek, not in Latin, not in shorthand,
but in plain American which cats and dogs can read! The letter *a*
    in psalm and calm when
pronounced with the sound of *a* in candle, is very noticeable, but

why should continents of misapprehension have to be accounted for
    by the
fact? Does it follow that because there are poisonous toadstools
which resemble mushrooms, both are dangerous? In the case of
    mettlesomeness which may be
mistaken for appetite, of heat which may appear to be haste,
    no con-   20

clusions may be drawn. To have misapprehended the matter is to
    have confessed
that one has not looked far enough. The sublimated wisdom
of China, Egyptian discernment, the cataclysmic torrent of emotion
    compressed
in the verbs of the Hebrew language, the books of the man who
    is able

to say, "I envy nobody but him, and him only, who catches more
    fish than
I do,"—the flower and fruit of all that noted superi-
ority—should one not have stumbled upon it in America, must
    one imagine
that it is not there? It has never been confined to one locality.

Look, stranger, on this island now

W. H. AUDEN

    Look, stranger, on this island now
    The leaping light for your delight discovers,
    Stand stable here
    And silent be,

That through the channels of the ear
May wander like a river
The swaying sound of the sea.

Here at the small field's ending pause
Where the chalk wall falls to the foam and its
   tall ledges
Oppose the pluck   10
And knock of the tide,
And the shingle scrambles after the suck-
   ing surf,
And the gull lodges
A moment on its sheer side.

Far off like floating seeds the ships
Diverge on urgent voluntary errands,
And the full view
Indeed may enter
And move in memory as now these clouds do,   20
That pass the harbour mirror
And all the summer through the water saunter.

Pur

W. H. AUDEN

This lunar beauty
Has no history,
Is complete and early;
If beauty later
Bear any feature,
It had a lover
And is another.

This like a dream
Keeps other time,
And daytime is   10
The loss of this;

Title: Pure (French).

For time is inches
And the heart's changes
Where ghost has haunted,
Lost and wanted.

But this was never
A ghost's endeavour
Nor, finished this,
Was ghost at ease;
And till it pass   20
Love shall not near
The sweetness here,
Nor sorrow take
His endless look.

I hear the cries of evening

STEPHEN SPENDER

I hear the cries of evening, while the paw
Of dark, creeps up the turf:
Sheep bleating, swaying gulls' cry, the rooks' "Caw,"
The hammering surf.

I am inconstant, yet this constancy
Of natural rest, pulls at my heart;
Town-bred, I feel the roots of each earth-cry
Tear me apart.

These are the creakings of the dusty day
When the dog Night bites sharp,   10
These fingers grip my soul and tear away
And pluck me like a harp.

I feel the huge sphere turn, the great wheel sing
While beasts move to their ease:
Sheep's love, gull's peace—I feel my chattering
Uncared by these.

What I expected

STEPHEN SPENDER

What I expected, was
Thunder, fighting,
Long struggles with men
And climbing.
After continual straining
I should grow strong;
Then the rocks would shake,
And I rest long.

What I had not foreseen
Was the gradual day
Weakening the will
Leaking the brightness away,
The lack of good to touch,
The fading of body and soul
—Smoke before wind,
Corrupt, unsubstantial.

The wearing of Time,
And the watching of cripples pass
With limbs shaped like questions
In their odd twist,
The pulverous grief
Melting the bones with pity,
The sick falling from earth—
These, I could not foresee.

Expecting always
Some brightness to hold in trust,
Some final innocence
Exempt from dust,
That, hanging solid,
Would dangle through all,
Like the created poem,
Or faceted crystal.

Sea Turtle

RICHARD O'CONNELL

Protected by an inch of glass,
I got close to him as I could;
And felt his overwhelming bulk
Envelop me and freeze my blood.

He didn't notice me at first
But kept on swimming back and forth;
Still measuring the cramping tank
Against his oceanic berth.

I thought: "Well, here he is. Himself.
The fabled old man of the seas . . ."   10
I felt I knew him so, I knocked—
He didn't open up his eyes;

But like an old priest saying mass
Prayed underwater in the shell
He made a church—too dumb to preach
And only good for ritual.

He turned: looked squarely at me with
Compassion—terror too, I guess;
I felt the pressure of his stare
Against the cold sweat on the glass.   20

Not man to beast, nor beast to man
But both of us alert, alive
Saw through each other to those depths
Few fathom and return alive.

~ V ~

The Sonnet

The sonnet was introduced into England in the sixteenth century, mainly as a result of the popularity throughout Europe of the sonnets of the Italian poet Petrarch. The dominant, though not the only, theme was love. In 1327, at church on Easter Friday, Petrarch had first seen "Laura," a married woman whose identity is not now known. From that moment till long after her death he loved her; and she became the subject of a series of lyrics, mainly sonnets, that were written in keeping with the tradition of "courtly love," in which a knight served with varying hope and despair a married, sometimes capricious or cruel fair lady. Petrarch recorded the changing moods and events of his love and, since he was a pious man, his conflicts between sensual love and spiritual devotion. The convention of the love sonnet, thus established, became the vehicle of a good deal of mechanical imitation but also of a surprisingly large amount of genuine poetry. The writer who introduced the convention into English was Sir Thomas Wyatt.

In form, though there have been many variations, the two chief types of sonnet in English are known as the Petrarchan or Italian and the Shakespearean or English. Both consist of fourteen lines of iambic pentameter. For the Italian form, the poet chooses a two-part subject, involving perhaps a question and answer, a problem and solution, a statement and retraction, or some other shift of thought or feeling that falls naturally into two parts, as the metrical form itself does. The first eight lines, or octave, are held together in a fixed rhyme scheme, *a b b a a b b a*. With the "turn" of thought the rhyme also changes in the sestet (the last six lines), where the poet has a freer choice. The rhyme may be *c d e c d e* or any of several other arrangements.

The English form, which receives its chief fame from Shakespeare, consists of three quatrains of alternate rhyme (*a b a b c d c d e f e f*), followed by a couplet. Sometimes the Shakespearean sonnet follows a two-part treatment of theme as the Italian does; more often its division of thought parallels the grouping of rhymes.

In the Elizabethan Age, when the vogue of the sonnet was at its height, many poets wrote "sonnet sequences," series of independent sonnets bound together by a single subject or carrying a thread of story, usually the poet's real or imagined love. Those of Shakespeare belong to such a sequence (or two sequences). But since that time the sonnet has most often been used for single isolated subjects.

The sonnet form, particularly the Italian version, is strict and narrow. In this chapter the two sonnets on the sonnet, by Wordsworth and Keats, give some idea of what the attraction of this form is to the poet himself. Other sonnets, some of them important ones, appear in other chapters (see especially Sidney's "With how sad steps" in the "Introduction," Hood's "On Mistress Nicely" in Chapter I, Yeats's "Meru" in Chapter VIII, and the important ones by Donne and Hopkins in Chapter VIII).

A Renouncing of Love

SIR THOMAS WYATT

Farewell, Love, and all thy laws for ever;
Thy baited hooks shall tangle me no more:
Senec and Plato call me from thy lore,
To perfect wealth my wit for to endeavour;

In blind errour when I did perséver,
Thy sharp repulse, that pricketh aye so sore,
Hath taught me to set in trifles no store;
And 'scape forth, since liberty is lever:
Therefore, farewell, go trouble younger hearts,
And in me claim no more authority;   10
With idle youth go use thy property,
And thereon spend thy many brittle darts:
For hitherto though I have lost all my time,
Me list no longer rotten boughs to clime.

8 lever: dearer.   11 property: power.   14 Me list no longer: it pleases me no longer, or I wish no longer.

The Lover Compareth His State to a Ship in Perilous Storm Tossed on the Sea

SIR THOMAS WYATT

My galley chargèd with forgetfulness,
Thorough sharp seas in winter nights doth pass,
'Tween rock and rock; and eke mine enemy, alas,
That is my lord steereth with cruelness;
And every oar a thought in readiness,
As though that death were light in such a case;
An endless wind doth tear the sail apace
Of forcèd sighs and trusty fearfulness;
A rain of tears, a cloud of dark disdain,
Hath done the wearied cords great hinderance;   10
Wreathèd with error and eke with ignorance,
The stars be hid that led me to this pain;
   Drownèd is Reason, that should me comfort;
   And I remain despairing of the port.

5 oar: possibly "hour." The old spellings produce uncertainty in the reading.
10 cords: cordage, ropes in the ship's rigging.

Leave me, O Love, which reachest but to dust

SIR PHILIP SIDNEY

Leave me, O Love, which reachest but to dust,
And thou, my mind, aspire to higher things:
Grow rich in that which never taketh rust:
Whatever fades, but fading pleasure brings.

Draw in thy beams, and humble all thy might,
To that sweet yoke, where lasting freedoms be:
Which breaks the clouds and opens forth the light,
That doth both shine and give us sight to see.

O take fast hold, let that light be thy guide,
In this small course which birth draws out to death,   10
And think how evil becometh him to slide,
Who seeketh heav'n, and comes of heav'nly breath.
   Then farewell world, thy uttermost I see,
   Eternal Love maintain thy life in me.

Since there's no help, come let us kiss and part

MICHAEL DRAYTON

Since there's no help, come let us kiss and part;
Nay, I have done, you get no more of me,
And I am glad, yea glad with all my heart
That thus so cleanly I myself can free;
Shake hands for ever, cancel all our vows,
And when we meet at any time again,
Be it not seen in either of our brows
That we one jot of former love retain.
Now at the last gasp of love's latest breath,
When, his pulse failing, passion speechless lies,   10

When faith is kneeling by his bed of death,
And innocence is closing up his eyes,
  Now if thou wouldst, when all have given him over,
  From death to life thou mightst him yet recover.

From *Amoretti*

EDMUND SPENSER

34

Lyke as a ship that through the Ocean wyde,
  by conduct of some star doth make her way,
  whenas a storme hath dimd her trusty guyde,
  out of her course doth wander far astray;
So I whose star, that wont with her bright ray,
  me to direct, with cloudes is overcast,
  doe wander now in darknesse and dismay,
  through hidden perils round about me plast.
Yet hope I well, that when this storme is past,
  my *Helice* the lodestar of my lyfe   10
  will shine again, and looke on me at last,
  with lovely light to cleare my cloudy grief.
Till then I wander carefull comfortlesse,
  in secret sorow and sad pensivenesse.

8 plast: placed.

75

One day I wrote her name upon the strand,
  but came the waves and washed it away:
  Agayne I wrote it with a second hand,
  but came the tyde, and made my paynes his pray.
Vayne man, sayd she, that doest in vaine assay
  a mortall thing so to immortalize,

4 pray: prey.

>   for I my selve shall lyke to this decay,
>   and eek my name bee wyped out lykewize.
>   Not so (quod I) let baser things devize
>   to dy in dust, but you shall live by fame: 10
>   my verse your vertues rare shall eternize,
>   and in the hevens wryte your glorious name;
>   Where, whenas death shall all the world subdew,
>   our love shall live, and later life renew.

8 eek: eke, also.

Sonnets

WILLIAM SHAKESPEARE

17

Who will believe my verse in time to come,
If it were fill'd with your most high deserts?
Though yet, heaven knows, it is but as a tomb
Which hides your life and shows not half your parts.
If I could write the beauty of your eyes
And in fresh numbers number all your graces,
The age to come would say "This poet lies;
Such heavenly touches ne'er touch'd earthly faces."
So should my papers yellow'd with their age,
Be scorn'd like old men of less truth than tongue,   10
And your true rights be term'd a poet's rage
And stretched metre of an antique song:
  But were some child of yours alive that time,
  You should live twice; in it and in my rhyme.

18

Shall I compare thee to a summer's day?
Thou art more lovely and more temperate:
Rough winds do shake the darling buds of May,
And summer's lease hath all too short a date:
Sometime too hot the eye of heaven shines,
And often is his gold complexion dimm'd;

And every fair from fair sometime declines,
By chance, or nature's changing course, untrimm'd;
But thy eternal summer shall not fade
Nor lose possession of that fair thou ow'st,   10
Nor shall Death brag thou wander'st in his shade,
When in eternal lines to time thou grow'st:
   So long as men can breathe, or eyes can see,
   So long lives this, and this gives life to thee.

10 ow'st: ownest.

19

Devouring Time, blunt thou the lion's paws,
And make the earth devour her own sweet brood;
Pluck the keen teeth from the fierce tiger's yaws,
And burn the long-lived phoenix in her blood;
Make glad and sorry seasons as thou fleet'st,
And do whate'er thou wilt, swift-footed Time,
To the wide world and all her fading sweets;
But I forbid thee one most heinous crime:
O, carve not with thy hours my love's fair brow,
Nor draw no lines there with thine antique pen;   10
Him in thy course untainted do allow
For beauty's pattern to succeeding men.
   Yet, do thy worst, old Time: despite thy wrong,
   My love shall in my verse ever live young.

3 yaws: jaws. 4 phoenix: sacred bird of middle eastern legend, of which only one existed at a time. It lived for 500 years, then burned itself in a self-created fire from the ashes of which another phoenix rose.

29

When in disgrace with fortune and men's eyes
I all alone beweep my outcast state,
And trouble deaf heaven with my bootless cries,
And look upon myself, and curse my fate,

Wishing me like to one more rich in hope,
Featur'd like him, like him with friends possess'd,
Desiring this man's art, and that man's scope,
With what I most enjoy contented least;
Yet in these thoughts myself almost despising,
Haply I think on thee, and then my state,   10
Like to the lark at break of day arising
From sullen earth, sings hymns at heaven's gate;
  For thy sweet love remember'd such wealth brings
  That then I scorn to change my state with kings.

30

When to the sessions of sweet silent thought
I summon up remembrance of things past,
I sigh the lack of many a thing I sought,
And with old woes new wail my dear time's waste:
Then can I drown an eye unus'd to flow,
For precious friends hid in death's dateless night,
And weep afresh love's long since cancell'd woe,
And moan th' expense of many a vanish'd sight;
Then can I grieve at grievances foregone,
And heavily from woe to woe tell o'er   10
The sad account of fore-bemoaned moan,
Which I new pay as if not paid before.
  But if the while I think on thee, dear friend,
  All losses are restor'd and sorrows end.

33

Full many a glorious morning have I seen
Flatter the mountain-tops with sovereign eye,
Kissing with golden face the meadows green,
Gilding pale streams with heavenly alchemy;
Anon permit the basest clouds to ride
With ugly rack on his celestial face,

6 rack: a wind-driven mass of high clouds.

And from the forlorn world his visage hide,
Stealing unseen to west with this disgrace.
Even so my sun one early morn did shine
With all triumphant splendour on my brow;   10
But out, alack! he was but one hour mine,
The region cloud hath mask'd him from me now.
   Yet him for this my love no whit disdaineth;
   Suns of the world may stain when heaven's sun staineth.

14 stain: become darkened.

55

Not marble, nor the gilded monuments
Of princes, shall outlive this powerful rhyme;
But you shall shine more bright in these contents
Than unswept stone besmear'd with sluttish time.
When wasteful war shall statues overturn,
And broils root out the work of masonry,
Nor Mars his sword nor war's quick fire shall burn
The living record of your memory.
'Gainst death and all oblivious enmity
Shall you pace forth; your praise shall still find room   10
Even in the eyes of all posterity
That wear this world out to the ending doom.
   So, till the judgment that yourself arise,
   You live in this, and dwell in lovers' eyes.

4 unswept stone: i.e., epitaphs inscribed (usually on bronze tablets) in the stone floors of churches.   *7* Mars his: Mars's.

57

Being your slave, what should I do but tend
Upon the hours and times of your desire?
I have no precious time at all to spend,
Nor services to do, till you require.
Nor dare I chide the world-without-end hour
Whilst I, my sovereign, watch the clock for you,

Nor think the bitterness of absence sour
When you have bid your servant once adieu;
Nor dare I question with my jealous thought
Where you may be, or your affairs suppose,
But, like a sad slave, stay and think of nought
Save where you are how happy you make those.
  So true a fool is love that in your Will,
  Though you do any thing, he thinks no ill.

60

Like as the waves make towards the pebbled shore,
So do our minutes hasten to their end,
Each changing place with that which goes before,
In sequent toil all forwards do contend.
Nativity, once in the main of light,
Crawls to maturity, wherewith being crown'd,
Crooked eclipses 'gainst his glory fight,
And Time that gave doth now his gift confound.
Time doth transfix the flourish set on youth
And delves the parallels in beauty's brow,
Feeds on the rarities of nature's truth,
And nothing stands but for his scythe to mow:
  And yet to times in hope my verse shall stand,
  Praising thy worth, despite his cruel hand.

62

Sin of self-love possesseth all mine eye
And all my soul and all my every part;
And for this sin there is no remedy,
It is so grounded inward in my heart:
Methinks no face so gracious is as mine,
No shape so true, no truth of such account;
And for myself mine own worth do define,
As I all other in all worths surmount.
But when my glass shows me myself indeed,
Beated and chopp'd with tann'd antiquity,

Mine own self-love quite contrary I read;
Self so self-loving were iniquity.
   'T is thee (myself) that for myself I praise,
   Painting my age with beauty of thy days.

65

Since brass, nor stone, nor earth, nor boundless sea,
But sad mortality o'er-sways their power,
How with this rage shall beauty hold a plea,
Whose action is no stronger than a flower?
O how shall summer's honey breath hold out
Against the wrackful siege of batt'ring days,
When rocks impregnable are not so stout,
Nor gates of steel so strong, but Time decays?
O fearful meditation! where, alack,
Shall Time's best jewel from Time's chest lie hid?   10
Or what strong hand can hold his swift foot back?
Or who his spoil of beauty can forbid?
   O none, unless this miracle have might,
   That in black ink my love may still shine bright.

6 batt'ring: The association is with battering rams used in the siege of a walled city.

71

No longer mourn for me when I am dead
Than you shall hear the surly sullen bell
Give warning to the world that I am fled
From this vile world, with vilest worms to dwell:
Nay, if you read this line, remember not
The hand that writ it; for I love you so,
That I in your sweet thoughts would be forgot,
If thinking on me then should make you woe.
O if, I say, you look upon this verse
When I perhaps compounded am with clay,   10
Do not so much as my poor name rehearse,
But let your love even with my life decay;
   Lest the wise world should look into your moan,
   And mock you with me after I am gone.

73

That time of year thou mayst in me behold
When yellow leaves, or none, or few, do hang
Upon those boughs which shake against the cold,
Bare ruin'd choirs, where late the sweet birds sang:
In me thou see'st the twilight of such day
As after sunset fadeth in the west,
Which by and by black night doth take away,
Death's second self, that seals up all in rest:
In me thou see'st the glowing of such fire,
That on the ashes of his youth doth lie,   10
As the death-bed whereon it must expire,
Consum'd with that which it was nourish'd by.
    This thou perceiv'st, which makes thy love more strong,
    To love that well which thou must leave ere long.

86

Was it the proud full sail of his great verse,
Bound for the prize of all too precious you,
That did my ripe thoughts in my brain inhearse,
Making their tomb the womb wherein they grew?
Was it his spirit, by spirits taught to write
Above a mortal pitch, that struck me dead?
No, neither he, nor his compeers by night
Giving him aid, my verse astonished.
He, nor that affable familiar ghost
Which nightly gulls him with intelligence,   10
As victors of my silence cannot boast;
I was not sick of any fear from thence:
    But when your countenance fill'd up his line,
    Then lack'd I matter; that enfeebled mine.

1 his: the rival poet's.   9–10 The allusion here remains a mystery.
13 countenance: favor.

87

Farewell! thou art too dear for my possessing,
And like enough thou know'st thy estimate:

The charter of thy worth gives thee releasing;
My bonds in thee are all determinate.
For how do I hold thee but by thy granting,
And for that riches where is my deserving?
The cause of this fair gift in me is wanting,
And so my patent back again is swerving.
Thyself thou gavest, thy own worth then not knowing,
Or me, to whom thou gav'st it, else mistaking;   10
So thy great gift, upon misprision growing,
Comes home again, on better judgment making.
  Thus have I had thee, as a dream doth flatter,
  In sleep a king, but waking, no such matter.

4 determinate: having a definite limit.   8 patent: right or privilege (legal).
11 upon misprision growing: which grew out of mistaken judgment.

90

Then hate me when thou wilt; if ever, now;
Now while the world is bent my deeds to cross,
Join with the spite of fortune, make me bow,
And do not drop in for an after loss:
Ah, do not, when my heart hath 'scap'd this sorrow,
Come in the rearward of a conquer'd woe;
Give not a windy night a rainy morrow,
To linger out a purpos'd overthrow.
If thou wilt leave me, do not leave me last,
When other petty griefs have done their spite,   10
But in the onset come: so shall I taste
At first the very worst of fortune's might;
  And other strains of woe, which now seem woe,
  Compar'd with loss of thee will not seem so.

97

How like a winter hath my absence been
From thee, the pleasure of the fleeting year!
What freezings have I felt, what dark days seen,
What old December's bareness everywhere!

And yet this time remov'd was summer's time;
The teeming autumn, big with rich increase,
Bearing the wanton burden of the prime,
Like widow'd wombs after their lords' decease:
Yet this abundant issue seem'd to me
But hope of orphans and unfather'd fruit; 10
For summer and his pleasures wait on thee,
And, thou away, the very birds are mute;
  Or, if they sing, 'tis with so dull a cheer,
  That leaves look pale, dreading the winter's near.

98

From you have I been absent in the spring,
When proud pied April, dress'd in all his trim,
Hath put a spirit of youth in every thing,
That heavy Saturn laugh'd and leapt with him.
Yet nor the lays of birds, nor the sweet smell
Of different flowers in odour and in hue
Could make me any summer's story tell,
Or from their proud lap pluck them where they grew;
Nor did I wonder at the lily's white,
Nor praise the deep vermilion in the rose; 10
They were but sweet, but figures of delight,
Drawn after you, you pattern of all those.
  Yet seem'd it winter still, and you away,
  As with your shadow I with these did play.

106

When in the chronicle of wasted time
I see descriptions of the fairest wights,
And beauty making beautiful old rhyme,
In praise of ladies dead and lovely knights,
Then, in the blazon of sweet beauty's best,
Of hand, of foot, of lip, of eye, of brow,
I see their antique pen would have express'd
Even such a beauty as you master now.

So all their praises are but prophecies
Of this our time, all you prefiguring;   10
And, for they look'd but with divining eyes,
They had not skill enough your worth to sing:
    For we which now behold these present days,
    Have eyes to wonder, but lack tongues to praise.

12 skill: so printed by most editors, though the 1609 edition has "still."

116

Let me not to the marriage of true minds
Admit impediments. Love is not love
Which alters when it alteration finds,
Or bends with the remover to remove:
O, no! it is an ever-fixed mark
That looks on tempests and is never shaken;
It is the star to every wand'ring bark,
Whose worth's unknown, although his height be taken.
Love's not Time's fool, though rosy lips and cheeks
Within his bending sickle's compass come;   10
Love alters not with his brief hours and weeks,
But bears it out even to the edge of doom.
    If this be error, and upon me prov'd,
    I never writ, nor no man ever lov'd.

7 star: North Star.

121

'Tis better to be vile than vile esteemed,
When not to be receives reproach of being,
And the just pleasure lost, which is so deemed
Not by our feeling but by others' seeing.
For why should others' false adulterate eyes
Give salutation to my sportive blood?
Or on my frailties why are frailer spies,
Which in their wills count bad what I think good?
No, I am that I am, and they that level
At my abuses reckon up their own: 10

I may be straight though they themselves be bevel;
By their rank thoughts my deeds must not be shown,
   Unless this general evil they maintain,
   All men are bad, and in their badness reign.

129

Th' expense of spirit in a waste of shame
Is lust in action; and till action, lust
Is perjur'd, murd'rous, bloody, full of blame,
Savage, extreme, rude, cruel, not to trust;
Enjoy'd no sooner but despised straight;
Past reason hunted, and no sooner had,
Past reason hated, as a swallow'd bait
On purpose laid to make the taker mad:
Mad in pursuit, and in possession so;
Had, having, and in quest to have, extreme;   10
A bliss in proof, and prov'd, a very woe;
Before, a joy propos'd; behind, a dream.
   All this the world well knows; yet none knows well
   To shun the heaven that leads men to this hell.

130

My mistress' eyes are nothing like the sun;
Coral is far more red than her lips' red;
If snow be white, why then her breasts are dun;
If hairs be wires, black wires grow on her head.
I have seen roses damask'd, red and white,
But no such roses see I in her cheeks;
And in some perfumes is there more delight
Than in the breath that from my mistress reeks.
I love to hear her speak, yet well I know
That music hath a far more pleasing sound: 10
I grant I never saw a goddess go;
My mistress, when she walks, treads on the ground.
   And yet, by heaven, I think my love as rare
   As any she belied with false compare.

11 go: walk.

138

When my love swears that she is made of truth,
I do believe her, though I know she lies,
That she might think me some untutor'd youth,
Unlearned in the world's false subtleties.
Thus vainly thinking that she thinks me young,
Although she knows my days are past the best,
Simply I credit her false-speaking tongue;
On both sides thus is simple truth suppress'd
But wherefore says she not she is unjust?
And wherefore say not I that I am old? 10
O, love's best habit is in seeming trust,
And age in love loves not to have years told.
　　Therefore I lie with her, and she with me,
　　And in our faults by lies we flatter'd be.

146

Poor soul, the centre of my sinful earth,
. . . . these rebel powers that thee array,
Why dost thou pine within and suffer dearth,
Painting thy outward walls so costly gay?
Why so large cost, having so short a lease,
Dost thou upon thy fading mansion spend?
Shall worms, inheritors of this excess,
Eat up thy charge? is this thy body's end?
Then, soul, live thou upon thy servant's loss,
And let that pine to aggravate thy store; 10
Buy terms divine in selling hours of dross;
Within be fed, without be rich no more:
　　So shalt thou feed on Death, that feeds on men,
　　And Death once dead, there's no more dying then.

---

1 earth: body.　2 An old printer's error at the beginning of this line leaves the reading a matter of guesswork. "Fool'd by" and "Thrall to" have been suggested.　10 aggravate: increase.

147

My love is as a fever, longing still
For that which longer nurseth the disease,
Feeding on that which doth preserve the ill,
The uncertain sickly appetite to please.
My reason, the physician to my love,
Angry that his prescriptions are not kept,
Hath left me, and I desperate now approve
Desire is death, which physic did except.
Past cure I am, now reason is past care,
And frantic-mad with evermore unrest; 10
My thoughts and my discourse as madmen's are,
At random from the truth vainly express'd;
  For I have sworn thee fair and thought thee bright,
  Who art as black as hell, as dark as night.

7 approve: prove.

On the Late Massacre in Piedmont

JOHN MILTON

Avenge O Lord thy slaughter'd Saints, whose bones
Lie scatter'd on the Alpine mountains cold,
Ev'n them who kept thy truth so pure of old
When all our Fathers worship't Stocks and Stones,
Forget not: in thy book record their groanes
Who were thy Sheep and in their antient Fold
Slayn by the bloody *Piemontese* that roll'd
Mother with Infant down the Rocks. Their moans
The Vales redoubl'd to the Hills, and they
To Heav'n. Their martyr'd blood and ashes sow 10
O're all th' *Italian* fields where still doth sway
The triple Tyrant: that from these may grow
A hunder'd-fold, who having learnt thy way
Early may fly the *Babylonian* wo.

12 triple Tyrant: the pope, who wears a triple-crowned tiara.

When I consider how my light is spent

JOHN MILTON

When I consider how my light is spent,
E're half my days, in this dark world and wide,
And that one Talent which is death to hide,
Lodg'd with me useless, though my Soul more bent
To serve therewith my Maker, and present
My true account, least he returning chide,
Doth God exact day-labour, light deny'd,
I fondly ask; But patience to prevent
That murmur, soon replies, God doth not need
Either man's work or his own gifts, who best   10
Bear his milde yoak, they serve him best, his State
Is Kingly. Thousands at his bidding speed
And post o're Land and Ocean without rest:
They also serve who only stand and waite.

Title: Also known as "On His Blindness."   3–7 Talent . . .: The reference is to the parable of the "talents" in Matt. 25.   6 least: lest.   8 fondly: foolishly.

On His Deceased Wife

JOHN MILTON

Methought I saw my late espoused Saint
Brought to me like *Alcestis* from the grave,
Whom *Joves* great Son to her glad Husband gave,
Rescu'd from death by force though pale and faint.
Mine as whom washt from spot of child-bed taint,
Purification in the old Law did save,
And such, as yet once more I trust to have
Full sight of her in Heaven without restraint,
Came vested all in white, pure as her mind:
Her face was vail'd, yet to my fancied sight,   10

2–3 Alcestis . . . Jove's great son: In the Greek legend, Hercules brought Alcestis back from the tomb to be reunited with her husband.

Love, sweetness, goodness, in her person shin'd
So clear, as in no face with more delight.
But O as to embrace me she enclin'd
I wak'd, she fled, and day brought back my night.

Nuns fret not at their convent's narrow room

WILLIAM WORDSWORTH

Nuns fret not at their convent's narrow room;
And hermits are contented with their cells;
And students with their pensive citadels;
Maids at the wheel, the weaver at his loom,
Sit blithe and happy; bees that soar for bloom,
High as the highest Peak of Furness-fells,
Will murmur by the hour in foxglove bells:
In truth, the prison, unto which we doom
Ourselves, no prison is: and hence for me,
In sundry moods, 't was pastime to be bound   10
Within the Sonnet's scanty plot of ground;
Pleased if some Souls (for such there needs must be)
Who have felt the weight of too much liberty,
Should find brief solace there, as I have found.

4 wheel: spinning wheel.   6 Furness-fells: mountains in the English Lake District.

Composed upon Westminster Bridge, September 3, 1802

WILLIAM WORDSWORTH

Earth has not anything to show more fair:
Dull would he be of soul who could pass by
A sight so touching in its majesty:
This City now doth, like a garment, wear

The beauty of the morning; silent, bare,
Ships, towers, domes, theatres, and temples lie
Open unto the fields, and to the sky;
All bright and glittering in the smokeless air.
Never did sun more beautifully steep
In his first splendour, valley, rock, or hill; 10
Ne'er saw I, never felt, a calm so deep!
The river glideth at his own sweet will:
Dear God! the very houses seem asleep;
And all that mighty heart is lying still!

The world is too much with us

WILLIAM WORDSWORTH

The world is too much with us; late and soon,
Getting and spending, we lay waste our powers:
Little we see in Nature that is ours;
We have given our hearts away, a sordid boon!
This Sea that bares her bosom to the moon;
The winds that will be howling at all hours,
And are up-gathered now like sleeping flowers;
For this, for everything, we are out of tune;
It moves us not.—Great God! I'd rather be
A Pagan suckled in a creed outworn 10
So might I, standing on this pleasant lea,
Have glimpses that would make me less forlorn;
Have sight of Proteus rising from the sea;
Or hear old Triton blow his wreathèd horn.

13–14 Proteus and Triton: sea gods of classical mythology.

Where lies the Land
WILLIAM WORDSWORTH

Where lies the Land to which yon Ship must go?
Fresh as a lark mounting at break of day,
Festively she puts forth in trim array;
Is she for tropic suns, or polar snow?
What boots the enquiry?—Neither friend nor foe
She cares for; let her travel where she may,
She finds familiar names, a beaten way
Ever before her, and a wind to blow.
Yet still I ask, what haven is her mark?
And, almost as it was when ships were rare,   10
(From time to time, like Pilgrims, here and there
Crossing the waters) doubt, and something dark,
Of the old Sea some reverential fear,
Is with me at thy farewell, joyous Bark!

With Ships the sea was sprinkled
WILLIAM WORDSWORTH

With Ships the sea was sprinkled far and nigh,
Like stars in heaven, and joyously it showed;
Some lying fast at anchor in the road,
Some veering up and down, one knew not why.
A goodly Vessel did I then espy
Come like a giant from a haven broad;
And lustily along the bay she strode,
Her tackling rich, and of apparel high.
This Ship was nought to me, nor I to her,
Yet I pursued her with a Lover's look;   10
This Ship to all the rest did I prefer:
When will she turn, and whither? She will brook
No tarrying; where She comes the winds must stir:
On went She, and due north her journey took.

3 road: roadstead.

Mutability

WILLIAM WORDSWORTH

From low to high doth dissolution climb,
And sink from high to low, along a scale
Of awful notes, whose concord shall not fail;
A musical but melancholy chime,
Which they can hear who meddle not with crime,
Nor avarice, nor over-anxious care.
Truth fails not; but her outward forms that bear
The longest date do melt like frosty rime,
That in the morning whitened hill and plain
And is no more; drop like the tower sublime   10
Of yesterday, which royally did wear
His crown of weeds, but could not even sustain
Some casual shout that broke the silent air,
Or the unimaginable touch of Time.

Ozymandias

PERCY BYSSHE SHELLEY

I met a traveler from an antique land
Who said: Two vast and trunkless legs of stone
Stand in the desert. Near them, on the sand,
Half sunk, a shattered visage lies, whose frown,
And wrinkled lip, and sneer of cold command,
Tell that its sculptor well those passions read
Which yet survive, stamped on these lifeless things,
The hand that mocked them, and the heart that fed;
And on the pedestal these words appear:
"My name is Ozymandias, king of kings: 10
Look on my works, ye Mighty, and despair!"
Nothing beside remains. Round the decay
Of that colossal wreck, boundless and bare
The lone and level sands stretch far away.

Keen, fitful gusts are whisp'ring here and there

JOHN KEATS

    Keen, fitful gusts are whisp'ring here and there
        Among the bushes half leafless, and dry;
        The stars look very cold about the sky,
    And I have many miles on foot to fare.
    Yet feel I little of the cool bleak air,
        Or of the dead leaves rustling drearily,
        Or of those silver lamps that burn on high,
    Or of the distance from home's pleasant lair:
    For I am brimfull of the friendliness
        That in a little cottage I have found;   10
    Of fair-hair'd Milton's eloquent distress,
        And all his love for gentle Lycid drown'd;
    Of lovely Laura in her light green dress,
        And faithful Petrarch gloriously crown'd.

On First Looking into Chapman's Homer

JOHN KEATS

    Much have I travell'd in the realms of gold,
        And many goodly states and kingdoms seen;
        Round many western islands have I been
    Which bards in fealty to Apollo hold.
    Oft of one wide expanse had I been told
        That deep-brow'd Homer ruled as his demesne;
        Yet did I never breathe its pure serene
    Till I heard Chapman speak out loud and bold:
    Then felt I like some watcher of the skies
        When a new planet swims into his ken;   10
    Or like stout Cortez when with eagle eyes
        He star'd at the Pacific—and all his men
    Look'd at each other with a wild surmise—
        Silent, upon a peak in Darien.

11 Cortez: a mistake for Balboa.

On the Grasshopper and Cricket

JOHN KEATS

The poetry of earth is never dead:
  When all the birds are faint with the hot sun,
  And hide in cooling trees, a voice will run
From hedge to hedge about the new-mown mead;
That is the Grasshopper's—he takes the lead
  In summer luxury,—he has never done
  With his delights; for when tired out with fun
He rests at ease beneath some pleasant weed.
The poetry of earth is ceasing never:
  On a lone winter evening, when the frost   10
    Has wrought a silence, from the stove there shrills
The Cricket's song, in warmth increasing ever,
  And seems to one in drowsiness half lost,
    The Grasshopper's among some grassy hills.

On the Sea

JOHN KEATS

It keeps eternal whisperings around
  Desolate shores, and with its mighty swell
  Gluts twice ten thousand caverns, till the spell
Of Hecate leaves them their old shadowy sound.
Often 'tis in such gentle temper found,
  That scarcely will the very smallest shell
  Be moved for days from where it sometime fell,
When last the winds of heaven were unbound.
Oh ye who have your eye-balls vex'd and tired,
  Feast them upon the wideness of the Sea;   10
    Oh ye whose ears are dinn'd with uproar rude,
  Or fed too much with cloying melody,—
    Sit ye near some old cavern's mouth, and brood
Until ye start, as if the sea-nymphs quired.

When I have fears that I may cease to be

JOHN KEATS

When I have fears that I may cease to be
  Before my pen has glean'd my teeming brain,
Before high-piled books, in charact'ry,
  Hold like rich garners the full-ripen'd grain;
When I behold, upon the night's starr'd face,
  Huge cloudy symbols of a high romance,
And think that I may never live to trace
  Their shadows, with the magic hand of chance;
And when I feel, fair creature of an hour!
  That I shall never look upon thee more,   10
Never have relish in the faery power
  Of unreflecting love!—then on the shore
Of the wide world I stand alone, and think
Till love and fame to nothingness do sink.

If by dull rhymes our English must be chain'd

JOHN KEATS

If by dull rhymes our English must be chain'd,
  And, like Andromeda, the Sonnet sweet
Fetter'd, in spite of pained loveliness;
Let us find out, if we must be constrain'd,
  Sandals more interwoven and complete
To fit the naked foot of poesy:
Let us inspect the lyre, and weigh the stress
Of every chord, and see what may be gain'd
  By ear industrious, and attention meet;
Misers of sound and syllable, no less   10
Than Midas of his coinage, let us be
  Jealous of dead leaves in the bay wreath crown;
So, if we may not let the Muse be free,
  She will be bound with garlands of her own.

Lucifer in Starlight
GEORGE MEREDITH

On a starred night Prince Lucifer uprose.
Tired of his dark dominion, swung the fiend
Above the rolling ball in cloud part screened,
Where sinners hugged their spectre of repose.
Poor prey to his hot fit of pride were those.
And now upon his western wing he leaned,
Now his huge bulk o'er Afric's sands careened,
Now the black planet shadowed Arctic snows.
Soaring through wider zones that pricked his scars
With memory of the old revolt from Awe,   10
He reached a middle height, and at the stars,
Which are the brain of heaven, he looked, and sank.
Around the ancient track marched, rank on rank,
The army of unalterable law.

Sonnet No. 23
From *The Growth of Love*
ROBERT BRIDGES

O weary pilgrims, chanting of your woe,
That turn your eyes to all the peaks that shine,
Hailing in each the citadel divine
The which ye thought to have enter'd long ago;
Until at length your feeble steps and slow
Falter upon the threshold of the shrine,
And your hearts overburden'd doubt in fine
Whether it be Jerusalem or no:

Dishearten'd pilgrims, I am one of you;
For, having worshipp'd many a barren face,   10
I scarce now greet the goal I journey'd to:
I stand a pagan in the holy place;
Beneath the lamp of truth I am found untrue,
And question with the God that I embrace.

Under Cover

ABBIE HUSTON EVANS

Rain with the old sound, with the country sough
From fields and meadows overpast and trees
That strip it into whip-lash, I hear now
Beat on this hill and cut about its knees.
Now while the lithe wind turns and springs again
On the spent tree, and rain floods down the glass,
I hear the sounds earth knew before we men
Came on, and shall know after we shall pass.
While ancient rumor rising to a shriek
Comes in to tell of matters we forget,   10
I am one more of the beasts of the field in bleak
Ecstatic cover, huddled from the wet.
   So stands the ox, so crouches now the mole,
   So sits the dry woodpecker in his hole.

Sunday Morning

LOUIS MacNEICE

Down the road some one is practising scales,
The notes like little fishes vanish with a wink of tails,
Man's heart expands to tinker with his car
For this is Sunday morning, Fate's great bazaar;
Regard these means as ends, concentrate on this Now,
And you may grow to music or drive beyond Hindhead anyhow,
Take corners on two wheels until you go so fast
That you can clutch a fringe or two of the windy past,
That you can abstract this day and make it to the week of time
A small eternity, a sonnet self-contained in rhyme.   10

But listen, up the road, something gulps, the church spire
Opens its eight bells out, skulls' mouths which will not tire
To tell how there is no music or movement that ensures
Escape from the weekday time. Which deadens and endures.

~ VI ~

Ironical Modes and the Grotesque

Irony is founded on contrast, but obviously not all contrast is ironic, for contrast is essential to every work of art. To produce irony, something double must be present that suggests an awareness of incongruity or contradiction; there must be an implied comment, a hint in the tone of the poem that the author does not stand quite where he appears to stand, that he is critical of what he appears to praise, that he is detached or not wholly involved. When a writer says the opposite of what he obviously means or speaks favorably of what he obviously wishes to condemn, he is making a double statement, the unspoken half being the ironic comment. When Housman wrote in cheerful-sounding, fast-moving anapests, "I 'listed at home for a lancer,/ Oh who would not sleep with the brave?/ I 'listed at home for a lancer/ To ride on a horse to my grave," the irony, conveyed largely though not entirely by the meter, is if anything too obvious though it is implied only. Understatement may be ironic when it is extreme enough to provide a contrast or opposition between what is said and what is thought or felt; so may an extreme overstatement or exaggeration by which a writer belittles what he appears to be magnifying. Whatever the contrast, in ironic writing it is present not primarily for the general sake of variety but for the specific purpose of making a double statement, usually implying mockery.

IRONICAL MODES AND THE GROTESQUE 211

Though originally it had to do only with human attitudes and language, the term "irony" came to be used also for a comparable double effect in the world of events. When an outcome proves dramatically contrary to what is expected or intended, it is commonly referred to as the irony of fate or of circumstance, or in certain instances as "poetic justice": a criminal unknowingly runs into a police station while trying to elude pursuit, or a poorly constructed statue falls at its unveiling and cracks the skull of the sculptor waiting for applause. When such events are used in a narrative or a play, they provide what is known as "dramatic irony." The most celebrated of all instances of this is Sophocles' *Oedipus Rex*, in which almost every word innocently uttered and every action innocently initiated by Oedipus is dramatically ironic, having for him one meaning and purpose but for the reader another.

Irony may be the mode of a piece of writing as a whole or it may be a flitting light, sometimes of wit, playing over the surface of a work not primarily ironic. When it is the latter, it often helps establish what is called "aesthetic distance." Even when a writer's emotions are deeply engaged in what he has to say, the hint of an ironic view may produce an effect of mastery and perspective without weakening the impact of the emotion itself. This play of irony or wit characterizes many of the serious poems in earlier chapters of the present volume—certain sonnets of Shakespeare, for example, and the poems of Marvell in Chapter IV. It is even more prominent in the poems of Donne and Yeats in Chapter VIII. But the reader who has gained an awareness of shades of tone and mood in poetry will find it in many places.

The present chapter is concerned essentially with the poem in which irony (or, in some poems, the grotesque) is the main mode—that is, with the ironic as a particular type of poem. The epigram is a minor form of this type: it is a brief, witty, ironical poem usually critical of something or someone and usually providing through its wit some small element of surprise. More important is satire, a larger literary form that holds up human beings, their doings, or their institutions to scorn or ridicule. In tone satire ranges from good-natured raillery to savage detraction. Though its method is sometimes that of direct invective, usually in English literature its primary weapon is irony.

The great period of satiric writing in English was that of the late seventeenth and early eighteenth centuries. From that period Pope is selected here as most characteristic among the poets. Nearly all his best works were satire, and of these *The Rape of the Lock* is the most amiable. It is also the most complex, for its mockery is double or even triple. In form it is a mock epic, so that in a sense it satirizes epic poetry; in content it satirizes both the behavior of certain fashionable persons on a particular occasion and, more generally, the triviality of the world of fashion.

The comic needs no discussion here apart from irony because, though in drama and fiction it sometimes remains fresh over many centuries, in poetry other than satire it has been exceedingly perishable. Ogden Nash amuses readers today, but yesterday's Ogden Nashes are usually unreadable. Parody, however, occasionally survives, particularly when the work parodied is well enough known to give it point; but parody, of course, is ironic. The good-humored comedy, however, blended with irony, of Robert Burns's "Tam O' Shanter," has retained its popularity in spite of its dialect, and the poem is reprinted here.

A genre somewhat related to the comic and the ironic, sometimes also to the tragic, is the grotesque. It too is founded on contrast, distortion, or incongruity, originally involving unnatural forms or combinations of forms such as those of demons and gargoyles. It differs from irony in the fact that it does not imply an unspoken comment: its contrasts are presented without being assimilated or reconciled; it provides no higher point of view from which contradictions are resolved in a higher truth. Nevertheless, often, and usually at its best, the grotesque is present not for its own sake but as an element in irony, tragedy, or comedy, serving some end beyond its own distortions. Perhaps the greatest of all uses of the grotesque occurs in Shakespeare's *King Lear;* unfortunately for our present discussion, there it is so integral a part of the whole play that it cannot be extricated for quotation or even described briefly for illustration. The witches in *Macbeth,* however, are grotesque, and they are easily extractable, partly because, though they themselves serve an important function in the play, the details of their grotesque chanting and brew do not. A few poems in which the grotesque is dominant—not all of the highest rank as poetry—are included in the present chapter in order to draw attention to the particular character of the grotesque itself, for it plays a larger part in serious poetry than we usually suppose; it often helps create the individual flavor or quality of a poem that is not as a whole grotesque, like a touch of acid or spice that sharpens a flavor. This is the case, for example, with de la Mare's "The Song of Finis," which is not essentially either an ironic or a grotesque poem. In the work of W. B. Yeats, as will appear in Chapter VIII (but see also Chapter I), it becomes an extremely important element.

The Rape of the Lock
An Heroic-Comical Poem

ALEXANDER POPE

[Letter of dedication to Miss Arabella Fermor]

Madam:
It will be in vain to deny that I have some regard for this piece, since I dedicate it to You. Yet you may bear me witness, it was intended only to divert a few young Ladies, who have good sense and good humour enough to laugh not only at their sex's little unguarded follies, but at their own. But as it was communicated with the air of a Secret, it soon found its way into the world. An

imperfect copy having been offered to a Bookseller, you had the good-nature for my sake to consent to the publication of one more correct: This I was forced to before I had executed half my design, for the Machinery was entirely wanting to complete it.

The Machinery, Madam, is a term invented by the Critics to signify that part which the Deities, Angels, or Daemons are made to act in a Poem; For the ancient Poets are in one respect like modern Ladies: let an action be never so trivial in itself, they always make it appear of the utmost importance. These Machines I determined to raise on a very new and odd foundation, the Rosicrucian doctrine of Spirits.

I know how disagreeable it is to make use of hard words before a Lady, but 't is so much the concern of a Poet to have his works understood, and particularly by your Sex, that you must give me leave to explain two or three difficult terms.

The Rosicrucians are a people I must bring you acquainted with. The best account I know of them is in a French book called Le Comte de Gabalis, which both by its title and size is so like a Novel, that many of the Fair Sex have read it for one by mistake. According to these Gentlemen, the four Elements are inhabited by Spirits, which they call Sylphs, Gnomes, Nymphs, and Salamanders. The Gnomes or Daemons of Earth delight in mischief; but the Sylphs, whose habitation is in the Air, are the best-conditioned creatures imaginable. For they say, any mortals may enjoy the most intimate familiarities with these gentle Spirits, upon a condition very easy to all true Adepts, an inviolate preservation of Chastity.

As to the following Cantos, all the passages of them are as fabulous, as the Vision at the beginning, or the Transformation at the end (except the loss of your Hair, which I always mention with reverence). The Human persons are as fictitious as the airy ones, and the character of Belinda, as it is now managed, resembles you in nothing but in Beauty.

If this Poem had as many Graces as there are in your Person, or in your Mind, yet I could never hope it should pass through the world half so Uncensured as You have done. But let its fortune be what it will, mine is happy enough to have given me this occasion of assuring you that I am, with the truest esteem, Madam,

Your most obedient, Humble Servant,

A. Pope.

CANTO I

What dire offense from am'rous causes springs,
What mighty contests rise from trivial things,
I sing—This verse to *Caryl,* Muse! is due;
This, ev'n Belinda may vouchsafe to view:
Slight is the subject, but not so the praise,
If She inspire, and He approve my lays.
  Say what strange motive, Goddess! could compel
A well-bred Lord t' assault a gentle Belle?
Oh say what stranger cause, yet unexplor'd,
Could make a gentle Belle reject a Lord?   10
In tasks so bold, can little men engage,
And in soft bosoms dwells such mighty Rage?
  Sol through white curtains shot a tim'rous ray,
And oped those eyes that must eclipse the day:
Now lap-dogs give themselves the rousing shake,
And sleepless lovers, just at twelve, awake:
Thrice rung the bell, the slipper knocked the ground,
And the pressed watch returned a silver sound.
Belinda still her downy pillow prest,
Her guardian *Sylph* prolonged the balmy rest.   20
'Twas he had summoned to her silent bed
The morning-dream that hovered o'er her head;
A Youth more glitt'ring than a Birth-night Beau,
(That ev'n in slumber caused her cheek to glow)
Seemed to her ear his winning lips to lay,
And thus in whispers said, or seemed to say.
  "Fairest of mortals, thou distinguished care
Of thousand bright Inhabitants of Air!
If e'er one vision touched thy infant thought,
Of all the Nurse and all the Priest have taught;   30
Of airy Elves by moonlight shadows seen,
The silver token, and the circled green,
Or virgins visited by Angel-pow'rs,
With golden crowns and wreaths of heav'nly flow'rs;

18 pressed watch: the fashionable "repeater" watch, which struck the preceding hour or quarter-hour when a spring was pressed.   *23 Birth-night Beau:* fashionable man dressed for the annual birthday ball of the Queen.

Hear and believe! thy own importance know,
Nor bound thy narrow views to things below.
Some secret truths, from learnèd pride concealed,
To Maids alone and Children are revealed:
What tho' no credit doubting Wits may give?
The Fair and Innocent shall still believe.   40
Know, then, unnumbered Spirits round thee fly,
The light Militia of the lower sky;
These, tho' unseen, are ever on the wing,
Hang o'er the Box, and hover round the Ring.
Think what an Equipage thou hast in Air,
And view with scorn Two Pages and a Chair.
As now your own, our beings were of old,
And once inclosed in Woman's beauteous mould;
Thence, by a soft transition, we repair
From earthly Vehicles to these of air.   50
Think not, when Woman's transient breath is fled,
That all her vanities at once are dead:
Succeeding vanities she still regards,
And tho' she plays no more, o'erlooks the cards.
Her joy in gilded Chariots, when alive,
And love of Ombre, after death survive.
For when the Fair in all their pride expire,
To their first Elements their Souls retire:
The Sprites of fiery Termagants in Flame
Mount up, and take a Salamander's name.   60
Soft yielding minds to Water glide away,
And sip, with Nymphs, their elemental Tea.
The graver Prude sinks downward to a Gnome,
In search of mischief still on Earth to roam.
The light Coquettes in Sylphs aloft repair,
And sport and flutter in the fields of Air.
    Know farther yet; whoever fair and chaste
Rejects mankind, is by some Sylph embraced:

---

44 Box: at the theater. Ring: a circular drive in Hyde Park. 46 Chair: a sedan chair. 58 first Elements: the four elements of earth, air, fire, and water. 60 The salamander is a fabled animal capable of enduring fire; also, in some mediaeval beliefs, a supernatural being whose habitation was the element of fire. 62 As pronounced in Pope's day, "tea" rhymed with "away."

For Spirits, freed from mortal laws, with ease
Assume what sexes and what shapes they please. 70
What guards the purity of melting Maids,
In courtly balls, and midnight masquerades,
Safe from the treach'rous Friend, the daring Spark,
The glance by day, the whisper in the dark;
When kind occasion prompts their warm desires,
When music softens, and when dancing fires?
'Tis but their Sylph, the wise Celestials know,
Though Honour is the word with Men below.
    Some nymphs there are, too conscious of their face,
For life predestined to the Gnomes' embrace. 80
These swell their prospects and exalt their pride,
When offers are disdained, and love denied.
Then gay Ideas crowd the vacant brain;
While Peers and Dukes, and all their sweeping train,
And Garters, Stars, and Coronets appear,
And in soft sounds, *Your Grace* salutes their ear.
'Tis these that early taint the female soul,
Instruct the eyes of young Coquettes to roll,
Teach Infant-cheeks a bidden blush to know,
And little hearts to flutter at a Beau. 90
    Oft when the world imagine women stray,
The *Sylphs* through mystic mazes guide their way,
Through all the giddy circle they pursue,
And old impertinence expel by new.
What tender maid but must a victim fall
To one man's treat, but for another's ball?
When Florio speaks what virgin could withstand,
If gentle Damon did not squeeze her hand?
With varying vanities, from ev'ry part,
They shift the moving Toyshop of their heart; 100
Where wigs with wigs, with sword-knots sword-knots strive,
Beaux banish beaux, and coaches coaches drive.
This erring mortals Levity may call;
Oh blind to truth! the *Sylphs* contrive it all.
    Of these am I, who thy protection claim,
A watchful sprite, and *Ariel* is my name.
Late, as I ranged the crystal wilds of air,

In the clear Mirror of thy ruling Star
I saw, alas! some dread event impend,
Ere to the main this morning sun descend, 110
But heav'n reveals not what, or how, or where:
Warned by the *Sylph*, oh Pious Maid, beware!
This to disclose is all thy guardian can:
Beware of all, but most beware of Man!"
   He said; when *Shock*, who thought she slept too long,
Leapt up, and waked his mistress with his tongue.
'Twas then, *Belinda,* if report say true,
Thy eyes first opened on a Billet-doux;
Wounds, Charms, and Ardors were no sooner read,
But all the Vision vanished from thy head. 120
   And now, unveiled, the Toilet stands displayed,
Each silver Vase in mystic order laid.
First, robed in white, the Nymph intent adores,
With head uncovered, the Cosmetic powers.
A heav'nly image in the glass appears,
To that she bends, to that her eyes she rears;
Th' inferior Priestess, at her altar's side,
Trembling, begins the sacred rites of Pride.
Unnumbered treasures ope at once, and here
The various off'rings of the world appear; 130
From each she nicely culls with curious toil,
And decks the Goddess with the glitt'ring spoil.
This casket India's glowing gems unlocks,
And all Arabia breathes from yonder box.
The Tortoise here and Elephant unite,
Transformed to combs, the speckled, and the white.
Here files of pins extend their shining rows,
Puffs, Powders, Patches, Bibles, Billet-doux.
Now awful Beauty puts on all its arms;
The fair each moment rises in her charms, 140
Repairs her smiles, awakens every grace,
And calls forth all the wonders of her face;
Sees by degrees a purer blush arise,

---

127 inferior priestess: Belinda's maid, Betty.

And keener lightnings quicken in her eyes.
The busy *Sylphs* surround their darling care;
These set the head, and those divide the hair,
Some fold the sleeve, whilst others plait the gown;
And *Betty's* praised for labours not her own.

CANTO II

Not with more glories, in th' etherial plain,
The Sun first rises o'er the purpled main,
Than issuing forth, the Rival of his Beams
Launched on the bosom of the silver Thames.
Fair Nymphs, and well-drest Youths around her shone,
But ev'ry eye was fixed on her alone.
On her white breast a sparkling Cross she wore,
Which Jews might kiss, and Infidels adore.
Her lively looks a sprightly mind disclose,
Quick as her eyes, and as unfixed as those: 10
Favours to none, to all she smiles extends,
Oft she rejects, but never once offends.
Bright as the sun, her eyes the gazers strike,
And, like the sun, they shine on all alike.
Yet graceful ease, and sweetness void of pride,
Might hide her faults, if Belles had faults to hide:
If to her share some female errors fall,
Look on her face, and you'll forget 'em all.
    This Nymph, to the destruction of mankind,
Nourished two Locks, which graceful hung behind 20
In equal curls, and well conspired to deck
With shining ringlets her smooth iv'ry neck.
Love in these labyrinths his slaves detains,
And mighty hearts are held in slender chains.
With hairy springes we the birds betray,
Slight lines of hair surprise the finny prey,
Fair tresses man's imperial race ensnare,
And beauty draws us with a single hair.
    Th' advent'rous Baron the bright locks admired;
He saw, he wished, and to the prize aspired. 30
Resolved to win, he mediates the way,
By force to ravish, or by fraud betray;

For when success a Lover's toil attends,
Few ask, if fraud or force attained his ends.
  For this, ere Phœbus rose, he had implored
Propitious Heav'n, and ev'ry Pow'r adored,
But chiefly *Love*—to *Love* an Altar built,
Of twelve vast French Romances, neatly gilt.
There lay three garters, half a pair of gloves;
And all the trophies of his former loves;   40
With tender Billet-doux he lights the pyre,
And breathes three am'rous sighs to raise the fire.
Then prostrate falls, and begs with ardent eyes
Soon to obtain, and long possess the prize:
The Pow'rs gave ear, and granted half his prayer,
The rest, the winds dispersed in empty air.
  But now secure the painted vessel glides,
The sun-beams trembling on the floating tides:
While melting music steals upon the sky,
And softened sounds along the waters die;   50
Smooth flow the waves, the Zephyrs gently play,
Belinda smiled, and all the world was gay.
All but the *Sylph*—with careful thoughts opprest,
Th' impending woe sate heavy on his breast.
He summons strait his Denizens of air;
The lucid squadrons round the sails repair:
Soft o'er the shrouds aërial whispers breathe,
That seemed but Zephyrs to the train beneath.
Some to the sun their insect-wings unfold,
Waft on the breeze, or sink in clouds of gold;   60
Transparent forms, too fine for mortal sight,
Their fluid bodies half dissolved in light,
Loose to the wind their airy garments flew,
Thin glitt'ring textures of the filmy dew;
Dipt in the richest tincture of the skies,
Where light disports in ever-mingling dyes,
While every beam new transient colours flings,
Colours that change whene'er they wave their wings.
Amid the circle, on the gilded mast,
Superior by the head, was *Ariel* placed;   70
His purple pinions opening to the sun,

He raised his azure wand, and thus begun.
  Ye *Sylphs* and *Sylphids*, to your Chief give ear!
Fays, Fairies, Genii, Elves, and *Dæmons* hear!
Ye know the spheres and various tasks assigned
By laws eternal to th' aërial kind.
Some in the fields of purest Æther play,
And bask and whiten in the blaze of day.
Some guide the course of wand'ring orbs on high,
Or roll the planets through the boundless sky.   80
Some less refined, beneath the moon's pale light
Pursue the stars that shoot athwart the night,
Or suck the mists in grosser air below,
Or dip their pinions in the painted bow,
Or brew fierce tempests on the wintry main,
Or o'er the glebe distil the kindly rain.
Others on earth o'er human race preside,
Watch all their ways, and all their actions guide:
Of these the Chief the care of Nations own,
And guard with Arms divine the British Throne.   90
  Our humbler province is to tend the Fair,
Not a less pleasing, tho' less glorious care;
To save the powder from too rude a gale,
Nor let th' imprisoned essences exhale;
To draw fresh colours from the vernal flow'rs;
To steal from rainbows e'er they drop in show'rs
A brighter wash; to curl their waving hairs,
Assist their blushes, and inspire their airs;
Nay oft, in dreams, invention we bestow,
To change a Flounce, or add a Furbelow.   100
  This day, black Omens threat the brightest Fair,
That e'er deserved a watchful spirit's care;
Some dire disaster, or by force, or slight;
But what, or where, the fates have wrapt in night.
Whether the nymph shall break Diana's law,
Or some frail China jar receive a flaw;
Or stain her honour or her new brocade;
Forget her prayers, or miss a masquerade;

105 Diana's law: the law of chastity.

Or lose her heart, or necklace, at a ball;
Or whether Heav'n has doomed that Shock must fall. 110
Haste then ye Spirits! to your Charge repair;
The flutt'ring fan be Zephyretta's care;
The drops to thee, Brillante, we consign;
And, Momentilla, let the watch be thine;
Do thou, Crispissa, tend her fav'rite Lock;
Ariel himself shall be the guard of *Shock*.
   To fifty chosen *Sylphs*, of special note,
We trust th' important charge, the Petticoat:
Oft have we known that sev'n-fold fence to fail,
Though stiff with hoops, and armed with ribs of whale; 120
Form a strong line about the silver bound,
And guard the wide circumference around.
   Whatever Spirit, careless of his charge,
His post neglects, or leaves the Fair at large,
Shall feel sharp vengeance soon o'ertake his sins,
Be stopt in vials, or transfixt with pins;
Or plunged in lakes of bitter washes lie,
Or wedged whole ages in a bodkin's eye:
Gums and Pomatums shall his flight restrain,
While clogged he beats his silken wings in vain; 130
Or alum styptics with contracting power
Shrink his thin essence like a riveled flower.
Or as Ixion fix'd, the wretch shall feel
The giddy motion of the whirling Mill,
In fumes of burning Chocolate shall glow,
And tremble at the sea that froths below!
   He spoke; the Spirits from the sails descend;
Some, orb in orb, around the Nymph extend;
Some thrid the mazy ringlets of her hair;
Some hang upon the pendants of her ear: 140
With beating hearts the dire event they wait,
Anxious, and trembling for the birth of Fate.

CANTO III

Close by those meads forever crowned with flow'rs,
Where Thames with pride surveys his rising tow'rs,

---

132 riveled: withered.

There stands a structure of majestic frame,
Which from the neighb'ring Hampton takes its name.
Here Britain's statesmen oft the fall foredoom
Of foreign Tyrants, and of Nymphs at home;
Here thou, great *Anna!* whom three realms obey,
Dost sometimes Counsel take—and sometimes Tea.
  Hither the Heroes and the Nymphs resort,
To taste awhile the pleasures of a Court;   10
In various talk th' instructive hours they past,
Who gave the ball, or paid the visit last;
One speaks the glory of the British Queen,
And one describes a charming Indian screen;
A third interprets motions, looks, and eyes;
At ev'ry word a reputation dies.
Snuff, or the fan, supply each pause of chat,
With singing, laughing, ogling, and all that.
  Meanwhile declining from the noon of day,
The Sun obliquely shoots his burning ray;   20
The hungry Judges soon the sentence sign,
And wretches hang that jury-men may dine;
The merchant from th' Exchange returns in peace,
And the long labours of the Toilet cease.
Belinda now, whom thirst of fame invites,
Burns to encounter two advent'rous Knights,
At Ombre singly to decide their doom;
And swells her breast with conquests yet to come.
Straight the three bands prepare in arms to join,
Each band the number of the sacred nine.   30
Soon as she spreads her hand, th' aërial guard
Descend, and sit on each important card:
First Ariel perched upon a Matadore,
Then each, according to the rank they bore;
For *Sylphs*, yet mindful of their ancient race,
Are, as when women, wondrous fond of place.
  Behold, four Kings in majesty revered,
With hoary whiskers and a forky beard;

3–4 Hampton Court Palace.   7 Anna: Queen Anne.   27 Ombre: a three-handed card game.   33 Matador: a principal trump.

And four fair Queens whose hands sustain a flow'r,
Th' expressive emblem of their softer pow'r; 40
Four Knaves in garbs succinct, a trusty band,
Caps on their heads, and halberts in their hand;
And particoloured troops, a shining train,
Draw forth to combat on the velvet plain.
   The skilful Nymph reviews her force with care:
Let Spades be trumps! she said, and trumps they were.
   Now move to war her sable Matadores,
In show like leaders of the swarthy Moors.
Spadillio first, unconquerable Lord!
Led off two captive trumps, and swept the board. 50
As many more Manillio forced to yield,
And marched a victor from the verdant field.
Him Basto followed, but his fate more hard
Gained but one trump and one Plebeian card.
With his broad sabre next, a chief in years,
The hoary Majesty of Spades appears,
Puts forth one manly leg, to sight revealed,
The rest, his many-coloured robe concealed.
The rebel Knave, who dares his prince engage,
Proves the just victim of his royal rage. 60
Ev'n mighty Pam, that Kings and Queens o'erthrew
And mowed down armies in the fights of Lu,
Sad chance of war! now, destitute of aid,
Falls undistinguished by the victor spade!
   Thus far both armies to Belinda yield;
Now to the Baron fate inclines the field.
His warlike Amazon her host invades,
Th' imperial consort of the crown of Spades.
The Club's black Tyrant first her victim dyed,
Spite of his haughty mien, and barb'rous pride: 70
What boots the regal circle on his head,
His giant limbs in state unwieldy spread?

---

49 Spadillio: the ace of spades.   51 Manillio: when spades are trump, the deuce.   53 Basto: the ace of clubs, which counts as a trump in this game. 61–62 Pam: the knave of clubs, which is the highest card in the game of Loo (Lu).

That long behind he trails his pompous robe,
And, of all monarchs, only grasps the globe?
　The Baron now his Diamonds pours apace;
Th' embroidered King who shows but half his face,
And his refulgent Queen, with pow'rs combined
Of broken troops an easy conquest find.
Clubs, Diamonds, Hearts, in wild disorder seen,
With throngs promiscuous strow the level green.　　80
Thus when dispersed a routed army runs,
Of Asia's troops, and Afric's sable sons,
With like confusion different nations fly,
Of various habit, and of various dye,
The pierced battalions dis-united fall,
In heaps on heaps; one Fate o'erwhelms them all.
　The Knave of Diamonds tries his wily arts,
And wins (oh shameful Chance!) the Queen of Hearts.
At this, the blood the virgin's cheek forsook,
A livid paleness spreads o'er all her look;　　90
She sees, and trembles at th' approaching ill,
Just in the jaws of ruin, and Codille.
And now (as oft in some distempered State)
On one nice Trick depends the general fate.
An Ace of Hearts steps forth: The King unseen
Lurked in her hand, and mourned his captive Queen:
He springs to Vengeance with an eager pace,
And falls like thunder on the prostrate Ace.
The nymph exulting fills with shouts the sky;
The walls, the woods, and long canals reply.　　100
　Oh thoughtless mortals! ever blind to Fate,
Too soon dejected, and too soon elate!
Sudden, these honours shall be snatched away,
And cursed for ever this victorious day.
　For lo! the board with cups and spoons is crowned,
The berries crackle, and the mill turns round.
On shining Altars of Japan they raise
The silver lamp; the fiery spirits blaze.

92 Codille: failure of the challenger to win the largest number of tricks.
107 berries . . . mill: Coffee beans were ground in a small mill at the table.
Altars of Japan: japanned (i.e., lacquered) tables.

From silver spouts the grateful liquors glide,
While China's earth receives the smoking tide. 110
At once they gratify their scent and taste,
And frequent cups prolong the rich repast.
Straight hover round the Fair her airy band;
Some, as she sipped, the fuming liquor fanned,
Some o'er her lap their careful plumes displayed,
Trembling, and conscious of the rich brocade.
Coffee, (which makes the politician wise,
And see thro' all things with his half-shut eyes)
Sent up in vapours to the Baron's brain
New Stratagems, the radiant Lock to gain. 120
Ah cease, rash Youth! desist ere 'tis too late,
Fear the just Gods, and think of Scylla's Fate!
Changed to a bird, and sent to flit in air,
She dearly pays for Nisus' injured hair!
  But when to mischief mortals bend their will,
How soon they find fit instruments of ill!
Just then, Clarissa drew with tempting grace
A two-edged weapon from her shining case:
So Ladies in Romance assist their Knight,
Present the spear, and arm him for the fight. 130
He takes the gift with rev'rence, and extends
The little engine on his fingers' ends;
This just behind Belinda's neck he spread,
As o'er the fragrant steams she bends her head.
Swift to the Lock a thousand Sprites repair,
A thousand wings, by turns, blow back the hair;
And thrice they twitched the diamond in her ear;
Thrice she looked back, and thrice the foe drew near.
Just in that instant, anxious *Ariel* sought
The close recesses of the Virgin's thought; 140
As on the nosegay in her breast reclined,
He watched th' Ideas rising in her mind,
Sudden he viewed, in spite of all her art,

122-124 The reference is to a story in Ovid. King Nisus had a magic hair which his daughter Scylla (not the monster Scylla of the *Odyssey*) plucked out and gave to the hostile Cretan leader Minos. For this she was changed into a bird.

An earthly Lover lurking at her heart.
Amazed, confused, he found his pow'r expired,
Resigned to fate, and with a sigh retired.
　The Peer now spreads the glitt'ring Forfex wide,
T' inclose the Lock; now joins it, to divide.
Ev'n then, before the fatal engine closed,
A wretched *Sylph* too fondly interposed;   150
Fate urged the shears, and cut the *Sylph* in twain,
(But Airy Substance soon unites again)
The meeting points the sacred hair dissever
From the fair head, for ever and for ever!
　Then flashed the living lightning from her eyes,
And screams of horror rend th' affrighted skies.
Not louder shrieks to pitying Heav'n are cast,
When husbands or when lap-dogs breathe their last;
Or when rich China vessels, fall'n from high,
In glitt'ring dust and painted fragments lie!   160
　Let wreaths of triumph now my temples twine,
(The victor cried) the glorious Prize is mine!
While fish in streams, or birds delight in air,
Or in a coach and six the British Fair,
As long as Atalantis shall be read,
Or the small pillow grace a Lady's bed,
While visits shall be paid on solemn days,
When num'rous wax-lights in bright order blaze,
While nymphs take treats, or assignations give,
So long my honour, name, and praise shall live!   170
What Time would spare, from Steel receives its date,
And monuments, like men, submit to fate!
Steel could the labour of the Gods destroy,
And strike to dust th' imperial tow'rs of Troy;
Steel could the works of mortal pride confound,
And hew triumphal arches to the ground.
What wonder then, fair Nymph! thy hairs should feel
The conq'ring force of unresisted steel?

---

147 Forfex: scissors.　　*165* Atalantis: *The New Atalantis,* a novel by Mrs. Mary Manley, containing scandalous anecdotes about contemporary society.

CANTO IV

But anxious cares the pensive Nymph oppresst,
And secret passions laboured in her breast.
Not youthful kings in battle seized alive,
Not scornful virgins who their charms survive,
Not ardent lovers robbed of all their bliss,
Not ancient ladies when refused a kiss,
Not tyrants fierce that unrepenting die,
Not Cynthia when her manteau's pinned awry,
E'er felt such rage, resentment and despair,
As thou, sad Virgin! for thy ravished Hair.   10
   For, that sad moment, when the *Sylphs* withdrew
And *Ariel* weeping from *Belinda* flew,
Umbriel, a dusky, melancholy sprite,
As ever sullied the fair face of light,
Down to the Central Earth, his proper scene,
Repaired to search the gloomy Cave of *Spleen*.
   Swift on his sooty pinions flits the Gnome,
And in a vapour reached the dismal dome.
No cheerful breeze this sullen region knows,
The dreaded East is all the wind that blows.   20
Here, in a grotto, sheltered close from air,
And screened in shades from day's detested glare,
She sighs forever on her pensive bed,
Pain at her side, and *Megrim* at her head.
   Two handmaids wait the throne: alike in place,
But diff'ring far in figure and in face.
Here stood *Ill-nature* like an ancient maid,
Her wrinkled form in black and white arrayed;
With store of prayers, for mornings, nights, and noons,
Her hand is filled; her bosom with lampoons.   30
   There *Affectation*, with a sickly mien,
Shows in her cheek the roses of eighteen,
Practised to lisp, and hang the head aside,
Faints into airs, and languishes with pride,
On the rich quilt sinks with becoming woe,

---

23 She: Spleen, or the Goddess of Spleen, representing bad temper, malice, anger.   24 Megrim: migraine.

Wrapt in a gown, for sickness, and for show.
The Fair-ones feel such maladies as these,
When each new night-dress gives a new disease.
   A constant Vapour o'er the palace flies;
Strange phantoms rising as the mists arise;   40
Dreadful, as hermit's dreams in haunted shades,
Or bright as visions of expiring maids.
Now glaring fiends, and snakes on rolling spires,
Pale spectres, gaping tombs, and purple fires:
Now lakes of liquid gold, Elysian scenes,
And crystal domes, and angels in machines.
   Unnumbered throngs on every side are seen,
Of bodies changed to various forms by *Spleen*.
Here living Tea-pots stand, one arm held out,
One bent; the handle this, and that the spout: 50
A Pipkin there like Homer's Tripod walks;
Here sighs a Jar, and there a Goose-pie talks;
Men prove with child, as pow'rful fancy works,
And maids turned bottles, call aloud for corks.
   Safe passed the Gnome through this fantastic band,
A branch of healing Spleenwort in his hand.
Then thus addressed the Pow'r: "Hail wayward Queen!
Who rule the sex to fifty from fifteen:
Parent of vapours and of female wit,
Who give th' hysteric or poetic fit,   60
On various tempers act by various ways,
Make some take physic, others scribble plays;
Who cause the proud their visits to delay,
And send the godly in a pet, to pray.
A Nymph there is, that all thy pow'r disdains,
And thousands more in equal mirth maintains.
But oh! if e'er thy Gnome could spoil a grace,
Or raise a pimple on a beauteous face,
Like Citron-waters matrons' cheeks inflame,
Or change complexions at a losing game;   70
If e'er with airy horns I planted heads,

39 Vapour: A fit of "the vapours" was an attack of hypochondria or melancholy, closely associated with attacks of "spleen."   71 airy horns: suspicion of being cuckolded.

Or rumpled petticoats, or tumbled beds,
Or caus'd suspicion when no soul was rude,
Or discomposed the head-dress of a Prude,
Or e'er to costive lap-dog gave disease,
Which not the tears of brightest eyes could ease:
Hear me, and touch *Belinda* with chagrin;
That single act gives half the world the spleen."
 The Goddess with a discontented air
Seems to reject him, though she grants his prayer.   80
A wondrous Bag with both her hands she binds,
Like that where once Ulysses held the winds;
There she collects the force of female lungs,
Sighs, sobs, and passions, and the war of tongues.
A Vial next she fills with fainting fears,
Soft sorrows, melting griefs, and flowing tears.
The *Gnome* rejoicing bears her gifts away,
Spreads his black wings, and slowly mounts to day.
 Sunk in *Thalestris'* arms the Nymph he found,
Her eyes dejected and her hair unbound.   90
Full o'er their heads the swelling bag he rent,
And all the Furies issued at the vent.
Belinda burns with more than mortal ire,
And fierce *Thalestris* fans the rising fire.
"O wretched maid!" she spread her hands, and cried,
(While Hampton's echoes, "Wretched maid!" replied)
"Was it for this you took such constant care
The bodkin, comb, and essence to prepare;
For this your locks in paper durance bound,
For this with torturing irons wreathed around?   100
For this with fillets strained your tender head,
And bravely bore the double loads of lead?
Gods! shall the ravisher display your hair,
While the Fops envy, and the Ladies stare!
Honour forbid! at whose unrivaled shrine
Ease, pleasure, virtue, all, our sex resign.
Methinks already I your tears survey,
Already hear the horrid things they say,

---

102 loads of lead: curlers, fastened with flexible lead.

Already see you a degraded toast,
And all your honour in a whisper lost! 110
How shall I, then, your helpless fame defend?
'Twill then be infamy to seem your friend!
And shall this prize, th' inestimable prize,
Exposed thro' crystal to the gazing eyes,
And heightened by the diamond's circling rays,
On that rapacious hand forever blaze?
Sooner shall grass in Hyde-park Circus grow,
And wits take lodgings in the sound of Bow;
Sooner let earth, air, sea, to Chaos fall,
Men, monkeys, lap-dogs, parrots, perish all!" 120
   She said; then raging to *Sir Plume* repairs,
And bids her Beau demand the precious hairs:
(*Sir Plume,* of amber snuff-box justly vain,
And the nice conduct of a clouded cane)
With earnest eyes, and round unthinking face,
He first the snuff-box opened, then the case,
And thus broke out—"My Lord, why, what the devil?
Z—ds! damn the lock! 'fore Gad, you must be civil!
Plague on't 'tis past a jest—nay prithee, pox!
Give her the hair"—he spoke, and rapped his box. 130
   "It grieves me much" (replied the Peer again)
"Who speaks so well should ever speak in vain.
But by this Lock, this sacred Lock I swear,
(Which never more shall join its parted hair;
Which never more its honours shall renew,
Clipt from the lovely head where late it grew)
That while my nostrils draw the vital air,
This hand, which won it, shall for ever wear."
He spoke, and speaking, in proud triumph spread
The long-contended honours of her head. 140
   But *Umbriel,* hateful *Gnome!* forbears not so;
He breaks the Vial whence the sorrows flow.
Then see! the Nymph in beauteous grief appears,
Her eyes half-languishing, half-drowned in tears;
On her heaved bosom hung her drooping head,

---

118 sound of Bow: within sound of the bells of the church of St. Mary-le-Bow, in an unfashionable section of London.

Which, with a sigh, she raised; and thus she said.
 "For ever curs'd be this detested day,
Which snatched my best, my fav'rite curl away!
Happy! ah ten times happy had I been,
If Hampton-Court these eyes had never seen!   150
Yet am not I the first mistaken maid,
By love of Courts to numerous ills betrayed.
Oh had I rather un-admired remained
In some lone isle, or distant Northern land;
Where the gilt Chariot never marks the way,
Where none learn Ombre, none e'er taste Bohea!
There kept my charms concealed from mortal eye,
Like roses, that in deserts bloom and die.
What moved my mind with youthful Lords to roam?
O had I stayed, and said my prayers at home!   160
'Twas this, the morning omens seemed to tell;
Thrice from my trembling hand the patch-box fell;
The tott'ring China shook without a wind,
Nay, *Poll* sate mute, and *Shock* was most unkind!
A *Sylph* too warned me of the threats of fate,
In mystic visions, now believed too late!
See the poor remnants of these slighted hairs!
My hands shall rend what ev'n thy rapine spares:
These, in two sable ringlets taught to break,
Once gave new beauties to the snowy neck;   170
The sister-lock now sits uncouth, alone,
And in its fellow's fate foresees its own;
Uncurled it hangs, the fatal shears demands,
And tempts once more, thy sacrilegious hands.
Oh hadst thou, cruel! been content to seize
Hairs less in sight, or any hairs but these!"

CANTO V

She said: the pitying audience melt in tears,
But Fate and Jove had stopped the Baron's ears.
In vain *Thalestris* with reproach assails,

---

162 patch-box: box containing patches of court plaster or black silk, applied to the face to heighten beauty by contrast.

For who can move when fair *Belinda* fails?
Not half so fixt the Trojan could remain,
While *Anna* begged and *Dido* raged in vain.
Then grave *Clarissa* graceful waved her fan;
Silence ensued, and thus the nymph began.
"Say, why are Beauties praised and honoured most,
The wise man's passion, and the vain man's toast?   10
Why decked with all that land and sea afford,
Why Angels called, and Angel-like adored?
Why round our coaches crowd the white-gloved Beaux,
Why bows the side-box from its inmost rows?
How vain are all these glories, all our pains,
Unless good sense preserve what beauty gains:
That men may say, when we the front-box grace:
'Behold the first in Virtue, as in face!'
Oh! if to dance all night, and dress all day,
Charmed the small-pox, or chased old-age away;   20
Who would not scorn what housewife's cares produce,
Or who would learn one earthly Thing of Use?
To patch, nay ogle, might become a Saint,
Nor could it sure be such a sin to paint.
But since, alas! frail beauty must decay,
Curled or uncurled, since Locks will turn to grey,
Since painted, or not painted, all shall fade,
And she who scorns a man, must die a maid;
What then remains but well our pow'r to use,
And keep good humuor still whate'er we lose?   30
And trust me, Dear! good humour can prevail,
When airs, and flights, and screams, and scolding fail.
Beauties in vain their pretty eyes may roll;
Charms strike the sight, but merit wins the soul."
   So spoke the Dame, but no applause ensued;
Belinda frowned, *Thalestris* called her Prude.
"To arms, to arms!" the fierce Virago cries,
And swift as lightning to the combat flies.
All side in parties, and begin th' attack;

---

5 The Trojan: Aeneas.   6 Anna: sister of Dido, Queen of Carthage, whom Aeneas left, by command of Jupiter, to continue his voyage.

Fans clap, silks rustle, and tough whalebones crack;　　40
Heroes' and Heroines' shouts confus'dly rise,
And bass and treble voices strike the skies.
No common weapons in their hands are found,
Like Gods they fight, nor dread a mortal wound.
　So when bold *Homer* makes the Gods engage,
And heav'nly breasts with human passions rage;
'Gainst *Pallas, Mars; Latona, Hermes* arms;
And all Olympus rings with loud alarms:
Jove's thunder roars, Heav'n trembles all around,
Blue *Neptune* storms, the bellowing deeps resound:　　50
Earth shakes her nodding tow'rs, the ground gives way,
And the pale ghosts start at the flash of day!
　Triumphant *Umbriel* on a sconce's height
Clapped his glad wings, and sate to view the fight:
Propt on their bodkin spears, the Sprites survey
The growing combat, or assist the fray.
　While through the press enraged *Thalestris* flies,
And scatters deaths around from both her eyes,
A Beau and Witling perished in the throng,
One died in *metaphor,* and one in *song.*　　60
"O cruel Nymph! a living death I bear,"
Cried *Dapperwit,* and sunk beside his chair.
A mournful glance Sir *Fopling* upwards cast,
"Those eyes are made so killing"—was his last:
Thus on Mæander's flow'ry margin lies
Th' expiring Swan, and as he sings he dies.
　When bold Sir *Plume* had drawn *Clarissa* down,
Chloe stepped in, and killed him with a frown;
She smiled to see the doughty hero slain,
But at her smile, the Beau revived again.　　70
　Now *Jove* suspends his golden scales in air,
Weighs the Men's wits against the Lady's hair;
The doubtful beam long nods from side to side;
At length the wits mount up, the hairs subside.

---

47 Pallas: Pallas Athene. Latona: goddess of night, mother of Apollo.
53–54 "Minerva in like manner, during the battle of Ulysses with the Suitors in *Oddyss.*, perches on a beam of the roof to behold it." (Note by Pope)
62–63 Dappermit and Sir Fopling were characters in well-known comedies.

See fierce *Belinda* on the *Baron* flies,
With more than usual lightning in her eyes;
Nor feared the Chief th' unequal fight to try,
Who sought no more than on his foe to die.
But this bold Lord, with manly strength endued,
She with one finger and a thumb subdued: 80
Just where the breath of life his nostrils drew,
A charge of Snuff the wily virgin threw;
The Gnomes direct, to every atom just,
The pungent grains of titillating dust.
Sudden, with starting tears each eye o'erflows,
And the high dome re-echoes to his nose.
　"Now meet thy fate," incensed *Belinda* cried,
And drew a deadly bodkin from her side.
(The same, his ancient personage to deck,
Her great great grandsire wore about his neck 90
In three seal-rings; which after, melted down,
Formed a vast buckle for his widow's gown:
Her infant grandame's whistle next it grew,
The bells she jingled, and the whistle blew;
Then in a bodkin graced her mother's hairs,
Which long she wore, and now *Belinda* wears.)
　"Boast not my fall" (he cried) "insulting foe!
Thou by some other shalt be laid as low.
Nor think, to die dejects my lofty mind;
All that I dread, is leaving you behind! 100
Rather than so, ah let me still survive,
And burn in Cupid's flames—but burn alive."
　"Restore the Lock!" she cries; and all around
"Restore the Lock!" the vaulted roofs rebound.
Not fierce *Othello* in so loud a strain
Roared for the handkerchief that caused his pain.
But see how oft ambitious aims are crossed,
And chiefs contend till all the prize is lost!
The Lock, obtained with guilt, and kept with pain,
In every place is sought, but sought in vain: 110

89–96 "In imitation of the progress of Agamemnon's scepter in Homer." (Note by Pope)

With such a prize no mortal must be blest,
So heaven decrees! with heaven who can contest?
  Some thought it mounted to the Lunar sphere,
Since all things lost on earth, are treasured there.
There Heroes' wits are kept in pond'rous vases,
And beaux' in Snuff-boxes and Tweezer-cases.
There broken vows and death-bed alms are found,
And lovers' hearts with ends of riband bound,
The courtier's promises, and sick man's prayers,
The smiles of harlots, and the tears of heirs,   120
Cages for gnats, and chains to yoke a flea,
Dried butterflies, and tomes of casuistry.
  But trust the Muse—she saw it upward rise,
Tho' marked by none but quick poetic eyes:
(So Rome's great founder to the Heav'ns withdrew,
To *Proculus* alone confessed in view)
A sudden Star, it shot through liquid air,
And drew behind a radiant Trail of Hair.
Not *Berenice's* Locks first rose so bright,
The Heav'ns bespangling with disheveled light.   130
The *Sylphs* behold it kindling as it flies,
And pleased pursue its progress through the skies.
  This the Beau monde shall from the Mall survey,
And hail with music its propitious ray.
This the blest Lover shall for Venus take,
And send up vows from Rosamonda's lake.
This *Partridge* soon shall view in cloudless skies,
When next he looks through *Galileo's* eyes;
And hence th' egregious wizard shall foredoom
The fate of *Louis,* and the fall of Rome.   140

---

125 founder: Romulus, said to have been raised to heaven and later to have communicated with the senator Proculus. 129–30 Berenice, wife of King Ptolemy III, dedicated her hair to a goddess for the safety of her husband. It became the constellation known as Coma Berenicis (Hair of Berenice). 136 Rosamonda's lake: a pond in St. James's Park, London. 137 Partridge: astrologer and publisher of almanacs. "John Partridge was a ridiculous Stargazer, who in his Almanacks every year, never failed to predict the downfall of the Pope, and the King of France, then at war with the English." (Note by Pope)

Then cease, bright Nymph! to mourn thy ravished hair,
Which adds new glory to the shining sphere!
Not all the tresses that fair head can boast,
Shall draw such envy as the Lock you lost.
For, after all the murders of your eye,
When, after millions slain, your self shall die:
When those fair suns shall set, as set they must,
And all those tresses shall be laid in dust,
This Lock, the Muse shall consecrate to Fame,
And 'midst the stars inscribe *Belinda's* name.   150

[*Epigram*]

Engraved on the Collar of a Dog, Which I Gave to His Royal Highness

ALEXANDER POPE

I am his Highness' dog at Kew;
Pray tell me, sir, whose dog are you?

[*Epigram*]

Of Treason

SIR JOHN HARINGTON

Treason doth never prosper; what's the reason?
For if it prosper, none dare call it treason.

Epitaph on King Charles II

JOHN WILMOT,
SECOND EARL OF ROCHESTER

Here lies a Great and Mighty King
Whose Promise none relies on,
Who never said a Foolish Thing
Nor ever did a Wise One.

[Epigram]

WILLIAM BLAKE

Her whole Life is an Epigram, smart, smooth, &
    neatly pen'd,
Platted quite neat to catch applause with a
    sliding noose at the end.

Imitation of Pope: A Compliment to the Ladies

WILLIAM BLAKE

Wondrous the Gods, more wondrous are the Men,
More Wondrous Wondrous still the Cock & Hen,
More Wondrous still the Table, Stool & Chair;
But Ah! More wondrous still the Charming Fair.

Tam O' Shanter
A Tale

ROBERT BURNS

When chapman billies leave the street,
And drouthy neebors, neebors meet;
As market-days are wearing late,
An' folk begin to tak the gate;
While we sit bousing at the nappy,
An' getting fou and unco happy,
We think na on the lang Scots miles,
The mosses, waters, slaps, and styles,
That lie between us and our hame,
Whare sits our sulky sullen dame, 10
Gathering her brows like gathering storm,
Nursing her wrath to keep it warm.

This truth fand honest Tam o' Shanter,
As he frae Ayr ae night did canter,
(Auld Ayr, wham ne'er a town surpasses,
For honest men and bonnie lasses).

O Tam! had'st thou but been sae wise,
As ta'en thy ain wife Kate's advice!
She tauld thee weel thou was a skellum,
A blethering, blustering, drunken blellum; 20
That frae November till October,
Ae market-day thou was nae sober;
That ilka melder, wi' the miller,
Thou sat as lang as thou had siller;

---

1 chapman billies: peddlers.   *4* tak the gate: take the road (for home).
5 nappy: ale.   *6* unco: extremely.   *7* Scots miles are longer than English miles.   *8* slaps: gateways. styles: stiles.   *13* fand: found.   *19* skellum: rogue.   *20* blethering: chattering. blellum: babbler.   *23* ilka melder: at every meal-grinding.   *24* siller: silver.

> That ev'ry naig was ca'd a shoe on,
> The smith and thee gat roaring fou on;
> That at the Lord's house, even on Sunday,
> Thou drank wi' Kirkton Jean till Monday.
> She prophesied that, late or soon,
> Thou would be found deep drown'd in Doon; 30
> Or catch'd wi' warlocks in the mirk,
> By Alloway's auld, haunted kirk.
>
> Ah! gentle dames, it gars me greet,
> To think how mony counsels sweet,
> How mony lengthen'd, sage advices,
> The husband frae the wife despises!
>
> But to our tale: Ae market-night,
> Tam had got planted unco right;
> Fast by an ingle, bleezing finely,
> Wi' reaming swats, that drank divinely; 40
> And at his elbow, Souter Johnny,
> His ancient, trusty, drouthy crony;
> Tam lo'ed him like a very brither;
> They had been fou for weeks thegither.
> The night drave on wi' sangs and clatter;
> And ay the ale was growing better:
> The landlady and Tam grew gracious,
> Wi' secret favours, sweet and precious:
> The Souter tauld his queerest stories;
> The landlord's laugh was ready chorus: 50
> The storm without might rair and rustle,
> Tam did na mind the storm a whistle.
>
> Care, mad to see a man sae happy,
> E'en drown'd himsel amang the nappy:
> As bees flee hame wi' lades o' treasure,
> The minutes wing'd their way wi' pleasure:

---

25 naig . . . : nag that was asked to be shod.   **31 warlocks:** wizards.   **mirk:** darkness.   **33 gars me greet:** makes me weep.   **40 reaming swats:** foaming ale.   **41 Souter:** shoemaker.   **55 lades:** loads.

Kings may be blest, but Tam was glorious,
O'er a' the ills o' life victorious!

But pleasures are like poppies spread:
You seize the flow'r, its bloom is shed; 60
Or like the snow falls in the river,
A moment white—then melts for ever;
Or like the Borealis race,
That flit ere you can point their place;
Or like the rainbow's lovely form
Evanishing amid the storm.—
Nae man can tether time or tide;
The hour approaches Tam maun ride;
That hour, o' night's black arch the key-stane,
That dreary hour Tam mounts his beast in; 70
And sic a night he taks the road in,
As ne'er poor sinner was abroad in.

The wind blew as 'twad blawn its last;
The rattling showers rose on the blast;
The speedy gleams the darkness swallow'd;
Loud, deep, and lang, the thunder bellow'd:
That night, a child might understand,
The Deil had business on his hand.

Weel mounted on his gray mare, Meg,
A better never lifted leg, 80
Tam skelpit on thro' dub and mire,
Despising wind, and rain, and fire;
Whiles holding fast his gude blue bonnet;
Whiles crooning o'er some auld Scots sonnet;
Whiles glow'ring round wi' prudent cares,
Lest bogles catch him unawares:
Kirk-Alloway was drawing nigh,
Whare ghaists and houlets nightly cry.

81 skelpit: dashed. dub: puddle. 84 sonnet: song. 86 bogles: ghosts, goblins. 88 ghaists: ghosts. houlets: owls.

By this time he was cross the ford,
Whare, in the snaw, the chapman smoor'd;   90
And past the birks and meikle stane,
Whare drunken Charlie brak's neck-bane;
And thro' the whins, and by the cairn,
Whare hunters fand the murder'd bairn;
And near the thorn, aboon the well,
Whare Mungo's mither hang'd hersel.
Before him Doon pours all his floods;
The doubling storm roars thro' the woods;
The lightnings flash from pole to pole;
Near and more near the thunders roll: 100
When, glimmering thro' the groaning trees,
Kirk-Alloway seem'd in a bleeze;
Thro' ilka bore the beams were glancing,
And loud resounded mirth and dancing.

   Inspiring, bold John Barleycorn!
What dangers thou canst make us scorn!
Wi' tippeny, we fear nae evil;
Wi' usquabae, we'll face the devil!
The swats sae ream'd in Tammie's noddle,
Fair play, he car'd na deils a boddle.   110
But Maggie stood, right sair astonish'd,
Till, by the heel and hand admonish'd,
She ventur'd forward on the light;
And, wow! Tam saw an unco sight!

   Warlocks and witches in a dance:
Nae cotillion, brent new frae France,
But hornpipes, jigs, strathspeys, and reels,
Put life and mettle in their heels.
A winnock-bunker in the east,
There sat auld Nick, in shape o' beast;   120

90 smoor'd: smothered.   91 birks: birches. meikle stane: great stone.   93 whins: gorse. cairn: pile of stones.   95 aboon: above.   103 ilka bore: every chink.   107 tippeny: two-penny ale.   108 usquabae: whisky.   110 deils: devils. boddle: farthing.   114 unco: wondrous, strange.   116 brent new: brand new.   17 strathspeys: a Scotch dance resembling a reel.   119 winnock-bunker: window-seat.

IRONICAL MODES AND THE GROTESQUE

A towzie tyke, black, grim, and large,
To gie them music was his charge:
He screw'd the pipes and gart them skirl,
Till roof and rafters a' did dirl.
Coffins stood round, like open presses,
That shaw'd the dead in their last dresses;
And, by some devilish cantraip sleight,
Each in its cauld hand held a light
By which heroic Tam was able
To note upon the haly table,   130
A murderer's banes in gibbet airns;
Twa span-lang, wee, unchristen'd bairns;
A thief, new-cutted frae a rape,
Wi' his last gasp his gab did gape;
Five tomahawks, wi' blude red-rusted;
Five scymitars, wi' murder crusted;
A garter which a babe had strangled;
A knife a father's throat had mangled—
Whom his ain son o' life bereft—
The grey hairs yet stack to the heft;   140
Wi' mair of horrible and awefu',
Which even to name wad be unlawfu'.

   As Tammie glowr'd, amaz'd, and curious,
The mirth and fun grew fast and furious;
The piper loud and louder blew;
The dancers quick and quicker flew;
They reel'd, they set, they cross'd, they cleekit,
Till ilka carlin swat and reekit,
And coost her duddies to the wark,
And linket at it in her sark!   150

   Now, Tam, O Tam! had thae been queans,
A' plump and strapping in their teens,

121 towzie tyke: shaggy dog.   *123* gart them skirl: made them scream.   *124* dirl: ring.   *127* cantraip sleight: magical trick.   *130* haly: holy.   *131* airns: irons.   *133* rape: rope.   *134* gab: mouth.   *147* cleekit: joined hands.   *148* carlin: witch. swat and reekit: sweated and steamed.   *149* coost . . . : cast off her rags for the work.   *150* linket: tripped. sark: shirt.   *151* queans: girls.

Their sarks, instead o' creeshie flannen,
Been snaw-white seventeen hunder linnen!
Thir breeks o' mine, my only pair,
That ance were plush, o' gude blue hair,
I wad hae gi'en them off my hurdies,
For ae blink o' the bonnie burdies!

But wither'd beldams, auld and droll,
Rigwoodie hags wad spean a foal,   160
Lowping and flinging on a crummock,
I wonder didna turn thy stomach.

But Tam kend what was what fu' brawlie,
There was ae winsome wench and wawlie,
That night enlisted in the core,
Lang after kend on Carrick shore
(For mony a beast to dead she shot,
And perish'd mony a bonnie boat,
And shook baith meikle corn and bear,
And kept the country-side in fear).   170
Her cutty sark, o' Paisley harn,
That while a lassie she had worn,
In longitude tho' sorely scanty,
It was her best, and she was vauntie.
Ah! little kend thy reverend grannie,
That sark she coft for her wee Nannie,
Wi' twa pund Scots ('twas a' her riches),
Wad ever grac'd a dance of witches!

But here my Muse her wing maun cour;
Sic flights are far beyond her pow'r;   180
To sing how Nannie lap and flang,

---

153 creeshie flannen: greasy flannel.   *154* seventeen hunder linnen: linen of fine quality.   *155* Thir breeks: These breeches.   *157* hurdies: hips. *158* burdies: lasses.   *160* Rigwoodie . . . : Lean hags [who] would wean a foal [with disgust].   *161* Lowping: leaping. crummock: crooked staff. *163* brawlie: well.   *164* wawlie: choice.   *169* corn and bear: wheat and barley.   *171* cutty: short. Paisley harn: coarse linen from Paisley.   *174* vauntie: proud.   *176* coft: bought.   *179* cour: lower.   *181* lap and flang: leaped and flung about.

(A souple jade she was, and strang),
And how Tam stood, like ane bewitch'd,
And thought his very een enrich'd;
Even Satan glowr'd, and fidg'd fu' fain,
And hotch'd and blew wi' might and main:
Till first ae caper, syne anither,
Tam tint his reason a' thegither,
And roars out, "Weel done, Cutty-sark!"
And in an instant all was dark: 190
And scarcely had he Maggie rallied,
When out the hellish legion sallied.

As bees bizz out wi' angry fyke,
When plundering herds assail their byke;
As open pussie's mortal foes,
When, pop! she starts before their nose;
As eager runs the market-crowd,
When "Catch the thief!" resounds aloud;
So Maggie runs, the witches follow,
Wi' mony an eldritch skreech and hollo. 200

Ah, Tam! Ah, Tam! thou'll get thy fairin!
In hell they'll roast thee like a herrin!
In vain thy Kate awaits thy comin!
Kate soon will be a woefu' woman!
Now, do thy speedy utmost, Meg,
And win the key-stane of the brig;
There, at them thou thy tail may toss,
A running stream they dare na cross!
But ere the key-stane she could make,
The fient a tail she had to shake! 210
For Nannie, far before the rest,
Hard upon noble Maggie prest,
And flew at Tam wi' furious ettle;
But little wist she Maggie's mettle!
Ae spring brought off her master hale,

185 fidgeted with delight.   *186* hotch'd: jerked.   *188* tint: lost.   *193* fyke: fuss.   *194* herds: shepherds. byke: hive.   *195* pussie's: the hare's.   *200* eldritch skreech: unearthly yell.   *201* fairin: deserts.   *206* brig: bridge.   *210* fient: devil.   *213* ettle: intent.

But left behind her ain grey tail:
The carlin claught her by the rump,
And left poor Maggie scarce a stump.

Now, wha this tale o' truth shall read,
Ilk man, and mother's son, take heed: 220
Whene'er to drink you are inclin'd,
Or cutty-sarks run in your mind,
Think! ye may buy the joys o'er dear,
Remember Tam o' Shanter's mare.

217 claught: clutched.

From *Macbeth*

WILLIAM SHAKESPEARE

ACT I, SC. I

Thunder and lightning. Enter three Witches.

 First Witch. When shall we three meet again
In thunder, lightning, or in rain?
 Sec. Witch. When the hurlyburly's done,
When the battle's lost and won.
 Third Witch. That will be ere the set of sun.
 First Witch. Where the place?
 Sec. Witch.   Upon the heath.
 Third Witch. There to meet with Macbeth.
 First Witch. I come, Graymalkin!
 Sec. Witch. Paddock calls.
 Third Witch. Anon. 10
 All. Fair is foul, and foul is fair:
Hover through the fog and filthy air. [*Exeunt.*

ACT I, SC. III

Thunder. Enter the three Witches.

 First Witch. Where hast thou been, sister?
 Sec. Witch. Killing swine.

Third Witch. Sister, where thou?
First Witch. A sailor's wife had chestnuts in
    her lap,
And munch'd, and munch'd, and munch'd:—
    'Give me,' quoth I:
'Aroint thee, witch!' the rump-fed ronyon cries.
Her husband's to Aleppo gone, master o' the Tiger:
But in a sieve I'll thither sail,
And, like a rat without a tail,
I'll do, I'll do, and I'll do.   10
    Sec. Witch. I'll give thee a wind.
    First Witch. Thou 'rt kind.
    Third Witch. And I another.
    First Witch. I myself have all the other,
And the very ports they blow,
All the quarters that they know
I' the shipman's card.
I will drain him dry as hay:
Sleep shall neither night nor day
Hang upon his pent-house lid;   20
He shall live a man forbid:
Weary se'nnights nine times nine
Shall he dwindle, peak and pine:
Though his bark cannot be lost,
Yet it shall be tempest-tost.
Look what I have.
    Sec. Witch. Show me, show me.
    First Witch. Here I have a pilot's thumb,
Wreck'd as homeward he did come. [*Drum within.*
    Third Witch. A drum, a drum!   30
Macbeth doth come.
    All. The weird sisters, hand in hand,
Posters of the sea and land,
Thus do go about, about:
Thrice to thine and thrice to mine
And thrice again, to make up nine.
Peace! the charm's wound up.

    Enter Macbeth *and* Banquo.

    Macb. So foul and fair a day I have not seen.

ACT IV, SC. I

Thunder. Enter the three Witches.

First Witch. Thrice the brinded cat hath mew'd.
Sec. Witch. Thrice and once the hedge-pig whined.
Third Witch. Harpier cries 'T is time, 't is time.
First Witch. Round about the cauldron go;
In the poison'd entrails throw.
Toad, that under cold stone
Days and nights has thirty-one
Swelter'd venom sleeping got,
Boil thou first i' the charmed pot.
   All. Double, double toil and trouble;   10
Fire burn and cauldron bubble.
   Sec. Witch. Fillet of a fenny snake,
In the cauldron boil and bake;
Eye of newt and toe of frog,
Wool of bat and tongue of dog,
Adder's fork and blind-worm's sting,
Lizard's leg and owlet's wing,
For a charm of powerful trouble,
Like a hell-broth boil and bubble.
   All. Double, double toil and trouble;   20
Fire burn and cauldron bubble.
   Third Witch. Scale of dragon, tooth of wolf,
Witches' mummy, maw and gulf
Of the ravin'd salt-sea shark,
Root of hemlock digg'd i' the dark,
Liver of blaspheming Jew,
Gall of goat, and slips of yew
Sliver'd in the moon's eclipse,
Nose of Turk and Tartar's lips,
Finger of birth-strangled babe   30
Ditch-deliver'd by a drab,
Make the gruel thick and slab:
Add thereto a tiger's chaudron,
For the ingredients of our cauldron.
   All. Double, double toil and trouble;
Fire burn and cauldron bubble.

Tom O' Bedlam's Song

ANON.

From the hag and hungry goblin
  That into rags would rend ye,
And the spirit that stands by the naked man
  In the book of moons, defend ye,
That of your five sound senses
  You never be forsaken,
Nor wander from yourselves with Tom,
  Abroad to beg your bacon.
    While I do sing: Any food, any feeding,
      Feeding, drink, or clothing? 10
    Come, dame or maid, be not afraid,
      Poor Tom will injure nothing.

Of thirty bare years have I
  Twice twenty been enragèd,
And of forty been three times fifteen
  In durance soundly cagèd
On the lordly lofts of Bedlam,
  With stubble soft and dainty,
Brave bracelets strong, sweet whips, ding-dong,
  With wholesome hunger plenty. 20
    And now I sing: Etc.

With a thought I took for Maudlin,
  And a cruse of cockle pottage,
With a thing thus tall, sky bless you all,
  I befell into this dotage.
I slept not since the Conquest,
  Till then I never wakèd, 30

4 The moon was thought to be a cause of madness. 25 Maudlin: The word has many meanings, none appropriate; it is probably part of the deliberate mixture of nonsense with sense. 26 cockle: any of several kinds of shell fish. 29 Conquest: the Norman Conquest, some fine hundred years before.

>   Till the roguish boy of love where I lay
>   Me found and stripped me naked.
>   And now I sing: Etc.
>
>   When I short have shorn my sour face,
>   And swigged my horny barrel,
>   In an oaken inn I pound my skin,
>   As a suit of gilt apparel.   40
>   The moon's my constant mistress,
>   And the lowly owl my morrow;
>   The flaming drake and the night-crow make
>   Me music to my sorrow.
>   While I do sing: Etc.
>
>   The palsy plagues my pulses,
>   When I prig your pigs or pullen,   50
>   Your culvers take, or matchless make
>   Your chanticleer or sullen.
>   When I want provant, with Humphry
>   I sup, and when benighted,
>   I repose in Powles with waking souls,
>   Yet never am affrighted.
>   But I do sing: Etc.
>
>   I know more than Apollo,   61
>   For oft when he lies sleeping,
>   I see the stars at bloody wars
>   In the wounded welkin weeping,
>   The moon embrace her shepherd,
>   And the queen of love her warrior,
>   While the first doth horn the star of morn,
>   And the next the heavenly Farrier.
>   While I do sing: Etc.

31 roguish boy of love: Cupid.   50 prig: steal. pullen: poultry.   53 provant: provender. Humphry: Duke Humphry, dead long before.   55 Powles: St. Paul's, in London.   65 moon . . . shepherd: Selene and Endymion.   66 Ares (Mars) was the lover of Aphrodite.   67 horn: cuckold (verb); star of morn: possibly the Sun, sometimes said to be Selene's husband.   68 Aphrodite cuckolds Hephaestus, her husband, god of metal working.

    The gipsey Snap and Pedro 73
      Are none of Tom's comradoes.
    The punk I scorn, and the cutpurse sworn,
      And the roaring boys' bravadoes.
    The meek, the white, the gentle,
      Me handle, touch, and spare not;
    But those that cross Tom Rynosseros
      Do what the panther dare not.
        Although I sing: Etc.

With an host of furious fancies
  Whereof I am commander,
With a burning spear and a horse of air
  To the wilderness I wander.
By a knight of ghosts and shadows
  I summoned am to tourney 90
Ten leagues beyond the wide world's end,
  Methinks it is no journey.
      Yet will I sing: Any food, any feeding,
        Feeding, drink, or clothing?
      Come, dame or maid, be not afraid,
        Poor Tom will injure nothing.

75 punk: prostitute.

The Madman's Song

JOHN WEBSTER
From *The Duchess of Malfi*

Oh, let us howl some heavy note,
  Some deadly doggèd howl,
Sounding, as from the threatening throat
  Of beasts and fatal fowl!
As ravens, screech-owls, bulls, and bears,
  We'll bell and bawl our parts
Till irksome noise have cloyed your ears,
  And còrrosived your hearts.

> At last, whenas our quire wants breath,
>   Our bodies being blessed,
> We'll sing, like swans, to welcome death,
>   And die in love and rest.

Alas, how soon

WALTER SAVAGE LANDOR

> Alas, how soon the hours are over
> Counted us out to play the lover!
> And how much narrower is the stage
> Allotted us to play the sage!
>
> But when we play the fool, how wide,
> The theater expands! beside,
> How long the audience sits before us!
> How many prompters! what a chorus!

[Epigram]

LORD BYRON

> The world is a bundle of hay,
>   Mankind are the asses who pull;
> Each tugs it a different way,—
>   And the greatest of all is John Bull!

Who Killed John Keats?

LORD BYRON

> Who killed John Keats?
>   "I," says the Quarterly,
>   So savage and Tartarly;
> " 'T was one of my feats."

Who shot the arrow?
"The poet-priest Milman"
(So ready to kill man)
"Or Southey, or Barrow."

Darkness

LORD BYRON

I had a dream, which was not all a dream.
The bright sun was extinguish'd, and the stars
Did wander darkling in the eternal space,
Rayless, and pathless, and the icy earth
Swung blind and blackening in the moonless air;
Morn came and went—and came, and brought no day,
And men forgot their passions in the dread
Of this their desolation; and all hearts
Were chill'd into a selfish prayer for light:
And they did live by watchfires—and the thrones, 10
The palaces of crowned kings—the huts,
The habitations of all things which dwell,
Were burnt for beacons; cities were consumed,
And men were gather'd round their blazing homes
To look once more into each other's face;
Happy were those who dwelt within the eye
Of the volcanos, and their mountain-torch:
A fearful hope was all the world contain'd;
Forests were set on fire—but hour by hour
They fell and faded—and the crackling trunks 20
Extinguish'd with a crash—and all was black.
The brows of men by the despairing light
Wore an unearthly aspect, as by fits
The flashes fell upon them; some lay down
And hid their eyes and wept; and some did rest
Their chins upon their clenched hands, and smiled;
And others hurried to and fro, and fed
Their funeral piles with fuel, and look'd up
With mad disquietude on the dull sky,

The pall of a past world; and then again 30
With curses cast them down upon the dust,
And gnash'd their teeth and howl'd: the wild birds shriek'd
And, terrified, did flutter on the ground,
And flap their useless wings; the wildest brutes
Came tame and tremulous; and vipers crawl'd
And twined themselves among the multitude,
Hissing, but stingless—they were slain for food.
And War, which for a moment was no more,
Did glut himself again:—a meal was bought
With blood, and each sate sullenly apart 40
Gorging himself in gloom: no love was left;
All earth was but one thought—and that was death
Immediate and inglorious; and the pang
Of famine fed upon all entrails—men
Died, and their bones were tombless as their flesh;
The meagre by the meagre were devour'd,
Even dogs assail'd their masters, all save one,
And he was faithful to a corse, and kept
The birds and beasts and famish'd men at bay,
Till hunger clung them, or the dropping dead 50
Lured their lank jaws; himself sought out no food,
But with a piteous and perpetual moan,
And a quick desolate cry, licking the hand
Which answered not with a caress—he died.
The crowd was famish'd by degrees; but two
Of an enormous city did survive,
And they were enemies: they met beside
The dying embers of an altar-place,
Where had been heap'd a mass of holy things
For an unholy usage; they raked up, 60
And shivering scraped with their cold skeleton hands
The feeble ashes, and their feeble breath
Blew for a little life, and made a flame
Which was a mockery; then they lifted up
Their eyes as it grew lighter, and beheld

50 clung: shriveled.

Each other's aspects—saw, and shriek'd, and died—
Even of their mutual hideousness they died,
Unknowing who he was upon whose brow
Famine had written Fiend. The world was void,
The populous and the powerful was a lump   70
Seasonless, herbless, treeless, manless, lifeless,
A lump of death—a chaos of hard clay.
The rivers, lakes, and ocean all stood still,
And nothing stirr'd within their silent depths;
Ships sailorless lay rotting on the sea,
And their masts fell down piecemeal: as they dropp'd
They slept on the abyss without a surge—
The waves were dead; the tides were in their grave,
The Moon, their mistress, had expired before;
The winds were wither'd in the stagnant air,   80
And the clouds perished; Darkness had no need
Of aid from them—She was the Universe.

The Song of Finis
WALTER DE LA MARE

At the edge of All the Ages
   A Knight sate on his steed,
His armour red and thin with rust,
   His soul from sorrow freed;
And he lifted up his visor
   From a face of skin and bone,
And his horse turned head and whinnied
   As the twain stood there alone.

No bird above that steep of time
   Sang of a livelong quest;   10
No wind breathed,
     Rest:
"Lone for an end!" cried Knight to steed,
   Loosed an eager rein—
Charged with his challenge into Space:
   And quiet did quiet remain.

The Great Day
WILLIAM BUTLER YEATS

Hurrah for revolution and more cannon-shot!
A beggar upon horseback lashes a beggar on foot.
Hurrah for revolution and cannon come again!
The beggars have changed places, but the lash goes on.

George III
EDMUND CLERIHEW BENTLEY

    George the Third
    Ought never to have occurred.
    One can only wonder
    At so grotesque a blunder.

The Old Man's Comforts
And How He Gained Them
ROBERT SOUTHEY

"You are old, Father William," the young man cried,
  "The few locks which are left you are gray;
You are hale, Father William, a hearty old man,
  Now tell me the reason, I pray."

"In the days of my youth," Father William replied,
  "I remembered that youth would fly fast,
And abused not my health, and my vigor at first,
  That I never might need them at last."

"You are old, Father William," the young man cried,
  "And pleasures with youth pass away;

And yet you lament not the days that are gone,
  Now tell me the reason, I pray."

"In the days of my youth," Father William replied,
  "I remembered that youth could not last;
I thought of the future, whatever I did,
  That I never might grieve for the past."

"You are old, Father William," the young man cried,
  "And life must be hastening away;
You are cheerful, and love to converse upon death,
  Now tell me the reason, I pray."   20

"I am cheerful, young man," Father William replied,
  "Let the cause thy attention engage;
In the days of my youth I remember'd my God!
  And He hath not forgotten my age."

Father William

"LEWIS CARROLL"
(Charles Lutwidge Dodgson)

"You are old, Father William," the young man said,
  "And your hair has become very white,
And yet you incessantly stand on your head—
  Do you think, at your age, it is right?"

"In my youth," Father William replied to his son,
  "I feared it might injure the brain;
But now that I'm perfectly sure I have none,
  Why, I do it again and again."

"You are old," said the youth, "as I mentioned before,
  And have grown uncommonly fat;   10
Yet you turned a back-somersault in at the door—
  Pray, what is the reason of that?"

"In my youth," said the sage, as he shook his gray locks,
  "I kept all my limbs very supple
By the use of this ointment—one shilling the box—
  Allow me to sell you a couple."

"You are old," said the youth, "and your jaws are too weak
  For anything tougher than suet;
Yet you finished the goose, with the bones and the beak;
  Pray, how did you manage to do it?"   20

"In my youth," said his father, "I took to the law,
  And argued each case with my wife;
And the muscular strength which it gave to my jaw
  Has lasted the rest of my life."

"You are old," said the youth, "one would hardly suppose
  That your eye was as steady as ever;
Yet you balanced an eel on the end of your nose—
  What made you so awfully clever?"

"I have answered three questions, and that is enough,"
  Said his father; "don't give yourself airs!   30
Do you think I can listen all day to such stuff?
  Be off, or I'll kick you downstairs!"

Ancient Music

EZRA POUND

Winter is icummen in,
Lhude sing Goddamm,
Raineth drop and staineth slop,
And how the wind doth ramm!
                Sing: Goddamm.

Skiddeth bus and sloppeth us,
An ague hath my ham.

---

1 Cf. "Sumer is icumen in" (p. 134).

Freezeth river, turneth liver,
        Damn you, sing: Goddamm.
Goddamm, Goddamm, 'tis why I am, Goddamm,   10

        So 'gainst the winter's balm.
Sing goddamm, damm, sing Goddamm,
Sing goddamm, sing goddamm, DAMM.

Salutation the Second

EZRA POUND

You were praised, my books,
    because I had just come from the country;
I was twenty years behind the times
    so you found an audience ready.
I do not disown you,
    do not you disown your progeny.

Here they stand without quaint devices,
Here they are with nothing archaic about them.
Watch the reporters spit,
Watch the anger of the professors,   10
Watch how the pretty ladies revile them:

"Is this," they say, "the nonsense
    that we expect of poets?"
"Where is the Picturesque?"
    "Where is the vertigo of emotion?"
"No! his first work was the best."
    "Poor Dear! he has lost his illusions."

Go, little naked and impudent songs,
Go with a light foot!
(Or with two light feet, if it please you!)   20
Go and dance shamelessly!

Go with an impertinent frolic!
Greet the grave and the stodgy,
Salute them with your thumbs at your noses.

Here are your bells and confetti.
Go! rejuvenate things!
Rejuvenate even "The Spectator."
   Go! and make cat calls!
Dance and make people blush,
Dance the dance of the phallus   30
   and tell anecdotes of Cybele!
Speak of the indecorous conduct of the Gods!
     (Tell it to Mr. Strachey)

Ruffle the skirts of prudes,
   speak of their knees and ankles.
But, above all, go to practical people—
   go! jangle their door-bells!
Say that you do no work
   and that you will live forever.

27 The Spectator: the English weekly periodical.   33 Mr. Strachey: Lytton Strachey, the writer of modern biographies.

The Lake Isle

EZRA POUND

O God, O Venus, O Mercury, patron of thieves,
Give me in due time, I beseech you, a little tobacco-shop,
With the little bright boxes
   piled up neatly upon the shelves
And the loose fragrant cavendish
   and the shag,
And the bright Virginia
   loose under the bright glass cases,

Title: An ironic reference to Yeats's *The Lake Isle of Innisfree* (p. 366), which should be read in order to understand Pound's satiric reply here.

And a pair of scales not too greasy,
And the whores dropping in for a word or two in passing,
For a flip word, and to tidy their hair a bit.

O God, O Venus, O Mercury, patron of thieves,
Lend me a little tobacco-shop,
    or install me in any profession
Save this damn'd profession of writing,
    where one needs one's brains all the time.

The Inquisitors

ROBINSON JEFFERS

Coming around a corner of the dark trail . . . what was
    wrong with the valley?
Azevedo checked his horse and sat staring: it was all
    changed. It was occupied. There were three hills
Where none had been: and firelight flickered red on their
    knees between them: if they were hills:
They were more like Red Indians around a camp-fire,
    grave and dark, mountain-high, hams on heels
Squatting around a little fire of hundred-foot logs.
    Azevedo remembers he felt an ice-brook
Glide on his spine; he slipped down from the saddle
    and hid
In the brush by the trail, above the black redwood forest.
    There was the Little Sur South Fork,
Its forest valley; the man had come in at nightfall over
    Bowcher's Gap, and a high moon hunted
Through running clouds. He heard the rumble of a voice,
    heavy not loud, saying, "I gathered some,
You can inspect them." One of the hills moved a huge
    hand
And poured its contents on a table-topped rock that
    stood in the firelight; men and women fell out;
Some crawled and some lay quiet; the hills leaned to eye
    them. One said: "It seems hardly possible

Such fragile creatures could be so noxious." Another answered,
"True, but we've seen. But it is only recently they have the power." The third answered, "That bomb?"
"Oh," he said, "—and the rest." He reached across and picked up one of the mites from the rock, and held it
Close to his eyes, and very carefully with finger and thumbnail peeled it: by chance a young female
With long black hair: it was too helpless even to scream. He held it by one white leg and stared at it:
"I can see nothing strange: only so fragile." The third hill answered, "We suppose it is something
Inside the head." Then the other split the skull with his thumbnail, squinting his eyes and peering, and said,
"A drop of marrow. How could that spoil the earth?"
"Nevertheless," he answered,   20
"They have that bomb. The blasts and the fires are nothing: freckles on the earth: the emanations
Might set the whole planet into a tricky fever
And destroy much." "Themselves," he answered. "Let them. Why not?" "No," he answered, "life."

                Azevedo
Still watched in horror, and all three of the hills
Picked little animals from the rock, peeled them and cracked them, or toasted them
On the red coals, or split their bodies from the crotch upward
To stare inside. They said, "It remains a mystery. However," they said,
"It is not likely they can destroy all life: the planet is capacious. Life would surely grow up again
From grubs in the soil, or the newt and toad level, and be beautiful again. And again perhaps break its legs
On its own cleverness: who can forecast the future?" The speaker yawned, and with his flat hand
Brushed the rock clean; the three slowly stood up,

Taller than Pico Blanco into the sky, their Indian-beaked
    heads in the moon-cloud,
And trampled their watchfire out and went away
    southward, stepping across the Ventana mountains.   10

Museums

LOUIS MacNEICE

Museums offer us, running from among the buses,
A centrally heated refuge, parquet floors and sarcophaguses,
Into whose tall fake porches we hurry without a sound
Like a beetle under a brick that lies, useless, on the ground.
Warmed and cajoled by the silence the cowed cypher revives,
Mirrors himself in the cases of pots, paces himself by marble lives,
Makes believe it was he that was the glory that was Rome,
Soft on his cheek the nimbus of other people's martyrdom,
And then returns to the street, his mind an arena where sprawls
Any number of consumptive Keatses and dying Gauls.   10

Bagpipe Music

LOUIS MacNEICE

It's no go the merry-go-round, it's no go the rickshaw,
All we want is a limousine and ticket for the peepshow.
Their knickers are made of crêpe-de-chine, their shoes are
    made of python,
Their halls are lined with tiger rugs and their walls with heads of
    bison.

John MacDonald found a corpse, put it under the sofa,
Waited till it came to life and hit it with a poker,
Sold its eyes for souvenirs, sold its blood for whiskey,
Kept its bones for dumb-bells to use when he was fifty.

It's no go the Yogi-Man, it's no go Blavatsky,
All we want is a bank balance and a bit of skirt in a taxi. 10

Annie MacDougall went to milk, caught her foot in the heather,
Woke to hear a dance record playing of Old Vienna.
It's no go your maidenheads, it's no go your culture,
All we want is a Dunlop tyre and the devil mend the puncture.

The Laird o'Phelps spent Hogmannay declaring he was sober;
Counted his feet to prove the fact and found he had one foot over.
Mrs. Carmichael had her fifth, looked at the job with repulsion,
Said to the midwife "Take it away; I'm through with over-
    production."

It's no go the gossip column, it's no go the Ceilidh,
All we want is a mother's help and a sugar-stick for the baby. 20

Willie Murray cut his thumb, couldn't count the damage,
Took the hide of an Ayrshire cow and used it for a bandage.
His brother caught three hundred cran when the seas were lavish,
Threw the bleeders back in the sea and went upon the parish.

It's no go the Herring Board, it's no go the Bible,
All we want is a packet of fags when our hands are idle.

15 Hogmannay: New Year's Eve in Scotland.   19 Ceilidh (pron. "Kaily"):
a social gathering.   23 cran: unit of measure for herring.   24 upon the parish:
on relief.

It's no go the picture palace, it's no go the stadium,
It's no go the country cot with a pot of pink geraniums.
It's no go the Government grants, it's no go the elections,
Sit on your arse for fifty years and hang your hat on a pension.   30

It's no go my honey love, it's no go my poppet;
Work your hands from day to day, the winds will blow the profit.
The glass is falling hour by hour, the glass will fall for ever,
But if you break the bloody glass you won't hold up the weather.

VII

Elegies, Odes, and Other Reflective Poems

Odes and elegies are usually serious reflective poems, dignified and as a rule deliberate in movement. The original Greek word from which the name "elegy" derives meant "a lament," but the term was also used as a name for any poem, regardless of subject, written in Greek elegiac meter. As a lament, its subject was likely to be either death or love. When the term was taken over into English and modern European languages, it continued to be used for various kinds of laments. More and more, death crowded out love and other themes, though never quite completely. In English, the elegy is not associated with any single metrical form.

The ode also dates back to Greek literature, and the term has meant a great many things in the intervening centuries. English odes are usually somewhat lofty, elaborate, even ceremonial in spirit; and they are most often poems of praise. Their subject may be anything that has sufficient magnitude to warrant a lofty tone and a rather formal treatment. A few English odes follow more or less closely the structure of the Greek odes of Pindar; others employ irregular rhyme and varied lengths of line and stanza; still others follow a regular stanza pattern.

As a rule, odes, elegies, and other poems of the kind are without the tightly unified intensity of the shorter lyric; they are broader, more inclusive, usually elaborate and rich in texture of sound and in sensuous imagery. They demand of the reader a more sustained concentration than is needed for the short lyric, somewhat, perhaps, as the sonata form does in music, in comparison with the song. Whatever their ostensible subject, they are usually concerned with large questions of philosophic belief or value, but these themes are treated dramatically rather than through direct philosophical discussion. The themes arise out of a situation, a time, a place, or even an object, which awakens and gives impetus to the creative movement of the poem. The center of gravity may rest in the specific occasion; it may lie in the philosophical view; or the occasion and the reflection may be so interwoven that one cannot fix upon either alone as central.

Note: Several of the greatest English odes, those of Keats, are printed in Chapter VIII.

Lycidas

JOHN MILTON

In this Monody the Author bewails a learned Friend, unfortunatly drown'd in his Passage from Chester on the Irish Seas, 1637. And by occasion fortels the ruine of our corrupted clergy then in their height.

Yet once more, O ye Laurels, and once more
Ye Myrtles brown, with Ivy never-sear,
I com to pluck your Berries harsh and crude,
And with forc'd fingers rude,
Shatter your leaves before the mellowing year.
Bitter constraint, and sad occasion dear,
Compels me to disturb your season due:
For *Lycidas* is dead, dead ere his prime
Young *Lycidas*, and hath not left his peer:
Who would not sing for *Lycidas*? he knew   10
Himself to sing, and build the lofty rhyme.

He must not flote upon his watry bear
Unwept, and welter to the parching wind,
Without the meed of som melodious tear.
   Begin then, Sisters of the sacred well,
That from beneath the seat of *Jove* doth spring,
Begin, and somwhat loudly sweep the string.
Hence with denial vain, and coy excuse,
So may som gentle Muse
With lucky words favour my destin'd Urn,   20
And as he passes turn,
And bid fair peace be to my sable shrowd.
For we were nurst upon the self-same hill,
Fed the same flock, by fountain, shade, and rill.
   Together both, ere the high Lawns appear'd
Under the opening eye-lids of the morn,
We drove a field, and both together heard
What time the Gray-fly winds her sultry horn,
Batt'ning our flocks with the fresh dews of night,
Oft till the Star that rose, at Ev'ning, bright   30
Toward Heav'ns descent had slop'd his westering wheel.
Mean while the Rural ditties were not mute,
Temper'd to th'Oaten Flute;
Rough *Satyrs* danc'd, and *Fauns* with clov'n heel,
From the glad sound would not be absent long,
And old *Damætas* lov'd to hear our song.
   But O the heavy change, now thou art gon,
Now thou art gon, and never must return!
Thee Shepherd, thee the Woods, and desert Caves,
With wilde Thyme and the gadding Vine o'regrown,   40
And all their echoes mourn.
The Willows, and the Hazle Copses green,
Shall now no more be seen,
Fanning their joyous Leaves to thy soft layes.
As killing as the Canker to the Rose,
Or Taint-worm to the weanling Herds that graze,
Or Frost to Flowers, that their gay wardrop wear,
When first the White thorn blows;
Such, *Lycidas*, thy loss to Shepherds ear.

12 bear: bier.   *15* Sisters . . . : the Muses.   *48* White thorn: hawthorn.

Where were ye Nymphs when the remorseless deep 50
Clos'd o're the head of your lov'd *Lycidas?*
For neither were ye playing on the steep,
Where your old *Bards,* the famous *Druids* ly,
Nor on the shaggy top of *Mona* high,
Nor yet where *Deva* spreads her wisard stream:
Ay me, I fondly dream!
Had ye bin there—for what could that have don?
What could the Muse her self that *Orpheus* bore,
The Muse her self, for her inchanting son
Whom Universal nature did lament, 60
When by the rout that made the hideous roar,
His goary visage down the stream was sent,
Down the swift *Hebrus* to the *Lesbian* shore.
  Alas! What boots it with uncessant care
To tend the homely slighted Shepherds trade,
And strictly meditate the thankles Muse,
Were it not better don as others use,
To sport with *Amaryllis* in the shade,
Or with the tangles of *Neæra's* hair?
Fame is the spur that the clear spirit doth raise 70
(That last infirmity of Noble mind)
To scorn delights, and live laborious dayes;
But the fair Guerdon when we hope to find,
And think to burst out into sudden blaze,
Comes the blind *Fury* with th'abhorred shears,
And slits the thin spun life. But not the praise,
Phœbus repli'd, and touch'd my trembling ears;
Fame is no plant that grows on mortal soil,
Nor in the glistering foil
Set off to th' world, nor in broad rumour lies, 80
But lives and spreds aloft by those pure eyes,
And perfet witnes of all judging *Jove;*
As he pronounces lastly on each deed,

---

54 Mona: island of Anglesey, near which King had drowned.   55 Deva: the river Dee.   58 Muse: Calliope, the Muse of epic poetry, was the mother of Orpheus, the Musician, inspirer of song, and center of a Greek religious cult. According to tradition, Maenads killed and dismembered him and threw him into a stream, from which his head floated, singing, to Lesbos.   79 glistering foil: glittering gold foil.

Of so much fame in Heav'n expect thy meed.
  O Fountain *Arethuse,* and thou honour'd floud,
Smooth-sliding *Mincius,* crown'd with vocall reeds,
That strain I heard was of a higher mood:
But now my Oate proceeds,
And listens to the Herald of the Sea
That came in *Neptune's* plea,   90
He ask'd the Waves, and ask'd the Fellon winds,
What hard mishap hath doom'd this gentle swain?
And question'd every gust of rugged wings
That blows from off each beaked Promontory,
They knew not of his story,
And sage *Hippotades* their answer brings,
That not a blast was from his dungeon stray'd,
The Ayr was calm, and on the level brine,
Sleek *Panope* with all her sisters play'd.
It was that fatall and perfidious Bark   100
Built in th'eclipse, and rigg'd with curses dark,
That sunk so low that sacred head of thine.
  Next *Camus,* reverend Sire, went footing slow,
His Mantle hairy, and his Bonnet sedge,
Inwrought with figures dim, and on the edge
Like to that sanguine flower inscrib'd with woe.
Ah; Who hath reft (quoth he) my dearest pledge?
Last came, and last did go,
The Pilot of the *Galilean* lake,

85 Arethuse: fountain in Sicily associated with the Greek pastoral poet Theocritus. 86 Mincius: river associated with Virgil, who wrote Latin pastoral poetry. 89–90 Herald of the Sea: Triton, a sea god, defends his father Neptune against the accusation of having drowned Lycidas. 96 Hippotades: Aeolus, god of the winds. 99 Panope: a sea nymph. 103 Camus: the river Cam, from which Cambridge receives its name. 106 sanguine flower: The youth Hyacinthus was loved but accidentally killed by Apollo. From his blood Apollo caused to spring up the hyacinth flower, whose petals were said to bear markings resembling the letters of the Greek word for "woe." 109 The Pilot: St. Peter, customarily represented as carrying the keys of Heaven. He had been a fisherman on the Sea of Galilee and was with Jesus during a storm at sea. As the founder of the Church he may be called its first "pastor." As the first bishop of Rome, he is represented with a bishop's headdress ("Miter'd," line 112).

Two massy Keyes he bore of metals twain, 110
(The Golden opes, the Iron shuts amain)
He shook his Miter'd locks, and stern bespake,
How well could I have spar'd for thee, young swain,
Anow of such as for their bellies sake,
Creep and intrude, and climb into the fold?
Of other care they little reck'ning make,
Then how to scramble at the shearers feast,
And shove away the worthy bidden guest.
Blind mouthes! that scarce themselves know how to hold
A Sheep-hook, or have learn'd ought els the least 120
That to the faithfull Herdmans art belongs!
What recks it them? What need they? They are sped;
And when they list, their lean and flashy songs
Grate on their scrannel Pipes of wretched straw,
The hungry Sheep look up, and are not fed,
But swoln with wind, and the rank mist they draw,
Rot inwardly, and foul contagion spread:
Besides what the grim Woolf with privy paw
Daily devours apace, and nothing sed,
But that two-handed engine at the door, 130
Stands ready to smite once, and smite no more.
   Return *Alpheus*, the dread voice is past,
That shrunk thy streams; Return *Sicilian* Muse,
And call the Vales, and bid them hither cast
Their Bels, and Flourets of a thousand hues.
Ye valleys low where the milde whispers use,
Of shades and wanton winds, and gushing brooks,
On whose fresh lap the swart Star sparely looks,
Throw hither all your quaint enameld eyes,
That on the green terf suck the honied showres, 140
And purple all the ground with vernal flowres.

114 Anow: enough.   *124* scrannel: thin and discordant.   *128* grim Woolf: the Roman Catholic Church, winning converts among Protestants.   privy: furtive, private.   *130–131* The "two-handed engine" has never been satisfactorily identified.   *132* Alpheus: god of the river Alpheus and lover of Arethusa (*1. 85*). He is associated here with pastoral poetry. In addressing him at this point, Milton returns to the theme with which the poem opened. *138* swart Star: Sirius, the Dog Star, whose name means "scorching."

Bring the rathe Primrose that forsaken dies.
The tufted Crow-toe, and pale Gessamine,
The white Pink, and the Pansie freakt with jeat,
The glowing Violet.
The Musk-rose, and the well attir'd Woodbine.
With Cowslips wan that hang the pensive hed,
And every flower that sad embroidery wears:
Bid *Amaranthus* all his beauty shed,
And Daffadillies fill their cups with tears,   150
To strew the Laureat Herse where *Lycid* lies.
For so to interpose a little ease,
Let our frail thoughts dally with false surmise.
Ay me! Whilst thee the shores, and sounding Seas
Wash far away, where ere thy bones are hurld,
Whether beyond the stormy *Hebrides,*
Where thou perhaps under the whelming tide
Visit'st the bottom of the monstrous world;
Or whether thou to our moist vows deny'd,
Sleep'st by the fable of *Bellerus* old,   160
Where the great vision of the guarded Mount
Looks toward *Namancos* and *Bayona's* hold;
Look homeward Angel now, and melt with ruth.
And, O ye *Dolphins*, waft the hapless youth.

    Weep no more, woful Shepherds weep no more,
For *Lycidas* your sorrow is not dead,
Sunk though he be beneath the watry floar,
So sinks the day-star in the Ocean bed,
And yet anon repairs his drooping head,
And tricks his beams, and with new spangled Ore,   170
Flames in the forehead of the morning sky:
So *Lycidas* sunk low, but mounted high,
Through the dear might of him that walk'd the waves
Where other groves, and other streams along,
With *Nectar* pure his oozy Lock's he laves,
And hears the unexpressive nuptiall Song,
In the blest Kingdoms meek of joy and love.

142 rathe: early.   *143* Crowtoe: crowfoot, ranunculus.   *144* freakt: streaked.
168 day-star: sun.   *173* Matt. 14:25–33.

There entertain him all the Saints above,
In solemn troops, and sweet Societies
That sing, and singing in their glory move, 180
And wipe the tears for ever from his eyes.
Now *Lycidas* the Shepherds weep no more;
Hence forth thou art the Genius of the shore,
In thy large recompense, and shalt be good
To all that wander in that perilous flood.
   Thus sang the uncouth Swain to th'Okes and rills,
While the still morn went out with Sandals gray,
He touch'd the tender stops of various Quills,
With eager thought warbling his *Dorick* lay:
And now the Sun had stretch'd out all the hills, 190
And now was dropt into the Western bay;
At last he rose, and twitch'd his Mantle blew:
Tomorrow to fresh Woods, and Pastures new.

183 genius: guardian spirit.   *186* uncouth: unknown or rustic.   *189* Doric: the dialect of Greek pastoral poetry.

Lines Composed a Few Miles Above Tintern Abbey, on Revisiting the Banks of the Wye...

WILLIAM WORDSWORTH

Five years have past; five summers, with the length
Of five long winters! and again I hear
These waters, rolling from their mountain-springs
With a soft inland murmur.—Once again
Do I behold these steep and lofty cliffs,
That on a wild secluded scene impress
Thoughts of more deep seclusion; and connect
The landscape with the quiet of the sky.
The day is come when I again repose
Here, under this dark sycamore, and view 10
These plots of cottage-ground, these orchard-tufts,

Which at this season, with their unripe fruits,
Are clad in one green hue, and lose themselves
'Mid groves and copses. Once again I see
These hedge-rows, hardly hedge-rows, little lines
Of sportive wood run wild: these pastoral farms,
Green to the very door; and wreaths of smoke
Sent up, in silence, from among the trees!
With some uncertain notice, as might seem
Of vagrant dwellers in the houseless woods,   20
Or of some Hermit's cave, where by his fire
The Hermit sits alone.
                    These beauteous forms,
Through a long absence, have not been to me
As is a landscape to a blind man's eye:
But oft, in lonely rooms, and 'mid the din
Of towns and cities, I have owed to them
In hours of weariness, sensations sweet,
Felt in the blood, and felt along the heart;
And passing even into my purer mind,
With tranquil restoration:—feelings too   30
Of unremembered pleasure: such, perhaps,
As have no slight or trivial influence
On that best portion of a good man's life,
His little, nameless, unremembered acts
Of kindness and of love. Nor less, I trust,
To them I may have owed another gift,
Of aspect more sublime; that blessed mood,
In which the burthen of the mystery,
In which the heavy and the weary weight
Of all this unintelligible world,   40
Is lightened:—that serene and blessed mood,
In which the affections gently lead us on,—
Until, the breath of this corporeal frame
And even the motion of our human blood
Almost suspended, we are laid asleep
In body, and become a living soul:
While with an eye made quiet by the power
Of harmony, and the deep power of joy,
We see into the life of things.

                    If this
Be but a vain belief, yet, oh! how oft—   50
In darkness and amid the many shapes
Of joyless daylight; when the fretful stir
Unprofitable, and the fever of the world,
Have hung upon the beatings of my heart—
How oft, in spirit, have I turned to thee,
O sylvan Wye! thou wanderer through the woods,
How often has my spirit turned to thee!

   And now, with gleams of half-extinguished thought,
With many recognitions dim and faint,
And somewhat of a sad perplexity,   60
The picture of the mind revives again:
While here I stand, not only with the sense
Of present pleasure, but with pleasing thoughts
That in this moment there is life and food
For future years. And so I dare to hope,
Though changed, no doubt, from what I was when first
I came among these hills; when like a roe
I bounded o'er the mountains, by the sides
Of the deep rivers, and the lonely streams,
Wherever nature led: more like a man   70
Flying from something that he dreads, than one
Who sought the thing he loved. For nature then
(The coarser pleasures of my boyish days,
And their glad animal movements all gone by)
To me was all in all.—I cannot paint
What then I was. The sounding cataract
Haunted me like a passion: the tall rock,
The mountain, and the deep and gloomy wood,
Their colours and their forms, were then to me
An appetite; a feeling and a love,   80
That had no need of a remoter charm,
By thought supplied, nor any interest
Unborrowed from the eye.—That time is past,
And all its aching joys are now no more,
And all its dizzy raptures. Not for this
Faint I, nor mourn nor murmur; other gifts

Have followed; for such loss, I would believe,
Abundant recompense. For I have learned
To look on nature, not as in the hour
Of thoughtless youth; but hearing oftentimes 90
The still, sad music of humanity,
Nor harsh nor grating, though of ample power
To chasten and subdue. And I have felt
A presence that disturbs me with the joy
Of elevated thoughts; a sense sublime
Of something far more deeply interfused,
Whose dwelling is the light of setting suns,
And the round ocean and the living air,
And the blue sky, and in the mind of man:
A motion and a spirit, that impels 100
All thinking things, all objects of all thought,
And rolls through all things. Therefore am I still
A lover of the meadows and the woods,
And mountains; and of all that we behold
From this green earth; of all the mighty world
Of eye, and ear,—both what they half create,
And what perceive; well pleased to recognize
In nature and the language of the sense
The anchor of my purest thoughts, the nurse,
The guide, the guardian of my heart, and soul 110
Of all my moral being.
                   Nor perchance,
If I were not thus taught, should I the more
Suffer my genial spirits to decay:
For thou art with me here upon the banks
Of this fair river; thou my dearest Friend,
My dear, dear Friend; and in thy voice I catch
The language of my former heart, and read
My former pleasures in the shooting lights
Of thy wild eyes. Oh! yet a little while
May I behold in thee what I was once, 120
My dear, dear Sister! and this prayer I make,
Knowing that Nature never did betray

---

115 Friend: Wordsworth's sister Dorothy.

The heart that loved her; 'tis her privilege,
Through all the years of this our life, to lead
From joy to joy: for she can so inform
The mind that is within us, so impress
With quietness and beauty, and so feed
With lofty thoughts, that neither evil tongues,
Rash judgments, nor the sneers of selfish men,
Nor greetings where no kindness is, nor all   130
The dreary intercourse of daily life,
Shall e'er prevail against us, or disturb
Our cheerful faith, that all which we behold
Is full of blessings. Therefore let the moon
Shine on thee in thy solitary walk;
And let the misty mountain-winds be free
To blow against thee: and, in after years,
When these wild ecstasies shall be matured
Into a sober pleasure; when thy mind
Shall be a mansion for all lovely forms,   140
Thy memory be as a dwelling-place
For all sweet sounds and harmonies; oh! then,
If solitude, or fear, or pain, or grief,
Should be thy portion, with what healing thoughts
Of tender joy wilt thou remember me,
And these my exhortations! Nor, perchance—
If I should be where I no more can hear
Thy voice, nor catch from thy wild eyes these gleams
Of past existence—wilt thou then forget
That on the banks of this delightful stream   150
We stood together; and that I, so long
A worshipper of Nature, hither came
Unwearied in that service: rather say
With warmer love—oh! with far deeper zeal
Of holier love. Nor wilt thou then forget,
That after many wanderings, many years
Of absence, these steep woods and lofty cliffs,
And this green pastoral landscape, were to me
More dear, both for themselves and for thy sake!

Ode

Intimations of Immortality from Recollections of Early Childhood

WILLIAM WORDSWORTH

The Child is father of the Man;
And I could wish my days to be
Bound each to each by natural piety.

I

There was a time when meadow, grove, and stream,
The earth, and every common sight,
  To me did seem
  Apparelled in celestial light,
The glory and the freshness of a dream.
It is not now as it hath been of yore;—
  Turn whereso'er I may,
   By night or day,
The things which I have seen I now can see no more.

II

  The Rainbow comes and goes,   10
  And lovely is the Rose,
  The Moon doth with delight
Look round her when the heavens are bare;
  Waters on a starry night
  Are beautiful and fair;
  The sunshine is a glorious birth;
  But yet I know, where'er I go,
That there hath past away a glory from the earth.

III

Now, while the birds thus sing a joyous song,
  And while the young lambs bound   20
   As to the tabor's sound,

To me alone there came a thought of grief:
A timely utterance gave that thought relief,
    And I again am strong:
The cataracts blow their trumpets from the steep;
No more shall grief of mine the season wrong;
I hear the Echoes through the mountains throng,
The Winds come to me from the fields of sleep,
    And all the earth is gay;
        Land and sea   30
    Give themselves up to jollity,
    And with the heart of May
    Doth every Beast keep holiday;—
        Thou Child of Joy,
Shout round me, let me hear thy shouts, thou happy
        Shepherd-boy!

IV

Ye blessed Creatures, I have heard the call
    Ye to each other make; I see
The heavens laugh with you in your jubilee;
    My heart is at your festival,
        My head hath its coronal,   40
The fulness of your bliss, I feel—I feel it all.
    Oh evil day! if I were sullen
      While Earth herself is adorning,
        This sweet May-morning,
    And the Children are culling
        On every side,
    In a thousand valleys far and wide,
    Fresh flowers; while the sun shines warm,
And the Babe leaps up on his Mother's arm:—
    I hear, I hear, with joy I hear!   50
  —But there's a Tree, of many, one,
A single Field which I have looked upon,
Both of them speak of something that is gone:
        The Pansy at my feet
        Doth the same tale repeat:
Whither is fled the visionary gleam?
Where is it now, the glory and the dream?

V

Our birth is but a sleep and a forgetting:
The Soul that rises with us, our life's Star,
    Hath had elsewhere its setting,
      And cometh from afar:
      Not in entire forgetfulness,
      And not in utter nakedness,
But trailing clouds of glory do we come
      From God, who is our home:
Heaven lies about us in our infancy!
Shades of the prison-house begin to close
    Upon the growing Boy,
      But He
Beholds the light, and whence it flows,
    He sees it in his joy;
The Youth, who daily farther from the east
    Must travel, still is Nature's Priest,
      And by the vision splendid
      Is on his way attended;
At length the Man perceives it die away,
And fade into the light of common day.

VI

Earth fills her lap with pleasures of her own;
Yearnings she hath in her own natural kind,
And, even with something of a Mother's mind,
      And no unworthy aim,
    The homely Nurse doth all she can
To make her Foster-child, her Inmate Man,
    Forget the glories he hath known,
And that imperial palace whence he came.

VII

Behold the Child among his new-born blisses,
A six years' Darling of a pigmy size!
See, where 'mid work of his own hand he lies,
Fretted by sallies of his mother's kisses,
With light upon him from his father's eyes!
See, at his feet, some little plan or chart,

Some fragment from his dream of human life,
Shaped by himself with newly-learned art;
  A wedding or a festival,
  A mourning or a funeral;
    And this hath now his heart,
    And unto this he frames his song:
      Then will he fit his tongue
To dialogues of business, love, or strife;
  But it will not be long   100
  Ere this be thrown aside,
  And with new joy and pride
The little Actor cons another part;
Filling from time to time his "humorous stage"
With all the Persons, down to palsied Age,
That Life brings with her in her equipage;
    As if his whole vocation
    Were endless imitation.

VIII

Thou, whose exterior semblance doth belie
  Thy Soul's immensity;   110
Thou best Philosopher, who yet dost keep
Thy heritage, thou Eye among the blind,
That, deaf and silent, read'st the eternal deep,
Haunted forever by the eternal mind,—
    Mighty Prophet! Seer blest!
    On whom those truths do rest,
Which we are toiling all our lives to find,
In darkness lost, the darkness of the grave;
Thou, over whom thy Immortality
Broods like the Day, a Master o'er a Slave,   120
A Presence which is not to be put by;
Thou little Child, yet glorious in the might
Of heaven-born freedom on thy being's height,
Why with such earnest pains dost thou provoke
The years to bring the inevitable yoke,
Thus blindly with thy blessedness at strife?
Full soon thy Soul shall have her earthly freight,
And custom lie upon thee with a weight,
Heavy as frost, and deep almost as life!

IX

      O joy! that in our embers 130
      Is something that doth live,
      That nature yet remembers
      What was so fugitive!
The thought of our past years in me doth breed
Perpetual benediction: not indeed
For that which is most worthy to be blest;
Delight and liberty, the simple creed
Of Childhood, whether busy or at rest,
With new-fledged hope still fluttering in his breast:—
      Not for these I raise 140
      The song of thanks and praise;
      But for those obstinate questionings
      Of sense and outward things,
      Fallings from us, vanishings;
      Blank misgivings of a Creature
Moving about in worlds not realised,
High instincts before which our mortal Nature
Did tremble like a guilty Thing surprised:
      But for those first affections,
      Those shadowy recollections, 150
      Which, be they what they may,
Are yet the fountain light of all our day,
Are yet a master light of all our seeing;
      Uphold us, cherish, and have power to make
Our noisy years seem moments in the being
Of the eternal Silence: truths that wake,
      To perish never;
Which neither listlessness, nor mad endeavour,
      Nor Man nor Boy,
Nor all that is at enmity with joy, 160
Can utterly abolish or destroy!
      Hence in a season of calm weather
      Though inland far we be,
Our Souls have sight of that immortal sea
      Which brought us hither,
      Can in a moment travel thither,
And see the Children sport upon the short,
And hear the mighty waters rolling evermore.

X

       Then sing, ye Birds, sing, sing a joyous song!
            And let the young Lambs bound   170
            As to the tabor's sound!
    We in thought will join your throng,
        Ye that pipe and ye that play,
        Ye that through your hearts to-day
         Feel the gladness of the May!
What though the radiance which was once so bright
Be now for ever taken from my sight,
      Though nothing can bring back the hour
Of splendour in the grass, of glory in the flower;
        We will grieve not, rather find   180
        Strength in what remains behind;
        In the primal sympathy
        Which having been must ever be;
        In the soothing thoughts that spring
        Out of human suffering;
        In the faith that looks through death,
In years that bring the philosophic mind.

XI

And O, ye Fountains, Meadows, Hills, and Groves,
Forbode not any severing of our loves!
Yet in my heart of hearts I feel your might;   190
I only have relinquished one delight
To live beneath your more habitual sway.
I love the Brooks which down their channels fret,
Even more than when I tripped lightly as they;
The innocent brightness of a new-born Day
            Is lovely yet;
The Clouds that gather round the setting sun
Do take a sober colouring from an eye
That hath kept watch o'er man's mortality;
Another race hath been, and other palms are won.   200
Thanks to the human heart by which we live,
Thanks to its tenderness, its joys, and fears,
To me the meanest flower that blows can give
Thoughts that do often lie too deep for tears.

Dejection: An Ode

SAMUEL TAYLOR COLERIDGE

Late, late yestreen I saw the new Moon,
With the old Moon in her arms;
And I fear, I fear, my Master dear!
We shall have a deadly storm.
—BALLAD OF SIR PATRICK SPENCE

I

Well! If the Bard was weather-wise, who made
  The grand old ballad of Sir Patrick Spence,
  This night, so tranquil now, will not go hence
Unroused by winds, that ply a busier trade
Than those which mould yon cloud in lazy flakes,
Or the dull sobbing draft, that moans and rakes
  Upon the strings of this Eolian lute,
  Which better far were mute.
For lo! the New-moon winter-bright!
And overspread with phantom light,   10
  (With swimming phantom light o'erspread
  But rimmed and circled by a silver thread)
I see the old Moon in her lap, foretelling
  The coming on of rain and squally blast.
And oh! that even now the gust were swelling,
  And the slant night-shower driving loud and fast!
Those sounds which oft have raised me, whilst they awed,
  And sent my soul abroad,
Might now perhaps their wonted impulse give,
Might startle this dull pain, and make it move and live!   20

II

A grief without a pang, void, dark, and drear,
  A stifled, drowsy, unimpassioned grief,

---

7 Eolian lute: The Aeolian harp, named from Aeolus, god of the winds, is an instrument that produces musical tones when placed in a strong current of air. It has generally eight or ten strings, stretched over a wooden sounding box.

Which finds no natural outlet, no relief,
   In word, or sigh, or tear—
O Lady! in this wan and heartless mood,
To other thoughts by yonder throstle woo'd,
   All this long eve, so balmy and serene,
Have I been gazing on the western sky,
   And its peculiar tint of yellow green:
And still I gaze—and with how blank an eye!   30
And those thin clouds above, in flakes and bars,
That give away their motion to the stars;
Those stars, that glide behind them or between,
Now sparkling, now bedimmed, but always seen:
Yon crescent Moon as fixed as if it grew
In its own cloudless, starless lake of blue;
I see them all so excellently fair,
I see, not feel, how beautiful they are!

III

   My genial spirits fail;
   And what can these avail   40
To lift the smothering weight from off my breast?
   It were a vain endeavour,
   Though I should gaze for ever
On that green light that lingers in the west:
I may not hope from outward forms to win
The passion and the life, whose fountains are within.

IV

O Lady! we receive but what we give,
And in our life alone does Nature live:
Ours is her wedding garment, ours her shroud!
   And would we aught behold, of higher worth,   50
Than that inanimate cold world allowed
To the poor loveless ever-anxious crowd,
   Ah! from the soul itself must issue forth
A light, a glory, a fair luminous cloud
     Enveloping the Earth—
And from the soul itself must there be sent

---

39 *genial spirits*: native, inborn spirits.

A sweet and potent voice, of its own birth,
Of all sweet sounds the life and element!

V

O pure of heart! thou need'st not ask of me
What this strong music in the soul may be!
What, and wherein it doth exist,
This light, this glory, this fair luminous mist,
This beautiful and beauty-making power.
    Joy, virtuous Lady! Joy that ne'er was given,
Save to the pure, and in their purest hour,
Life, and Life's effluence, cloud at once and shower,
Joy, Lady! is the spirit and the power,
Which wedding Nature to us gives in dower
    A new Earth and new Heaven,
Undreamt of by the sensual and the proud—
Joy is the sweet voice, Joy the luminous cloud—
    We in ourselves rejoice!
And thence flows all that charms or ear or sight,
    All melodies the echoes of that voice,
All colours a suffusion from that light.

VI

There was a time when, though my path was rough,
    This joy within me dallied with distress,
And all misfortunes were but as the stuff
    Whence Fancy made me dreams of happiness:
For hope grew round me, like the twining vine,
And fruits, and foliage, not my own, seemed mine.
But now afflictions bow me down to earth:
Nor care I that they rob me of my mirth;
    But oh! each visitation
Suspends what nature gave me at my birth,
    My shaping spirit of Imagination.
For not to think of what I needs must feel,
    But to be still and patient, all I can;
And haply by abstruse research to steal
    From my own nature all the natural man—
    This was my sole resource, my only plan:

Till that which suits a part infects the whole,
And now is almost grown the habit of my soul.

VII

Hence, viper thoughts, that coil around my mind,
   Reality's dark dream!
I turn from you, and listen to the wind,
   Which long has raved unnoticed. What a scream
Of agony by torture lengthened out
That lute sent forth! Thou Wind, that rav'st without,
   Bare crag, or mountain-tairn, or blasted tree,   100
Or pine-grove whither woodman never clomb,
Or lonely house, long held the witches' home,
   Methinks were fitter instruments for thee,
Mad Lutanist! who in this month of showers,
Of dark brown gardens, and of peeping flowers,
   Mak'st Devils' yule, with worse than wintry song,
The blossoms, buds, and timorous leaves among.
   Thou Actor, perfect in all tragic sounds!
Thou mighty Poet, e'en to frenzy bold!
     What tell'st thou now about?   110
   'Tis of the rushing of an host in rout,
With groans, of trampled men, with smarting wounds—
At once they groan with pain, and shudder with the cold!
But hush! there is a pause of deepest silence!
   And all that noise, as of a rushing crowd,
With groans, and tremulous shudderings—all is over—
   It tells another tale, with sounds less deep and loud!
     A tale of less affright,
     And tempered with delight,
As Otway's self had framed the tender lay,—   120
     'Tis of a little child
     Upon a lonesome wild,
Not far from home, but she hath lost her way:

---

99 This address to the Storm-wind will not appear extravagant to those who have heard it at night and in a mountainous country (Coleridge's note).
100 tairn: tarn, small mountain lake.

And now moans low in bitter grief and fear,
And now screams loud, and hopes to make her mother hear.

VIII

'Tis midnight, but small thoughts have I of sleep:
Full seldom may my friend such vigils keep!
Visit her, gentle Sleep! with wings of healing,
  And may this storm be but a mountain-birth,
May all the stars hang bright above her dwelling,   130
  Silent as though they watched the sleeping Earth!
    With light heart may she rise,
    Gay fancy, cheerful eyes,
  Joy lift her spirit, joy attune her voice;
To her may all things live, from pole to pole,
Their life the eddying of her living soul!
  O simple spirit, guided from above,
Dear Lady! friend devoutest of my choice,
Thus mayest thou ever, evermore rejoice.

Ode to the West Wind

PERCY BYSSHE SHELLEY

1

O wild West Wind, thou breath of Autumn's being,
Thou, from whose unseen presence the leaves dead
Are driven, like ghosts from an enchanter fleeing,

Yellow, and black, and pale, and hectic red,
Pestilence-stricken multitudes: O thou,
Who chariotest to their dark wintry bed

The wingèd seeds, where they lie cold and low,
Each like a corpse within its grave, until
Thine azure sister of the Spring shall blow

Her clarion o'er the dreaming earth, and fill
(Driving sweet buds like flocks to feed in air)
With living hues and odours plain and hill:
Wild Spirit, which art moving everywhere;
Destroyer and preserver; hear! oh, hear!

2

Thou on whose stream, mid the steep sky's commotion,
Loose clouds like earth's decaying leaves are shed,
Shook from the tangled boughs of Heaven and Ocean,

Angels of rain and lightning: there are spread
On the blue surface of thine aëry surge,
Like the bright hair uplifted from the head

Of some fierce Mænad, even from the dim verge
Of the horizon to the zenith's height,
The locks of the approaching storm. Thou dirge

Of the dying year, to which this closing night
Will be the dome of a vast sepulchre,
Vaulted with all thy congregated might

Of vapours, from whose solid atmosphere
Black rain, and fire, and hail will burst: oh, hear!

3

Thou who didst waken from his summer dreams
The blue Mediterranean, where he lay,
Lulled by the coil of his crystàlline streams,

Beside a pumice isle in Baiæ's bay,
And saw in sleep old palaces and towers
Quivering within the wave's intenser day,

All overgrown with azure moss and flowers
So sweet, the sense faints picturing them! Thou
For whose path the Atlantic's level powers

32 pumice isle: island of volcanic rock.

Cleave themselves into chasms, while far below
The sea-blooms and the oozy woods which wear
The sapless foliage of the ocean, know   40
Thy voice, and suddenly grow gray with fear,
And tremble and despoil themselves: oh, hear!

4

If I were a dead leaf thou mightest bear;
If I were a swift cloud to fly with thee;
A wave to pant beneath thy power, and share

The impulse of thy strength, only less free
Than thou, O uncontrollable! If even
I were as in my boyhood, and could be

The comrade of thy wanderings over Heaven,
As then, when to outstrip thy skiey speed   50
Scarce seemed a vision; I would ne'er have striven

As thus with thee in prayer in my sore need.
Oh, lift me as a wave, a leaf, a cloud!
I fall upon the thorns of life! I bleed!

A heavy weight of hours has chained and bowed
One too like thee—tameless, and swift, and proud.

5

Make me thy lyre, even as the forest is:
What if my leaves are falling like its own!
The tumult of thy mighty harmonies

Will take from both a deep, autumnal tone,   60
Sweet though in sadness. Be thou, Spirit fierce,
My spirit! Be thou me, impetuous one!

Drive my dead thoughts over the universe
Like withered leaves to quicken a new birth!
And, by the incantation of this verse,

Scatter, as from an unextinguished hearth
Ashes and sparks, my words among mankind!
Be through my lips to unawakened earth

The trumpet of a prophecy! O, Wind,
If Winter comes, can Spring be far behind? 70

Ulysses

ALFRED, LORD TENNYSON

It little profits that an idle king,
By this still hearth, among these barren crags,
Match'd with an aged wife, I mete and dole
Unequal laws unto a savage race,
That hoard, and sleep, and feed, and know not me.
I cannot rest from travel: I will drink
Life to the lees: all times I have enjoy'd
Greatly, have suffer'd greatly, both with those
That loved me, and alone; on shore, and when
Thro' scudding drifts the rainy Hyades 10
Vext the dim sea. I am become a name;
For always roaming with a hungry heart
Much have I seen and known; cities of men
And manners, climates, councils, governments,
Myself not least, but honour'd of them all;
And drunk delight of battle with my peers,
Far on the ringing plains of windy Troy.
I am a part of all that I have met;
Yet all experience is an arch wherethro'
Gleams that untravel'd world, whose margin fades 20
For ever and for ever when I move.
How dull it is to pause, to make an end,
To rust unburnish'd, not to shine in use!
As tho' to breathe were life. Life piled on life
Were all too little, and of one to me
Little remains: but every hour is saved
From that eternal silence, something more,

A bringer of new things; and vile it were
For some three suns to store and hoard myself,
And this gray spirit yearning in desire   30
To follow knowledge like a sinking star,
Beyond the utmost bound of human thought.
  This is my son, mine own Telemachus,
To whom I leave the sceptre and the isle—
Well-loved of me, discerning to fulfill
This labour, by slow prudence to make mild
A rugged people, and thro' soft degrees
Subdue them to the useful and the good.
Most blameless is he, centered in the sphere
Of common duties, decent not to fail   40
In offices of tenderness, and pay
Meet adoration to my household gods,
When I am gone. He works his work, I mine.
  There lies the port; the vessel puffs her sail:
There gloom the dark broad seas. My mariners,
Souls that have toil'd, and wrought, and thought with me—
That ever with a frolic welcome took
The thunder and the sunshine, and opposed
Free hearts, free foreheads—you and I are old;
Old age hath yet his honour and his toil;   50
Death closes all: but something ere the end,
Some work of noble note, may yet be done,
Not unbecoming men that strove with Gods.
The lights begin to twinkle from the rocks:
The long day wanes: the slow moon climbs: the deep
Moans round with many voices. Come, my friends,
'T is not too late to seek a newer world.
Push off, and sitting well in order smite
The sounding furrows; for my purpose holds
To sail beyond the sunset, and the baths   60
Of all the western stars, until I die.
It may be that the gulfs will wash us down:
It may be we shall touch the Happy Isles,

---

63 Happy Isles: the Isles of the Blest in the western ocean, where heroes especially favored by the gods might live exempt from death.

And see the great Achilles, whom we knew.
Tho' much is taken, much abides; and tho'
We are not now that strength which in old days
Moved earth and heaven, that which we are, we are;
One equal temper of heroic hearts,
Made weak by time and fate, but strong in will
To strive, to seek, to find, and not to yield. 70

The Lotos-Eaters

ALFRED, LORD TENNYSON

"Courage!" he said, and pointed toward the land,
"This mounting wave will roll us shoreward soon."
In the afternoon they came unto a land
In which it seemèd always afternoon.
All round the coast the languid air did swoon,
Breathing like one that hath a weary dream.
Full-faced above the valley stood the moon;
And like a downward smoke, the slender stream
Along the cliff to fall and pause and fall did seem.

A land of streams! some, like a downward smoke,   10
Slow-dropping veils of thinnest lawn, did go;
And some thro' wavering lights and shadows broke,
Rolling a slumbrous sheet of foam below.
They saw the gleaming river seaward flow
From the inner land: far off, three mountain-tops,
Three silent pinnacles of agèd snow,
Stood sunset-flush'd: and, dew'd with showery drops,
Up-clomb the shadowy pine above the woven copse.

The charmèd sunset linger'd low adown
In the red West: thro' mountain clefts the dale   20
Was seen far inland, and the yellow down
Border'd with palm, and many a winding vale

21 down: open hilly land.

And meadow, set with slender galingale;
A land where all things always seem'd the same!
And round about the keel with faces pale,
Dark faces pale against that rosy flame,
The mild-eyed melancholy Lotos-eaters came.

Branches they bore of that enchanted stem,
Laden with flower and fruit, whereof they gave
To each, but whoso did receive of them   30
And taste, to him the gushing of the wave
Far far away did seem to mourn and rave
On alien shores; and if his fellow spake,
His voice was thin, as voices from the grave;
And deep-asleep he seem'd, yet all awake,
And music in his ears his beating heart did make.

They sat them down upon the yellow sand,
Between the sun and moon upon the shore;
And sweet it was to dream of Fatherland,
Of child, and wife, and slave; but evermore   40
Most weary seem'd the sea, weary the oar,
Weary the wandering fields of barren foam.
Then someone said, "We will return no more,"
And all at once they sang, "Our island home
Is far beyond the wave; we will no longer roam."

CHORIC SONG

I

There is sweet music here that softer falls
Than petals from blown roses on the grass,
Or night-dews on still waters between walls
Of shadowy granite, in a gleaming pass;
Music that gentlier on the spirit lies,   50
Than tir'd eyelids upon tir'd eyes;
Music that brings sweet sleep down from the
    blissful skies.
Here are cool mosses deep,
And thro' the moss the ivies creep,

And in the stream the long-leaved flowers weep,
And from the craggy ledge the poppy hangs in sleep.

II

Why are we weigh'd upon with heaviness,
And utterly consumed with sharp distress,
While all things else have rest from weariness?
All things have rest: why should we toil alone,   60
We only toil, who are the first of things,
And make perpetual moan,
Still from one sorrow to another thrown:
Nor ever fold our wings,
And cease from wanderings,
Nor steep our brows in slumber's holy balm;
Nor harken what the inner spirit sings,
"There is no joy but calm!"
Why should we only toil, the roof and crown of things?

III

Lo! in the middle of the wood,   70
The folded leaf is woo'd from out the bud
With winds upon the branch, and there
Grows green and broad, and takes no care,
Sun-steep'd at noon, and in the moon
Nightly dew-fed; and turning yellow
Falls, and floats adown the air.
Lo! sweeten'd with the summer light,
The full-juiced apple, waxing over-mellow,
Drops in a silent autumn night.
All its allotted length of days,   80
The flower ripens in its place,
Ripens and fades, and falls, and hath no toil,
Fast-rooted in the fruitful soil.

IV

Hateful is the dark-blue sky,
Vaulted o'er the dark-blue sea.
Death is the end of life; ah, why
Should life all labour be?

Let us alone. Time driveth onward fast,
And in a little while our lips are dumb.
Let us alone. What is it that will last? 90
All things are taken from us, and become
Portions and parcels of the dreadful Past.
Let us alone. What pleasure can we have
To war with evil? Is there any peace
In ever climbing up the climbing wave?
All things have rest, and ripen toward the grave
In silence; ripen, fall, and cease:
Give us long rest or death, dark death, or dreamful
    ease.

V

How sweet it were, hearing the downward stream
With half-shut eyes ever to seem 100
Falling asleep in a half-dream!
To dream and dream, like yonder amber light,
Which will not leave the myrrh-bush on the height;
To hear each other's whispered speech;
Eating the Lotos day by day,
To watch the crisping ripples on the beach,
And tender curving lines of creamy spray;
To lend our hearts and spirits wholly
To the influence of mild-minded melancholy;
To muse and brood and live again in memory, 110
With those old faces of our infancy
Heap'd over with a mound of grass,
Two handfuls of white dust, shut in an urn of brass!

VI

Dear is the memory of our wedded lives,
And dear the last embraces of our wives
And their warm tears; but all hath suffered change:
For surely now our household hearts are cold:
Our sons inherit us: our looks are strange:
And we should come like ghosts to trouble joy.

106 crisping: curling.

Or else the island princes over-bold 120
Have eat our substance, and the minstrel sings
Before them of the ten years' war in Troy,
And our great deeds, as half-forgotten things.
Is there confusion in the little isle?
Let what is broken so remain.
The gods are hard to reconcile:
'Tis hard to settle order once again.
There *is* confusion worse than death,
Trouble on trouble, pain on pain,
Long labour unto aged breath, 130
Sore task to hearts worn out by many wars
And eyes grown dim with gazing on the pilot-stars.

VII

But, propt on beds of amaranth and moly,
How sweet (while warm airs lull us, blowing lowly)
With half-dropt eyelid still,
Beneath a heaven dark and holy,
To watch the long bright river drawing slowly
His waters from the purple hill—
To hear the dewy echoes calling
From cave to cave thro' the thick-twined vine— 140
To watch the emerald-coloured water falling
Thro' many a wov'n acanthus-wreath divine!
Only to hear and see the far-off sparkling brine,
Only to hear were sweet, stretch'd out beneath the pine.

VIII

The Lotos blooms below the barren peak:
The Lotos blows by every winding creek:
All day the wind breathes low with mellower tone:
Thro' every hollow cave and alley lone
Round and round the spicy downs the yellow
    Lotos-dust is blown.
We have had enough of action, and of motion we, 150
Roll'd to starboard, roll'd to larboard, when the surge
    was seething free,

Where the wallowing monster spouted his foam-
  fountains in the sea.
Let us swear an oath, and keep it with an equal mind,
In the hollow Lotos-land to live and lie reclined
On the hills like Gods together, careless of mankind.
For they lie beside their nectar, and the bolts are
  hurl'd
Far below them in the valleys, and the clouds are
  lightly curl'd
Round their golden houses, girdled with the gleaming
  world:
Where they smile in secret, looking over wasted lands,
Blight and famine, plague and earthquake, roaring
  deeps and fiery sands,   160
Clanging fights, and flaming towns, and sinking ships,
  and praying hands.
But they smile, they find a music centred in a doleful
  song
Steaming up, a lamentation and an ancient tale of
  wrong,
Like a tale of little meaning tho' the words are
  strong;
Chanted from an ill-used race of men that cleave the
  soil,
Sow the seed, and reap the harvest with enduring toil,
Storing yearly little dues of wheat, and wine and oil;
Till they perish and they suffer—some, 'tis whisper'd—
  down in hell
Suffer endless anguish, others in Elysian valleys dwell,
Resting weary limbs at last on beds of asphodel.   170
Surely, surely, slumber is more sweet than toil, the shore
Than labour in the deep mid-ocean, wind and wave
  and oar;
O rest ye, brother mariners, we will not wander more.

Dover Beach

MATTHEW ARNOLD

The sea is calm to-night.
The tide is full, the moon lies fair
Upon the straits;—on the French coast the light
Gleams and is gone; the cliffs of England stand,
Glimmering and vast, out in the tranquil bay.
Come to the window, sweet is the night-air!

Only, from the long line of spray
Where the sea meets the moon-blanch'd land,
Listen! you hear the grating roar
Of pebbles which the waves draw back, and fling,   10
At their return, up the high strand,
Begin, and cease, and then again begin,
With tremulous cadence slow, and bring
The eternal note of sadness in.

Sophocles long ago
Heard it on the Ægæan, and it brought
Into his mind the turbid ebb and flow
Of human misery; we
Find also in the sound a thought,
Hearing it by this distant northern sea.   20

The Sea of Faith
Was once, too, at the full, and round earth's shore
Lay like the folds of a bright girdle furl'd.
But now I only hear
Its melancholy, long, withdrawing roar,
Retreating, to the breath
Of the night-wind, down the vast edges drear
And naked shingles of the world.

Ah, love, let us be true
To one another! for the world, which seems   30
To lie before us like a land of dreams,
So various, so beautiful, so new,
Hath really neither joy, nor love, nor light,
Nor certitude, nor peace, nor help for pain;
And we are here as on a darkling plain
Swept with confused alarms of struggle and flight,
Where ignorant armies clash by night.

Philomela

MATTHEW ARNOLD

Hark! ah, the nightingale—
The tawny-throated!
Hark, from that moonlit cedar what a burst!
What triumph! hark!—what pain!

O wanderer from a Grecian shore,
Still, after many years, in distant lands,
Still nourishing in thy bewilder'd brain
That wild, unquench'd, deep-sunken, old-world pain—
Say, will it never heal?
And can this fragrant lawn   10
With its cool trees, and night,
And the sweet, tranquil Thames,
And moonshine, and the dew,
To thy rack'd heart and brain
Afford no balm?

Dost thou to-night behold,
Here, through the moonlight on this English grass,
The unfriendly palace in the Thracian wild?
Dost thou again peruse
With hot cheeks and sear'd eyes   20
The too clear web, and thy dumb sister's shame?
Dost thou once more assay

Thy flight, and feel come over thee,
Poor fugitive, the feathery change
Once more, and once more seem to make resound
With love and hate, triumph and agony,
Lone Daulis, and the high Cephissian vale?
Listen, Eugenia—
How thick the bursts come crowding through the leaves!
Again—thou hearest? 30
Eternal passion!
Eternal pain!

When lilacs last in the dooryard bloom'd

WALT WHITMAN

1

When lilacs last in the dooryard bloom'd,
And the great star early droop'd in the western sky in the night,
I mourn'd, and yet shall mourn with ever-returning spring.

Ever-returning spring, trinity sure to me you bring,
Lilac blooming perennial and drooping star in the west,
And thought of him I love.

2

O powerful western fallen star!
O shades of night—O moody, tearful night!
O great star disappear'd—O the black murk that hides the star!
O cruel hands that hold me powerless—O helpless soul of me! 10
O harsh surrounding cloud that will not free my soul.

3

In the dooryard fronting an old farm-house near the whitewash'd palings,
Stands the lilac-bush tall-growing with heart-shaped leaves of rich green,
With many a pointed blossom rising delicate, with the perfume strong I love,

With every leaf a miracle—and from this bush in the dooryard,
With delicate-color'd blossoms and heart-shaped leaves of rich
    green,
A sprig with its flower I break.

4

In the swamp in secluded recesses,
A shy and hidden bird is warbling a song.

Solitary the thrush,   20
The hermit withdrawn to himself, avoiding the settlements,
Sings by himself a song.

Song of the bleeding throat,
Death's outlet song of life, (for well dear brother I know,
If thou wast not granted to sing thou would'st surely die.)

5

Over the breast of the spring, the land, amid cities,
Amid lanes and through old woods, where lately the violets peep'd
    from the ground, spotting the gray debris,
Amid the grass in the fields each side of the lanes, passing the
    endless grass,
Passing the yellow-spear'd wheat, every grain from its shroud in
    the dark-brown fields uprisen,
Passing the apple-tree blows of white and pink in the orchards,   30
Carrying a corpse to where it shall rest in the grave,
Night and day journeys a coffin.

6

Coffin that passes through lanes and streets,
Through day and night with the great cloud darkening the land,
With the pomp of the inloop'd flags with the cities draped in black,
With the show of the States themselves as of crape-veil'd women
    standing,
With processions long and winding and the flambeaus of the night,
With the countless torches lit, with the silent sea of faces and the
    unbared heads,
With the waiting depot, the arriving coffin, and the somber faces,

With dirges through the night, with the thousand voices rising
    strong and solemn, 40
With all the mournful voices of the dirges pour'd around the coffin,
The dim-lit churches and the shuddering organs—where amid these
    you journey,
With the tolling tolling bells' perpetual clang,
Here, coffin that slowly passes,
I give you my sprig of lilac.

7

(Nor for you, for one alone,
Blossoms and branches green to coffins all I bring,
For fresh as the morning, thus would I chant a song for you O sane
    and sacred death.
All over bouquets of roses,
O death, I cover you over with roses and early lilies, 50
But mostly and now the lilac that blooms the first,
Copious I break, I break the sprigs from the bushes,
With loaded arms I come, pouring for you,
For you and the coffins all of you O death.)

8

O western orb sailing the heaven,
Now I know what you must have meant as a month since I walk'd,
As I walk'd in silence the transparent shadowy night,
As I saw you had something to tell as you bent to me night after
    night,
As you droop'd from the sky low down as if to my side, (while the
    other stars all look'd on,)
As we wander'd together the solemn night, (for something I know
    not what kept me from sleep,) 60
As the night advanced, and I saw on the rim of the west how full
    you were of woe,
As I stood on the rising ground in the breeze in the cool
    transparent night,
As I watch'd where you pass'd and was lost in the netherward
    black of the night,
As my soul in its trouble dissatisfied sank, as where you sad orb,
Concluded, dropt in the night, and was gone.

9

Sing on there in the swamp,
O singer bashful and tender, I hear your notes, I hear your call,
I hear, I come presently, I understand you,
But a moment I linger, for the lustrous star has detain'd me,
The star my departing comrade holds and detains me. 70

10

O how shall I warble myself for the dead one there I loved?
And how shall I deck my song for the large sweet soul that has gone?
And what shall my perfume be for the grave of him I love?

Sea-winds blown from east and west,
Blown from the Eastern sea and blown from the Western sea, till there on the prairies meeting,
These and with these and the breath of my chant,
I'll perfume the grave of him I love.

11

O what shall I hang on the chamber walls?
And what shall the pictures be that I hang on the walls,
To adorn the burial-house of him I love? 80
Pictures of growing spring and farms and homes,
With the Fourth-month eve at sundown, and the gray smoke lucid and bright,
With floods of the yellow gold of the gorgeous, indolent, sinking sun, burning, expanding the air,
With the fresh sweet herbage under foot, and the pale green leaves of the trees prolific,
In the distance the flowing glaze, the breast of the river, with a wind-dapple here and there,
With ranging hills on the banks, with many a line against the sky, and shadows,
And the city at hand with dwellings so dense, and stacks of chimneys,
And all the scenes of life and the workshops, and the workmen homeward returning.

12

Lo, body and soul—this land,
My own Manhattan with spires, and the sparkling and hurrying
    tides, and the ships, 90
The varied and ample land, the South and the North in the light,
    Ohio's shores and flashing Missouri,
And ever the far-spreading prairies cover'd with grass and corn.

Lo, the most excellent sun so calm and haughty,
The violet and purple morn with just-felt breezes,
The gentle soft-born measureless light,
The miracle spreading bathing all, the fulfill'd noon,
The coming eve delicious, the welcome night and the stars,
Over my cities shining all, enveloping man and land.

13

Sing on, sing on you gray-brown bird,
Sing from the swamps, the recesses, pour your chant from the
    bushes, 100
Limitless out of the dusk, out of the cedars and pines.
Sing on dearest brother, warble your reedy song,
Loud human song, with voice of uttermost woe.

O wild and loose to my soul—O wondrous singer!
You only I hear—yet the star holds me, (but will soon depart,)
Yet the lilac with mastering odor holds me.

14

Now while I sat in the day and look'd forth,
In the close of the day with its light and the fields of spring, and
    the farmers preparing their crops,
In the large unconscious scenery of my land with its lakes and
    forests, 110
In the heavenly aerial beauty, (after the perturb'd winds and the
    storms,)
Under the arching heavens of the afternoon swift passing, and the
    voices of children and women,
The many-moving sea-tides, and I saw the ships how they sail'd,

And the summer approaching with richness, and the fields all
    busy with labor,
And the infinite separate houses, how they all went on, each with
    its meals and minutia of daily usages,
And the streets how their throbbings throbb'd, and the cities pent—
    lo, then and there,
Falling upon them all and among them all, enveloping me with the
    rest,
Appear'd the cloud, appear'd the long black trail,
And I knew death, its thought, and the sacred knowledge of death.

Then with the knowledge of death as walking one side of me,   120
And the thought of death close-walking the other side of me,
And I in the middle as with companions, and as holding the hands
    of companions,
I fled forth to the hiding receiving night that talks not,
Down to the shores of the water, the path by the swamp in the
    dimness,
To the solemn shadowy cedars and ghostly pines so still.

And the singer so shy to the rest receiv'd me,
The gray-brown bird I know receiv'd us comrades three,
And he sang the carol of death, and a verse for him I love.

From deep secluded recesses,
From the fragrant cedars and the ghostly pines so still,   130
Came the carol of the bird.

And the charm of the carol rapt me,
As I held as if by their hands my comrades in the night,
And the voice of my spirit tallied the song of the bird.

Come lovely and soothing death,
Undulate round the world, serenely arriving, arriving,
In the day, in the night, to all, to each,
Sooner or later delicate death.

Prais'd be the fathomless universe,
For life and joy, and for objects and knowledge curious,   140

And for love, sweet love—but praise! praise! praise!
For the sure-enwinding arms of cool-enfolding death.

Dark mother always gliding near with soft feet,
Have none chanted for thee a chant of fullest welcome?
Then I chant it for thee, I glorify thee above all,
I bring thee a song that when thou must indeed come, come
    unfalteringly.

Approach strong deliveress,
When it is so, when thou hast taken them I joyously sing the dead,
Lost in the loving floating ocean of thee,
Laved in the flood of thy bliss O death.   150

From me to thee glad serenades,
Dances for thee I propose saluting thee, adornments and feastings
    for thee,
And the sights of the open landscape and the high-spread sky are
    fitting,
And life and the fields, and the huge and thoughtful night.

The night in silence under many a star,
The ocean shore and the husky whispering wave whose voice I
    know,
And the soul turning to thee O vast and well-veil'd death,
And the body gratefully nestling close to thee.

Over the tree-tops I float thee a song,
Over the rising and sinking waves, over the myriad fields and the
    prairies wide,   160
Over the dense-pack'd cities all and the teeming wharves and ways,
I float this carol with joy, with joy to thee O death.

15

To the tally of my soul,
Loud and strong kept up the gray-brown bird,
With pure deliberate notes spreading filling the night.

Loud in the pines and cedars dim,
Clear in the freshness moist and the swamp-perfume,
And I with my comrades there in the night.

While my sight that was bound in my eyes unclosed,
As to long panoramas of visions. 170

And I saw askant the armies,
I saw as in noiseless dreams hundreds of battle-flags,
Borne through the smoke of the battles and pierc'd with missiles
    I saw them,
And carried hither and yon through the smoke, and torn and
    bloody,
And at last but a few shreds left on the staffs, (and all in silence,)
And the staffs all splinter'd and broken.

I saw battle-corpses, myriads of them,
And the white skeletons of young men, I saw them,
I saw the debris and debris of all the slain soldiers of the war,
But I saw they were not as was thought, 180
They themselves were fully at rest, they suffer'd not,
The living remain'd and suffer'd, the mother suffer'd,
And the wife and the child and the musing comrade suffer'd,
And the armies that remain'd suffer'd.

16

Passing the visions, passing the night,
Passing, unloosing the hold of my comrades' hands,
Passing the song of the hermit bird and the tallying song of my soul,
Victorious song, death's outlet song, yet varying ever-altering song,
As low and wailing, yet clear the notes, rising and falling, flooding
    the night,
Sadly sinking and fainting, as warning and warning, and yet again
    bursting with joy, 190
Covering the earth and filling the spread of the heaven,
As that powerful psalm in the night I heard from recesses,
Passing, I leave thee lilac with heart-shaped leaves,
I leave thee there in the dooryard, blooming, returning with spring.

I cease from my song for thee,
From my gaze on thee in the west, fronting the west, communing
    with thee,
O comrade lustrous with silver face in the night.
Yet each to keep and all, retrievements out of the night,

The song, the wondrous chant of the gray-brown bird,
And the tallying chant, the echo arous'd in my soul,   200
With the lustrous and drooping star with the countenance full
    of woe,
With the holders holding my hand nearing the call of the bird,
Comrades mine and I in the midst, and their memory ever to keep,
    for the dead I loved so well,
For the sweetest, wisest soul of all my days and lands—and this
    for his dear sake,
Lilac and star and bird twined with the chant of my soul,
There in the fragrant pines and the cedars dusk and dim.

Musée Des Beaux Arts

W. H. AUDEN

About suffering they were never wrong,
The Old Masters: how well they understood
Its human position; how it takes place
While someone else is eating or opening a window or just
    walking dully along;
How, when the aged are reverently, passionately waiting
For the miraculous birth, there always must be
Children who did not specially want it to happen, skating
On a pond at the edge of the wood:
They never forgot   10
That even the dreadful martyrdom must run its course
Anyhow in a corner, some untidy spot
Where the dogs go on with their doggy life and the
    torturer's horse
Scratches its innocent behind on a tree.

In Brueghel's *Icarus*, for instance: how everything turns away
Quite leisurely from the disaster; the ploughman may

---

16 Brueghel: Pieter Brueghel the elder (1520–69), Flemish painter. Icarus: According to Greek legend, Daedalus built wings by means of which he and his son Icarus escaped from the labyrinth in Crete. Icarus flew too close to the sun and was drowned when the wax of his wings melted.

Have heard the splash, the forsaken cry,
But for him it was not an important failure; the sun shone
As it had to on the white legs disappearing into the green   20
Water; and the expensive delicate ship that must have seen
Something amazing, a boy falling out of the sky,
Had somewhere to get to and sailed calmly on.

In Memory of W. B. Yeats[1]
(d. Jan. 1939)

W. H. AUDEN

I

He disappeared in the dead of winter:
The brooks were frozen, the airports almost deserted,
And snow disfigured the public statues;
The mercury sank in the mouth of the dying day.
O all the instruments agree
The day of his death was a dark cold day.

Far from his illness
The wolves ran on through the evergreen forests,
The peasant river was untempted by the fashionable quays;
By mourning tongues   10
The death of the poet was kept from his poems.

But for him it was his last afternoon as himself,
An afternoon of nurses and rumours;
The provinces of his body revolted,
The squares of his mind were empty,
Silence invaded the suburbs,
The current of his feeling failed: he became his admirers.

---

[1] Note: This is the first of a group of three poems published under the same title.

Now he is scattered among a hundred cities
And wholly given over to unfamiliar affections;
To find his happiness in another kind of wood   20
And be punished under a foreign code of conscience.
The words of a dead man
Are modified in the guts of the living.

But in the importance and noise of tomorrow
When the brokers are roaring like beasts on the floor of
   the Bourse,
And the poor have the sufferings to which they are
   fairly accustomed,
And each in the cell of himself is almost convinced of
   his freedom;
A few thousand will think of this day
As one thinks of a day when one did something slightly
   unusual.

O all the instruments agree
The day of his death was a dark cold day.

After the Funeral
(In memory of Ann Jones)

DYLAN THOMAS

After the funeral, mule praises, brays,
Windshake of sailshaped ears, muffle-toed tap
Tap happily of one peg in the thick
Grave's foot, blinds down the lids, the teeth in black,
The spittled eyes, the salt ponds in the sleeves,
Morning smack of the spade that wakes up sleep,
Shakes a desolate boy who slits his throat
In the dark of the coffin and sheds dry leaves,
That breaks one bone to light with a judgment clout,
After the feast of tear-stuffed time and thistles   10

In a room with a stuffed fox and a stale fern,
I stand, for this memorial's sake, alone
In the snivelling hours with dead, humped Ann
Whose hooded, fountain heart once fell in puddles
Round the parched worlds of Wales and drowned each sun
(Though this for her is a monstrous image blindly
Magnified out of praise; her death was a still drop;
She would not have me sinking in the holy
Flood of her heart's fame; she would lie dumb and deep
And need no druid of her broken body).   20
But I, Ann's bard on a raised hearth, call all
The seas to service that her wood-tongued virtue
Babble like a bellbuoy over the hymning heads,
Bow down the walls of the ferned and foxy woods
That her love sing and swing through a brown chapel,
Bless her bent spirit with four, crossing birds.
Her flesh was meek as milk, but this skyward statue
With the wild breast and blessed and giant skull
Is carved from her in a room with a wet window
In a fiercely mourning house in a crooked year.   30
I know her scrubbed and sour humble hands
Lie with religion in their cramp, her threadbare
Whisper in a damp word, her wits drilled hollow,
Her fist of a face died clenched on a round pain;
And sculptured Ann is seventy years of stone.
These cloud-sopped, marble hands, this monumental
Argument of the hewn voice, gesture and psalm
Storm me forever over her grave until
The stuffed lung of the fox twitch and cry Love
And the strutting fern lay seeds on the black sill.   40

VIII

Individual Poets

From a purely theoretical aesthetic point of view, every poem stands alone, a complete, self-contained unit; and a few modern critics have maintained this view so rigidly as to discourage any reference to the poet or to any other work than the single poem under consideration. No human activities, however, including the aesthetic, are of quite such absolute purity or singleness as this view implies. The reader does not come to the poem as a pure perceiver and absorber; he comes to it with his own temperament, interests, prejudices. Equally, the poet makes his poem not entirely as a pure, isolated creator but as a creator with his own temperament, interests, and prejudices; and every poet speaks his own special language. The successful poem is nearly always both a self-contained whole and part of a larger body of work. Hence, while a poem is ultimately to be read for its own sake as an aesthetic entity, it often gains from being read, and sometimes needs to be read, in the light of the author's other work as well. His idiom may be so unusual that we need to get used to it before we can fully appreciate the separate poems; certain symbols may recur in different contexts and may become clearer or richer to the reader who can follow them from poem to poem. The individual flavor of a writer's style in a particular poem can often be more clearly recognized when we see how it has been adapted elsewhere to his changing themes and moods. In painting, a one-man exhibition incalculably deepens the spectator's appreciation of the individual pictures, and so it is with the equivalent of a one-man show for musical composers, and for poets.

The present chapter, then, is composed of groups of poems by some writers who particularly gain from being read in bulk and who have not been so represented—that is, by long poems or sequences of short ones—in earlier chapters. What can appear in any anthology is, of course, only a taste. If the taste pleases or interests the reader, both collected and selected editions of almost all the poets in this volume are available, often at very modest prices for the purchaser, as well as in most libraries for the borrower.

JOHN DONNE

Song

Go and catch a falling star,
    Get with child a mandrake root,
Tell me where all past years are,
    Or who cleft the Devil's foot,
Teach me to hear mermaids singing,
Or to keep off envy's stinging,
      And find
      What wind
Serves to advance an honest mind.

If thou be'st borne to strange sights,   10
    Things invisible to see,
Ride ten thousand days and nights,
    Till age snow white hairs on thee;
Thou, when thou return'st, wilt tell me
All strange wonders that befell thee,
      And swear
      Nowhere
Lives a woman true, and fair.

2 mandrake (mandragora): a plant that has been the subject of many superstitions. It has a forked root which is said to resemble the human form.

>   If thou findst one, let me know,
>   Such a pilgrimage were sweet;—   20
>   Yet do not, I would not go,
>   Though at next door we might meet;
>   Though she were true, when you met her,
>   And last, till you write your letter,
>   Yet she
>   Will be
>   False, ere I come, to two, or three.

The Indifferent

I can love both fair and brown,
Her whom abundance melts, and her whom want betrays,
Her who loves loneness best, and her who masks and plays,
Her whom the country form'd, and whom the town,
Her who believes, and her who tries,
Her who still weeps with spongy eyes,
And her who is dry cork and never cries;
I can love her, and her, and you, and you,
I can love any, so she be not true.

Will no other vice content you?   10
Will it not serve your turn to do as did your mothers?
Or have you all old vices spent, and now would find out others?
Or doth a fear, that men are true, torment you?
O we are not, be not you so.
Let me, and do you, twenty know.
Rob me, but bind me not, and let me go.
Must I, who came to travail thorough you,
Grow your fix'd subject, because you are true?

Venus heard me sigh this song,
And by love's sweetest part, variety, she swore   20
She heard not this till now; and that it should be so no more.
She went, examin'd, and return'd ere long,
And said, "Alas, some two or three

Poor heretics in love there be,
Which think to stablish dangerous constancy.
But I have told them, 'Since you will be true,
You shall be true to them, who are false to you.' "

The Bait

Come live with me, and be my love,
And we will some new pleasures prove
Of golden sands, and crystal brooks:
With silken lines, and silver hooks.

There will the river whispering run
Warm'd by thy eyes, more than the Sun;
And there the enamour'd fish will stay,
Begging themselves they may betray.

When thou wilt swim in that live bath,
Each fish, which every channel hath,   10
Will amorously to thee swim,
Gladder to catch thee, than thou him.

If thou to be so seen be'st loath
By Sun, or Moon, thou dark'nest both,
And if myself have leave to see,
I need not their light, having thee.

Let others freeze with angling reeds,
And cut their legs with shells and weeds,
Or treacherously poor fish beset,
With strangling snare, or windowy net: 20

Let coarse bold hands, from slimy nest
The bedded fish in banks out-wrest;
Or curious traitors, sleave-silk flies,
Bewitch poor fishes' wand'ring eyes.

17 reeds: rods.   *23* sleave-silk flies: artificial flies made of floss or raw silk.

For thee, thou need'st no such deceit,
For thou thyself art thine own bait;
That fish that is not catch'd thereby,
Alas, is wiser far than I.

The Flea

Mark but this flea, and mark in this
How little that which thou deny'st me is;
Me it suck'd first, and now sucks thee,
And in this flea our two bloods mingled be;
Confess it: this cannot be said
A sin, or shame, or loss of maidenhead;
   Yet this enjoys before it woo,
     And pamper'd swells with one blood made of two,
   And this, alas, is more than we would do.

Oh stay, three lives in one flea spare,   10
Where we almost, yea, more than married are.
This flea is you and I, and this
Our marriage bed, and marriage temple is;
Though parents grudge, and you, we're met
And cloister'd in these living walls of jet.
   Though use make you apt to kill me,
   Let not to that, self-murder added be,
   And sacrilege, three sins in killing three.

Cruel and sudden, hast thou since
Purpled thy nail in blood of innocence?   20
In what could this flea guilty be,
Except in that drop which it suck'd from thee?
Yet thou triumph'st, and say'st that thou
Find'st not thyself, nor me, the weaker now:
   'Tis true; then learn how false, fears be:
   Just so much honour, when thou yield'st to me,
   Will waste, as this flea's death took life from thee.

The Triple Fool

I am two fools, I know,
For loving, and for saying so
   In whining Poetry;
But where's that wiseman, that would not be I,
   If she would not deny?
Then, as the earth's inward narrow crooked lanes
Do purge sea-water's fretful salt away,
   I thought, if I could draw my pains,
Through Rime's vexation, I should them allay:
Grief brought to numbers cannot be so fierce,   10
For he tames it, that fetters it in verse.

   But when I have done so,
Some man, his art and voice to show,
   Doth set and sing my pain,
And, by delighting many, frees again
   Grief, which verse did restrain.
To Love and Grief tribute of Verse belongs,
But not of such as pleases when 'tis read;
   Both are increasèd by such songs:
For both their triumphs so are publishèd,   20
And I, which was two fools, do so grow three;
Who are a little wise, the best fools be.

14 set: set to music.

The Ecstasy

Where, like a pillow on a bed,
   A pregnant bank swell'd up, to rest
The violet's reclining head,
   Sat we two, one another's best.

Our hands were firmly cèmented
   With a fast balm, which thence did spring;

Our eye-beams twisted, and did thread
  Our eyes upon one double string;

So to entergraft our hands, as yet
  Was all the means to make us one,
And pictures in our eyes to get
  Was all our propagation.

As, 'twixt two equal armies, Fate
  Suspends uncertain victory,
Our souls (which to advance their state
  Were gone out) hung 'twixt her and me.

And whilst our souls negotiate there,
  We like sepulchral statues lay;
All day, the same our postures were,
  And we said nothing, all the day.

If any, so by love refin'd
  That he soul's language understood,
And by good love were grown all mind,
  Within convenient distance stood,

He (though he knew not which soul spake,
  Because both meant, both spake the same)
Might thence a new concoction take
  And part far purer than he came.

"This ecstasy doth unperplex,"
  We said, "and tell us what we love:
We see by this it was not sex;
  We see we saw not what did move;

But as all several souls contain
  Mixture of things, they know not what,
Love these mix'd souls doth mix again,
  And makes both one, each this and that.

---

27 concoction: a purification by heat, as of metals in a furnace.

A single violet transplant,—
  The strength, the colour, and the size,
All which before was poor, and scant,
  Redoubles still, and multiplies.   40

When love, with one another so
  Interinanimates two souls,
That abler soul, which thence doth flow,
  Defects of loneliness controls.

We then, who are this new soul, know
  Of what we are composed and made,
For th' atomies of which we grow
  Are souls, whom no change can invade.

But oh alas, so long, so far
  Our bodies why do we forbear?   50
They are ours, though they are not we; we are
  The intelligences, they the sphere.

We owe them thanks, because they thus
  Did us to us at first convey,
Yielded their forces, sense, to us,
  Nor are dross to us, but allay.

On man heaven's influence works not so,
  But that it first imprints the air;
So soul into the soul may flow,
  Though it to body first repair.   60

As our blood labours to beget
  Spirits, as like souls as it can,
Because such fingers need to knit
  That subtle knot which makes us man,

So must pure lovers' souls descend
  To affections, and to faculties,

56 allay: alloy.   66 affections: passions. faculties: powers of action.

>   Which sense may reach and apprehend,
>   Else a great Prince in prison lies.
>
>   To our bodies turn we then, that so
>   Weak men on love reveal'd may look;
>   Love's mysteries in souls do grow,
>   But yet the body is his book.
>
>   And if some lover, such as we,
>   Have heard this dialogue of one,
>   Let him still mark us, he shall see
>   Small change, when we are to bodies gone."

74 dialogue of one: two speaking as one.

The Good-Morrow

> I wonder, by my troth, what thou and I
> Did, till we lov'd? Were we not wean'd till then?
> But suck'd on country pleasures, childishly?
> Or snorted we in the Seven Sleepers' den?
> 'Twas so; but this, all pleasures fancies be:
> If ever any beauty I did see,
> Which I desir'd, and got, 'twas but a dream of thee.
>
> And now good-morrow to our waking souls,
> Which watch not one another out of fear;
> For love, all love of other sights controls,
> And makes one little room, an everywhere.
> Let sea-discoverers to new worlds have gone,
> Let maps to others, worlds on worlds have shown,
> Let us possess one world, each hath one, and is one.
>
> My face in thine eye, thine in mine appears,
> And true plain hearts do in the faces rest;

4 The Seven Sleepers of Ephesus, legendary Christians fleeing from persecution, hid in a cave, were walled in, and slept till they were rescued two hundred years later.

Where can we find two better hemispheres,
Without sharp North, without declining West?
Whatever dies, was not mix'd equally;
If our two loves be one, or, thou and I   20
Love so alike, that none do slacken, none can die.

21 none: neither.

The Sun Rising

Busy old fool, unruly sun,
    Why dost thou thus,
Through windows, and through curtains, call on us?
Must to thy motions lovers' seasons run?
    Saucy pedantic wretch, go chide
    Late schoolboys and sour prentices,
  Go tell court-huntsmen that the King will ride,
  Call country ants to harvest offices;
Love, all alike, no season knows nor clime,
Nor hours, days, months, which are the rags of time.   10

    Thy beams, so reverend and strong
    Why shouldst thou think?
I could eclipse and cloud them with a wink,
But that I would not lose her sight so long.
    If her eyes have not blinded thine,
    Look, and to-morrow late tell me,
  Whether both the Indias of spice and mine
  Be where thou leftst them, or lie here with me.
Ask for those Kings whom thou saw'st yesterday,
And thou shalt hear: "All here in one bed lay."   20

    She is all States, and all Princes I;
    Nothing else is:
Princes do but play us; compar'd to this,
All honour's mimic, all wealth alchemy.

17 The East Indies, associated with spice, and the West Indies, associated by Donne elsewhere with gold mines.

Thou, Sun, art half as happy as we,
In that the world's contracted thus;
Thine age asks ease, and since thy duties be
To warm the world, that's done in warming us.
Shine here to us, and thou art everywhere;
This bed thy centre is, these walls thy sphere.   30

The Anniversary

All Kings, and all their favourites,
All glory of honours, beauties, wits,
The Sun itself, which makes times, as they pass,
Is elder by a year, now, than it was
When thou and I first one another saw:
All other things to their destruction draw,
Only our love hath no decay;
This, no tomorrow hath, nor yesterday;
Running it never runs from us away,
But truly keeps his first, last, everlasting day.   10

Two graves must hide thine and my corse;
If one might, death were no divorce:
Alas, as well as other Princes, we
(Who Prince enough in one another be)
Must leave at last in death, these eyes, and ears,
Oft fed with true oaths, and with sweet salt tears;
But souls where nothing dwells but love
(All other thoughts being inmates) then shall prove
This, or a love increasèd there above,
When bodies to their graves, souls from their graves
  remove.   20

And then we shall be throughly blest,
But we no more than all the rest;
Here upon earth, we are Kings, and none but we

11 corse: corpse.   *18* inmates: lodgers, not permanent dwellers.   prove: test out, or experience.

Can be such kings, nor of such subjects be:
Who is so safe as we, where none can do
Treason to us, except one of us two?
   True and false fears let us refrain,
   Let us love nobly, and live, and add again
Years and years unto years, till we attain
To write threescore; this is the second of our reign.   30

The Canonization

For God's sake hold your tongue, and let me love,
   Or chide my palsy, or my gout,
My five gray hairs, or ruin'd fortune flout,
With wealth your state, your mind with arts improve,
     Take you a course, get you a place,
     Observe his honour, or his grace,
Or the King's real, or his stamped face
   Contemplate; what you will, approve,
   So you will let me love.

Alas, alas, who's injured by my love?   10
   What merchant's ships have my sighs drown'd?
Who says my tears have overflow'd his ground?
When did my colds a forward spring remove?
     When did the heats which my veins fill
     Add one man to the plaguy bill?
Soldiers find wars, and lawyers find out still
   Litigious men, which quarrels move,
   Though she and I do love.

Call us what you will, we are made such by love;
   Call her one, me another fly,   20
We are tapers too, and at our own cost die,

---

5 course: either a course of study or a career. place: position, at court or elsewhere (often with the implication of political patronage).   7 stamped: on coins; i.e., pursue the King's favor or go and get rich.   8 approve: experience, test out.   13–14 colds . . . heats: chills and fevers of love. 15 plaguy bill: the published list of those who have died of plague.

    And we in us find the Eagle and the Dove.
        The Phoenix riddle hath more wit
        By us; we two being one, are it.
So to one neutral thing both sexes fit,
    We die and rise the same, and prove
    Mysterious by this love.

We can die by it, if not live by love,
    And if unfit for tombs and hearse
Our legend be, it will be fit for verse;   30
And if no piece of chronicle we prove,
        We'll build in sonnets pretty rooms;
        As well a well-wrought urn becomes
The greatest ashes, as half-acre tombs,
    And by these hymns, all shall approve
    Us *canoniz'd* for Love:

And thus invoke us: "You, whom reverend love
    Made one another's hermitage;
You, to whome love was peace, that now is rage;
Who did the whole world's soul contract, and drove   40
        Into the glasses of your eyes
        (So made such mirrors, and such spies,
That they did all to you epitomize)
    Countries, towns, courts: beg from above
    A pattern of your love!"

22 Eagle . . . Dove: strength and gentleness.   23 Phoenix: Since it reproduces itself, it may be considered as a union of both sexes.

A Valediction: Forbidding Mourning

    As virtuous men pass mildly away,
        And whisper to their souls, to go,
    Whilst some of their sad friends do say,
        "The breath goes now," and some say, "No":

    So let us melt, and make no noise,
        No tear-floods, nor sigh-tempests move;

'Twere profanation of our joys
    To tell the laity our love.

Moving of the earth brings harms and fears;
    Men reckon what it did and meant:
But trepidation of the spheres,
    Though greater far, is innocent.

Dull sublunary lovers' love
    (Whose soul is sense) cannot admit
Absence, because it doth remove
    Those things which elemented it.

But we by a love so much refin'd
    That ourselves know not what it is,
Inter-assurèd of the mind,
    Care less, eyes, lips, and hands to miss.

Our two souls therefore, which are one,
    Though I must go, endure not yet
A breach, but an expansïon,
    Like gold to airy thinness beat.

If they be two, they are two so
    As stiff twin compasses are two;
Thy soul, the fix'd foot, makes no show
    To move, but doth, if the other do;

And though it in the center sit,
    Yet when the other far doth roam,
It leans, and hearkens after it,
    And grows erect, as that comes home.

Such wilt thou be to me who must,
    Like the other foot, obliquely run:
Thy firmness makes my circle just,
    And makes me end where I begun.

---

9 moving of the earth: earthquake.   11 Trepidation of the spheres: according to ancient astronomy, movement in one of the heavenly spheres, believed to cause variation in the times of the equinox.   12 innocent: harmless.   24 gold beaten into gold-leaf.

The Funeral

Whoever comes to shroud me, do not harm
    Nor question much
That subtle wreath of hair, which crowns my arm;
The mystery, the sign, you must not touch,
    For 'tis my outward Soul,
Viceroy to that, which then to heaven being gone,
    Will leave this to control,
And keep these limbs, her provinces, from dissolutïon.

For if the sinewy thread my brain lets fall
    Through every part,   10
Can tie those parts, and make me one of all;
These hairs which upward grew, and strength and art
    Have from a better brain,
Can better do it; except she meant that I
    By this should know my pain,
As prisoners then are manacled, when they're condem'd to die.

Whate'er she meant by it, bury it with me,
    For since I am
Love's martyr, it might breed idolatry
If into others' hands these relics came;   20
    As 'twas humility
To afford to it all that a soul can do,
    So, 'tis some bravery,
That since you would save none of me, I bury some of you.

9 sinewy thread: the nervous system.   23 bravery: boldness.

The Blossom

Little think'st thou, poor flower,
    Whom I have watch'd six or seven days,
And seen thy birth, and seen what every hour
Gave to thy growth, thee to this height to raise,

And now dost laugh and triumph on this bough,
    Little think'st thou
That it will freeze anon, and that I shall
Tomorrow find thee fall'n, or not at all.

    Little think'st thou, poor heart,
        That labour'st yet to nestle thee,   10
And think'st by hovering here to get a part
In a forbidden or forbidding tree,
And hop'st her stiffness by long siege to bow:
    Little think'st thou,
That thou tomorrow, ere that Sun doth wake,
Must with this sun, and me, a journey take.

    But thou, which lov'st to be
        Subtle to plague thyself, wilt say:
"Alas! if you must go, what's that to me?
Here lies my business, and here I will stay: 20
You go to friends, whose love and means present
    Various content
To your eyes, ears, and tongue, and every part.
If then your body go, what need you a heart?"

    Well then, stay here; but know,
        When thou hast stay'd and done thy most,
A naked thinking heart, that makes no show,
Is, to a woman, but a kind of ghost;
How shall she know my heart; or, having none,
    Know thee for one?   30
Practise may make her know some other part,
But take my word, she doth not know a heart.

    Meet me at London, then,
        Twenty days hence, and thou shalt see
Me fresher, and more fat, by being with men,
Than if I had stay'd still with her and thee.
For God's sake, if you can, be you so too:
    I would give you
There, to another friend, whom we shall find
As glad to have my body, as my mind.   40

Twickenham Garden

Blasted with sighs, and surrounded with tears,
    Hither I come to seek the spring,
    And at mine eyes, and at mine ears,
Receive such balms as else cure every thing;
    But oh, self-traitor, I do bring
The spider love, which transubstantiates all,
    And can convert manna to gall;
And that this place may thoroughly be thought
True Paradise, I have the serpent brought.

'Twere wholesomer for me, that winter did
    Benight the glory of this place,
    And that a grave frost did forbid
These trees to laugh, and mock me to my face;
    But that I may not this disgrace
Endure, nor yet leave loving, Love, let me
    Some senseless piece of this place be;
Make me a mandrake, so I may groan here,
Or a stone fountain weeping out my year.

Hither with crystal vials, lovers, come,
    And take my tears, which are love's wine,
    And try your mistress' tears at home,
For all are false, that taste not just like mine;
    Alas, hearts do not in eyes shine,
Nor can you more judge woman's thoughts by tears,
    Than by her shadow, what she wears.
O perverse sex, where none is true but she,
Who's therefore true, because her truth kills me.

Title: Twickenham was the home of the Countess of Bedford, to whom the poem is believed to have been addressed.   17 The mandrake was supposed to groan when uprooted.

A Nocturnal upon St. Lucy's Day;
being the Shortest Day

'Tis the year's midnight, and it is the day's,
Lucy's, who scarce seven hours herself unmasks;
    The sun is spent, and now his flasks
    Send forth light squibs, no constant rays;
    The world's whole sap is sunk;
The general balm the hydroptic earth hath drunk,
Whither, as to the bed's feet, life is shrunk,
Dead and interr'd; yet all these seem to laugh,
Compar'd with me, who am their epitaph.

Study me then, you who shall lovers be   10
At the next world, that is, at the next Spring:
    For I am every dead thing,
    In whom love wrought new alchemy.
    For his art did express
A quintessence even from nothingness,
From dull privations, and lean emptiness:
He ruin'd me, and I am re-begot
Of absence, darkness, death; things which are not.

All others, from all things, draw all that's good,
Life, soul, form, spirit, whence they being have;   20
    I, by Love's limbeck, am the grave
    Of all that's nothing. Oft a flood
    Have we two wept, and so
Drown'd the whole world, us two; oft did we grow
To be two Chaoses, when we did show
Care to aught else; and often absences
Withdrew our souls, and made us carcases.

2 St. Lucy's Day: December 13 (not in fact quite the shortest day either under the old Julian calendar or now).   3 flasks: powder-horns.   4 squib: half-charges of powder used for practice by recruits (note by T. Redpath). 14 express: press out.   17 ruin'd me: destroyed me.   21 limbeck: alembic, an apparatus used in Donne's day for distilling.

But I am by her death (which word wrongs her),
Of the first nothing the Elixir grown;
>   Were I a man, that I were one 30
>   I needs must know; I should prefer,
>   If I were any beast,
Some ends, some means; yea plants, yea stones, detest,
And love; all, all, some properties invest;
If I an ordinary nothing were,
As shadow, a light and body must be here.

But I am none; nor will my Sun renew.
You lovers, for whose sake the lesser sun
>   At this time to the Goat is run
>   To fetch new lust, and give it you, 40
>   Enjoy your summer all;
Since she enjoys her long night's festival,
Let me prepare towards her, and let me call
This hour her Vigil, and her Eve, since this
Both the year's, and the day's, deep midnight is.

39 Goat: the tenth sign of the zodiac into which the sun enters in December; also the animal goat, which formerly symbolized lust.

At the round earth's imagin'd corners

At the round earth's imagin'd corners, blow
Your trumpets, Angels, and arise, arise
From death, you numberless infinities
Of souls, and to your scatter'd bodies go;
All whom the flood did, and fire shall o'erthrow,
All whom war, dearth, age, agues, tyrannies,
Despair, law, chance, hath slain, and you whose eyes
Shall behold God, and never taste death's woe.
But let them sleep, Lord, and me mourn a space;
For, if above all these my sins abound, 10

5 flood . . . fire: i.e., all who have died from the time of Noah's flood to the final destruction of the world by fire.

'Tis late to ask abundance of thy grace,
When we are there. Here on this lowly ground,
Teach me how to repent, for that's as good
As if thou hadst seal'd my pardon with thy blood.

If poisonous minerals

If poisonous minerals, and if that tree,
Whose fruit threw death on else immortal us,
If lecherous goats, if serpents envious
Cannot be damn'd; Alas, why should I be?
Why should intent or reason, born in me,
Make sins, else equal, in me more heinous?
And mercy being easy, and glorious
To God; in his stern wrath, why threatens he?
But who am I, that dare dispute with thee
O God? Oh! of thine only worthy blood,　　　　10
And my tears, make a heavenly Lethean flood,
And drown in it my sins' black memory;
That thou remember them, some claim as debt,
I think it mercy, if thou wilt forget.

1–2 tree, Whose fruit: the fatal tree in Eden.

Death, be not proud

Death, be not proud, though some have called thee
Mighty and dreadful, for thou art not so;
For those, whom thou think'st thou dost overthrow,
Die not, poor death, nor yet canst thou kill me.
From rest and sleep, which but thy pictures be,
Much pleasure; then from thee much more must flow,
And soonest our best men with thee do go,
Rest of their bones, and souls' delivery.
Thou art slave to Fate, Chance, kings, and desperate men,
And dost with poison, war, and sickness dwell;　　　　10

And poppy, or charms can make us sleep as well,
And better than thy stroke; why swell'st thou then?
One short sleep past, we wake eternally,
And death shall be no more; death, thou shalt die.

GEORGE HERBERT

The Collar

I struck the board, and cry'd, No more;
    I will abroad.
What? shall I ever sigh and pine?
My lines and life are free, free as the road,
    Loose as the wind, as large as store.
        Shall I be still in suit?
    Have I no harvest but a thorn
    To let me blood, and not restore
    What I have lost with cordial fruit?
        Sure there was wine   10
Before my sighs did dry it; there was corn
    Before my tears did drown it;
    Is the year only lost to me?
        Have I no bays to crown it?
    No flowers, no garlands gay? all blasted,
        All wasted?

    Not so, my heart: but there is fruit,
        And thou hast hands.
    Recover all thy sigh-blown age
On double pleasures: Leave thy cold dispute   20
Of what is fit, and not. Forsake thy cage,
        Thy rope of sands,
Which petty thoughts have made, and made to thee
    Good cable, to enforce and draw,
        And be thy law,

---

1 board: table.   5 store: abundance.   6 in suit: in attendance upon a superior to gain favors.   9 cordial: restorative.

While thou didst wink and wouldst not see.
  Away! take heed:
  I will abroad.
Call in thy death's-head there: tie up thy fears.
  He that forbears
    To suit and serve his need,
    Deserves his load.
But as I rav'd and grew more fierce and wild
  At every word,
  Methought I heard one calling, "Child";
  And I reply'd, "My Lord."

The Pulley

When God at first made man,
Having a glass of blessings standing by,
Let us (said he) pour on him all we can:
Let the world's riches, which dispersèd lie,
  Contract into a span.

So strength first made a way;
Then beauty flow'd, then wisdom, honour, pleasure:
When almost all was out, God made a stay,
Perceiving that, alone of all his treasure,
  Rest in the bottom lay.

For if I should (said he)
Bestow this jewel also on my creature,
He would adore my gifts instead of me,
And rest in Nature, not the God of Nature:
  So both should losers be.

Yet let him keep the rest,
But keep them with repining restlessness;
Let him be rich and weary, that at least,
If goodness lead him not, yet weariness
  May toss him to my breast.

Denial

When my devotions could not pierce
    Thy silent ears;
Then was my heart broken, as was my verse;
    My breast was full of fears
        And disorder,

My bent thoughts, like a brittle bow,
    Did fly asunder:
Each took his way; some would to pleasures go,
    Some to the wars and thunder
        Of alarms.

As good go any where, they say,
    As to benumb
Both knees and heart, in crying night and day,
    Come, come, my God, O come,
        But no hearing.

O that thou shouldst give dust a tongue
    To cry to thee,
And then not hear it crying! all day long
    My heart was in my knee,
        But no hearing.

Therefore my soul lay out of sight,
    Untun'd, unstrung:
My feeble spirit, unable to look right,
    Like a nipt blossom, hung
        Discontented.

O cheer and tune my heartless breast,
    Defer no time;
That so thy favours granting my request,
    They and my mind may chime,
        And mend my rhyme.

Peace

Sweet Peace, where dost thou dwell? I humbly crave,
    Let me once know.
I sought thee in a secret cave,
    And ask'd if Peace were there.
A hollow wind did seem to answer, "No:
    Go seek elsewhere."

I did; and going did a rainbow note:
    Surely, thought I,
This is the lace of Peace's coat:
    I will search out the matter.   10
But while I lookt, the clouds immediately
    Did break and scatter.

Then went I to a garden, and did spy
    A gallant flower,
The Crown Imperiall. Sure, said I,
    Peace at the root must dwell.
But when I digg'd, I saw a worm devour
    What show'd so well.

At length I met a rev'rend good old man,
    Whom when for Peace   20
I did demand, he thus began:
    "There was a Prince of old
At Salem dwelt, Who liv'd with good increase
    Of flock and fold.

"He sweetly liv'd; yet sweetness did not save
    His life from foes.
But after death out of His grave

---

15 Crown Imperiall: Fritillaria imperialis, a spring-blooming plant with clusters of pendent bell-shaped flowers.   22ff. Prince . . . Salem: Melchisedec, "King of Salem, which is, King of peace," in the Old Testament blessed Abraham, and was later represented as prefiguring Christ.

There sprang twelve stalks of wheat;
Which many wond'ring at, got some of those
    To plant and set.   30

"It prosper'd strangely, and did soon disperse
    Through all the earth;
For they that taste it do rehearse
    That virtue lies therein;
A secret virtue, bringing peace and mirth
    By flight of sin.

"Take of this grain, which in my garden grows,
    And grows for you;
Make bread of it; and that repose
    And peace, which ev'ry where   40
With so much earnestness you do pursue,
    Is only there."

28 twelve stalks of wheat: the twelve Apostles.

WILLIAM BLAKE

To the Muses

Whether on Ida's shady brow,
    Or in the chambers of the East,
The chambers of the sun, that now
    From ancient melody have ceas'd;

Whether in Heav'n ye wander fair,
    Or the green corners of the earth,
Or the blue regions of the air
    Where the melodious winds have birth;

Whether on crystal rocks ye rove,
    Beneath the bosom of the sea   10
Wand'ring in many a coral grove,
    Fair Nine, forsaking Poetry!

How have you left the ancient love
That bards of old enjoy'd in you!
The languid strings do scarcely move!
The sound is forc'd, the notes are few!

Mad Song

The wild winds weep,
And the night is a-cold;
Come hither, Sleep,
And my griefs unfold:
But lo! the morning peeps
Over the eastern steeps,
And the rustling birds of dawn
The earth do scorn.

Lo! to the vault
Of pavèd heaven, 10
With sorrow fraught
My notes are driven:
They strike the ear of night,
Make weep the eyes of day;
They make mad the roaring winds,
And with tempests play.

Like a fiend in a cloud,
With howling woe
After night I do crowd,
And with night will go; 20
I turn my back to the east,
From whence comforts have increas'd;
For light doth seize my brain
With frantic pain.

The Tyger
From *Songs of Experience*

Tyger! Tyger! burning bright
In the forests of the night,
What immortal hand or eye
Could frame thy fearful symmetry?

In what distant deeps or skies
Burnt the fire of thine eyes?
On what wings dare he aspire?
What the hand dare seize the fire?

And what shoulder, & what art,
Could twist the sinews of thy heart?   10
And when thy heart began to beat,
What dread hand? & what dread feet?

What the hammer? what the chain?
In what furnace was thy brain?
What the anvil? what dread grasp
Dare its deadly terrors clasp?

When the stars threw down their spears,
And water'd heaven with their tears,
Did he smile his work to see?
Did he who made the Lamb make thee?   20

Tyger! Tyger! burning bright
In the forests of the night,
What immortal hand or eye,
Dare frame thy fearful symmetry?

A Poison Tree

I was angry with my friend:
I told my wrath, my wrath did end.
I was angry with my foe:
I told it not, my wrath did grow.

And I water'd it in fears,
Night & morning with my tears;
And I sunnèd it with smiles,
And with soft deceitful wiles.

And it grew both day and night,
Till it bore an apple bright;　　　　　　　10
And my foe beheld it shine,
And he knew that it was mine,

And into my garden stole
When the night had veil'd the pole:
In the morning glad I see
My foe outstretch'd beneath the tree.

The Sick Rose

O Rose, thou art sick!
The invisible worm,
That flies in the night,
In the howling storm,

Has found out thy bed
Of crimson joy;
And his dark secret love
Does thy life destroy.

Ah Sun-flower!

Ah, Sun-flower! weary of time,
Who countest the steps of the Sun;
Seeking after that sweet golden clime,
Where the traveller's journey is done;

Where the Youth pined away with desire,
And the pale Virgin shrouded in snow,
Arise from their graves, and aspire
Where my Sun-flower wishes to go.

The Garden of Love

I went to the Garden of Love,
And saw what I never had seen:
A Chapel was built in the midst,
Where I used to play on the green.

And the gates of this Chapel were shut,
And 'Thou shalt not' writ over the door;
So I turn'd to the Garden of Love
That so many sweet flowers bore;

And I saw it was fillèd with graves,
And tomb-stones where flowers should be; 10
And Priests in black gowns were walking
    their rounds,
And binding with briars my joys & desires.

London

I wander thro' each charter'd street,
Near where the charter'd Thames does flow,
And mark in every face I meet
Marks of weakness, marks of woe.

In every cry of every Man,
In every Infant's cry of fear,
In every voice, in every ban,
The mind-forg'd manacles I hear.

How the Chimney-sweeper's cry
Every black'ning church appalls; 10
And the hapless Soldier's sigh
Runs in blood down Palace walls.

But most thro' midnight streets I hear
How the youthful Harlot's curse
Blasts the newborn Infant's tear,
And blights with plagues the Marriage hearse.

The Human Abstract

Pity would be no more
If we did not make somebody Poor;
And Mercy no more could be
If all were as happy as we.

And mutual fear brings peace,
Till the selfish loves increase;
Then Cruelty knits a snare,
And spreads his baits with care.

He sits down with holy fears,
And waters the ground with tears;   10
Then Humility takes its root
Underneath his foot.

Soon spreads the dismal shade
Of Mystery over his head;
And the Catterpiller and Fly
Feed on the Mystery.

And it bears the fruit of Deceit,
Ruddy and sweet to eat;
And the Raven his nest has made
In its thickest shade.   20

The Gods of the earth and sea
Sought thro' Nature to find this Tree;
But their search was all in vain:
There grows one in the Human Brain.

From *Auguries of Innocence*

To see a World in a Grain of Sand,
And a Heaven in a Wild Flower,
Hold Infinity in the palm of your hand,
And Eternity in an hour.

From *Milton*

And did those feet in ancient time
 Walk upon England's mountains green?
And was the holy Lamb of God
 On England's pleasant pastures seen?

And did the Countenance Divine
 Shine forth upon our clouded hills?
And was Jerusalem builded here
 Among these dark Satanic Mills?

Bring me my Bow of burning gold!
 Bring me my Arrows of desire! 10
Bring me my Spear! O clouds, unfold!
 Bring me my chariot of fire!

I will not cease from Mental Fight,
 Nor shall my Sword sleep in my hand,
Till we have built Jerusalem
 In England's green & pleasant Land.

Mock on, mock on, Voltaire, Rousseau

Mock on, Mock on, Voltaire, Rousseau;
Mock on, Mock on; 'tis all in vain!
You throw the sand against the wind,
And the wind blows it back again.

And every sand becomes a Gem
Reflected in the beams divine;
Blown back they blind the mocking Eye,
But still in Israel's paths they shine.

The Atoms of Democritus
And Newton's Particles of light 10
Are sands upon the Red sea shore,
Where Israel's tents do shine so bright.

---

9 Democritus: ancient Greek philosopher who developed an atomic theory of matter.

To the Accuser who is The God of This World

From For the Sexes: The Gates of Paradise

Truly, My Satan, thou art but a Dunce,
And dost not know the Garment from the Man;
Every Harlot was a Virgin once,
Nor canst thou ever change Kate into Nan.

Tho' thou art Worshippèd by the Names Divine
Of Jesus and Jehovah, thou art still
The Son of Morn in weary Night's decline,
The lost Traveller's Dream under the Hill.

JOHN KEATS

La Belle Dame sans Merci

  O what can ail thee, knight-at-arms,
    Alone and palely loitering?
  The sedge has wither'd from the lake,
    And no birds sing.

  O what can ail thee, knight-at-arms!
    So haggard and so woe-begone?
  The squirrel's granary is full,
    And the harvest's done.

  I see a lily on thy brow,
    With anguish moist and fever dew,   10
  And on thy cheeks a fading rose
    Fast withereth too.

  I met a lady in the meads,
    Full beautiful—a faery's child,
  Her hair was long, her foot was light,
    And her eyes were wild.

Title: The beautiful lady without mercy.

I made a garland for her head,
    And bracelets too, and fragrant zone;
She look'd at me as she did love,
    And made sweet moan.

I set her on my pacing steed,
    And nothing else saw all day long,
For sidelong would she bend, and sing
    A faery's song.

She found me roots of relish sweet,
    And honey wild, and manna dew,
And sure in language strange she said—
    "I love thee true."

She took me to her elfin grot,
    And there she wept, and sigh'd full sore,
And there I shut her wild wild eyes
    With kisses four.

And there she lulled me asleep,
    And there I dream'd—Ah! woe betide!
The latest dream I ever dream'd
    On the cold hill side.

I saw pale kings and princes too,
    Pale warriors, death-pale were they all;
They cried—"La Belle Dame sans Merci
    Hath thee in thrall!"

I saw their starv'd lips in the gloam,
    With horrid warning gaped wide,
And I awoke and found me here,
    On the cold hill's side.

And this is why I sojourn here,
    Alone and palely loitering,
Though the sedge has wither'd from the lake,
    And no birds sing.

---

18 fragrant zone: girdle, presumably of flowers.

Ode to a Nightingale

1

My heart aches, and a drowsy numbness pains
   My sense, as though of hemlock I had drunk,
Or emptied some dull opiate to the drains
   One minute past, and Lethe-wards had sunk:
'Tis not through envy of thy happy lot,
   But being too happy in thine happiness,—
     That thou, light-winged Dryad of the trees,
       In some melodious plot
   Of beechen green, and shadows numberless,
     Singest of summer in full-throated ease.   10

2

O, for a draught of vintage! that hath been
   Cool'd a long age in the deep-delved earth,
Tasting of Flora and the country green,
   Dance, and Provençal song, and sunburnt mirth!
O for a beaker full of the warm South,
   Full of the true, the blushful Hippocrene,
     With beaded bubbles winking at the brim,
       And purple-stained mouth;
   That I might drink, and leave the world unseen,
     And with thee fade away into the forest dim: 20

3

Fade far away, dissolve, and quite forget
   What thou among the leaves hast never known,
The weariness, the fever, and the fret
   Here, where men sit and hear each other groan;
Where palsy shakes a few, sad, last gray hairs,
   Where youth grows pale, and spectre-thin, and dies;
     Where but to think is to be full of sorrow
       And leaden-eyed despairs,
   Where Beauty cannot keep her lustrous eyes,
     Or new Love pine at them beyond tomorrow.   30

14 Provence was the center of the revival of lyric poetry in the Middle Ages.

4

Away! away! for I will fly to thee,
  Not charioted by Bacchus and his pards,
But on the viewless wings of Poesy,
  Though the dull brain perplexes and retards:
Already with thee! tender is the night,
  And haply the Queen-Moon is on her throne,
    Cluster'd around by all her starry Fays;
      But here there is no light,
  Save what from heaven is with the breezes blown
    Through verdurous glooms and winding mossy ways.   40

5

I cannot see what flowers are at my feet,
  Nor what soft incense hangs upon the boughs,
But, in embalmed darkness, guess each sweet
  Wherewith the seasonable month endows
The grass, the thicket, and the fruit-tree wild;
  White hawthorn, and the pastoral eglantine;
    Fast fading violets cover'd up in leaves;
      And mid-May's eldest child,
  The coming musk-rose, full of dewy wine,
    The murmurous haunt of flies on summer eves.   50

6

Darkling I listen; and, for many a time
  I have been half in love with easeful Death,
Call'd him soft names in many a mused rhyme,
  To take into the air my quiet breath;
Now more than ever seems it rich to die,
  To cease upon the midnight with no pain,
    While thou art pouring forth thy soul abroad
      In such an ecstasy!
  Still wouldst thou sing, and I have ears in vain—
    To thy high requiem become a sod.   60

7

Thou wast not born for death, immortal Bird!
  No hungry generations tread thee down;
The voice I hear this passing night was heard

      In ancient days by emperor and clown:
   Perhaps the self-same song that found a path
      Through the sad heart of Ruth, when, sick for home,
         She stood in tears amid the alien corn;
            The same that oft-times hath
      Charm'd magic casements, opening on the foam
         Of perilous seas, in faery lands forlorn.   70

8

Forlorn! the very word is like a bell
   To toll me back from thee to my sole self!
Adieu! the fancy cannot cheat so well
   As she is fam'd to do, deceiving elf.
Adieu! adieu! thy plaintive anthem fades
   Past the near meadows, over the still stream,
      Up the hill-side; and now 't is buried deep
         In the next valley-glades:
   Was it a vision, or a waking dream?
      Fled is that music:—Do I wake or sleep?   80

Ode on a Grecian Urn

1

Thou still unravish'd bride of quietness,
   Thou foster-child of silence and slow time,
Sylvan historian, who canst thus express
   A flowery tale more sweetly than our rhyme:
What leaf-fring'd legend haunts about thy shape
   Of deities or mortals, or of both,
         In Tempe or the dales of Arcady?
   What men or gods are these? What maidens loth?
   What mad pursuit? What struggle to escape?
      What pipes and timbrels? What wild ecstasy?   10

2

Heard melodies are sweet, but those unheard
   Are sweeter; therefore, ye soft pipes, play on;

Not to the sensual ear, but, more endear'd,
  Pipe to the spirit ditties of no tone:
Fair youth, beneath the trees, thou canst not leave
  Thy song, nor ever can those trees be bare;
    Bold Lover, never, never canst thou kiss,
Though winning near the goal—yet, do not grieve;
  She cannot fade, though thou hast not thy bliss,
    For ever wilt thou love, and she be fair!   20

3

Ah, happy, happy boughs! that cannot shed
  Your leaves, nor ever bid the Spring adieu;
And, happy melodist, unwearied,
  For ever piping songs for ever new;
More happy love! more happy, happy love!
  For ever warm and still to be enjoy'd,
    For ever panting, and for ever young;
All breathing human passion far above,
  That leaves a heart high-sorrowful and cloy'd,
    A burning forehead, and a parching tongue.   30

4

Who are these coming to the sacrifice?
  To what green altar, O mysterious priest,
Lead'st thou that heifer lowing at the skies,
  And all her silken flanks with garlands drest?
What little town by river or sea shore,
  Or mountain-built with peaceful citadel,
    Is emptied of this folk, this pious morn?
And, little town, thy streets for evermore
  Will silent be; and not a soul to tell
    Why thou art desolate, can e'er return.   40

5

O Attic shape! Fair attitude! with brede
  Of marble men and maidens overwrought,
With forest branches and the trodden weed;
  Thou, silent form, dost tease us out of thought

---

13 sensual: sensuous.   *41 brede:* embroidery.

As doth eternity: Cold Pastoral!
   When old age shall this generation waste,
     Thou shalt remain, in midst of other woe
Than ours, a friend to man, to whom thou say'st,
   Beauty is truth, truth beauty,—that is all
     Ye know on earth, and all ye need to know.   50

To Autumn

1

Season of mists and mellow fruitfulness,
   Close bosom-friend of the maturing sun;
Conspiring with him how to load and bless
   With fruit the vines that round the thatch-eaves run;
To bend with apples the moss'd cottage-trees,
   And fill all fruit with ripeness to the core;
     To swell the gourd, and plump the hazel shells
With a sweet kernel; to set budding more,
   And still more, later flowers for the bees,
     Until they think warm days will never cease,   10
        For Summer has o'er-brimm'd their clammy cells.

2

Who hath not seen thee oft amid thy store?
   Sometimes whoever seeks abroad may find
Thee sitting careless on a granary floor,
   Thy hair soft-lifted by the winnowing wind;
Or on a half-reap'd furrow sound asleep,
   Drows'd with the fume of poppies, while thy hook
     Spares the next swath and all its twined flowers:
And sometimes like a gleaner thou dost keep
   Steady thy laden head across a brook;   20
   Or by a cyder-press, with patient look,
     Thou watchest the last oozings hours by hours.

3

Where are the songs of Spring? Ay, where are they?
   Think not of them, thou hast thy music too,—

> While barred clouds bloom the soft-dying day,
>   And touch the stubble-plains with rosy hue;
> Then in a wailful choir the small gnats mourn
>   Among the river shallows, borne aloft
>   Or sinking as the light wind lives or dies;
> And full-grown lambs loud bleat from hilly bourn; 30
>   Hedge-crickets sing; and now with treble soft
>   The redbreast whistles from a gardencroft;
> And gathering swallows twitter in the skies.

Ode on Melancholy

1

> No, no, go not to Lethe, neither twist
>   Wolf's-bane, tight-rooted, for its poisonous wine;
> Nor suffer thy pale forehead to be kiss'd
>   By nightshade, ruby grape of Proserpine;
> Make not your rosary of yew-berries,
>   Nor let the beetle, nor the death-moth be
>   Your mournful Psyche, nor the downy owl
> A partner in your sorrow's mysteries;
>   For shade to shade will come too drowsily,
>   And drown the wakeful anguish of the soul. 10

2

> But when the melancholy fit shall fall
>   Sudden from heaven like a weeping cloud,
> That fosters the droop-headed flowers all,
>   And hides the green hill in an April shroud;
> Then glut thy sorrow on a morning rose,
>   Or on the rainbow of the salt sand-wave,
>   Or on the wealth of globed peonies;
> Or if thy mistress some rich anger shows,
>   Emprison her soft hand, and let her rave,
>   And feed deep, deep upon her peerless eyes. 20

2 Wolf's-bane: aconite (monkshood). 4 nightshade: a poisonous red-berried nightshade common in England, not (unless Keats confused the two) the related "deadly nightshade" or belladonna, which has black berries.

3

    She dwells with Beauty—Beauty that must die;
      And Joy, whose hand is ever at his lips
    Bidding adieu; and aching Pleasure nigh,
      Turning to poison while the bee-mouth sips:
    Ay, in the very temple of Delight
      Veil'd Melancholy has her sovran shrine,
        Though seen of none save him whose strenuous tongue
      Can burst Joy's grape against his palate fine;
    His soul shall taste the sadness of her might,
      And be among her cloudy trophies hung.   30

GERARD MANLEY HOPKINS

Heaven-Haven
A Nun Takes the Veil

    I have desired to go
      Where springs not fail,
    To fields where flies no sharp and sided hail
      And a few lilies blow.

    And I have asked to be
      Where no storms come,
    Where the green swell is in the havens dumb,
      And out of the swing of the sea.

Title: The title of the earliest draft of this poem was "Rest."   3 sided: shaped "like the cut of diamonds called brilliants" (description of hailstones in Hopkins's notebook; a mistaken nineteenth-century belief).

I must hunt down the prize

[Unfinished lines from Hopkins's notebook, intended as a companion piece to "Heaven-Haven"]

    I must hunt down the prize
      Where my heart lists.

    Must see the eagle's bulk, render'd in mists,
       Hang of a treble size.
      Must see the waters roll
        Where the seas set
Towards wastes where round the ice-blocks tilt and fret
      Not so far from the pole.

or

      Must see the green seas roll
        Where waters set
Towards those wastes where the ice-blocks tilt and fret,
      Not so far from the pole.

The Sea and the Skylark

On ear and ear two noises too old to end
   Trench—right, the tide that ramps against the shore;
   With a flood or a fall, low lull-off or all roar,
Frequenting there while moon shall wear and wend.

Left hand, off land, I hear the lark ascend,
   His rash-fresh re-winded new-skeinèd score
   In crisps of curl off wild winch whirl, and pour
And pelt music, till none's to spill nor spend.

How these two shame this shallow and frail town!
   How ring right out our sordid turbid time,   10
Being pure! We, life's pride and cared-for crown,

   Have lost that cheer and charm of earth's past **prime:**
Our make and making break, are breaking, down
   To man's last dust, drain fast towards man's first slime.

7 crisps: frills, ripples.

Pied Beauty

Glory be to God for dappled things—
  For skies of couple-colour as a brinded cow;
    For rose-moles all in stipple upon trout that swim;
Fresh-firecoal chestnut-falls; finches' wings;
  Landscape plotted and pieced—fold, fallow, and plough;
    And áll trádes, their gear and tackle and trim.

All things counter, original, spare, strange;
  Whatever is fickle, freckled (who knows how?)
    With swift, slow; sweet, sour; adazzle, dim;
He fathers-forth whose beauty is past change: 10
    Praise him.

4 newly fallen chestnuts "as bright as coals" (Hopkins's notebook).

The Windhover:
To Christ Our Lord

I caught this morning morning's minion, king-
  dom of daylight's dauphin, dapple-dawn-drawn Falcon, in
    his riding
Of the rolling level underneath him steady air, and striding
High there, how he rung upon the rein of a wimpling wing
In his ecstasy! then off, off forth on swing,
  As a skate's heel sweeps smooth on a bow-bend: the hurl
    and gliding
Rebuffed the big wind. My heart in hiding
Stirred for a bird,—the achieve of, the mastery of the thing!

Brute beauty and valour and act, oh, air, pride, plume, here
  Buckle! AND the fire that breaks from thee then, a billion   10
Times told lovelier, more dangerous, O my chevalier!

  No wonder of it: shéer plód makes plough down sillion
Shine, and blue-bleak embers, ah my dear,
  Fall, gall themselves, and gash gold-vermilion.

Felix Randal

Felix Randal the farrier, O he is dead then? my duty all ended,
Who have watched his mould of man, big-boned and hardy-
    handsome
Pining, pining, till time when reason rambled in it and some
Fatal four disorders, fleshed there, all contended?

Sickness broke him. Impatient he cursed at first, but mended
Being anointed and all; though a heavenlier heart began some
Months earlier, since I had our sweet reprieve and ransom
Tendered to him. Ah well, God rest him all road ever he offended!

This seeing the sick endears them to us, us too it endears.
My tongue had taught thee comfort, touch had quenched thy tears, 10
Thy tears that touched my heart, child, Felix, poor Felix Randal;

How far from then forethought of, all thy more boisterous years,
When thou at the random grim forge, powerful amidst peers,
Didst fettle for the great grey drayhorse his bright and battering
    sandal!

No worst, there is none

No worst, there is none. Pitched past pitch of grief,
More pangs will, schooled at forepangs, wilder wring.
Comforter, where, where is your comforting?
Mary, mother of us, where is your relief?
My cries heave, herds-long; huddle in a main, a chief
Woe, world-sorrow; on an age-old anvil wince and sing—
Then lull, then leave off. Fury had shrieked "No ling-
ering! Let me be fell: force I must be brief."

   O the mind, mind has mountains; cliffs of fall
Frightful, sheer, no-man-fathomed. Hold them cheap   10

May who ne'er hung there. Nor does long our small
Durance deal with that steep or deep. Here! creep,
Wretch, under a comfort serves in a whirlwind: all
Life death does end and each day dies with sleep.

12 durance: power of endurance.

I wake and feel the fell of dark

I wake and feel the fell of dark, not day.
What hours, O what black hoürs we have spent
This night! what sights you, heart, saw; ways you went!
And more must, in yet longer light's delay.
   With witness I speak this. But where I say
Hours I mean years, mean life. And my lament
Is cries countless, cries like dead letters sent
To dearest him that lives alas! away.

   I am gall, I am heartburn. God's most deep decree
Bitter would have me taste: my taste was me;   10
Bones built in me, flesh filled, blood brimmed the curse.
   Selfyeast of spirit a dull dough sours. I see
The lost are like this, and their scourge to be
As I am mine, their sweating selves; but worse.

My own heart let me more have pity on

My own heart let me more have pity on; let
Me live to my sad self hereafter kind,
Charitable; not live this tormented mind
With this tormented mind tormenting yet.
   I cast for comfort I can no more get
By groping round my comfortless, than blind
Eyes in their dark can day or thirst can find
Thirst's all-in-all in all a world of wet.

Soul, self; come, poor Jackself, I do advise
You, jaded, let be; call off thoughts awhile   10
Elsewhere; leave comfort root-room; let joy size
At God knows when to God knows what; whose smile
's not wrung, see you; unforeseen times rather—as skies
Betweenpie mountains—lights a lovely mile.

That Nature Is a Heraclitean Fire and of the Comfort of the Resurrection

Cloud-puffball, torn tufts, tossed pillows ǀ flaunt forth, then chevy on an air-
built thoroughfare: heaven-roysterers, in gay-gangs ǀ they throng; they glitter in marches.
Down roughcast, down dazzling whitewash, ǀ wherever an elm arches,
Shivelights and shadowtackle in long ǀ lashes lace, lance, and pair.
Delightfully the bright wind boisterous ǀ ropes, wrestles, beats earth bare
Of yestertempest's creases; ǀ in pool and rut peel parches
Squandering ooze to squeezed ǀ dough, crust, dust; stanches, starches
Squadroned masks and manmarks ǀ treadmire toil there
Footfretted in it. Million-fuelèd, ǀ nature's bonfire burns on.
But quench her bonniest, dearest ǀ to her, her clearest-selvèd spark   10
Man, how fast his firedint, ǀ his mark on mind, is gone!
Both are in an unfathomable, all is in an enormous dark
Drowned. O pity and indig ǀ nation! Manshape, that shone
Sheer off, disseveral, a star, ǀ death blots black out; nor mark
  Is any of him at all so stark

---

4 Shivelights: slices of light. shadowtackle: patterns of shadow resembling the complicated patterns made by the rigging of a ship.   9 Footfretted: "fret" in the sense of fretwork, making a pattern.   14 disseveral: each one separate, distinct, individual.

But vastness blurs and time | beats level. Enough! the
   Resurrection,
A heart's-clarion! Away grief's gasping, | joyless days, dejection.
   Across my foundering deck shone
A beacon, an eternal beam. | Flesh fade, and mortal trash
Fall to the residuary worm; | world's wildfire, leave but ash: 20
   In a flash, at a trumpet crash,
I am all at once what Christ is, | since he was what I am, and
This Jack, joke, poor potsherd, | patch, matchwood, immortal
   diamond,
       Is immortal diamond.

Thou art indeed just, Lord

Justus quidem tu es, Domine, si disputem tecum:
verumtamen justa loquar ad te: Quare via impiorum
prosperatur? &c. [JEREMIAH xii.i]

Thou art indeed just, Lord, if I contend
With thee; but, sir, so what I plead is just.
Why do sinners' ways prosper? and why must
Disappointment all I endeavour end?
   Wert thou my enemy, O thou my friend,
How wouldst thou worse, I wonder, than thou dost
Defeat, thwart me? Oh, the sots and thralls of lust
Do in spare hours more thrive than I that spend,
Sir, life upon thy cause. See, banks and brakes
Now, leavèd how thick! lacèd they are again   10
With fretty chervil, look, and fresh wind shakes
Them; birds build—but not I build; no, but strain,
Time's eunuch, and not breed one work that wakes.
Mine, O thou lord of life, send my roots rain.

1–3 These lines translate the epigraph.   **11** fretty: elaborately patterned, as in fretwork or lace.

To R. B.

The fine delight that fathers thought; the strong
Spur, live and lancing like the blowpipe flame,
Breathes once and, quenchèd faster than it came,
Leaves yet the mind a mother of immortal song.
Nine months she then, nay years, nine years she long
Within her wears, bears, cares and combs the same:
The widow of an insight lost she lives, with aim
Now known and hand at work now never wrong.
 Sweet fire the sire of muse, my soul needs this;
I want the one rapture of an inspiration.   10
O then if in my lagging lines you miss
The roll, the rise, the carol, the creation,
My winter world, that scarcely breathes that bliss
Now, yields you, with some sighs, our explanation.

Title: Robert Bridges the poet, the friend who preserved and later published Hopkins's poems.

ROBERT BRIDGES

A Passer-By

Whither, O splendid ship, thy white sails crowding,
 Leaning across the bosom of the urgent West,
That fearest nor sea rising nor sky clouding,
 Whither away, fair rover, and what thy quest?
 Ah! soon, when Winter has all our vales opprest,
When skies are cold and misty, and hail is hurling,
 Wilt thóu glíde on the blue Pacific, or rest
In a summer haven asleep, thy white sails furling.

I there before thee, in the country that well thou knowest,
 Already arrived am inhaling the odorous air: 10
I watch thee enter unerringly where thou goest,
 And anchor queen of the strange shipping there,
 Thy sails for awnings spread, thy masts bare;

Nor is aught from the foaming reef to the snow-capped, grandest
   Peak, that is over the feathery palms more fair
Than thou, so upright, so stately, and still thou standest.

And yet, O splendid ship, unhailed and nameless,
   I know not if, aiming a fancy, I rightly divine
That thou hast a purpose joyful, a courage blameless,
   Thy port assured in a happier land than mine.   20
   But for all I have given thee, beauty enough is thine,
As thou, aslant with trim tackle and shrouding,
   From the proud nostril curve of a prow's line
In the offing scatterest foam, thy white sails crowding.

London Snow

When men were all asleep the snow came flying,
In large white flakes falling on the city brown,
Stealthily and perpetually settling and loosely lying,
   Hushing the latest traffic of the drowsy town;
Deadening, muffling, stifling its murmurs failing;
Lazily and incessantly floating down and down:
   Silently sifting and veiling road, roof and railing;
Hiding difference, making unevenness even,
Into angles and crevices softly drifting and sailing.
   All night it fell, and when full inches seven   10
It lay in the depth of its uncompacted lightness,
The clouds blew off from a high and frosty heaven;
   And all woke earlier for the unaccustomed brightness
Of the winter dawning, the strange unheavenly glare:
The eye marveled—marveled at the dazzling whiteness;
   The ear hearkened to the stillness of the solemn air;
No sound of wheel rumbling nor of foot falling,
And the busy morning cries came thin and spare.
   Then boys I heard, as they went to school, calling;
They gathered up the crystal manna to freeze   20
Their tongues with tasting, their hands with snowballing;
   Or rioted in a drift, plunging up to the knees;

Or peering up from under the white-mossed wonder,
"O look at the trees!" they cried, "O look at the trees!"
    With lessened load, a few carts creak and blunder,
Following along the white deserted way,
A country company long dispersed asunder:
    When now already the sun, in pale display
Standing by Paul's high dome, spread forth below
His sparkling beams, and awoke the stir of the day.   30
    For now doors open, and war is waged with the snow;
And trains of sombre men, past tale of number,
Tread long brown paths, as toward their toil they go:
    But even for them awhile no cares encumber
Their minds diverted; the daily word is unspoken,
The daily thoughts of labour and sorrow slumber
At the sight of the beauty that greets them, for the charm
    they have broken.

Nightingales

Beautiful must be the mountains whence ye come,
And bright in the fruitful valleys the streams, wherefrom
        Ye learn your song:
Where are those starry woods? O might I wander there,
    Among the flowers, which in that heavenly air
        Bloom the year long!

Nay, barren are those mountains and spent the streams:
Our song is the voice of desire, that haunts our dreams,
        A throe of the heart,
Whose pining visions dim, forbidden hopes profound,   10
    No dying cadence nor long sigh can sound,
        For all our art.

Alone, aloud in the raptured ear of men
We pour our dark nocturnal secret; and then,
        As night is withdrawn
From these sweet-springing meads and bursting boughs of May,
    Dream, while the innumerable choir of day
        Welcome the dawn.

November

The lonely season in lonely lands, when fled
Are half the birds, and mists lie low, and the sun
Is rarely seen, nor strayeth far from his bed;
The short days pass unwelcomed one by one.

  Out by the ricks the mantled engine stands
Crestfallen, deserted,—for now all hands
Are told to the plough,—and ere it is dawn appear
The teams following and crossing far and near,
As hour by hour they broaden the brown bands
Of the striped fields; and behind them firk and prance   10
The heavy rooks, and daws grey-pated dance:
As awhile, surmounting a crest, in sharp outline
(A miniature of toil, a gem's design,)
They are pictured, horses and men, or now near by
Above the lane they shout lifting the share,
By the trim hedgerow bloom'd with purple air;
Where, under the thorns, dead leaves in huddle lie
Packed by the gales of Autumn, and in and out
The small wrens glide
With a happy note of cheer,   20
And yellow amorets flutter above and about,
Gay, familiar in fear.

  And now, if the night shall be cold, across the sky
Linnets and twites, in small flocks helter-skelter,
All the afternoon to the gardens fly,
From thistle-pastures hurrying to gain the shelter
Of American rhododendron or cherry-laurel:
And here and there, near chilly setting of sun,
In an isolated tree a congregation
Of starlings chatter and chide,   30
Thickset as summer leaves, in garrulous quarrel:

10 firk: hasten or be frisky.   11 Rooks and daws resemble crows.   15 share: plowshare.   16 bloom'd: silvered over with autumn haze.   24 twite or twite finch: another kind of linnet.

Suddenly they hush as one,—
The tree top springs,—
And off, with a whirr of wings,
They fly by the score
To the holly-thicket, and there with myriads more
Dispute for the roosts; and from the unseen nation
A babel of tongues, like running water unceasing,
Makes live the wood, the flocking cries increasing,
Wrangling discordantly, incessantly,   40
While falls the night on them self-occupied;
The long dark night, that lengthens slow,
Deepening with Winter to starve grass and tree,
And soon to bury in snow
The Earth, that, sleeping 'neath her frozen stole,
Shall dream a dream crept from the sunless pole
Of how her end shall be.

In der Fremde

Ah! wild-hearted wand'rer
 far in the world away
Restless nor knowest why
 only thou canst not stay
And now turnest trembling
 hearing the wind to sigh:
'Twas thy lover calling
 whom thou didst leave forby.

So faint and yet so far
 so far and yet so fain—   10
'Return belov'd to me'
 but thou must onward strain:
Thy trembling is in vain
 as thy wand'ring shall be.
What so well thou lovest
 thou nevermore shalt see.

Title: In a foreign land, abroad. The poem is a translation of a lyric by **Heine**.

Narcissus

Almighty wondrous everlasting
Whether in a cradle of astral whirlfire
Or globed in a piercing star thou slumb'rest
    The impassive body of God:
Thou deep i' the core of earth—Almighty!—
From numbing stress and gloom profound
Madest escape in life desirous
    To embroider her thin-spun robe.

'Twas down in a wood—they tell—
In a running water thou sawest thyself   10
Or leaning over a pool: The sedges
    Were twinn'd at the mirror's brim
The sky was there and the trees—Almighty!—
A bird of a bird and white clouds floating
And seeing thou knewest thine own image
    To love it beyond all else.

Then wondering didst thou speak
Of beauty and wisdom of art and worship
Didst build the fanes of Zeus and Apollo
    The high cathedrals of Christ: 20
All that we love is thine—Almighty!—
Heart-felt music and lyric song
Language the eager grasp of knowledge
    All that we think is thine.

But whence?—Beauteous everlasting!—
Whence and whither? Hast thou mistaken?
Or dost forget? Look again! Thou seest
    A shadow and not thyself.

Low Barometer

The south-wind strengthens to a gale,
Across the moon the clouds fly fast,
The house is smitten as with a flail,
The chimney shudders to the blast.

On such a night, when Air has loosed
Its guardian grasp on blood and brain,
Old terrors then of god or ghost
Creep from their caves to life again;

And Reason kens he herits in
A haunted house. Tenants unknown 10
Assert their squalid lease of sin
With earlier title than his own.

Unbodied presences, the pack'd
Pollution and remorse of Time,
Slipp'd from oblivion reënact
The horrors of unhouseld crime.

Some men would quell the thing with prayer
Whose sightless footsteps pad the floor,
Whose fearful trespass mounts the stair
Or bursts the lock'd forbidden door. 20

Some have seen corpses long interr'd
Escape from hallowing control,
Pale charnel forms—nay ev'n have heard
The shrilling of a troubled soul,

That wanders till the dawn hath cross'd
The dolorous dark, or Earth hath wound
Closer her storm-spredd cloke, and thrust
The baleful phantoms underground.

9 herits: dwells in by inheritance.

WILLIAM BUTLER YEATS

The Lake Isle of Innisfree

I will arise and go now, and go to Innisfree,
And a small cabin build there, of clay and wattles made;
Nine bean rows will I have there, a hive for the honey bee,
    And live alone in the bee-loud glade.

And I shall have some peace there, for peace comes dropping slow,
Dropping from the veils of the morning to where the cricket sings;
There midnight's all a glimmer, and noon a purple glow,
    And evening full of the linnet's wings.

I will arise and go now, for always night and day
I hear lake water lapping with low sounds by the shore;   10
While I stand on the roadway, or on the pavements gray,
    I hear it in the deep heart's core.

Cuchulain's Fight With the Sea

A man came slowly from the setting sun,
To Emer, raddling raiment in her dun,
And said, "I am that swineherd whom you bid
Go watch the road between the wood and tide,
But now I have no need to watch it more."

Then Emer cast the web upon the floor,
And raising arms all raddled with the dye,
Parted her lips with a loud sudden cry.
That swineherd stared upon her face and said,
"No man alive, no man among the dead,   10
Has won the gold his cars of battle bring."

"But if your master comes home triumphing
Why must you blench and shake from foot to crown?"
Thereon he shook the more and cast him down

---

2 **raddling**: dyeing with red ochre.   **dun**: a fortified dwelling in ancient Ireland.

Upon the web-heaped floor, and cried his word:
"With him is one sweet-throated like a bird."

"You dare me to my face," and thereupon
She smote with raddled fist, and where her son
Herded the cattle came with stumbling feet,
And cried with angry voice, "It is not meet   20
To idle life away, a common herd."

"I have long waited, mother, for that word:
But wherefore now?"

          "There is a man to die;
You have the heaviest arm under the sky."

"Whether under its daylight or its stars
My father stands amid his battle-cars."

"But you have grown to be the taller man."

"Yet somewhere under starlight or the sun
My father stands."

          "Aged, worn out with wars
On foot, on horseback or in battle-cars."   30

"I only ask what way my journey lies,
For He who made you bitter made you wise."

"The Red Branch camp in a great company
Between wood's rim and the horses of the sea.
Go there, and light a camp-fire at wood's rim;
But tell your name and lineage to him
Whose blade compels, and wait till they have found
Some feasting man that the same oath has bound."

Among those feasting men Cuchulain dwelt,
And his young sweetheart close beside him knelt,   40
Stared on the mournful wonder of his eyes,
Even as Spring upon the ancient skies,

---

36 to him: i.e., only to him.

And pondered on the glory of his days;
And all around the harp-string told his praise,
And Conchubar, the Red Branch king of kings,
With his own fingers touched the brazen strings.

At last Cuchulain spake, "Some man has made
His evening fire amid the leafy shade.
I have often heard him singing to and fro,
I have often heard the sweet sound of his bow.
Seek out what man he is."
      One went and came.
"He bade me let all know he gives his name
At the sword-point, and waits till we have found
Some feasting man that the same oath has bound."

Cuchulain cried, "I am the only man
Of all this host so bound from childhood on."

After short fighting in the leafy shade,
He spake to the young man, "Is there no maid
Who loves you, no white arms to wrap you round,
Or do you long for the dim sleepy ground,
That you have come and dared me to my face?" 60

"The dooms of men are in God's hidden place."

"Your head a while seemed like a woman's head
That I loved once."
    Again the fighting sped,
But now the war-rage in Cuchulain woke,
And through that new blade's guard the old blade broke,
And pierced him.
    "Speak before your breath is done."

"Cuchulain I, mighty Cuchulain's son."

"I put you from your pain. I can no more."

---

45 **Conchubar:** king of all the Red Branch warriors.

While day its burden on to evening bore, 70
With head bowed on his knees Cuchulain stayed;
Then Conchubar sent that sweet-throated maid,
And she, to win him, his grey hair caressed;
In vain her arms, in vain her soft white breast.
Then Conchubar, the subtlest of all men,
Ranking his Druids round him ten by ten,
Spake thus: "Cuchulain will dwell there and brood
For three days more in dreadful quietude,
And then arise, and raving slay us all.
Chaunt in his ear delusions magical, 80
That he may fight the horses of the sea."
The Druids took them to their mystery,
And chaunted for three days.
      Cuchulain stirred,
Stared on the horses of the sea, and heard
The cars of battle and his own name cried;
And fought with the invulnerable tide.

No Second Troy

Why should I blame her that she filled my days
With misery, or that she would of late
Have taught to ignorant men most violent ways,
Or hurled the little streets upon the great,
Had they but courage equal to desire?
What could have made her peaceful with a mind
That nobleness made simple as a fire,
With beauty like a tightened bow, a kind
That is not natural in an age like this,
Being high and solitary and most stern? 10
Why, what could she have done, being what she is?
Was there another Troy for her to burn?

2–5 Maud Gonne had been urging violent rebellion in Ireland.

That the Night Come

She lived in storm and strife,
Her soul had such desire
For what proud death may bring
That it could not endure
The common good of life,
But lived as 'twere a king
That packed his marriage day
With banneret and pennon,
Trumpet and kettledrum,
And the outrageous cannon,   10
To bundle time away
That the night come.

The Cold Heaven

Suddenly I saw the cold and rook-delighting heaven
That seemed as though ice burned and was but the more ice,
And thereupon imagination and heart were driven
So wild that every casual thought of that and this
Vanished, and left but memories, that should be out of season
With the hot blood of youth, of love crossed long ago;
And I took all the blame out of all sense and reason,
Until I cried and trembled and rocked to and fro,
Riddled with light. Ah! when the ghost begins to quicken,
Confusion of the death-bed over, is it sent   10
Out naked on the roads, as the books say, and stricken
By the injustice of the skies for punishment?

The Magi

Now as at all times I can see in the mind's eye,
In their stiff, painted clothes, the pale unsatisfied ones
Appear and disappear in the blue depth of the sky
With all their ancient faces like rain-beaten stones,

And all their helms of silver hovering side by side,
And all their eyes still fixed, hoping to find once more,
Being by Calvary's turbulence unsatisfied,
The uncontrollable mystery on the bestial floor.

The Hawk

"Call down the hawk from the air:
Let him be hooded or caged
Till the yellow eye has grown mild,
For larder and spit are bare,
The old cook enraged,
The scullion gone wild."

"I will not be clapped in a hood,
Nor a cage, nor alight upon wrist,
Now I have learnt to be proud
Hovering over the wood   10
In the broken mist
Or tumbling cloud."

"What tumbling cloud did you cleave,
Yellow-eyed hawk of the mind,
Last evening? that I, who had sat
Dumbfounded before a knave,
Should give to my friend
A pretence of wit."

The Wild Swans at Coole

The trees are in their autumn beauty,
The woodland paths are dry,
Under the October twilight the water
Mirrors a still sky;
Upon the brimming water among the stones
Are nine-and-fifty swans.

Title: Coole was the name of the estate of Yeats's friend, Lady Gregory.

The nineteenth autumn has come upon me
Since I first made my count;
I saw, before I had well finished,
All suddenly mount
And scatter wheeling in great broken rings
Upon their clamorous wings.

I have looked upon those brilliant creatures,
And now my heart is sore.
All's changed since I, hearing at twilight,
The first time on this shore,
The bell-beat of their wings above my head,
Trod with a lighter tread.

Unwearied still, lover by lover,
They paddle in the cold
Companionable streams or climb the air;
Their hearts have not grown old;
Passion or conquest, wander where they will,
Attend upon them still.

But now they drift on the still water,
Mysterious, beautiful;
Among what rushes will they build,
By what lake's edge or pool
Delight men's eyes when I awake some day
To find they have flown away?

Under the Round Tower

"Although I'd lie lapped up in linen
A deal I'd sweat and little earn
If I should live as live the neighbours,"
Cried the beggar, Billy Byrne;
"Stretch bones till the daylight come
On great-grandfather's battered tomb."

Upon a grey old battered tombstone
In Glendalough beside the stream,
Where the O'Byrnes and Byrnes are buried,
He stretched his bones and fell in a dream   10
Of sun and moon that a good hour
Bellowed and pranced in the round tower;

Of golden king and silver lady,
Bellowing up and bellowing round,
Till toes mastered a sweet measure,
Mouth mastered a sweet sound,
Prancing round and prancing up
Until they pranced upon the top.

That golden king and that wild lady
Sang till stars began to fade,   20
Hands gripped in hands, toes close together,
Hair spread on the wind they made;
That lady and that golden king
Could like a brace of blackbirds sing.

"It's certain that my luck is broken,"
That rambling jailbird Billy said;
"Before nightfall I'll pick a pocket
And snug it in a feather-bed.
I cannot find the peace of home
On great-grandfather's battered tomb."   30

The Second Coming

Turning and turning in the widening gyre
The falcon cannot hear the falconer;
Things fall apart; the centre cannot hold;
Mere anarchy is loosed upon the world,
The blood-dimmed tide is loosed, and everywhere
The ceremony of innocence is drowned;
The best lack of all conviction, while the worst
Are full of passionate intensity.

Surely some revelation is at hand;
Surely the Second Coming is at hand. 10
The Second Coming! Hardly are those words out
When a vast image out of *Spiritus Mundi*
Troubles my sight: somewhere in sands of the desert
A shape with lion body and the head of a man,
A gaze blank and pitiless as the sun,
Is moving its slow thighs, while all about it
Reel shadows of the indignant desert birds.
The darkness drops again; but now I know
That twenty centuries of stony sleep
Were vexed to nightmare by a rocking cradle, 20
And what rough beast, its hour come round at last,
Slouches towards Bethlehem to be born?

12 *Spiritus Mundi:* a "general store house of images which have ceased to be a property of any personality or spirit" (Yeats), much like the unconscious racial memory described by Jung. 14 The image here suggests a sphinx and a "brazen winged beast," as well as other combinations of man and beast such as the centaur, all of which Yeats wrote about elsewhere. 20 rocking cradle: a reference to the Nativity and the subsequent worship of Mary and the infant Christ.

Leda and the Swan

A sudden blow: the great wings beating still
Above the staggering girl, her thighs caressed
By the dark webs, her nape caught in his bill,
He holds her helpless breast upon his breast.

How can those terrified vague fingers push
The feathered glory from her loosening thighs?
And how can body, laid in that white rush,
But feel the strange heart beating where it lies?

A shudder in the loins engenders there
The broken wall, the burning roof and tower 10
And Agamemnon dead.

Being so caught up,
So mastered by the brute blood of the air,
Did she put on his knowledge with his power
Before the indifferent beak could let her drop?

Among School Children

I

I walk through the long schoolroom questioning;
A kind old nun in a white hood replies;
The children learn to cipher and to sing,
To study reading-books and histories,
To cut and sew, be neat in everything
In the best modern way—the children's eyes
In momentary wonder stare upon
A sixty-year-old smiling public man.

II

I dream of a Ledaean body, bent
Above a sinking fire, a tale that she   10
Told of a harsh reproof, or trivial event
That changed some childish day to tragedy—
Told, and it seemed that our two natures blent
Into a sphere from youthful sympathy,
Or else, to alter Plato's parable,
Into the yolk and white of the one shell.

III

And thinking of that fit of grief or rage
I look upon one child or t'other there
And wonder if she stood so at that age—
For even daughters of the swan can share   20

9 Ledaean: referring to Helen, daughter of Leda.   15–16 A story of the origin of love told in Plato's *Symposium*. Man, originally whole, attacked the gods and for this was punished by Zeus, who split him in two "as you might divide an egg with a hair." Since then, the halves forever try to unite: "the pursuit of the whole is called love."

Something of every paddler's heritage—
And had that colour upon cheek or hair,
And thereupon my heart is driven wild:
She stands before me as a living child.

IV

Her present image floats into the mind—
Did Quattrocento finger fashion it
Hollow of cheek as though it drank the wind
And took a mess of shadows for its meat?
And I though never of Ledaean kind
Had pretty plumage once—enough of that,   30
Better to smile on all that smile, and show
There is a comfortable kind of scarecrow.

V

What youthful mother, a shape upon her lap
Honey of generation had betrayed,
And that must sleep, shriek, struggle to escape
As recollection or the drug decide,
Would think her son, did she but see that shape
With sixty or more winters on its head,
A compensation for the pang of his birth,
Or the uncertainty of his setting forth?   40

VI

Plato thought nature but a spume that plays
Upon a ghostly paradigm of things;
Solider Aristotle played the taws
Upon the bottom of a king of kings;
World-famous golden-thighed Pythagoras
Fingered upon a fiddle-stick or strings

41–42 refer to Plato's theory of reality.   *43–44* Aristotle was the tutor of Alexander the Great. taws: whips.   *45–47* Pythagoras (who was believed by his followers to have golden thighs) discovered the mathematical relation between the harmony of the octave and the length of strings. He therefore reasoned that the order of the whole universe consists of number. Applying the theory to the heavenly bodies produced the famous nation of the "music of the spheres" ("what a star sang," line *47*).

What a star sang and careless Muses heard:
Old clothes upon old sticks to scare a bird.

VII

Both nuns and mothers worship images,
But those the candles light are not as those   50
That animate a mother's reveries,
But keep a marble or a bronze repose.
And yet they too break hearts—O Presences
That passion, piety or affection knows,
And that all heavenly glory symbolise—
O self-born mockers of man's enterprise;

VIII

Labour is blossoming or dancing where
The body is not bruised to pleasure soul,
Nor beauty born out of its own despair,
Nor blear-eyed wisdom out of midnight oil.   60
O chestnut tree, great-rooted blossomer,
Are you the leaf, the blossom or the bole?
O body swayed to music, O brightening glance,
How can we know the dancer from the dance?

Sailing to Byzantium

I

That is no country for old men. The young
In one another's arms, birds in the trees
—Those dying generations—at their song,
The salmon-falls, the mackerel-crowded seas,
Fish, flesh, or fowl, commend all summer long
Whatever is begotten, born, and dies.
Caught in that sensual music all neglect
Monuments of unaging intellect.

II

An aged man is but a paltry thing,
A tattered coat upon a stick, unless   10

Soul clap its hands and sing, and louder sing
For every tatter in its mortal dress,
Nor is there singing school but studying
Monuments of its own magnificence;
And therefore I have sailed the seas and come
To the holy city of Byzantium.

III

O sages standing in God's holy fire
As in the gold mosaic of a wall,
Come from the holy fire, perne in a gyre,
And be the singing-masters of my soul. 20
Consume my heart away; sick with desire
And fastened to a dying animal
It knows not what it is; and gather me
Into the artifice of eternity.

IV

Once out of nature I shall never take
My bodily form from any natural thing,
But such a form as Grecian goldsmiths make
Of hammered gold and gold enamelling
To keep a drowsy Emperor awake;
Or set upon a golden bough to sing 30
To lords and ladies of Byzantium
Of what is past, or passing, or to come.

19 perne: circle.　27 Grecian: i.e., Byzantine, not classical Greek.

Byzantium

The unpurged images of day recede;
The Emperor's drunken soldiery are abed;
Night resonance recedes, night-walkers' song
After great cathedral gong;
A starlit or a moonlit dome disdains
All that man is,

All mere complexities,
The fury and the mire of human veins.
Before me floats an image, man or shade,
Shade more than man, more image than a shade;
For Hades' bobbin bound in mummy-cloth
May unwind the winding path;
A mouth that has no moisture and no breath
Breathless mouths may summon;
I hail the superhuman;
I call it death-in-life and life-in-death.

Miracle, bird or golden handiwork,
More miracle than bird or handiwork,
Planted on the star-lit golden bough,
Can like the cocks of Hades crow,
Or, by the moon embittered, scorn aloud
In glory of changeless metal
Common bird or petal
And all complexities of mire or blood.

At midnight on the Emperor's pavement flit
Flames that no faggot feeds, nor steel has lit,
Nor storm disturbs, flames begotten of flame,
Where blood-begotten spirits come
And all complexities of fury leave,
Dying into a dance,
An agony of trance,
An agony of flame that cannot singe a sleeve.

Astraddle on the dolphin's mire and blood,
Spirit after spirit! The smithies break the flood,
The golden smithies of the Emperor!
Marbles of the dancing floor
Break bitter furies of complexity,
Those images that yet
Fresh images beget,
That dolphin-torn, that gong-tormented sea.

Meru

Civilisation is hooped together, brought
Under a rule, under the semblance of peace
By manifold illusion; but man's life is thought,
And he, despite his terror, cannot cease
Ravening through century after century,
Ravening, raging, and uprooting that he may come
Into the desolation of reality:
Egypt and Greece, good-bye, and good-bye, Rome!
Hermits upon Mount Meru or Everest,
Caverned in night under the drifted snow,   10
Or where that snow and winter's dreadful blast
Beat down upon their naked bodies, know
That day brings round the night, that before dawn
His glory and his monuments are gone.

Title: a mythical high mountain at the center of the world, dwelling place of the god Vishnu, who has gone through many incarnations.

The Circus Animals' Desertion

I

I sought a theme and sought for it in vain,
I sought it daily for six weeks or so.
Maybe at last, being but a broken man,
I must be satisfied with my heart, although
Winter and summer till old age began
My circus animals were all on show,
Those stilted boys, that burnished chariot,
Lion and woman and the Lord knows what.

II

What can I but enumerate old themes?

7 stilted boys: in the play *The King's Threshold* (1904).   7-8 burnished chariot . . . Lion and woman: in *The Unicorn from the Stars* (1908).

First that sea-rider Oisin led by the nose   10
Through three enchanted islands, allegorical dreams,
Vain gaiety, vain battle, vain repose,
Themes of the embittered heart, or so it seems,
That might adorn old songs or courtly shows;
But what cared I that set him on to ride,
I, starved for the bosom of his faery bride?

And then a counter-truth filled out its play,
The Countess Cathleen was the name I gave it;
She, pity-crazed, had given her soul away,
But masterful Heaven had intervened to save it.   20
I thought my dear must her own soul destroy,
So did fanaticism and hate enslave it,
And this brought forth a dream and soon enough
This dream itself had all my thought and love.

And when the Fool and Blind Man stole the bread
Cuchulain fought the ungovernable sea;
Heart-mysteries there, and yet when all is said
It was the dream itself enchanted me:
Character isolated by a deed
To engross the present and dominate memory.   30
Players and painted stage took all my love,
And not those things that they were emblems of.

III

Those masterful images because complete
Grew in pure mind, but out of what began?
A mound of refuse or the sweepings of a street,
Old kettles, old bottles, and a broken can,
Old iron, old bones, old rags, that raving slut
Who keeps the till. Now that my ladder's gone,
I must lie down where all the ladders start,
In the foul rag-and-bone shop of the heart.   40

10–16 Oisin . . . : in the narrative poem *The Wanderings of Oisin* (1889).
17–20 *The Countess Cathleen:* a play (1892).   21–24 . . . my dear . . . :
Maud Gonne, associated by Yeats with *The Countess Cathleen*.   25–30 . . .
Fool . . . : in *On Baile's Strand* (1904), a dramatic version of the death of
Cuchulain.

ROBERT FROST

After Apple-Picking

My long two-pointed ladder's sticking through a tree
Toward heaven still,
And there's a barrel that I didn't fill
Beside it, and there may be two or three
Apples I didn't pick upon some bough.
But I am done with apple-picking now.
Essence of winter sleep is on the night,
The scent of apples: I am drowsing off.
I cannot rub the strangeness from my sight
I got from looking through a pane of glass   10
I skimmed this morning from the drinking trough
And held against the world of hoary grass.
It melted, and I let it fall and break.
But I was well
Upon my way to sleep before it fell,
And I could tell
What form my dreaming was about to take.
Magnified apples appear and disappear,
Stem end and blossom end,
And every fleck of russet showing clear.   20
My instep arch not only keeps the ache,
It keeps the pressure of a ladder-round.
I feel the ladder sway as the boughs bend.
And I keep hearing from the cellar bin
The rumbling sound
Of load on load of apples coming in.
For I have had too much
Of apple-picking: I am overtired
Of the great harvest I myself desired.
There were ten thousand thousand fruit to touch,   30
Cherish in hand, lift down, and not let fall.
For all
That struck the earth,
No matter if not bruised or spiked with stubble,

Went surely to the cider-apple heap
As of no worth.
One can see what will trouble
This sleep of mine, whatever sleep it is.
Were he not gone,
The woodchuck could say whether it's like his 40
Long sleep, as I describe its coming on,
Or just some human sleep.

Fire and Ice

Some say the world will end in fire,
Some say in ice.
From what I've tasted of desire
I hold with those who favor fire.
But if it had to perish twice,
I think I know enough of hate
To say that for destruction ice
Is also great
And would suffice.

Nothing Gold Can Stay

Nature's first green is gold,
Her hardest hue to hold.
Her early leaf's a flower;
But only so an hour.
Then leaf subsides to leaf.
So Eden sank to grief,
So dawn goes down to day.
Nothing gold can stay.

Stopping by Woods on a Snowy Evening

Whose woods these are I think I know.
His house is in the village though;
He will not see me stopping here
To watch his woods fill up with snow.

My little horse must think it queer
To stop without a farmhouse near
Between the woods and frozen lake
The darkest evening of the year.

He gives his harness bells a shake
To ask if there is some mistake. 10
The only other sound's the sweep
Of easy wind and downy flake.

The woods are lovely, dark and deep,
But I have promises to keep,
And miles to go before I sleep,
And miles to go before I sleep.

Desert Places

Snow falling and night falling fast, oh, fast
In a field I looked into going past,
And the ground almost covered smooth in snow,
But a few weeds and stubble showing last.

The woods around it have it—it is theirs.
All animals are smothered in their lairs.
I am too absent-spirited to count;
The loneliness includes me unawares.

And lonely as it is that loneliness
Will be more lonely ere it will be less— 10
A blanker whiteness of benighted snow
With no expression, nothing to express.

They cannot scare me with their empty spaces
Between stars—on stars where no human race is.
I have it in me so much nearer home
To scare myself with my own desert places.

WALLACE STEVENS

Domination of Black

At night, by the fire,
The colors of the bushes
And of the fallen leaves,
Repeating themselves,
Turned in the room,
Like the leaves themselves
Turning in the wind.
Yes: but the color of the heavy
    hemlocks
Came striding.
And I remembered the cry of the
    peacocks.   10

The colors of their tails
Were like the leaves themselves
Turning in the wind,
In the twilight wind.
They swept over the room,
Just as they flew from the boughs
    of the hemlocks
Down to the ground.
I heard them cry—the peacocks.
Was it a cry against the twilight
Or against the leaves themselves   20
Turning in the wind,
Turning as the flames
Turned in the fire,
Turning as the tails of the peacocks
Turned in the loud fire,
Loud as the hemlocks
Full of the cry of the peacocks?
Or was it a cry against the hemlocks?

Out of the window,
I saw how the planets gathered   30

Like the leaves themselves
Turning in the wind.
I saw how the night came,
Came striding like the color of the
    heavy hemlocks.
I felt afraid.
And I remembered the cry of the
    peacocks.

The Snow Man

One must have a mind of winter
To regard the frost and the boughs
Of the pine-trees crusted with snow;

And have been cold a long time
To behold the junipers shagged with ice,
The spruces rough in the distant glitter

Of the January sun; and not to think
Of any misery in the sound of the wind,
In the sound of a few leaves,

Which is the sound of the land   10
Full of the same wind
That is blowing in the same bare place

For the listener, who listens in the snow,
And, nothing himself, beholds
Nothing that is not there and the nothing that is.

Disillusionment of Ten O'Clock

The houses are haunted
By white night-gowns.
None are green,
Or purple with green rings,

Or green with yellow rings,
Or yellow with blue rings.
None of them are strange,
With socks of lace
And beaded ceintures.
People are not going   10
To dream of baboons and periwinkles.
Only, here and there, an old sailor,
Drunk and asleep in his boots,
Catches tigers
In red weather.

Sunday Morning

I

Complacencies of the peignoir, and late
Coffee and oranges in a sunny chair,
And the green freedom of a cockatoo
Upon a rug mingle to dissipate
The holy hush of ancient sacrifice.
She dreams a little, and she feels the dark
Encroachment of that old catastrophe,
As a calm darkens among water-lights.
The pungent oranges and bright, green wings
Seem things in some procession of the dead,   10
Winding across wide water, without sound.
The day is like wide water, without sound,
Stilled for the passing of her dreaming feet
Over the seas, to silent Palestine,
Dominion of the blood and sepulchre.

II

Why should she give her bounty to the dead?
What is divinity if it can come
Only in silent shadows and in dreams?
Shall she not find in comforts of the sun,
In pungent fruit and bright, green wings, or else   20

In any balm or beauty of the earth,
Things to be cherished like the thought of heaven?
Divinity must live within herself:
Passions of rain, or moods in falling snow;
Grievings in loneliness, or unsubdued
Elations when the forest blooms; gusty
Emotions on wet roads on autumn nights;
All pleasures and all pains, remembering
The bough of summer and the winter branch.
These are the measures destined for her soul.   30

III

Jove in the clouds had his inhuman birth.
No mother suckled him, no sweet land gave
Large-mannered motions to his mythy mind.
He moved among us, as a muttering king,
Magnificent, would move among his hinds,
Until our blood, commingling, virginal,
With heaven, brought such requital to desire
The very hinds discerned it, in a star.
Shall our blood fail? Or shall it come to be
The blood of paradise? And shall the earth   40
Seem all of paradise that we shall know?
The sky will be much friendlier then than now,
A part of labor and a part of pain,
And next in glory to enduring love,
Not this dividing and indifferent blue.

IV

She says, "I am content when wakened birds,
Before they fly, test the reality
Of misty fields, by their sweet questionings;
But when the birds are gone, and their warm fields
Return no more, where, then, is paradise?"   50
There is not any haunt of prophecy,
Nor any old chimera of the grave,
Neither the golden underground, nor isle
Melodious, where spirits gat them home,
Nor visionary south, nor cloudy palm

Remote on heaven's hill, that has endured
As April's green endures; or will endure
Like her remembrance of awakened birds,
Or her desire for June and evening, tipped
By the consummation of the swallow's wings.

V

She says, "But in contentment I still feel
The need of some imperishable bliss."
Death is the mother of beauty; hence from her,
Alone, shall come fulfillment to our dreams
And our desires. Although she strews the leaves
Of sure obliteration on our paths,
The path sick sorrow took, the many paths
Where triumph rang its brassy phrase, or love
Whispered a little out of tenderness,
She makes the willow shiver in the sun
For maidens who were wont to sit and gaze
Upon the grass, relingquished to their feet.
She causes boys to pile new plums and pears
On disregarded plate. The maidens taste
And stray impassioned in the littering leaves.

VI

Is there no change of death in paradise?
Does ripe fruit never fall? Or do the boughs
Hang always heavy in that perfect sky,
Unchanging, yet so like our perishing earth,
With rivers like our own that seek for seas
They never find, the same receding shores
That never touch with inarticulate pang?
Why set the pear upon those river-banks
Or spice the shores with odors of the plum?
Alas, that they should wear our colors there,
The silken weavings of our afternoons,
And pick the strings of our insipid lutes!
Death is the mother of beauty, mystical,
Within whose burning bosom we devise
Our earthly mothers waiting, sleeplessly.

VII

Supple and turbulent, a ring of men
Shall chant in orgy on a summer morn
Their boisterous devotion to the sun,
Not as a god, but as a god might be,
Naked among them, like a savage source.
Their chant shall be a chant of paradise,
Out of their blood, returning to the sky;
And in their chant shall enter, voice by voice,
The windy lake wherein their lord delights,
The trees, like serafin, and echoing hills,   100
That choir among themselves long afterward.
They shall know well the heavenly fellowship
Of men that perish and of summer morn.
And whence they came and whither they shall go
The dew upon their feet shall manifest.

VIII

She hears, upon that water without sound,
A voice that cries, "The tomb in Palestine
Is not the porch of spirits lingering.
It is the grave of Jesus, where he lay."
We live in an old chaos of the sun,   110
Or old dependency of day and night,
Or island solitude, unsponsored, free,
Of that wide water, inescapable.
Deer walk upon our mountains, and the quail
Whistle about us their spontaneous cries;
Sweet berries ripen in the wilderness;
And, in the isolation of the sky,
At evening, casual flocks of pigeons make
Ambiguous undulations as they sink,
Downward to darkness, on extended wings.   120

The Death of a Soldier

Life contracts and death is expected,
As in a season of autumn.
The soldier falls.

He does not become a three-days personage,
Imposing his separation,
Calling for pomp.

Death is absolute and without memorial,
As in a season of autumn,
When the wind stops,

When the wind stops and, over the heavens,
The clouds go, nevertheless,
In their direction.

The Idea of Order at Key West

She sang beyond the genius of the sea.
The water never formed to mind or voice,
Like a body wholly body, fluttering
Its empty sleeves; and yet its mimic motion
Made constant cry, caused constantly a cry,
That was not ours although we understood,
Inhuman, of the veritable ocean.

The sea was not a mask. No more was she.
The song and water were not medleyed sound
Even if what she sang was what she heard,
Since what she sang was uttered word by word.
It may be that in all her phrases stirred
The grinding water and the gasping wind;
But it was she and not the sea we heard.

For she was the maker of the song she sang.
The ever-hooded, tragic-gestured sea
Was merely a place by which she walked to sing.
Whose spirit is this? we said, because we knew
It was the spirit that we sought and knew
That we should ask this often as she sang.

If it was only the dark voice of the sea
That rose, or even colored by many waves;

If it was only the outer voice of sky
And cloud, of the sunken coral water-walled,
However clear, it would have been deep air,
The heaving speech of air, a summer sound
Repeated in a summer without end
And sound alone. But it was more than that,
More even than her voice, and ours, among
The meaningless plungings of water and the wind,   30
Theatrical distances, bronze shadows heaped
On high horizons, mountainous atmospheres
Of sky and sea.

                  It was her voice that made
The sky acutest at its vanishing.
She measured to the hour its solitude.
She was the single artificer of the world
In which she sang. And when she sang, the sea,
Whatever self it had, became the self
That was her song, for she was the maker. Then we,
As we beheld her striding there alone,   40
Knew that there never was a world for her
Except the one she sang and, singing, made.

Ramon Fernandez, tell me, if you know,
Why, when the singing ended and we turned
Toward the town, tell why the glassy lights,
The lights in the fishing boats at anchor there,
As the night descended, tilting in the air,
Mastered the night and portioned out the sea,
Fixing emblazoned zones and fiery poles,
Arranging, deepening, enchanting night.   50

Oh! Blessed rage for order, pale Ramon,
The maker's rage to order words of the sea,
Words of the fragrant portals, dimly-starred,
And of ourselves and of our origins,
In ghostlier demarcations, keener sounds.

---

43 Stevens said he had chosen two common names at random. In fact, however, Ramon Fernandez is a modern humanist philosopher.

Autumn Refrain

The skreak and skritter of evening gone
And grackles gone and sorrows of the sun,
The sorrows of sun, too, gone . . . the moon and moon,
The yellow moon of words about the nightingale
In measureless measures, not a bird for me
But the name of a bird and the name of a nameless air
I have never—shall never hear. And yet beneath
The stillness of everything gone, and being still,
Being and sitting still, something resides,
Some skreaking and skrittering residuum,   10
And grates these evasions of the nightingale
Though I have never—shall never hear that bird.
And the stillness is in the key, all of it is,
The stillness is all in the key of that desolate sound.

The Candle a Saint

Green is the night, green kindled and apparelled.
It is she that walks among astronomers.

She strides above the rabbit and the cat,
Like a noble figure, out of the sky,

Moving among the sleepers, the men,
Those that lie chanting *green is the night.*

Green is the night and out of madness woven,
The self-same madness of the astronomers

And of him that sees, beyond the astronomers,
The topaz rabbit and the emerald cat,   10

That sees above them, that sees rise up above them,
The noble figure, the essential shadow,

Moving and being, the image at its source,
The abstract, the archaic queen. Green is the night.

Asides on the Oboe

The prologues are over. It is a question, now,
Of final belief. So, say that final belief
Must be in a fiction. It is time to choose.

I

That obsolete fiction of the wide river in
An empty land; the gods that Boucher killed;
And the metal heroes that time granulates—
The philosophers' man alone still walks in dew,
Still by the sea-side mutters milky lines
Concerning an immaculate imagery.
If you say on the hautboy man is not enough,   10
Can never stand as god, is ever wrong
In the end, however naked, tall, there is still
The impossible possible philosophers' man,
The man who has had the time to think enough,
The central man, the human globe, responsive
As a mirror with a voice, the man of glass,
Who in a million diamonds sums us up.

II

He is the transparence of the place in which
He is and in his poems we find peace.
He sets this peddler's pie and cries in summer,   20
The glass man, cold and numbered, dewily cries,
"Thou art not August unless I make thee so."
Clandestine steps upon imagined stairs
Climb through the night, because his cuckoos call.

III

One year, death and war prevented the jasmine scent
And the jasmine islands were bloody martyrdoms.
How was it then with the central man? Did we

---

5 Boucher: François Boucher, eighteenth-century French painter of mythological subjects. In his pictures the classical gods of earlier art are reduced in dignity until they become little more than artificial shepherd and shepherdess figures.

Find peace? We found the sum of men. We found,
If we found the central evil, the central good.
We buried the fallen without jasmine crowns.   30
There was nothing he did not suffer, no; nor we.

It was not as if the jasmine ever returned.
But we and the diamond globe at last were one.
We had always been partly one. It was as we came
To see him, that we were wholly one, as we heard
Him chanting for those buried in their blood,
In the jasmine haunted forests, that we knew
The glass man, without external reference.

The Motive for Metaphor

You like it under the trees in autumn,
Because everything is half dead.
The wind moves like a cripple among the leaves
And repeats words without meaning.

In the same way, you were happy in spring,
With the half colors of quarter-things,
The slightly brighter sky, the melting clouds,
The single bird, the obscure moon—

The obscure moon lighting an obscure world
Of things that would never be quite expressed,   10
Where you yourself were never quite yourself
And did not want nor have to be,

Desiring the exhilarations of changes:
The motive for metaphor, shrinking from
The weight of primary noon,
The A B C of being,

The ruddy temper, the hammer
Of red and blue, the hard sound—
Steel against intimation—the sharp flash,
The vital, arrogant, fatal, dominant X.   20

EDITH SITWELL

Said King Pompey

Said King Pompey the emperor's ape,
Shuddering black in his temporal cape
Of dust, 'The dust is everything—
The heart to love and the voice to sing,
Indianapolis
And the Acropolis,
Also the hairy sky that we
Take for a coverlet comfortably.'
Said the Bishop, 'The world is flat. . . .
But the see-saw Crowd sent the emperor down   10
To the howling dust—and up went the Clown
With his face that is filched from the new young
    Dead. . . .
And the Tyrant's ghost and the Low-Man-Flea
Are emperor-brothers, throw shades that are red
From the tide of blood (Red Sea, Dead Sea),
And Attila's voice or the hum of a gnat
Can usher in Eternity.'

Dark Song

The fire was furry as a bear
And the flames purr . . .
The brown bear rambles in his chain
Captive to cruel men
Through the dark and hairy wood . . .
The maid sighed, 'All my blood
Is animal. They thought I sat
Like a household cat;
But through the dark woods rambled I . . .
Oh, if my blood would die!'   10
The fire had a bear's fur;
It heard and knew. . . .
The dark earth, furry as a bear,
Grumbled too!

The Little Ghost Who Died for Love
for Allanah Harper

Deborah Churchill, born 1678, was hanged in 1708 for shielding her lover in a duel. His opponent was killed, her lover fled to Holland, and she was hanged in his stead, according to the law of the time. The chronicle said, 'Though she died at peace with God, this malefactor could never understand the justice of her sentence, to the last moment of her life.'

'Fear not, O maidens, shivering
As bunches of the dew-drenched leaves
In the calm moonlight . . . it is the cold sends quivering
My voice, a little nightingale that grieves.

Now Time beats not, and dead Love is forgotten . . .
The spirit too is dead and dank and rotten,

And I forget the moment when I ran
Between my lover and the sworded man—

Blinded with terror lest I lose his heart.
The sworded man dropped, and I saw depart   10

Love and my lover and my life . . . he fled
And I was strung and hung upon the tree.
It is so cold now that my heart is dead
And drops through time . . . night is too dark to see

Him still. . . . But it is spring; upon the fruit-boughs of your lips,
Young maids, the dew like India's splendor drips.
Pass by among the strawberry beds, and pluck the berries
Cooled by the silver moon; pluck boughs of cherries

That seem the lovely lucent coral bough
(From streams of starry milk those branches grow)   20
That Cassiopeia feeds with her faint light,
Like Ethiopia ever jeweled bright.

Those lovely cherries do enclose
Deep in their sweet hearts the silver snows,

And the small budding flowers upon the trees
Are filled with sweetness like the bags of bees.

Forget my fate . . . but I, a moonlight ghost,
Creep down the strawberry paths and seek the lost

World, the apothecary at the Fair.
I, Deborah, in my long cloak of brown, 30
Like the small nightingale that dances down
The cherried boughs, creep to the doctor's bare
Booth . . . cold as ivy in the air,

And, where I stand, the brown and ragged light
Holds something still beyond, hid from my sight.

Once, plumaged like the sea, his swanskin head
Had wintry white quills . . . "Hearken to the Dead . . .
I was a nightingale, but now I croak
Like some dark harpy hidden in night's cloak
Upon the walls; among the Dead, am quick; 40
Oh, give me medicine, for the world is sick;
Not medicines, planet-spotted like fritillaries
For country sins and old stupidities,
Nor potions you may give a country maid
When she is lovesick . . . love in earth is laid,
Grown dead and rotten". . . so I sank me down,
Poor Deborah in my long cloak of brown.
Though cockcrow marches, crying of false dawns,
Shall bury my dark voice, yet still it mourns
Among the ruins—for it is not I, 50
But this old world, is sick and soon must die!'

Heart and Mind

Said the Lion to the Lioness—'When you are amber dust—
No more a raging fire like the heat of the Sun
(No liking but all lust)—
Remember still the flowering of the amber blood and bone,

The rippling of bright muscles like a sea,
Remember the rose-prickles of bright paws,
Though we shall mate no more
Till the fire of that sun the heart and the moon-cold bone are one.'

Said the Skeleton lying upon the sands of Time—
'The great gold planet that is the mourning heat of the Sun   10
Is greater than all gold, more powerful
Than the tawny body of a Lion that fire consumes
Like all that grows or leaps . . . so is the heart
More powerful than all dust. Once I was Hercules
Or Samson, strong as the pillars of the seas:
But the flames of the heart consumed me, and the mind
Is but a foolish wind.'

Said the Sun to the Moon—'When you are but a lonely white crone,
And I, a dead King in my golden armor somewhere in a dark wood,
Remember only this of our hopeless love: 20
That never till Time is done
Will the fire of the heart and the fire of the mind be one.'

T. S. ELIOT

The Love Song of J. Alfred Prufrock

> S'io credesse che mia risposta fosse
> A persona che mai tornasse al mondo,
> Questa fiamma staria senza piu scosse.
> Ma perciocche giammai di questo fondo
> Non torno vivo alcun, s'i'odo il vero,
> Senza tema d'infamia ti rispondo.

Let us go then, you and I,
When the evening is spread out against the sky
Like a patient etherised upon a table;
Let us go, through certain half-deserted streets,
The muttering retreats
Of restless nights in one-night cheap hotels
And sawdust restaurants with oyster-shells:

Streets that follow like a tedious argument
Of insidious intent
To lead you to an overwhelming question . . .   10
Oh, do not ask, "What is it?"
Let us go and make our visit.

    In the room the women come and go
Talking of Michelangelo.

    The yellow fog that rubs its back upon the window-panes,
The yellow smoke that rubs its muzzle on the window-panes
Licked its tongue into the corners of the evening,
Lingered upon the pools that stand in drains,
Let fall upon its back the soot that falls from chimneys,
Slipped by the terrace, made a sudden leap,   20
And seeing that it was a soft October night,
Curled once about the house, and fell asleep.

    And indeed there will be time
For the yellow smoke that slides along the street,
Rubbing its back upon the window-panes;
There will be time, there will be time
To prepare a face to meet the faces that you meet;
There will be time to murder and create,
And time for all the works and days of hands
That lift and drop a question on your plate;   30
Time for you and time for me,
And time yet for a hundred indecisions,
And for a hundred visions and revisions,
Before the taking of a toast and tea.

    In the room the women come and go
Talking of Michelangelo.

    And indeed there will be time
To wonder, "Do I dare?" and, "Do I dare?"
Time to turn back and descend the stair,

With a bald spot in the middle of my hair— 40
[They will say: "How his hair is growing thin!"]
My morning coat, my collar mounting firmly to the chin,
My necktie rich and modest, but asserted by a simple pin—
[They will say: "But how his arms and legs are thin!"]
Do I dare
Disturb the universe?
In a minute there is time
For decisions and revisions which a minute will reverse.

   For I have known them all already, known them all:—
Have known the evenings, mornings, afternoons, 50
I have measured out my life with coffee spoons;
I know the voices dying with a dying fall
Beneath the music from a farther room.
     So how should I presume?

   And I have known the eyes already, known them all—
The eyes that fix you in a formulated phrase,
And when I am formulated, sprawling on a pin,
When I am pinned and wriggling on the wall,
Then how should I begin
To spit out all the butt-ends of my days and ways? 60
     And how should I presume?

   And I have known the arms already, known them all—
Arms that are braceleted and white and bare
[But in the lamplight, downed with light brown hair!]
Is it perfume from a dress
That makes me so digress?
Arms that lie along a table, or wrap about a shawl.
     And should I then presume?
     And how should I begin?

      .   .   .   .   .

Shall I say, I have gone at dusk through narrow streets 70
And watched the smoke that rises from the pipes
Of lonely men in shirt-sleeves, leaning out of windows? . . .

I should have been a pair of ragged claws
Scuttling across the floors of silent seas.

. . . . .

And the afternoon, the evening, sleeps so peacefully!
Smoothed by long fingers,
Asleep ... tired ... or it malingers,
Stretched on the floor, here beside you and me.
Should I, after tea and cakes and ices,
Have the strength to force the moment to its crisis?   80
But though I have wept and fasted, wept and prayed,
Though I have seen my head [grown slightly bald] brought
    in upon a platter,
I am no prophet—and here's no great matter;
I have seen the moment of my greatness flicker,
And I have seen the eternal Footman hold my coat, and
    snicker,
And in short, I was afraid.

And would it have been worth it, after all,
After the cups, the marmalade, the tea,
Among the porcelain, among some talk of you and me,
Would it have been worth while,   90
To have bitten off the matter with a smile,
To have squeezed the universe into a ball
To roll it toward some overwhelming question,
To say: "I am Lazarus, come from the dead,
Come back to tell you all, I shall tell you all"—
If one, settling a pillow by her head,
    Should say: "That is not what I meant at all.
    That is not it, at all."

And would it have been worth it, after all,
Would it have been worth while,   100
After the sunsets and the dooryards and the sprinkled streets,
After the novels, after the teacups, after the skirts that trail
    along the floor—

And this, and so much more?—
It is impossible to say just what I mean!
But as if a magic lantern threw the nerves in patterns on a
    screen:
Would it have been worth while
If one, settling a pillow or throwing off a shawl,
And turning toward the window, should say:
    "That is not it at all,
    That is not what I meant, at all."   110

      .   .   .   .   .

No! I am not Prince Hamlet, nor was meant to be;
Am an attendant lord, one that will do
To swell a progress, start a scene or two,
Advise the prince; no doubt, an easy tool,
Deferential, glad to be of use,
Politic, cautious, and meticulous;
Full of high sentence, but a bit obtuse;
At times, indeed, almost ridiculous—
Almost, at times, the Fool.

    I grow old . . . I grow old . . .   120
I shall wear the bottoms of my trousers rolled.

    Shall I part my hair behind? Do I dare to eat a peach?
I shall wear white flannel trousers, and walk upon the beach.
I have heard the mermaids singing, each to each.

    I do not think that they will sing to me.

    I have seen them riding seaward on the waves
Combing the white hair of the waves blown back
When the wind blows the water white and black.

    We have lingered in the chambers of the sea
By sea-girls wreathed with seaweed red and brown   130
Till human voices wake us, and we drown.

From "Landscapes"
IV. *Rannoch, by Glencoe*

Here the crow starves, here the patient stag
Breeds for the rifle. Between the soft moor
And the soft sky, scarcely room
To leap or soar. Substance crumbles, in the thin air
Moon cold or moon hot. The road winds in
Listlessness of ancient war
Languor of broken steel,
Clamour of confused wrong, apt
In silence. Memory is strong
Beyond the bone. Pride snapped,   10
Shadow of pride is long, in the long pass
No concurrence of bone.

Journey of the Magi

'A cold coming we had of it,
Just the worst time of the year
For a journey, and such a long journey:
The ways deep and the weather sharp,
The very dead of winter.'
And the camels galled, sore-footed, refractory,
Lying down in the melting snow.
There were times we regretted
The summer palaces on slopes, the terraces,
And the silken girls bringing sherbet.   10
Then the camel men cursing and grumbling
And running away, and wanting their liquor and women,
And the night-fires going out, and the lack of shelters,
And the cities hostile and the towns unfriendly
And the villages dirty and charging high prices:
A hard time we had of it.
At the end we preferred to travel all night,

Sleeping in snatches,
With the voices singing in our ears, saying
That this was all folly. 20

Then at dawn we came down to a temperate valley,
Wet, below the snow line, smelling of vegetation;
With a running stream and a water-mill beating the darkness,
And three trees on the low sky,
And an old white horse galloped away in the meadow.
Then we came to a tavern with vine-leaves over the lintel,
Six hands at an open door dicing for pieces of silver,
And feet kicking the empty wine-skins.
But there was no information, and so we continued
And arrived at evening, not a moment too soon 30
Finding the place; it was (you may say) satisfactory.

All this was a long time ago, I remember,
And I would do it again, but set down
This set down
This: were we led all that way for
Birth or Death? There was a Birth, certainly,
We had evidence and no doubt. I had seen birth and death,
But had thought they were different; this Birth was
Hard and bitter agony for us, like Death, our death.
We returned to our places, these Kingdoms, 40
But no longer at ease here, in the old dispensation,
With an alien people clutching their gods.
I should be glad of another death.

Marina

Quis hic locus, quae regio, quae mundi plaga?

What seas what shores what grey rocks and what islands
What water lapping the bow
And scent of pine and the woodthrush singing through the fog
What images return
O my daughter.

Those who sharpen the tooth of the dog, meaning
Death
Those who glitter with the glory of the humming-bird, meaning
Death   10
Those who sit in the sty of contentment, meaning
Death
Those who suffer the ecstasy of the animals, meaning
Death

Are become unsubstantial, reduced by a wind,
A breath of pine, and the woodsong fog
By this grace dissolved in place

What is this face, less clear and clearer
The pulse in the arm, less strong and stronger—
Given or lent? more distant than stars and nearer than the eye   20

Whispers and small laughter between leaves and hurrying feet
Under sleep, where all the waters meet.

Bowsprit cracked with ice and paint cracked with heat.
I made this, I have forgotten
And remember.
The rigging weak and the canvas rotten
Between one June and another September.
Made this unknowing, half conscious, unknown, my own.

The garboard strake leaks, the seams need calking.
This form, this face, this life   30
Living to live in a world of time beyond me; let me
Resign my life for this life, my speech for that unspoken,
The awakened, lips parted, the hope, the new ships.

What seas what shores what granite islands towards my timbers
And woodthrush calling through the fog
My daughter.

Burnt Norton

I

Time present and time past
Are both perhaps present in time future,
And time future contained in time past.
If all time is eternally present
All time is unredeemable.
What might have been is an abstraction
Remaining a perpetual possibility
Only in a world of speculation.
What might have been and what has been
Point to one end, which is always present.   10
Footfalls echo in the memory
Down the passage which we did not take
Towards the door we never opened
Into the rose-garden. My words echo
Thus, in your mind.
                    But to what purpose
Disturbing the dust on a bowl of rose-leaves
I do not know.
              Other echoes
Inhabit the garden. Shall we follow?
Quick, said the bird, find them, find them,
Round the corner. Through the first gate,   20
Into our first world, shall we follow
The deception of the thrush? Into our first world.
There they were, dignified, invisible,
Moving without pressure, over the dead leaves,
In the autumn heat, through the vibrant air,
And the bird called, in response to
The unheard music hidden in the shrubbery,
And the unseen eyebeam crossed, for the roses

Title: An old English country house. The scene is its deserted garden.
16 bowl of rose leaves: the once fashionable rose bowl (often a Chinese jar [cf. line 142] containing dried rose petals spiced for enhanced fragrance. With its reminder of last summer's flowers, it is a natural symbol of memory.

Had the look of flowers that are looked at.
There they were as our guests, accepted and accepting.
So we moved, and they, in a formal pattern,
Along the empty alley, into the box circle,
To look down into the drained pool.

Dry the pool, dry concrete, brown edged,
And the pool was filled with water out of sunlight,
And the lotos rose, quietly, quietly,
The surface glittered out of heart of light,
And they were behind us, reflected in the pool.
Then a cloud passed, and the pool was empty.
Go, said the bird, for the leaves were full of children,
Hidden excitedly, containing laughter.
Go, go, go, said the bird: human kind
Cannot bear very much reality.
Time past and time future
What might have been and what has been
Point to one end, which is always present.

II

Garlic and sapphires in the mud
Clot the bedded axle-tree.
The trilling wire in the blood
Sings below inveterate scars
And reconciles forgotten wars.
The dance along the artery
The circulation of the lymph
Are figured in the drift of stars
Ascend to summer in the tree
We move above the moving tree
In light upon the figured leaf
And hear upon the sodden floor
Below, the boarhound and the boar
Pursue their pattern as before
But reconciled among the stars.

At the still point of the turning world. Neither flesh nor
    fleshless;
Neither from nor towards; at the still point, there the
    dance is,
But neither arrest nor movement. And do not call it
    fixity,
Where past and future are gathered. Neither movement
    from nor towards,
Neither ascent nor decline. Except for the point, the
    still point,
There would be no dance, and there is only the
    dance.
I can only say, *there* we have been: but I cannot say
    where.
And I cannot say, how long, for that is to place it
    in time.

The inner freedom from the practical desire,   70
The release from action and suffering, release from the inner
And the outer compulsion, yet surrounded
By a grace of sense, a white light still and moving,
Erhebung without motion, concentration
Without elimination, both a new world
And the old made explicit, understood
In the completion of its partial ecstasy,
The resolution of its partial horror.
Yet the enchainment of past and future
Woven in the weakness of the changing body,   80
Protects mankind from heaven and damnation
Which flesh cannot endure.
                      Time past and time future
Allow but a little consciousness.
To be conscious is not to be in time
But only in time can the moment in the rose-garden,
The moment in the arbour where the rain beat,
The moment in the draughty church at smokefall

---

74 *Erhebung:* elevation, exaltation (literally, a lifting up).

Be remembered; involved with past and future.
Only through time time is conquered.

III

Here is a place of disaffection
Time before and time after
In a dim light: neither daylight
Investing form with lucid stillness
Turning shadow into transient beauty
With slow rotation suggesting permanence
Nor darkness to purify the soul
Emptying the sensual with deprivation
Cleansing affection from the temporal.
Neither plenitude nor vacancy. Only a flicker
Over the strained time-ridden faces
Distracted from distraction by distraction
Filled with fancies and empty of meaning
Tumid apathy with no concentration
Men and bits of paper, whirled by the cold wind
That blows before and after time,
Wind in and out of unwholesome lungs
Time before and time after.
Eructation of unhealthy souls
Into the faded air, the torpid
Driven on the wind that sweeps the gloomy hills of
    London,
Hampstead and Clerkenwell, Campden and Putney,
Highgate, Primrose and Ludgate. Not here
Not here the darkness, in this twittering world.

Descend lower, descend only
Into the world of perpetual solitude,
World not world, but that which is not world,
Internal darkness, deprivation
And destitution of all property,
Dessication of the world of sense,
Evacuation of the world of fancy,
Inoperancy of the world of spirit;
This is the one way, and the other

Is the same, not in movement
But abstention from movement; while the world moves
In appetency, on its metalled ways
Of time past and time future.

IV

Time and the bell have buried the day,
The black cloud carries the sun away.
Will the sunflower turn to us, will the clematis
Stray down, bend to us; tendril and spray   130
Clutch and cling?
Chill
Fingers of yew be curled
Down on us? After the kingfisher's wing
Has answered light to light, and is silent, the light is still
At the still point of the turning world.

V

Words move, music moves
Only in time; but that which is only living
Can only die. Words, after speech, reach
Into the silence. Only by the form, the pattern,   140
Can words or music reach
The stillness, as a Chinese jar still
Moves perpetually in its stillness.
Not the stillness of the violin, while the note lasts,
Not that only, but the co-existence,
Or say that the end precedes the beginning,
And the end and the beginning were always there
Before the beginning and after the end.
And all is always now. Words strain,
Crack and sometimes break, under the burden,   150
Under the tension, slip, slide, perish,
Decay with imprecision, will not stay in place,
Will not stay still. Shrieking voices
Scolding, mocking, or merely chattering,
Always assail them. The Word in the desert
Is most attacked by voices of temptation,

The crying shadow in the funeral dance,
The loud lament of the disconsolate chimera.

The detail of the pattern is movement,
As in the figure of the ten stairs.	160
Desire itself is movement
Not in itself desirable;
Love is itself unmoving,
Only the cause and end of movement,
Timeless, and undesiring
Except in the aspect of time
Caught in the form of limitation
Between un-being and being.
Sudden in a shaft of sunlight
Even while the dust moves	170
There rises the hidden laughter
Of children in the foliage
Quick now, here, now, always—
Ridiculous the waste sad time
Stretching before and after.

160 the ten stairs: St. John of the Cross's symbol of ascent toward God.

Notes

I

P. 37. "Mr. Flood's Party"
  Is the poet's attitude toward his subject sympathetic, or mocking, or both? Point out some of the details that influence your opinion. Compare the tone and the attitude toward failure in this and the next two poems, observing particularly the key words and images that establish the tone.

P. 42. "Of Jeoffrey, His Cat"
  This selection forms part of a long, fragmentary work called *Jubilate Agno* (Rejoice in the Lamb), written in 1759–63 during Smart's confinement in a madhouse but not published till 1939. One part is known as the "Let" section, since all but two of the lines begin with "Let"; the other is the "For" section. The two were perhaps intended to be grouped in alternate, antiphonal pairs of lines, but there is no "Let" section corresponding to the "Jeoffrey" lines. Smart worked carefully on the *Jubilate*, attempting to apply to English verse the principles of Hebrew versification, which is based on parallelism rather than meter.

P. 46. "My Last Duchess"
  This and the following selections from Browning are dramatic monologues, poems in which the author speaks as someone other than himself. Browning constructs a specific scene and situation in which a character reveals himself by talking.

P. 47. "The Bishop Orders His Tomb at
        St. Praxed's Church"
  The Bishop is meant to typify some incongruous aspects of the Italian Renaissance: love of beauty, genuine Christian belief mingling with pagan tastes, worldliness, cynical immorality.

P. 53. "Bonny Barbara Allan"
This ballad combines stock materials ("She had not gane a mile but twa" and "make my bed," the latter as a token of approaching death) with unusually individual and complex motivation, that of a girl who destroys herself and her lover out of injured pride.

P. 55. "Marie Hamilton"
The emotional impact of the last stanza is worth considering. It merely makes the objective statement that tomorrow there will be one Mary fewer in her circle and then names those who will be left. What is the effect of this?

P. 57. "The Three Ravens"
This is an example of the ballad with refrain and repeated lines, all the stanzas being sung according to the pattern printed in the first stanza.
M. J. C. Hodgart (*The Ballads*, London, 1950) believes that an older ballad lies behind this one: he thinks "a magical transformation of a maiden into a deer lies in the background but has become suppressed." There are other unexplained elements in the poem, some perhaps remnants of symbolism in the earlier poem. It is a good example of what the uncertainties of oral tradition may do to or for a ballad.

P. 58. "The Twa Corbies"
Though this is commonly accepted as an authentic folk ballad, Hodgart is of the opinion that it is largely the work of Sir Walter Scott, who first printed it with other Scottish ballads. Compare the treatment of similar materials in this and the preceding poem.

P. 59. "Sir Patrick Spence"
33-40 Note how the waiting is stretched out through two stanzas and how it is emphasized by the only details given about the wives, the fans in their hands and the gold combs in their hair; they are dressed and waiting idly, "lang, lang."

P. 66.   "The Castaway"
Ṭhis and most of the remaining narratives are less simple than the preceding ballads. It is important to see as clearly as possible both the surface and the submerged meanings, to see how one reveals or is influenced by the other, and to appreciate the interweaving of the strands into a unified whole.

The incident upon which "The Castaway" is based was reported in Admiral George Anson's "A Voyage Round the World" (see line 52). In the story of the dead seaman, Cowper saw an emblem of his own spiritual despair. A deeply religious and gentle man, Cowper several times sank into a state of horror in which he believed himself abandoned by God, his soul doomed to eternal Hell. Long struggles against despair won him some years of cheerful friendliness and sanity, but the dream in which a voice had once announced his doom continued to haunt him. "The Castaway" was written not long before his final descent into insanity. In line 3 and the conclusion he makes explicit the parallel between his state and that of Anson's seaman. Consider what effect this double meaning has on the poem as a whole.

P. 68.   "The Rime of the Ancient Mariner"
So many essays and even full-length books (the most famous is John Livingstone Lowes's *The Road to Xanadu* [1927]) have been written to interpret this poem that the only possible course here is to let the reader read and make of it what he chooses or what he can give a reasonable defence of. There is no difficulty about the upper layer or two of meaning; the only question is whether there are other layers and, if so, what they represent. These are the questions that cannot be answered here.

Briefly, the poem is a literary ballad influenced by the earlier folk ballad and employing what is known as ballad meter (see Chapter II) with sophistication and skill. Many of the descriptive details and the main narrative of the outbound voyage —its log—are derived from various books of travel and voyages, favorite reading with Coleridge. The story is one of sin (the wanton killing of a harmless and innocent living being), punishment (storm, polar ice, heat, calm, drought, death of all but the one mariner) repentance (through recognition of the beauty of living beings), a miraculous journey home, and penance. The voyage out is natural; the supernatural enters with the spectre ship that is seen when the men are near death from drought; then for a time the natural and supernatural mingle; in the voyage home the supernatural is in the ascendant. Thus it is possible to construe the supernatural events as hallucinations of drought and starvation, but Coleridge does not suggest this. The whole is placed within a contrasting frame of wedding, wedding-guest, piety, and innocent mirth.

Many critics believe that a deeper symbolism underlies this story, but there is little agreement on the nature of it; many others feel that no such symbolism is present. A self-disciplined reader will carefully test out any symbolic interpretation by asking himself (1) precisely what *in the poem* suggests such a meaning, (2) whether there is anything that is not accounted for by the story and the explicit theme without other symbolism, and (3) whether the poem as a whole is consistent with the deeper symbolic interpretation.

P. 88. "The Host of the Air"

Yeats said this poem was founded on an old Irish folk ballad. The title refers to the "trooping fairies" of Irish legend, described by Yeats in *Irish Fairy and Folk Tales*. The name "Sidhe" (pronounced "shee"), he explained, in Gaelic means wind as well as fairies. The Sidhe ride the wind; and country people, seeing in the road a whirlwind of straws and leaves, say it is the fairies passing. The Sidhe are not always little but take what size and shape they choose. They like to feast, fight, dance, and make love; and they play the most beautiful music. They are inconstant and irresponsible.

When Yeats wrote this poem he added a note explaining, "Any one who tastes fairy food or drink is glamoured and stolen by the fairies. This is why Bridget sets O'Driscoll to play cards." He also made the conclusion explicit in an additional stanza: O'Driscoll recognized his companions as "the folk of the air"; filled with dread, he ran home, where he found old women keening his dead wife. Yeats thought the meaning was evident without this stanza and discarded it because it had no "rhythmical charm" and broke the unity of mood.

Can the mood or tone of the poem be described? Does it owe anything to contradictory words and images?

26   The phrase has a double meaning. The trooping fairies were themselves the "Fairy Host" or the "Host of the Air"; but the bread of the Eucharist is also the Host, and the bread and wine here represent consecration to the powers of the air.

II

P. 101.   "She dwelt among the untrodden ways"

This poem and the next are examples of typical, rather simple iambic meter. They employ the ballad stanza, with first and third as well as second and fourth lines rhyming. They have some of the common variations—substitutions of trochaic and other feet here and there—though the first has fewer such substitutions than most poems have. They provide easy practice in scansion for those who desire it. But beyond this they provide a study in the poetic effects of meter, which are in the end what we look for.

The two poems deal with the same subject, the death of a girl loved by the poet. On first acquaintance, many readers prefer the first poem because its conclusion is more directly personal—how he misses her! the poet exclaims—and because violets, mossy stones, and "springs of Dove" (the name of a river) are prettier than any of the more cosmic but sterner and more impersonal images in the second poem, where, writing with more restraint, the poet says only that he had been utterly unprepared for her death and that she has now become one with the great and permanent elements in nature. Regardless of immediate appeal, however, the second is the better poem, and this is true largely for metrical reasons: its meter is less monotonous, more flexible and alive, and more expressively fitted to the mood.

Ballad meter can be a trap to a momentarily insensitive ear (either poet's or reader's) if its feet are too regular and its pauses too monotonously fixed, as they sometimes are, with a half-pause at the end of the first line, a full or nearly full stop at the end of the second, then again a half-pause, and so on, with the result that every four-stressed line ends with a half cadence and, alternately, every three-stressed line with a full cadence. Such a fixed rhythm has its uses on occasion; but it produces a mechanical effect that can make an emotional statement sound flat or even insincere, however genuine the original emotion may have been. Compare, then, from this standpoint, and *listen to* the spacing of the cadences in these two poems. Then also consider the much greater regularity of the feet in most lines of "She dwelt. . . ." In the second, third, and fourth lines, for example, nearly all the stressed syllables are about equally stressed and nearly all the unstressed ones are equally light and short; whereas in "A slumber did my spirit seal" both the heavy and the light syllables vary greatly in the degree of their stress and in their length (duration).

The two poems should be studied in detail, with every departure from the standard form noted, and with the sound of the lines constantly in mind. Finally, the *speed* of the last two lines of each should be compared, in the light of the meaning and of what would seem to be the intended mood of the poems.

P. 102.   "Fear no more"
The metrical irregularity of lines 19–22 may be due to music for which the song was written, but the original music has not survived.

P. 102.   "Full fathom five"
In this song, "Ding-dong" is a "burden" or undersong, proba-

bly to be sung softly as an accompaniment while the other words are sung more distinctly by one voice. Hence, in line 8 it does not count as part of the metrical structure.

P. 103. "Dust of Snow"
Iambic meter, as such, has no distinctive character of its own and conveys no particular mood. All depends on what is done with it. This poem and the next illustrate the importance of something that is not often enough noticed in the study of verse, the relation between the metrical unit and the word or phrasal unit. Both poems are in iambic verse; yet the metrical effects are very different, and the difference is not due primarily to the length of the lines, though one is dimeter and the other (except for its third line) pentameter. If one examines the units, one finds that in "Dust of Snow" the words are nearly all monosyllables and—more important—that the foot and the word groupings coincide except in one instance: The way/ a crow/, shook down/ on me, etc., except for the line "From a hem/lock tree," where the foot ends in the middle of a word. (The next line might be considered an exception too, but in actual reading one would say "giv'n/" more nearly than "giv/en."). In Shelley's "Fragment," the words obviously are much longer, and this in itself creates a different effect but is not the whole story. The poem scans as follows:

He wan/ders, like/ a day-/appear/ing dream;

Through the/ dim wil/derness/es of/ the mind;

Through des/ert woods/ and tracts,/ which seem

Like o/cean, home/less, bound/less, un/confined.

The brackets below the line mark the points at which the word or phrase crosses and therefore tends to obliterate or at least minimize the foot unit.

These two poems represent extremes of overlapping and

nonoverlapping units and of long and short words. Most poems are more mixed, but always variety of movement, speed, smoothness, emphasis, and other things having to do with expressiveness are affected by such differences as these.

P. 103. "The Sluggard"
This and the four following poems employ anapestic meter with varying degrees of success and freedom. They are not all great poems. All should be studied, however, for the relation between meter, tone, and meaning. In those that succeed best as serious poetry, the variations from the anapestic foot should be noticed.

P. 104. "The Chimney Sweeper"
3 'weep: a bitter pun made from the lisped cry of the small "sweep" as he went through the streets calling out his occupation. The enforced employment of small boys as "climbing boys" was widely condemned but still practiced in Blake's time.

This poem was probably influenced by Blake's early familiarity with the didactic verses of Watts. Is it possible to tell whether the conclusion is intended to be ironical or straight? Is the tone of the poem as a whole clear to you, or is it ambiguous? Has the meter anything to do with this problem if you are uncertain?

P. 105. Lines: "When the lamp is shattered"
Note the pattern of masculine and feminine rhyme, and study the meter of this poem with particular care.

P. 107. "The Listeners"
This poem is metrically much more irregular than the preceding ones. Note that the gallop is avoided both by the elimination of light syllables through the substitution of iambic and spondaic feet and by an unexpected, quite opposite means, the frequent use of even more than the usual number of light, unaccented syllables and the presence of soft sounds in many

of the accented syllables, with the consequent effect of softness and silence throughout. With few abrupt, strong accents, there is little contrast and hence no gallop.

As to the meaning of the poem, de la Mare is reported to have said that the Traveler is the ghost.

P. 108. "A Lament for Our Lady's Shrine at Walsingham"
This sixteenth-century poem also is extremely irregular. Consider how ordinary ballad meter is altered to make the tone and movement expressive of lamentation. Note also the metrical ambiguity of the first half-dozen lines, which could be read less expressively as swifter, two-stress lines. The rhythm of subsequent lines, however, makes clear what is intended, though the rhyming lines vary in length.

P. 110. "Upon Julia's Clothes"
The cool neatness, finish, and symmetry of this light poem is lost if the reader does not recognize the literal meaning: Herrick admires first the beauty of Julia's movement as she walks in bright flowing silk and next her beauty as she walks in "glittering" nakedness. Each tercet contains its own picture, which changes when the rhyme and stanza change; and each tercet has for its highlight one long, unromantic, and in Herrick's day technical or scientific term, "liquefaction" and "vibration." The poem is an excellent small example of the interdependence of form, meter, meaning, and tone.

1.   goes: In Herrick's time the meaning of "go" was more specific than it is now. It meant "walk."

5   vibration: Bentham in the eighteenth century described his walking (for exercise) as "vibrating." Earlier, the word was used in scientific discussions having to do with gravity, oscillation of pendulums, and so on.

P. 110. "Birds at Winter Nightfall"
This triolet should be compared with the one by Bridges in the introduction to the next chapter.

3   cotonea-aster (usually written as one word, *cotoneaster,* but pronounced as Hardy's spelling and the rhyme suggest): A flowering shrub of which some varieties bear bright berries that remain into the winter.

5   crumb-outcaster: Undoubtedly one of the most ingenious rhymes in English poetry. Is it so forced as to be a defect?

P. 110.   From *Song of Myself,* Section 32

However Whitman may be ranked as a poet—and he is ranked very differently by different people—he is of some importance in the history of versification for the impetus he gave to free verse. There was free verse before Whitman, but it was he who can be said to have declared it free and who materially influenced later writers. With Whitman the line is the primary unit. In this selection from *Song of Myself,* each line makes an independent statement; each uses the simplest word order. The lines therefore are end stopped, and they fall into similar cadences because they make similar statements in parallel constructions. This produces a semirhythmical, though somewhat monotonous, effect.

III

P. 118.   "A Lyke-Wake Dirge"

This poem is often printed among folk ballads, which it resembles in certain respects, though it is not a narrative. How is the ballad meter managed in the opening stanza so as to make the movement, from the beginning, exceptionally slow?

The refrain of the fourth line is obviously a prayer for the dead, but that in the second line is not. What purpose does it serve?

How does the homely, concrete, yet severely schematic imagery contribute to the mood? What, specifically in the poem, do we mean by "schematic" here?

3   fleet: The word sometimes meant a paved floor, but its meaning here is not certainly known. Scholars have suggested that it is a copyist's error for "sleet," since the old form of *s* resembles *f*. Since this, though possible, would place an outdoor image between the two related indoor images of fire and candlelight, the reading remains doubtful.

P. 119.   "Cupid and my Campaspe played"
The poem consists entirely of the elaboration of a single "conceit." The subject, Campaspe's literally devastating beauty, is developed through the figure of a card game, which is announced at the beginning with alliteration (Cupid, Campaspe, cards, kisses) and then is exploited to its utmost with ingeniously matched details. Campaspe wins all his beauty from the young god of Love himself (Cupid, son of Venus, is not the debased modern fat doll but the ideally beautiful, though for obvious symbolic reasons blind, young god of older tradition).

Compare the different effects of tightly organized imagery such as this with the looser, more varied imagery in the poem by Herrick in this chapter.

P. 120.   "Follow thy fair sun"
This and the following poem by Campion might well have been included in Chapter II, for Campion was intensely interested in the development of English meters, and his metrical effects are carefully calculated. Study the meter of this poem, observing how even the irregularities are made regular by being ranged in a symmetrical pattern.

Trace the progression of thought through the elaboration of the double image of sun and shadow.

P. 121.   "Rose-cheekt Laura, come"
This is among the few English lyrics written without rhyme. Campion printed it in his *Observations on the Art of English Poesie* (1602), a pamphlet attacking the use of rhyme as a bar-

barous and vulgar modern device that he thought should be replaced by a return to the Greek and Latin unrhymed quantitative verse, though he himself had previously written rhymed verse. The type of stanza used in this particular poem he described as "voluble, and fit to express any amorous conceit." Of his unrhymed verse in general, he wrote: "Some ears accustomed altogether to the fatness of rime may perhaps except against the cadences of these numbers; but let any man judicially examine them, and he shall find they close of themselves so perfectly that the help of rime were not only in them superfluous but also absurd."

What is the meter of this poem? Is the absence of rhyme noticed? Study the patterns of sound, and try to hear and describe the particular character of the musical effects.

Can you find in the poems the "perfectly" closed cadences that Campion claims for them?

P. 121.   From the twelfth chapter of Ecclesiastes

The King James translators of the Bible, adapting what they knew of the principles of Hebrew poetry to the English language, produced what would now be described as free verse. Consider how nearly this passage approaches regular meter, and try to see what other elements increase the rhythmical, measured movement.

What kinds of repetition are used?

Notice that the imagery is all concrete, yet all universal, none specific: "house," "doors" (but no particular house or door); "silver cord," "golden bowl" (but whose, what for, and where?). What connection has this with the meaning and how does it affect the character, tone, and unity of mood of the passage as a whole?

P. 122.   "Corinna's Going a-Maying"

The subject is "bringing in the May," a May-day celebration in which young people went out to woods and fields and brought back flowers and flowering branches, particularly of "may" (white hawthorn or white-thorn) to decorate houses and doorways. In lines 14 and 44 the word "May" is a pun, meaning both the month and the flower. Most of the imagery is what the subject naturally dictates, the delights of nature on a fine spring morning. It is heightened, however, in several respects. English pastoral poetry owed much to a tradition stemming from Greek and Latin writers and had become highly conventionalized: nature was not ordinary nature but always a little better than real; the people were usually shepherds and shepherdesses with classical names and little to do but sing songs, compose verses, and make love. Within this tradition there was room for treatment of a wide range of themes, both light and serious (for the latter, see Milton's *Lycidas*, p. 267) but, whatever the subject, the imagery usually tended toward the ornate, as in this poem of Herrick, rather than the simple. The pastoral tradition, then, and the fact that May-day itself is a ceremonial occasion influence the choice of imagery in "Corinna's Going a-Maying." Note how some of the most exaggerated images of nature are those used in compliment to Corinna, rather than to nature, and note also the use in the early stanzas of religious images. Do they suggest a religious mood here or, by contrast, a pagan one?

P. 124. "Kubla Khan"
Coleridge had been reading from an old account of Eastern travel (Purchas's *Pilgrimage*): "In Xamdu did Cublai Can build a stately Palace, encompassing sixteene miles of plaine ground with a wall, wherein are fertile meddowes, pleasant Springs, delightful Streames, . . . and in the middest thereof a sumptuous house of pleasure." Lines 1–36 describe the pleasure-grounds. The latter part is Coleridge's poetic explanation of why he had not completed the poem: he had lost his inspiration. In a vision, he says, he had once heard music (that of the Abyssinian Maid) which, if only he could revive it, would inspire him to create the scene of Kubla's paradise

in such poetry as the world would listen to in awe. The imagery of magic circle, flashing eyes, floating hair, milk and honey are ancient conventional properties of divinely inspired poet-prophets. So much for the literal statement made in the poem. The rest is atmosphere, created by the sounds and images. The poem is celebrated for its incantatory music, and its patterns of assonance and alliteration are not easily matched for elaboration: X*an* . . . Kh*an* (pronounced Can). *K*ubla *K*han, *d*ome *d*ecree, Alph . . . rive*r* ra*n*—these are but a few instances. Notice some of the others, consider what effect they have, and consider also the effect of the changing lengths of lines and the fluctuating meter when the shorter lines begin.

P. 126. Fragment ("Strike, churl")
Comment on the alliteration and assonance in this fragment.
What is the effect of all the imperative verbs? of the epithet "giant"?
What feeling is being conveyed?

P. 126. "To an Athlete Dying Young"
See pp. 24–25 for comments on the imagery of the first two stanzas.

11 laurel: The European laurel, or bay tree, whose evergreen leaves provide the traditional crown of victory or fame (not to be confused with the unrelated American flowering laurel, so named because its leaves resemble those of the bay). Why does Housman deliberately reverse the facts of nature in using this image? Obviously, the laurel long outlasts the rose. What meaning does this deliberate misstatement convey? Is it important for the theme? See, in this connection, the last line.

21–28 The imagery here derives from the Greek conception of the world—or, as it was sometimes thought to be, the house—of the dead, where the souls existed only as dim "shades."

Study and comment on the patterning of imagery throughout. Does the underlying theme by implication seem to be regret over the brevity of youth, or is it literally the good fortune of the athlete who will never be defeated?

P. 127. "We'll to the woods no more"
Like Bridges' "Triolet," this poem is created out of almost nothing, for it consists of little more than two worn-out symbolic images (Muses and laurel) and a structure of sound. Partly adapted from a French poem of Theodore de Banville, it was printed by Housman as the introduction to *Last Poems*, and its theme is obviously his farewell to poetry. This is never mentioned, however; all we have are the traditionally symbolic laurel and Muses and the naturally symbolic references to the closing day and year. The rest is a repetitive but progressive structure of sound. It begins with predominantly low-pitched and relaxed rounded vowels. Tension increases in the ninth line with the slightly exclamatory "Oh," the doubling of "no more," and then the doubling of "to the woods," where, first, the epithet "leafy" is added and finally, with hitherto unused, higher, and more tense vowels, the double epithets "high wild," simple words but in their context of sound and sense almost violent.

In this poem, then, the symbolism is initiated by laurel and Muses, but their staleness is transformed and the whole brought to life and rendered expressive by a structure of interdependent sound and sense. With little change the poem might have been a flat statement about woodcutters instead of an emotionally charged farewell to poetry.

P. 128. "Easter Hymn"
Essentially the poem turns on the question of the validity of Christianity: Was Christ divine, and does he still exist, or not? A second thought is involved also: the state of the world is crucial.

It is not often that thought of such magnitude can be stated and its weight of charged emotion successfully conveyed in only two sentences. The feeling of weight and magnitude is established partly by the imagery, with its Biblical associations, and partly by the grammatical and rhetorical pattern, with its two long, parallel periodic sentences, each filling a stanza and each maintaining the tension of grammatical suspense till the last line. Within each sentence, short phrasal units are played off against long ones, and these together form a varied counterpoint over the fixed, decasyllabic couplet rhyme pattern. Once these technical means have been noticed, they may quite properly be ignored and only the impressive and moving quality of the poem as a whole attended to; but they have a great deal to do with its impressiveness.

P. 129. "Conversion"
7-9 river . . . in a sack . . . peeping Turk: an allusion to the punishment by drowning in a weighted sack of men who attempt to invade the privacy of a harem and who catch even a glimpse of the beauties.

What does the poem mean, and how much beyond the bare meaning is conveyed by the symbolic image?

P. 129. "Lethe"
Title: In Greek mythology, Lethe is the river of forgetfulness in the world of the dead. It may therefore be thought of as the kindest thing death can offer to those who did not wish to die.

The structure of this Imagist poem is unusual, with its parallel negative statements concerning identical or nearly identical concrete things—skin, hide, fleece; cedar, fir, pine (all needle- and cone-bearing evergreens); whin, gorse, flowering bush ("whin" and "gorse" being merely two names for the same flowering bush); and the several birds—followed by the single affirmative statement in the poem, containing the only word that is subjective and that directly refers to feeling, "long" —"you shall long only for this"—which, however, itself becomes negative in substance, for "this" that is desired is the "tide" of oblivion, Lethe. The reader should be aware of the relation between the positive living images and the negative pattern of anaphora that provides a repetitive formula for those images and creates by its flatness the feeling of unending monotony and deprivation.

P. 130. "Question"
Study the movement of this poem and the means by which the movement is secured. Study also the rhyme and other sound patterns and the relation of all these things to the theme and tone of the whole.

P. 131. "Fern Hill"
The theme is an obvious one, the loss of the carefree joy of childhood. The poet re-creates the joy even while he takes it away. Crudely expressed in prose, the thought runs somewhat like this: As a boy, he and the farm together were a single world. Each day was fresh and full of delight. At night the farm vanished while he slept, only to appear next morning as fresh and new as Eden. He had not thought that this would end, or that all the while time held him prisoner until a night would come when time would fly away with the farm—that is, with his childhood.

The poem is sprinkled with wayward variations on set phrases from children's stories—"happy as the day is long," "once upon a time," "all the day long"—and with an extension of an ancient poetic device called the "transferred epithet," by which, for special effects, a descriptive word is attached not to the object to which it logically applies but to some other. Thomas carries this device to an extreme, using it constantly instead of only occasionally, and producing by it a series of rather surrealistic images: the house sings, the yard is happy, the boy is green, the stable is green and whinnies. This apparently irresponsible distortion of imagery does much to recreate the irresponsible mood of happy childhood.

What passages particularly convey the bursting egotism of childhood, the feeling of the child that the universe is his apple?

Study in some detail the ways in which the natural imagery is made expressive of both the child's and the grown poet's feeling. Try to show how this double mood is maintained.

IV

P. 135. "Westron winde, when will thou blow"
For so short a poem, this one has caused a good deal of speculation. Is the speaker a man or woman? And what logical link can there be between the first two lines and the last two? But these questions scarcely matter, for the essence of the poem is longing, and every word conveys this directly, with little need for explanation.

P. 137. "To a Lady to Answer Directly with Yea or Nay"
Try to describe the tone of the poem. Consider in this connection the handling of the meter and the style. Notice, for example, that there are no descriptive adjectives or adverbs.

P. 137. "The Lover Showeth How He Is Forsaken of such as He Sometime Enjoyed"
The image underlying the first stanza has been shown by Mr. A. K. Moore to be probably that of a falcon: "flee" often meant "fly," "gentle" was a common epithet for a female falcon, and falcons were often kept in their master's chamber. The women, then, who once came to the poet "gentle, tame, and meek" now have flown off like falcons reverting to the wild.

Some writers have chosen to believe that the lady of the second and third stanzas is Fortune personified, instead of a flesh-and-blood woman. Considering the poem as a whole, does this seem likely?

The poem is notable for its grace and musical expressiveness, though it is metrically quite irregular. Observe, for instance, the effect of the occasional inversion of the accent. "Stalking," in line 2, is a good example of an inverted accent that serves to emphasize the meaning of the word. Notice also how the run-on lines and imperfect but harmonious rhymes help carry the movement forward through the first stanza.

The verse form is the seven-line stanza known as rhyme royal, which rhymes *a b a b b c c.*

P. 139. "Brown is my Love"
Though blondness was conventionally associated with beauty, poets as well as other men often found brunettes beautiful too.

P. 139. "The Passionate Shepherd to His Love"
This is an example of Elizabethan pastoral poetry in which artificial shepherds are presented in an artificial country scene where the fields are never muddy, the shepherds never work, and life consists largely of love and conversation. Cf. the poem by Herrick in Chapter III.

P. 140. "The Nymph's Reply to the Shepherd"
Notice the different degrees of simplicity in the thought of this and the preceding poem. Marlowe's poem is precisely and only what its title declares. This one is the girl's reply, with something added. Is it a mockery of pastoral convention or of a romantic view of life, or both? Is its tone serious?

P. 141. Song: "Adieu farewell earth's bliss" (Often printed under the title "Litany in Time of Plague")
This is a song from the masque *A Pleasant Comedie, called Summers last will and Testament,* sung in response to Summer's request, "Sing me some doleful ditty to the Lute,/ That may complain my neere approaching death." It belongs to the year 1592–93, when the plague was raging in London.

P. 143. "Spring"
This and the next poem form a slightly mocking conclusion to the comedy *Love's Labour's Lost.* They are introduced as a "dialog" that two "learned men have compiled in praise of the owl and the cuckoo." The singers are the two seasons.

This apparently simple poem is double edged, for its pretty, cheerful picture of Spring is given a cynical twist. The song of the cuckoo is loved by the English as a sign of Spring. But it is a bird that lays its eggs in other birds' nests, and from this circumstance is derived the word "cuckold," a mocking term for a man whose wife is unfaithful.

P. 144. "Tell me where is fancy bred"
What is the meaning of this song? Is it cynical or romantic?

P. 149. "To the Virgins, to Make Much of Time"
The theme here is the ancient *carpe diem* theme: literally, "seize the day"—enjoy today before it vanishes, for age and death come all too soon.

Compare the treatment of "Time" in this and numerous other poems in the present chapter.

P. 151. "To His Coy Mistress"
Here the *carpe diem* theme is magnified until it becomes something quite different, a love poem within a space-time frame.

5–7 Ganges . . . Humber. The lovers would begin their leisurely approach to each other from the opposite ends of the earth. The Humber is an English river.

11 Why would their loves be "vegetable"?

Try to describe the tone or the attitude of the poet toward his subject. What words and images particularly help set the tone?

P. 153. "The Mower against Gardens"
Marvel wrote a number of rural "mower" poems, in which the mower of fields celebrates nature, sometimes in conjunction with the theme of love. In this poem he speaks as the defender of untouched nature in opposition to cultivated gardens. He decries all that is artificial: walls or hedges; fertilizing, artificial breeding or crossing of plants; propagation by grafting; the

breeding of a double flower from the single "Pink" (Dianthus); the recent craze for "broken colors," as striped or variegated shades were called in tulips, a craze so great that it caused wild financial speculation; the artificial breeding of sterile hybrids ("eunuchs," line 27; cf. the seedless grape and orange, which cannot be propagated by the "natural" means of seeds); importation of novel flowers (the Marvel-of-Peru or four o'clock, *Mirabilis jalapa*); and garden statuary.

P. 156. "The Convergence of the Twain"
In 1912 the *Titanic*, then the world's largest ship, struck an iceberg on her maiden voyage and sank, though she had been supposed unsinkable.
Stanza VI. The Immanent Will. Hardy expressed a fatalistic view of the world in various terms at different times. The primary power was "fate"; or "chance"; or the "Immanent Will," which was unconscious and nonhuman; or some other form of blind and irresponsible power.

P. 158. "Waiting Both"
What does the repetition at the end of each stanza contribute to the meaning or the mood? How do you think this final line should be read aloud in relation to the preceding lines?

P. 158. "When smoke stood up from Ludlow"
Note the use of the bird as a symbol here.
In this poem and the next, Housman employs an unusual five-line stanza that resembles an ordinary quatrain with an extra rhyming line added. Study the effect of this extra line throughout both poems.

P. 159. "Bredon Hill"
A successful poem seldom arises from the poet's attacking an important subject directly and squarely as a whole. More often it develops when an image, a line or two, or an oblique slant upon the subject occurs to the writer. "Bredon Hill" is

a good poem in which to study this indirect treatment of a theme. Its real subject, obviously, is the death of a girl and the grief of the lover who had hoped to marry her and who would now like to die too. But the poet says almost nothing directly about this. Instead, he writes about church bells, about going or not going to church, and about sitting on a hill. The whole seems very simple. Is it? There is no direct statement of emotion in the poem. Is emotion communicated?

P. 160. "The rain, it streams on stone and hillock"
In three of the five stanzas the speaker is telling himself that he will miss his friend less once he has got over the shock of his death. This is the kind of condolence often uselessly given to a bereaved person by friends. Does it make the poem more sad or less? Can you tell why?

Does the image in line 2 suggest more than the physical surroundings of rain and a freshly dug grave? Notice the inversion of the accent in the second foot and the prominence this gives to the word "clings."

P. 162. "The Gallows"
The animals referred to here, as country-bred readers will know, are destructive and so may be shot by farmers, who sometimes hang them up afterwards to keep other marauders away.

Is this an S.P.C.A. poem? If not, what is the poet's evident attitude toward his subject? Comment on the effect of the imagery and the refrain.

P. 164. "At the Keyhole"
On the surface, de la Mare's subjects frequently seem conventional and out of date: horsemen, ghosts, the fairies and elves of old-fashioned children's stories. Beneath this surface, however, there is often the sadness of universal themes of death and separation, primitive fears of the mysterious, often also a chilly hint of evil or malice at work behind the visible

world, and sometimes a hint of modern psychological interpretations of folk superstition.

Grilled or broiled bones are a meat dish for which recipes may be found in English cookbooks. Do they seem to have been selected as a refrain here, in preference to other dishes, for any reason having to do with this particular poem? The slight metrical irregularity of the first line places particular stress on "grill" and "bones." What is the effect?

Do you regard this as a children's poem, or a grown-ups' poem, or both?

P. 165. "The Mocking Fairy"

What the Fairy says might be paraphrased as a taunt, "Yah! you're dead, aren't you!" Almost everything mentioned is beautiful or dainty. How do the nastiness and horror creep in? Do the words "mimbling mambling" (line 16) suggest a witless, subhuman mumbling?

P. 166. "Peak and Puke"

Here the old belief about changelings—that the fairies sometimes steal the real child and substitute a wrong or a bewitched one—seems to have psychological symbolic overtones. Assuming a bond with its mother against the infant interloper, the elder child rejects the new baby ("it isn't ours, we won't have this one"). What is the effect of the high proportion of close-mouthed and almost close-mouthed sounds: *w, m, o, oo, u,* and so on?

P. 166. "The Old Men"

For the theme, cf. R. L. Stevenson's "Aes Triplex": "By the time a man gets well into the seventies, his continued existence is a mere miracle; and when he lays his old bones in bed for the night, there is an overwhelming probability that he will never see the day. Do the old men mind it, as a matter of fact? Why, no . . . they hear of the death of people about their own age, or even younger, not as if it was a grisly warning, but with a simple childlike pleasure at having outlived someone else."

2   What is meant by "caged" and "riddle-rid"? The answer is specifically given in lines 3 and 4.

10   Comment on the epithet "ruinous."

14   The phrase "in their sockets" is a good example of poetic economy of language. In one sense it is altogether unnecessary, since all human eyes are in sockets. But on the other hand, the mere fact that the word "socket" is not needed for literal statement makes it particularly emphatic and vivid as a descriptive word. It is thus both more vivid and more economical than a longer phrase describing deep-sunken eyes.

P. 168.   "Maerchen"

Observe how de la Mare turns to serious use the proverbial expression, "Even a cat can look at a king."

Study the clogged effect of the sounds in the earlier part of the poem. What is their relation to the theme?

Study carefully the imagery to see how it points to a symbolic meaning: Do kings die (or sleep) alone with bats, cats, and mice while the court carouses? What of the change in the last stanza to an outdoor image? Whose is the robe "enstarred"? These are some of the keys to interpretation of the poem.

P. 169.   "The River-Merchant's Wife: A Letter"

This poem and the next are adaptations of ancient Chinese poems by Li Po (eighth century), whom Pound calls by his Japanese name, Rihaku.

Are these poems in free verse? What means are used to heighten the writing beyond what would be only prose?

P. 173.   "You, Andrew Marvell"

The title is an acknowledgement of the source of MacLeish's inspiration in Marvell's "To His Coy Mistress." MacLeish omits the love element of the earlier poem and develops the space-time theme alone.

Perhaps the most notable feature of the poem is its grammatical structure: there is not a single sentence. There is not even a subordinate clause or a finite verb until the very last line, where a single dependent clause is hung upon an infinitive. Everywhere else, instead of verbs there are only infinitives depending on other infinitives, and participles and gerunds depending on infinitives: "To feel . . . chill . . . creep up . . . and . . . shadow grow . . . and . . . trees take leaf by leaf the evening . . . [to feel] . . . the mountains . . . change . . . and Baghdad darken . . . and Spain go under. . . ." This linked structure is continuous and never reaches completion because there is no sentence, no end, no cessation of the movement of time. Thus the grammar itself is expressive of the theme.

The poet traces less than half a revolution of the earth, and even that only in imagination, as he lies beneath the noonday sun somewhere in America, thinking of the edge of night approaching from the other side of the earth. Within this still moment in time and space which frames the poem, he opens out the vastness and remoteness of past ages and distance. The place names, which mark the advance of the westward-moving shadow, are rich in associations that go back through the Middle Ages to antiquity, and along with these names go many images suggesting evening and time past, such as the "earthy chill of dusk," the "ever-climbing shadow," and the "wheel rut in the ruined stone."

P. 174. "The Fish"

Marianne Moore usually writes syllabic rather than accentual verse—her metrical form, that is, is secured not by the number or placing of accents in the line and not by the time value of units as in music, but simply by the number of syllables in the line. The number varies from line to line within the stanza, but corresponding lines in all the stanzas have the same number of syllables. In "The Fish," all the first lines have one syllable, all the second lines three, the third lines nine, and so on. This would seem merely an arbitrary form of symmetry, perceptible only to a computing machine and not to the human ear and therefore without value as an element of poetic form, particularly when the lines are long, as they often are, and when they end without a rhetorical pause—or even in the middle of a word, as they often do. Miss Moore, however, does mark the ends of her lines with rhyme, and this to a sufficiently trained ear often brings the lines into a perceptible pattern except in poems where the lines are very long. The rhyme is rarely conspicuous. She has said that she likes "light" rhyme, in which an unaccented syllable rhymes with an accented one; and often her pattern calls for rhyming of only some of the lines. In "The Fish," for example, the last line of each stanza is unrhymed and usually its sense runs on to the next stanza. Some readers may feel that often she takes too literally the notion that "heard melodies are sweet, but those unheard are sweeter." Or, to put the matter more accurately, her form is apprehensible by logic but not always by the ear.

There can be no question, however, of her extraordinary power of precise yet imaginative visual perceptions and her equally remarkable power of finding accurate, imaginative language in which to convey these perceptions: the swan with its "gondoliering legs," elephants with "fog-coloured skin," the cat carrying off a mouse with its (the mouse's) "limp tail hanging like a shoelace," the often-quoted statement that poetry creates "imaginary gardens with real toads in them."

In "The Fish," the poet's miscroscopic eye is focused upon a rock crevice or chasm at the edge of the sea with the marks of time and weather upon it, the changing surface of the water in sunlight, and the minutiae of marine life inhabiting it. Possibly only those who have watched such crevices along the coast of Maine or the Pacific coast will appreciate fully the brilliant imaginative precision of the poem.

    8   The "barnacles" here are probably not the real ones on the rock but the air bubbles on the under side of waves, which suggest the look of barnacles.

    20–22   Starfish, sometimes called "stars," with their pink granular surface.

    24–25   Submarine toadstools: Limpets, shaped much like

toadstools, are commonly known for their power of clinging to rock, but when feeding undisturbed they slide along.

P. 176. "England"
The title represents the first word but not the primary subject of the poem. One can guess at but not be sure of a reason for its being so used.

11 victoria: Carriages such as the victoria and the surrey were still used in southern cities, sometimes in competition with taxis.

24–26 the man who is able to say: Isaac Walton in *The Compleat Angler* (Miss Moore's note).

P. 177. "Look, stranger, on this island now"
The island is of course England, the scene evidently somewhere on the chalk cliffs of the southern coast.

The poem contains numerous echoes from other poets, particularly Hopkins and Bridges. The imagery and the metrical and other sound patterns will repay close study for their complexity and their creation of a mood.

V

P. 184. "The Lover Compareth His State to a Ship in Perilous Storm Tossed on the Sea"
This is an early translation by Wyatt of a sonnet by Petrarch. Wyatt's (or Petrarch's) metaphor of the storm-tossed ship representing a love affair was taken up later by many of the Elizabethan sonnet writers. Obscurities in the first three lines have been cleared up by E. M. W. Tillyard and others by comparison with the original: his ship is so weighted down (chargèd) by love that he forgets all else; the "enemy" is Cupid.

P. 185. "Since there's no help, come let us kiss and part"
This sonnet is remarkable for its modern, colloquial tone.

Notice the extreme plainness and the high proportion of everyday, one-syllable words in the first part and the change in style that accompanies the turn of thought in the third quatrain, which with the final couplet casts a new light on the meaning of the preceding lines. This is a particularly fine example of a sonnet that combines the Petrarchan two-part handling of a theme with the non-Petrarchan "Shakespearean" rhyme scheme.

P. 186.   From *Amoretti*

Spenser's sonnet sequence recorded the progress of his courtship of his future wife. The second of those selected here presents a theme that, like the ship-and-storm metaphor, became popular with the Elizabethans: the poet boasts or promises that he will confer immortality upon his lover by praising her in immortal verse. These sonnet writers sought not originality of theme but excellence, and sometimes originality, in the *expression* of it. A theme already treated by others was therefore a challenge to be met by emulation without exact imitation.

Note that Spenser's sonnets do not conform precisely to either the Italian or the "Shakespearean" form.

P. 187.   Sonnets (Shakespeare)

Shakespeare's sonnets appear to have been composed in two connected sequences, the first and longer series addressed to a man (Sonnets 1–126) and the second (Sonnets 127–152) to a woman who, being a brunette, has come to be known as the mysterious Dark Lady. The first series is concerned with the writer's devotion to his friend, a young man evidently of superior station in the world, handsome, brilliant, gifted, and noble, whom Shakespeare urges to marry in order to have children through whom his beauty and gifts will survive, as one form of immortality. The poet will bestow or do his best to bestow another kind through the immortality of verse. The friendship is not smooth, however, for other poets, one in particular, gain the friend's favor and threaten to eclipse the poet. Nor is his affair with the Dark Lady happy; she deserts him for the friend. There are bitter sonnets on lust and broken faith.

The identity of the persons involved has long been a subject for scholars' research and guesses, with no positive conclusions. There has also been unprofitable speculation concerning the nature of the friendship of the two men. Undoubtedly many of the sonnets to or about the friend seem to a modern reader like love poems, and they may have been that; we do not know. Common usage in the language, however, has changed since Shakespeare's day: the word "love" was a customary name for devoted friendship as well as sexual love; the word "beauty" sometimes described a man's as well as a woman's good looks. We know also that strong friendship between men at that time was approved as a virtue. Whatever the character of Shakespeare's devotion may have been, there is no indication that his contemporaries thought it anything out of the way, for the sonnets were known and admired during his lifetime.

The rhyme scheme is the same throughout all except one or two of Shakespeare's sonnets, but the internal structure of thought, the sentence pattern, the imagery, and the range of emotion and tone are remarkably varied. Sometimes, for example, each quatrain develops a separate image and the final couplet sums them all up or expresses the point toward which all are directed; sometimes one metaphor is elaborated through a whole sonnet; sometimes the Petrarchan octave-sestet division of thought is employed.

Shakespeare's sonnets are not all poetic masterpieces. Some are; others are evidently exercises in ingenuity: the quality is uneven. The present selection includes a number of the less famous ones in order to give the reader an impression of the sequence itself.

Sonnet 18
One of the most celebrated examples of Shakespeare's elabo-

ration of a single image. Trace in detail the relation between image and meaning.

Sonnet 29

In sonnets 29 and 30 the poet presents two moods of depression. But notice how distinct they are, and how vividly and precisely each is imagined and portrayed: one an almost paranoid mood in which the writer feels as if everything is conspiring against him, the other a mood of sadness and loss. In the first, the structure is mainly that of grammatical suspense; in the following one the unity is created by assonance, alliteration, and other forms of repetition, and by the imagery. Though the mood of No. 30 is one of personal sadness, the imagery is drawn from the harsh impersonal world of commerce, finance, and law. In Shakespeare's day "sessions" (line 1) used with "summon" would have brought immediately to mind the session of a court of law; to "tell" (line 10) is to count (cf. our bank "teller"); "dateless" (line 6), meaning "without fixed due date or date of termination," implies payments, debts, and the law; and besides these there are "cancell'd" (line 7), "expense" (line 8), "account" (line 11), "pay" and "paid" (line 12), and "losses" (line 14). Consider the effect on the tone of the poem of this contrast between the imagery and the themes of grief and love.

Sonnet 33

Note again how a single metaphor controls the language throughout.

Sonnet 62

10   In several sonnets Shakespeare refers to himself as old. Though the date of most poems in the series is not known, he is believed to have been not much more than thirty and therefore old only in momentary feeling or by comparison with his younger friend.

Sonnet 87
What is unusual about the rhyme? Does it seem to have any effect on the tone of the poem as a whole?
Comment on the character of the metaphorical language.

Sonnet 147
8   The meaning of the latter half of this line has not been satisfactorily explained.

P. 199.   "On the Late Massacre in Piedmont"
The occasion of this sonnet was the Catholic persecution, in 1655, of an ancient Protestant sect in northern Italy.

The relation between sound and sense is worth studying in these lines with their sonorous vowel sounds, particularly the long *o*'s that dominate the rhymes.

Note that in Milton's sonnets the "turn" of the thought does not always coincide with the close of the octave.

P. 201.   "Composed upon Westminster Bridge, September 3, 1802"
Though Wordsworth idealized nature and country life and disliked the city, this (on an exceptional subject for him) is one of his best sonnets. With these facts in mind, consider the imagery and the sound, the quiet character of which is established by the first line with the vowels of "earth," "anything," and "air," and the absence of all stopped consonants.

P. 203.   "Where lies the Land"
With this and the next sonnet, compare Bridge's "A Passerby" (p. 359).

P. 204.   "Mutability"
10–13   A tower so old that weeds have grown on its roof (not uncommon in England's moist climate) and so fragile that sound waves could destroy it.

Consider the effect of the last line, with its abstract language and six-syllable word, in relation to the sonnet as a whole.

P. 205. "On First Looking into Chapman's Homer"
George Chapman's translation of Homer appeared in 1598–1616.
What key idea unifies the thought and imagery of this sonnet? When does the reader first know what the real subject is?

P. 206. "On the Grasshopper and Cricket"
A sonnet written on an agreed subject in competition with his friend Leigh Hunt.

P. 207. "When I have fears that I may cease to be"
The possibility of early death had immediacy for Keats; it was not a poet's conventional imagining. What, in detail, does this poem mean?

P. 208. From *The Growth of Love*
Observe how, as in some of Shakespeare's sonnets, a single analogy controls the language of this love poem. Consider also the nature of the moment of doubt which is Bridges' subject, doubt at the moment of commitment to love, of course, not religion. The theme is quite original as far as English poetry goes. Does it seem "true" as well as "new"?

P. 209. "Sunday Morning"
Precisely what is the thought in the first ten lines? What is significant in the particular choice of the details of practicing scales and tinkering with the car? The key is in the fifth line.

VI

P. 213. *The Rape of the Lock*
The germ of the poem was an actual event—the theft of a lock of Miss Arabella Fermor's hair by young Lord Petre—which, though trifling, occasioned a quarrel between the two families. John Caryll, a friend of all three, suggested the sub-

ject to Pope as a means of healing the breach. The first short version of the poem was replaced by a longer and more polished one, as Pope explained in his letter of dedication.

As a "mock" epic or heroic poem, *The Rape of the Lock* imitates lightly and ironically the conventions followed by epic poets: announcement of theme ("I sing"), invocation to the Muses, intervention of supernatural beings in human affairs, the long voyage (an afternoon's sail up the Thames), the battle (a game of cards), feasting (refreshments at Hampton Court Palace, where Queen Anne entertained guests), a journey to the lower world (the Cave of Spleen), and "epic" similes—long, often elaborately wrought comparisons.

The poem is written in heroic couplets, the favorite verse form of the late seventeenth century and most of the eighteenth. It consists of two rhyming lines of iambic pentameter in which the close of the rhyme and the close of the thought coincide. A sentence may be two lines long, or four with an almost complete break after the second line. When the form is strictly maintained, run-on lines are avoided and the number of syllables in the line is always held to ten. The pitfall of such a form is monotony. Pope, with his wit and polish, successfully avoids this for the most part and, instead, makes the form work in his favor. He maintains it nearly, but not quite invariably, at its strictest, securing variety by subtle variation in the timing and especially in the pauses within the lines. The style is marked by a high proportion of balanced and antithetical sentences, which are a particularly effective vehicle for Pope's kind of wit.

Because the poem is full of the vanished trivia of eighteenth-century society, it requires a good deal of annotation. Furthermore, it requires alert reading, for Pope does not underscore or explain his satiric thrusts, and he deals them out in many directions, as when he remarks quite incidentally, in describing the opening of a fashionable day, "And *sleepless* lovers, just at *twelve, awake*" (the italics are not Pope's; he expects the reader to catch the point without the aid of typography).

Canto III, ll. 5–8 Here Pope employs the rhetorical device of anticlimax for ironic effect. Note other instances later in the poem.

P. 238. "Epitaph on King Charles II"
An epigram in the form of an epitaph, written while Charles II was still living.

P. 238. "Imitation of Pope: A Compliment to the Ladies"
What particular trick of Pope is Blake imitating?

P. 239. "Tam O' Shanter"
According to Burns, his story was based on an actual legend of a farmer who saw witches dancing in Alloway Kirk and was chased by them.

164–70 Those with little experience of witches may need to be reminded that, unlike ghosts, they are living people. If you see a dance of witches, you may recognize there your next-door neighbor.

P. 249. "Tom o'Bedlam's Song"
"Tom-o'-Bedlam" or "mad" songs were once fairly common. Compare these with the later one by Blake (p. 338).

P. 252. "Who killed John Keats?"
It was widely rumored that the death of Keats had been hastened by despair over a contemptuous review of his *Endymion* in the influential *Quarterly Review*. Though the rumor was unfounded, Byron's parody of "Cock Robin" helped perpetuate it. Reviews in all the leading journals of that day were anonymous, but Milman, Southey, and Barrow were known as frequent contributors to the *Quarterly* and as supporters of its Tory politics. Byron was a liberal whig.

P. 253. "Darkness"
The nineteenth century saw a good deal of pre-atomic speculation concerning the end of the world, different in character

from the medieval religious preoccupation with the theme. Early in the century, a popular novel called *The Last Man* (1806) seems to have inspired a number of poems, of which Byron's "Darkness" is the best. For a treatment that is altogether grotesque on a considerably lower level, the reader may look up Thomas Hood's "The Last Man," which strains for a gruesome effect through the use of empty skulls, a dirty beggar, a jocular hangman, wild man-eating dogs, and the like. Along with de la Mare's "The Song of Finis," these provide an instructive study in the treatment of similar themes and in different uses of grotesque elements.

P. 256. "The Great Day"
Toward the end of his life, Yeats wrote to a friend that this (along with two other similar epigrams) gives "the essence of my politics."

P. 256. "The Old Man's Comforts"
These verses are printed for the sake of the parody that follows. They provide, however, a good basis for study of an author's insensitivity to the relation between rhythm and theme, and of the effect of that insensitivity on the tone—or lack of tone—of a poem. The subject is serious, though not solemn. Is the tone serious? and if not, is the absence of seriousness justified or does it seem accidental? Can you tell, in other words, what effect Southey wished to secure? Many mediocre poems of this sort raise similar questions.

P. 263. "Museums"
3 tall fake porches: modern imitations of classical buildings with columned entrances.
What is MacNeice being ironical about? Most people approve of visits to museums and of a sympathetic appreciation of the past. Is this MacNeice's subject? Is his irony making a valid point or not?

P. 263. "Bagpipe Music"

The scene is Scotland (hence the Scottish words); the time, the depression of the 1930's. The title suggests not only the place but the tone—shrill, plaintive, and, like the cockeyed rhymes in the poem, off key.

9   Mme. Blavatsky was a Theosophist leader. This cult, as well as Yoga, had attracted a good many persons who were searching for salvation or truth through mystical religions.

VII

Some English elegies adopt the conventions of pastoral poetry, using as a background nature and the life of shepherds, with idealized and conventionalized scenes and classical names. Though pastoral elegies are artificial in their borrowing of these elements from classical poetry, they, like their prototypes, follow the natural course of human experience. When someone dies in youth or in his prime, the first feeling of the mourner is one of irreparable loss. Why should death, he feels, have struck down this particular person? Why was death not prevented? Then, if he is not overwhelmed by personal grief —if he is a friend, say, and not a lover of the dead—his thought turns to himself ("There but for the grace of God . . .") and to an examination of his own life and his values, in the face of death. Finally, his thought returns to the dead man, but now he has become more reconciled and perhaps turns to faith or some sort of hope: the friend, after all, is not really dead, or has not died in vain, or has left something of himself that will survive.

The conventional design of the elegy, then, like the normal course of a sorrow that is less than overwhelming, runs through three stages: (1) the unreconciled cry: "Weep, he is gone forever. Why could he not have been saved?"; (2) the taking stock of oneself and sometimes more broadly of the values of the living; (3) the reconciliation: "Do not weep; something of value survives."

In *Lycidas* Milton mourns the death by shipwreck of Edward King, a young man whom he had known, probably not with great intimacy, when both were students at Cambridge. He follows the tradition of the pastoral elegy, writing of himself and King as shepherds whose poems are songs sung to the accompaniment of an "oaten flute" (a simple flute made from a hollow stem). But King had intended to become a clergyman, and so the other sense of "pastor" and "pastoral" enters into the poem too: King was to have been not only a poet but also a spiritual shepherd of a flock.

In lines 23–36 Milton translates the fact that he and King had attended the university together into its elaborate pastoral equivalent. Like Lycidas, the name Damætus is common in pastoral poetry. The identity of the person referred to is not known.

64–84 What argument does the poet carry on with himself in this paragraph, and what is its place in the poem as a whole?

75 blind Fury: The Furies and the three Fates of mythology are not actually the same, though Milton identifies them here. Two Fates prepare and spin the thread of life; the third, Atropos the "inflexible" one, who is blindfold, cuts it.

In lines 113–31 Milton attacks the contemporary English clergy. What does he mean by the daring image "blind mouths" in line 119?

The poet has imagined a suitable flowery funeral but at line 152 reminds himself that the body of Lycidas was never found. Imagining then the real places to which it may have drifted, he enriches these place-names with associations of grandeur more impressive than the preceding flowery tribute. Bellerus and the guarded Mount refer to Land's End, the southwestern promontory of England, and St. Michael's Mount near Land's End, which looks toward Spain (Namancos and Bayona). The Mount is supposed to be guarded by the Archangel

Michael. Milton urges him to turn and look homeward, for the dangers are now domestic rather than foreign—a hint of the theme touched upon earlier (lines 113–31).

To what extent is *Lycidas* unified by recurring or related themes and images, such as those of shepherds (in both senses) and of water and shipwreck? Trace these through the poem to show the variety as well as the unity in Milton's use of them.

Study the sound patterns, and *listen to the verse.*

The central contrasting section attacking the clergy of the English Church and the Church of Rome has been a subject of controversy among critics. No one disputes the high poetic quality of its strong-flavored language, but some consider the passage an intrusion that destroys the unity of the poem. Others maintain that it provides a fine contrast in tone without disturbing the unity of the whole, which properly includes the poet's reflections concerning the conflicting values of self-indulgence, devotion to duty, and nobility of ambition. Milton had an unquestionably great gift for denunciatory eloquence, which he exercised only occasionally in his poetry (cf. the sonnet "On the Late Massacre in Piedmont"). Those who like it in *Lycidas* feel that the passage lends a needed touch of severity in the midst of so much that is luxuriant in language and imagery and that it prepares the way for the passage of what might be called the geographical, followed by the spiritual, sublime (lines 154–81) immediately preceding the quiet pastoral close.

P. 273. "Lines Composed . . . above Tintern Abbey . . ."

The scene, perhaps it should be noted, is not that of the ruined abbey but of picturesque country along the river. The poem combines natural scenery, autobiography, and a transcendental philosophical statement. The linking of these provides the theme.

What is the meaning of the two key passages, lines 35–49 and 93–101? Notice how the movement of the blank verse heightens the impressiveness of these two passages by causing many of the lines and phrases to be read more slowly than they would be ordinarily (in line 40, "unintelligible" occupies the position of three metrical stresses and the time of three feet, for example), and how the movement then picks up speed immediately afterwards, an effect analogous to that of *rubato* in music, which gives it the springiness of life. How else does the blank verse of the poem secure movement, life, and variety without loss of dignity?

Some critics feel that the poem falls off in the concluding lines, from about line 115. Does it seem so to you? If so, can you tell why? (This is not a question to which a categorical answer need be given.)

P. 278. "Ode: Intimations of Immortality from Recollections of Early Childhood

The "Ode" is founded on the neo-Platonic belief that the human soul exists in Heaven before being born on earth and that it brings with it into earthly life faint memories of its heavenly past. This notion fits well with the idealizing of childhood that followed from the wide popularity of the writings of Rousseau in the eighteenth century: the belief in the "natural goodness of man" that is the child's inheritance and that he loses only because of corrupted human institutions and the consequently faulty education he receives. Wordsworth describes the child as the wisest and best of mortals because the "clouds of glory" only gradually fade from his memory as the cares and evils of this world close around him.

This idea leads further to the question of what the grown man can do. Must he simply mope over his lost childhood? Wordsworth's answer is no. Through sympathetic devotion to nature and children, through experience and conscious reflection, he may arrive once more within sight and sound of that sea of immortality from which he came.

The development of this central train of thought is set within a frame: the country scene, this particular May morning, the singing birds, the instinctive joyous life of young lambs and the shepherd boy. How does Wordsworth combine symmetry with variety in this frame (Stanzas I–III, X–XI)?

In form, the poem is one of the English irregular odes. Consider the effect upon the mood of the poem of the varying length of lines, the irregularly placed rhyme, the patterns of sound and imagery, and the long, complicated sentences.

Stanzas VII–VIII. The child's play all has to do with imitation of grown-up living: marriage, business, war, funerals. Why, the poet asks, is he in such haste to take on the "yoke" of maturity when he is so blessed as a child? Notice the elaborate suspended grammar of the single sentence that makes up most of Stanza VIII.

P. 284. "Dejection: An Ode"

This poem was composed shortly after Coleridge had read the opening stanzas of his friend Wordsworth's "Ode," and one passage (Stanzas IV–V) was a reply to Wordsworth's ideas about man and nature. Nature, Coleridge said, is not the source of man's strength or inspiration; we only seem to receive this from her if we already possess it in the form of an inner joy and harmony from which we derive our creative imagination. In its original form, "Dejection" was a verse letter addressed to Sara Hutchinson, with whom Coleridge, already unhappily married, was hopelessly in love (in subsequent versions the name "Sara" was changed to "William" [Wordsworth], "Edmund," and eventually, as here, "Lady"). In the revised version Coleridge omitted much personal matter and improved the whole structurally and poetically.

120   Otway: Thomas Otway (1652–1685), an English playwright once considered a master of pathos. The name here replaces "William" in the original version. The story in lines 118–125 is that of Wordsworth's poem "Lucy Gray."

How does Coleridge use his frame—the progress of the weather from calm evening to violent mountain storm—to develop his theme?

Compare the relation between man and nature as set forth in this and the two preceding poems.

P. 288. "Ode to the West Wind"
"This poem was conceived and chiefly written in a wood that skirts the Arno, near Florence, and on a day when that tempestuous wind, whose temperature is at once mild and animating, was collecting the vapours which pour down the autumnal rains. They began, as I foresaw, at sunset with a violent tempest of hail and rain, attended by that magnificent thunder and lightning peculiar to the Cisalpine regions.

"The Phenomenon alluded to at the conclusion of the third stanza is well known to naturalists. The vegetation at the bottom of the sea, of rivers, and of lakes, sympathizes with that of the land in the changes of seasons, and is consequently influenced by the winds which announce it." (Shelley's note).

The verse form is founded on the Italian *terza rima*, a three-line grouping with linked rhyme between the groups: *a b a, b c b, c d c,* etc. Shelley combines these into larger stanzaic units with a couplet at the end of each.

To what extent is the imagery used to produce the formal structure of the poem? Consider also the effect of Shelley's having combined wild subject matter—the wild wind—with an exceptionally rigid formal structure.

P. 291. "Ulysses"
This poem and the next are not odes or elegies but rather, wholly or partly, dramatic monologues. Their subject, however, is not the dramatic representation of a particular character so much as it is reflection upon human aims and values. The subjects of both poems derive from the *Odyssey*, but the scene imagined by Tennyson in *Ulysses* obviously follows some time after the close of the Homeric poem.

The time of day that one most often associates with Homer's *Odyssey* is morning, the time of the "rosy-fingered Dawn" and of the beginnings of journeys. Before the invention of the compass, one would not usually choose to set sail in the evening. Comment on the time of day, and the reason for it, in *Ulysses*. What is its effect on the tone of the poem as a whole?

Line 18 is regarded as an exceptionally fine line, though it is made up of simple words. Consider it.

4   savage race: Ulysses' island kingdom of Ithaca was on the fringes rather than at the center of Greek culture.

P. 293.   "The Lotos-Eaters"

In the land of the Lotos-Eaters, those who ate the lotos flower or fruit became languid and lost all desire for action.

Why is the land described as a place "in which it seemed always afternoon"? Consider the part played by imagery, sound, and movement of the verse in establishing the mood.

The first part of the poem is written in the Spenserian stanza, a difficult and elaborate form consisting of eight lines of iambic pentameter followed by a ninth line of hexameter (an Alexandrine), rhyming *a b a b b c b c c*. Because of the complex arrangement of the rhymes (each rhyme occurring a different number of times in the stanza), the reader does not automatically predict the rhyming sound, as he does with simple couplets or quatrains. After eight pentameter lines, the extended last line, too, has an unusual effect when skilfully prepared for. It can produce a rallentando cadence, a linking, or a smoothing-out effect.

57ff.   Who are the "we" of this stanza?

P. 300.   "Philomela"

The title and theme hark back to one of the violent Greek legends, best known to English poets in the Latin version of Ovid. King Tereus of Thrace had raped Philomela, his wife Procne's sister (in earlier versions the sisters' names are reversed), and cut out her tongue to prevent her speaking against him. She wove her story into a tapestry, however, which she sent to Procne. The sisters then united in revenge, killed the child Itys, son of Tereus and Procne, and served him as meat to his father, who learned the truth only after he had eaten his meal with, according to Ovid, a strange and profound pleasure. The women fled; he pursued. Philomela was transformed by the gods into a nightingale, Procne into a swallow, and Tereus into a hawk pursuing them. In English poetry the nightingale is often called Philomel or Philomela, from the story. Arnold uses a version in which Philomela is the wife.

18 Thracian wild: The sisters were Athenian; Thrace was on the outskirts of Greek civilization.

What does Arnold put into the poem that is not part of the original story? What effect has this on the poem as a whole? What elements has this poem in common with "Dover Beach"?

P. 301.   When lilacs last in the dooryard bloom'd

This elegy on the death of Lincoln lacks the concentration and distinction of language that characterizes the greatest poetry, but it has long been a favorite with American readers. Diffuse though it is, some degree of organization and unity is attained through the thematic use of certain images, particularly the lilac and the bird.

P. 309.   "Musée des Beaux Arts"

Religious paintings of the Renaissance often contained figures of people and animals from everyday life that had little or nothing to do with the theme of the picture. These were painted with realistic and sometimes humorous detail. The same combination of the lofty and the commonplace occasionally appears in paintings of mythological subjects.

P. 311.   "After the Funeral"

Two features of Thomas's poetry should be borne in mind. In the first place, more perhaps than with any other writer, patterns of sound dominate the poem. Interlaced alliteration and assonance have never been woven into more complex designs. In the second place, the language of Thomas is addressed directly to the imagination and the emotions, often seeming to defy logic: Thomas writes almost entirely in images.

"After the Funeral" honors the poet's aunt, Ann Jones, old and disfigured from work and suffering, for whom he feels an affection that goes back to his boyhood. In general outline the poem is clear enough.

Thomas first describes the actual, unsatisfactory funeral, with its "mule praises, brays," the stupid praise of those with sail-shaped (mules', asses') ears, who do not recognize Ann's worth. But the sound of the spade "wakes" him back into his boyhood, so that he feels her death as he would have felt it then (lines 6–9). Afterwards, in her room with its shabby "stuffed fox" and "stale fern," he holds his own memorial service for her. The hearth of her room is now the "raised hearth" (line 21)—that is, the altar. He praises her in images magnified beyond what she would have expected or thought suitable (lines 15–20), but that are true and genuinely felt, unlike the "mule praises" of the public funeral. He calls upon the seas to make her inarticulate virtue "babble" and upon "the ferned and foxy woods" to make her love "sing and swing through a brown chapel" (perhaps the woods or her room but more probably both); and he blesses her with the sign of the cross made by flying birds. Then he describes her as she truly was. His praises are a monument ("this skyward statue"), and the monument is this poem that he is writing, which "storms" at him over her grave until by writing it he can bring to life again her love: "the stuffed fox cries Love and the stale fern is fertile." This is the bare skeleton; the poetry resides in the union of this with the complex patterns of sound, image, and symbol. Thomas should always be read aloud.

The only real difficulty in the poem lies in the few phrases in which two or three images are telescoped into one. In "Blinds down the lids" (line 4), for example, are telescoped the window blinds drawn down in the house as a sign of mourning, the closed eyelids of the dead, which are "blinds" of another sort, and the coffin lid. The phrase just before this, "muffle-toed . . . one peg in the thick grave's foot," seems to fit both the perfunctory mourners, indifferent old people who themselves have "one foot in the grave" (Thomas's words are a variation on this cliché), and the nailing of the coffin lid.

VIII

JOHN DONNE

John Donne was the first of a group that almost by chance came to be called the "metaphysical" poets, chiefly because of Dryden's remark that Donne "affects the metaphysics." But he is scarcely metaphysical in the modern philosophical sense. In style, imagery, and tone, Donne's poetry departed from—even while it grew out of—that of his contemporaries and immediate predecessors in the Elizabethan Age. Like them, he employed ingenious and farfetched "conceits." His, however, are apt to be more extreme and more apparently antipoetic, as well as more ironic. Unlike his contemporaries, he had little to say about the beauty of nature. Whereas in Shakespeare the sun may "gild pale streams with heavenly alchemy," in Donne it is the "busy old fool, unruly Sun." His serious love poem may center about a flea, not a flower; or if about a flower, the flower is scarcely a visual presence (cf. "The Blossom" with Shakespeare's "daisies pied"). Shakespeare uses imagery derived from law and commerce in sonnets about love or friendship, but even this language, heightened as it is with emotion, becomes poetic in the usual sense; one does not think of it as being at all antipoetic. Donne, too, uses the language of commerce and law, and the language of science, the cosmos, daily life, and the intrigues of the royal court. His imagination found most unlikely, sometimes eccentric resemblances between these things and his immediate subject, which was usually personal emotion under specific circumstances. In his poetry, however, the emotion, instead of transforming or subordinating the intellectual elements as Shakespeare's does, seems rather to sharpen the tension of those elements. Intellectual thought, therefore, expressed in witty, concrete, and often extremely colloquial language, stands out as the immediately striking feature of Donne's poetry.

Because the date of composition of most of his poems is uncertain, they are arranged here according to theme. There is, first, cynical poetry about love and women, believed to have been written for the most part during the poet's early, profligate years. Then there is serious love poetry, most (but probably not all) addressed to the woman he married. From his friend Isaac Walton's biography of him, we know that his most serious love affair was beset by difficulties. The girl's father disapproved the match; the pair were married secretly; and when this was discovered Donne was dismissed from his post and imprisoned. Efforts to have the marriage annulled failed, however, and eventually the personal and financial obstacles were overcome. This, in brief, is the frame of reference of many of the love poems, though it is not thought that all the serious poems belong to this group. Finally, there are religious poems, represented here by three of the "Holy Sonnets." Born a Catholic, Donne eventually accepted the Church of England and became one of its greatest preachers.

The reader should notice the wide variety of rhyme schemes and stanza forms used by Donne. Often in the longer stanzas one rhyme will be used three times, the others twice. One effect of this is to satisfy what Bridges called expectancy without too obvious predictability. The effect of Donne's metrical irregularities is worth attention, as is his preference for colloquial to musical inflections.

P. 314. "Song"

About what else besides women is Donne passingly cynical in the first stanza? Has this any effect on the tone of the poem as a whole?

Consider the effect of the closely placed rhymes toward the end of each stanza.

P. 315. "The Indifferent"
What light does this poem throw on the preceding one? A recent editor, Theodore Redpath, suggests the following interpretations:
2   The woman "made amorous by living in luxury, and the woman who gives herself because she needs money."
5   believes [him] ... tries (i.e., tests) [him].

P. 316. "The Bait"
Trace the working out of the conceit through each stanza. Compare the tone of this with that of Marlowe's "The Passionate Shepherd to His Love" (p. 316).

P. 318. "The Triple Fool"
The "two fools" are explicit in the beginning. The third is the fool who through his second action—writing the poem—enables a composer to make a delightful song that, when the poet hears it sung, arouses again, through the alluring music, the grief which his verse writing had brought under control.

P. 321. "The Good-Morrow"
How should the first stanza be read aloud, with what inflections and in what spirit?
19   not mixed equally: An old scientific belief held that compound substances whose elements are equally mixed are stable and cannot be dissolved.

P. 323. "The Anniversary"
3   The "times" are hours, days, seasons, etc. It is not certain whether Donne meant "they" to refer to "Kings," etc., or to "times." If the latter, he probably meant that though the sun is the cause of "times," the very passing of these times makes the sun itself older.
18–20   The general meaning is that their loving souls will be even happier after death.
25–26   What is meant here?

P. 324.   "The Canonization"

29–34   An almost identical thought is repeated three times in these lines: if we are not important enough in a worldly way for a big funeral, a "half-acre tomb," or a place in history ("chronicle"), we shall at any rate be a fit subject for poems.

36–45   The subject of "invoke" is "all" (line 35). "Beg" (line 44) is imperative. Since the lovers are now canonized (have become saints), they are asked to intercede with heaven to send down a pattern by which others may have as perfect a love.

P. 325.   "A Valediction: Forbidding Mourning"

The title refers to parting, not death. Walton says the poem was written to his wife before he left on a mission to France in 1611.

The image of the pair of compasses is one of Donne's most celebrated conceits, but its apparent inconsistency remains a puzzle. Does it refer to drawing a circle, or to the bringing together of the two feet after the circle is drawn, or to one of these in the eighth and the other in the ninth stanza? The last explanation seems to fit the words best, though if both meanings are intended, their order is the reverse of what we should expect.

P. 327.   "The Funeral"

3   wreath of hair. For sentimental reasons, bracelets used sometimes to be made from a lock of someone's hair, woven or braided with strands of gold thread.

5–8   What is meant by the image involving "Viceroy" and "provinces"?

12–13   The superior power of the bracelet is fancifully reasoned. Hair grows up from the brain, the nerves down; and the lady's brain that bore the hair is better than his. Surely this bracelet, then, after his death will hold him together as a unified being better than the network of his nerves ever did

—unless, he adds, she gave it to him only to remind him that he is still her manacled prisoner.

22   The meaning is uncertain. Redpath suggests that it may be "to confer on it all that a Soul can confer."

P. 330.   "A Nocturnal upon Saint Lucy's Day"
Most of the poem is engaged, with great ingenuity, in doubling and redoubling images and ideas of nothingness. By the death of his love he has become, he says, not merely nothing but the quintessence of nothingness; and this thought is elaborated at length. Does the intellectual ingenuity chill, or does it intensify the emotional impact of the poem?

GEORGE HERBERT

Though essentially a very different kind of poet (and man), Herbert felt the influence of Donne's style, and his poetry too is called "metaphysical," chiefly because of its use of everyday, yet farfetched, metaphors for religious themes. After a young manhood spent in fashionable secular life, Herbert entered the church. His poetry, published under the general title of *The Temple*, nearly all concerns the church and the relation of the true Christian to his God.

P. 333.   "The Collar"
The suggestion has been made that "Collar" is simply Herbert's spelling of "Choler." Most readers, however, understand the title as drawn from the collar of a dray-horse or other beast of burden, symbolizing the restraint upon the individual will that is required of one who would serve God. This interpretation gains support from the images of the rope in lines 22–25 and "load" in line 32.

Note that the rebellious speech does not end, as a hasty reading may lead one to suppose, with the end of the question in line 16, but only with line 32.

P. 334.   "The Pulley"
What is the "pulley" of the title?

How does the five-line stanza here differ from that used by Housman in rhyme scheme? in poetic effect?

On the basis of these few poems, try to compare and distinguish the individual qualities of the poetry of Donne and Herbert. Consider the style, the tone, and the character of the thought and of the temperaments revealed in the poems.

WILLIAM BLAKE

Blake was an artist and engraver as well as a poet. Often he seems to have conceived poem and picture as parts of a single whole. The reader interested in his poetry should try to see some of the facsimile editions of his works, nearly all of which he engraved and illustrated himself.

Living through the era of the French Revolution and the Napoleonic wars, Blake was a passionate humanitarian, a passionate hater of tyranny, and if possible an even more passionate hater of hypocrisy.

The selections presented here are from the shorter poems; he also wrote a number of long, obscure but interesting works based on strange symbols which he invented and did not explain. There has never been complete agreement on the interpretation of these works, and some of the shorter poems share their obscurity. On the other hand, many are simple and a few, not printed here, possibly simple-minded.

P. 338. "Mad Song"
Compare this with the earlier "mad songs" in Chapter VI.

P. 339. "The Tyger"
Ordinarily, lamb and tiger, used as symbols, are likely to represent good and evil or gentleness and ferocity. This is not quite what Blake meant. His tiger is fearful but beautiful. He had never seen a real tiger, and his beast is rather a vision than a live animal. The meaning of the poem has been much dis-

puted. The tiger is sometimes thought to represent divine Wrath, in contrast with Forgiveness of the lamb; or Experience in contrast with Innocence. In Blake's *Songs of Innocence*, the poem "The Lamb" asks much the same question ("Little Lamb, who made thee?"). The answer partly identifies the lamb with Jesus. "The Tyger" is the corresponding poem in *Songs of Experience*.

What is the effect of the poem's being written entirely in the form of questions? Is the overall feeling one of questioning? of exclamation? or neither?

12   The grammatical incompleteness is explained by an early version in which "What dread hand? & what dread feet?" was followed by a stanza, eventually dropped, beginning, "Could fetch it from the furnace deep." Later changes were considered but not published.

17–18   The key to this image has been found in lines from Blake's long symbolic work, *Vala; or the Four Zoas*:

> I went not forth: I hid myself in black clouds of my wrath;
> I call'd the stars around my feet in the night of councils dark;
> The stars threw down their spears and fled naked away.
>   (Night the Fifth, Urizen speaking)

The trouble is that one cannot be quite sure of what the key unlocks, and a discussion of the problem here would be overlong and still inconclusive.

P. 339.   "A Poison Tree"

An alternate title for this poem, "Christian Forbearance," should make the meaning clear if it is in doubt. To understand Blake's irony on Christian forbearance, however, one must take into account every detail in the poem. In an early version, for example, line 9 reads: "And I gave it to my foe." This was deleted: in the finished form of the poem, the forbearing Christian simply leaves the bright apple enticingly there for his foe to steal.

P. 340. "The Sick Rose"

This poem and the next, like many of Blake's poems, are symbolic but not in such a way as to dictate a specific allegorical equivalent. They are at the same time clear, precise—and indefinite. One could name various forms of evil that might be symbolized by the worm, but the poem itself does not point to any one meaning, not even to the worm as embodied evil itself, or destruction, or death. It fits any and all and should therefore not be limited by a closed interpretation.

Blake often uses anapestic meter for serious poetry and often (not always) succeeds with it. Study the meter of this and the next two poems in the light of the discussions in Chapter II. What does the meter do to or for the tone?

P. 341. "London"

Study the choice of language in this poem, and be sure to take in the precise meaning of all the words as they stand in their context. The language is much stronger and more specific than a cursory reading will suggest.

P. 342. "The Human Abstract"

The poem attacks conventional religion. The tree of "Mystery" in the last three stanzas is what Blake calls elsewhere the "deadly tree" that England has named "Moral Virtue, and the Law/of God, who dwells in Chaos, hidden from the human sight." The Caterpillar and Fly are priests. In some of Blake's engravings priests are represented in the form of caterpillars, and in *Proverbs of Hell* he wrote: "As the caterpillar chooses the fairest leaves to lay her eggs, so the priest lays his curse on the fairest joys."

JOHN KEATS

Keats had an unusually keen feeling for sensuous experience and an exceptional power of communicating it. His short life, however, was not one of easy pleasure but was heavily burdened with responsibility, sickness, and death. His father died early, and he watched first his mother and then his younger brother die of tuberculosis with, perhaps, toward the end a guess that he himself might follow. The desire to escape sorrow and responsibility is a frequent theme in his poetry. It is always balanced by the recognition that there is no escape, that one must, after all, live in the real world and meet whatever comes. More than commonly susceptible to pleasure, and more than commonly experienced in pain, he often brings the two extremes together in his poetry. In a letter to a friend, he wrote: "I scarcely remember counting upon any Happiness —I look not for it if it be not in the present hour—nothing startles me beyond the Moment. The setting Sun will always set me to rights—or if a Sparrow come before my Window I take part in its existence and pick about the Gravel." This power of empathy and this double sense of unhappiness and pleasure are distinguishing features of his work. It is the latter that most often governs the structure of the poems. "La Belle Dame sans Merci" begins with a lonely knight wandering by withered sedge and a desolate lake, and ends as it began when the knight's false fairyland has collapsed. "The Eve of St. Agnes" (not reprinted here) is a sensuously luxuriant tale of youthful love with a happy ending; but it is placed within a frame of old age, poverty, cold, and death. The "Ode to the Nightingale" has a similar, though not a narrative structure. They all represent Keats's essentially realistic view of the inescapable condition of man.

P. 346. "Ode to a Nightingale"

Trace the theme of escape through its transformations in this ode.

Study carefully the language of the poem and the meter. What, for example, is the effect, at the very beginning of the poem, of the unusual inversion of accent and the pronounced pause in the second foot of the first line?

Comment on the relation between sound and meaning in line 17.

26   Keats's brother Tom had died a few months before this was written.

66–67   alien corn: a poetic epitome of part of the Old Testament book of Ruth. Note how this foreshadows the later "forlorn."

Stanza 7 introduces the distant past. It also makes the obviously false statement that the nightingale does not die (to the human listener one nightingale's song sounds like another; hence they create the illusion of continuity). What is the general meaning of this stanza, and what is its function in relation to the rest of the poem?

P. 348.   "Ode on a Grecian Urn"

This is one of the most discussed, and perhaps overdiscussed, of English poems, chiefly because of the closing statement about truth and beauty. As a universal principle, it seems to many people false, absurd, or immoral. By various ingenious explanations, critics have tried to rescue Keats from what appears to be a weak position. The question cannot be argued out here, but readers should keep in mind that Keats was using a commonplace as old as Plato, whose ultimate values—his triad of the good, the true, and the beautiful—were regarded as approximately three aspects of the same thing. In a letter, Keats once wrote of the "truth" of creative imagination, "What the imagination seizes as Beauty must be truth—whether it existed before or not." "Truth" and "beauty" were a pair of terms almost interchangeable in the eighteenth and early nineteenth centuries, on the assumption that beauty (particularly in sculpture and painting) is "essential" truth, purged of individual imperfections.

2   foster-child. "Time" and "silence," though not the original creators (parents), were the foster-parents who had preserved the urn through the ages.

44–45   dost tease: taxes our thought or imagination beyond its capacity, as does the attempt to imagine eternity.

P. 350.   "To Autumn"
25   bloom. Keats may have two different senses of this word in mind: the common one, having to do with blossoming; and the other, not quite as common but not at all unusual, meaning to cover with a soft, powdery silver, such as often appears on plums and other fruit. Or he may have meant only the latter.
28   Some texts of the poem have sallows (willows) for shallows.
What time of autumn is described here? What images contribute most to the feeling of ripeness and fulfillment?
What change in tone or mood accompanies the change in time of day between the beginning and end? What images bring this about?

P. 351.   "Ode on Melancholy"
4   The word "grape," by an ironic metaphor, transforms this line into a contrast between extremes of life and death, Dionysus and Persephone (Proserpina). Dionysus, crowned with the grape vine, was a god not only of wine but, much more importantly in Greek religion, of fertility (hence, life) and intensified vitality. Persephone, as Queen of the Dead, is his opposite; and Keats crowns her with something quite opposite to the grape.

This poem will repay an attempt to work out a prose statement of the meaning in the light of all the imagery and all the statements.

GERARD MANLEY HOPKINS

Almost none of the poetry of Hopkins was printed till 1918, though he died in 1889; hence the influence of his revolutionary style has been felt only in the present century. The central fact of his life, which put its mark on nearly all his writing, was his conversion from the Anglican to the Catholic Church and his entrance into the Jesuit order as soon as his undergraduate years at Oxford were over. His poetry reflects a temperament in which two opposing impulses are balanced. He is as sensuous as Keats, and more self-willed: his language is filled almost to bursting with images of physical sensation. But an impulse toward asceticism was equally fundamental in him, and his poetry is the product of tension between these contradictory impulses.

Like Whitman, Hopkins broke away from established metrical forms—but not in the direction of free verse. Instead, he worked out his own system, new but with roots in the practice of earlier poets. His chief departures were two. He introduced what he called "counterpointed" rhythm: that is, standard meter in which for several successive feet the accents are reversed. The mind continues to be aware of the ground rhythm, which is normally iambic, while the ear hears, superimposed upon this, for a time, the new reversed rhythm. In musical terms, "syncopation" possibly provides a closer analogy than "counterpoint." Hopkins's other invention he called "sprung rhythm." This already existed in nursery rhymes and some other verse intended for song or chant. In it, every foot has one accented syllable followed by unaccented syllables ranging from none at all to four (occasionally more). These disparate feet are to some extent equalized and a rhythmical effect secured by the fact that, as the number of light syllables in the foot decreases, the accented syllable grows heavier and longer. The most easily identified feature of sprung rhythm is the frequent presence of two or three strongly accented syllables in immediate succession. As Hopkins said, the effect is of a strongly marked, emphatic rhythm, as in the line: "Áll things/ coúnter, or/-íginal,/spáre,/stránge." The timing and weight of these juxtaposed accents is different from that of standard meter, in which a spondaic foot is substituted. The second line, for example, of Wordsworth's "A slumber did my spirit seal," which is read "I had/nó hú/man feárs," in sprung rhythm would become "I had/nó/húman/feárs," which gives "no" a great deal more time and weight. Once a reader becomes accustomed to them, Hopkins's rhythms as a rule are clearly defined, though sometimes further elaborations of his system or uncertainties of meaning or emphasis render the reading uncertain. He also, however, had a fine ear for the handling of conventional meters (cf. "Heaven-Haven"). Most of his best-known poems employ the sonnet form or some variation of it.

The idiosyncrasies of Hopkins's style reflect the dual impulses already referred to. On the one hand, the language must be as rich, as bursting with all kinds of physical sensation, as it can be; and on the other hand, it must be as rigidly controlled and ascetically stripped as possible. What he usually sacrifices in the stripping process is words that serve only as grammatical connectives; it is his pruning away of these that causes much of the obscurity in his poetry.

Practically all Hopkins's poetry is religious. Intense love of the material world, intensely ascetic devotion to God, and the reconciling of these provide the theme of many of his poems. His other major theme is that of spiritual suffering.

P. 353. "The Sea and the Skylark"
11–14 The play on "make" and "break" obscures the grammar. Our make (our kind, man) and our making (that which we make, our deeds) break down, and are continually in process of breaking down to man's "last dust" or his "first slime." Hopkins noted elsewhere, probably with the modern Darwinian parallel in mind, that the ancient Greek philosopher Parmenides thought men "had sprung from slime."

P. 354. "Pied Beauty"
The theme resembles an inverted pyramid: variety and multiplicity are reduced first to pairs of opposites and then to unity at the end.

P. 354. "The Windhover"

Title. The windhover is a small falcon, said to be named for its habit of hovering almost motionless, staying itself in the air with its head against the wind.

The meaning of this sonnet has been much in dispute, but the interpretation given here is, in the editor's opinion, the only one that draws all the parts of the poem together into a coherent whole.

In the octave, the poet describes the bird of which he caught sight this morning. It is the favorite ("minion"), the crown prince ("dauphin") of the morning because of the beauty of its movement and its mastery over its element, the air. The poet's heart, which before had been stagnant and unwilling to feel anything ("in hiding"), was stirred by the bird's power and mastery.

When the sestet opens, the individual bird is universalized so that it stands for the whole of material creation or nature: "brute [i.e., animal] beauty . . . air, pride, plume." But as the poet contemplates it, this material world of nature, with all its beauty and power, seems to buckle, break open, collapse —like a structure that is burning from within. AND (the capitalization makes the word equivalent to "and behold!") through and beyond the material reality "breaks" the infinitely more beautiful, and more daring or dangerous, fire of the spirit of Christ ("my chevalier"), whom the poet is now addressing directly. No wonder this happens, he says, for the most commonplace things break open to show inward beauty. The ordinary labor of ploughing breaks dull-colored earth into a shining furrow (sillion) of fresh soil (Hopkins's journal describes a recently ploughed hill "glistening with very bright newly turned sods"). And the coals of a fire (the English use very large chunks of coal in fireplaces) that seem dead on the outside (blue-bleak embers) fall open and show the still-bright fire ("gold-vermilion") inside.

This train of thought was common in Hopkins: the beauty of the material world stirred him for its own sake, then led

NOTES 471

him on to think of the spiritual beauty dwelling in or beyond the material.

4 rung upon the rein: a term used in the training of a horse: at the end of a long rein the horse describes a circle. Here the falcon, using one wing as pivot, swings the circle.

6 skate's heel . . . bow-bend: another image of smooth circling, drawn from figure skating.

11 chevalier: a term of honor: a chivalrous man, a knight. Here it is Christ, to whom the poem is addressed. Hopkins did not follow the modern custom of capitalizing nouns and pronouns referring to God or Christ (in another poem he addressed God as "sir").

P. 355. "No worst, there is none"

This and several of the following sonnets deal with extremes of spiritual suffering. The feeling itself is presented, not the cause.

11–14 The only limit to this suffering is that the soul cannot endure it long. The only "comfort [that] serves in a whirlwind"—the rock or crevice of cliff under which one can hide—is the knowledge that oblivion comes through sleep and finally death. The omission of a relative pronoun in unusual places ("comfort [that] serves") is frequent in Hopkins.

P. 356. "I wake and feel the fell of dark"

1 "Fell" here is a tactual image ("fell" meaning the pelt of an animal), like "velvet darkness" but primitive, coarse, and so thick as to be almost palpable. It is not the "fell" (cruel, evil, deadly) of line 8 in the preceding sonnet.

P. 356. "My own heart let me more have pity on"

The general sense is clear. The poet urges himself to cease his self-tormenting, to allow his spirit to relax and be natural, to give himself a little mental freedom. Hopkins stretches and twists his grammar but does not break it. In lines 2–4 he says: Let me live hereafter kind to myself, not live tormenting my [already] tormented mind by means of my tormented mind. The redoubling of tormented thus emphasizes the intensification of torment that feeds upon itself. He continues: I can no more get comfort from within my comfortless [mind] than blind eyes can find daylight or than those adrift at sea can find water [to drink]. The language and images of the octave are thus tied together by the idea of doubling and redoubling back on the self. In the sestet he urges himself to relax and look outward: Let joy size [a verb: to grow in size] spontaneously at any time in response to anything. There is a play on "God knows": it is to be taken in both the religious and the slang sense. "Whose" refers back to "joy": joy . . . whose smile is not wrung [cannot be compelled], but rather, at unforeseen times lights a lovely mile [of the road of life] in the same way as "skies betweenpie [a verb: make a variegated pattern between] mountains" along a mile of road.

Once the tortured grammar, reflection of the inner torture, is understood, the force of the poem can be felt. Consider, within the context of the poem, the attitude toward the self expressed in the epithet "poor Jackself."

P. 357.   "That Nature Is a Heraclitean Fire and of the Comfort of the Resurrection"

The Greek philosopher Heraclitus believed that fire is the underlying primary substance: the world is an "ever-living fire with measures of it kindling and measures of it going out." It is perpetually in process of being transformed into water and earth, which in turn are continually changing back through vapor to fire.

Like a number of other sonnets, including "The Windhover," this one (Hopkins called it a sonnet with two codas) moves from the theme at first of something beautiful or impressive in nature that has moved him and that he describes in passionately exact physical detail, to a devotional conclusion. The scene is a bright windy day with flying clouds, when the earth is drying up after "yestertemptest." In pool (i.e., puddle) and wheel rut the earth changes as it dries to the texture, in turn, of dough, crust, dust. The grammar of the last part of this sentence (lines 5–9) is obscure; perhaps "wind" is the subject of all the verbs. At any rate, the general meaning is evident: the drying process stiffens the patterned footprints of men going about their work—the "manmarks [that] treadmire [mudtreading] toil" had made—but these will crumble to dust and in the next rain become mud again. The Heraclitean change is continuous. But it is sad that man, nature's "clearest-selvèd spark," her most highly individualized creation, vanishes utterly when he dies and his "mark" on the mind of the world disappears and leaves no trace (lines 10–15); the poet seems to be thinking of his own life and work, of which he often despaired). But the thought of the Resurrection breaks into his lament. "Flesh [may] fade" and "mortal trash [may] fall" to the worm that inherits all flesh; the "world's wildfire [may] leave but ash"; Heraclitus may be right, that is, about the material world. Nevertheless, because Christ lived and sacrificed himself as a man, "I" (and other souls) who on my own account am nothing (Jack, joke, potsherd) am, through Christ, diamond (symbol of value and permanence, in contrast to the earlier mud and dust)—and immortal.

The only manuscript of this poem was marked by Hopkins "provisional only," and the poem does seem imperfectly finished. It contains, however, some of his finest images and lines, and some memorable phrases, such as the rather Shakespearean "mortal trash/Fall to the residuary worm."

P. 359. "To R. B."

The theme, of course, is poetic creation as Hopkins knew it, what is requisite for its success and how it often failed him. Note the elaborately wrought symbolism based on sexual intercourse and human reproduction. Like Coleridge, Hopkins associated creative inspiration with some sort of inner delight or joy.

ROBERT BRIDGES

The distinguished poetry of Bridges has gained recognition only slowly, particularly in America, for his work is not striking or ostentatiously modern in either subject or style. Yeats once said of it, ". . . every metaphor, every thought a commonplace, emptiness everywhere, the whole magnificent"; Housman, with less ambivalence, called Bridges' volume *Shorter Poems* "the most perfect single volume of English verse ever published." Bridges' excellence lies partly in his power of completely realizing (that is, of *making real* to the reader as well as, for himself, being fully conscious of) the precise character and quality of whatever experience he writes about, partly in his love of beauty in nature and language, and partly in what he described as "the inexhaustible satisfaction of form." His realization of commonly unnoticed aspects of love—the moment of abysmal doubt in the very hour of happiness and the "hard master" that love can be ("O weary pilgrims," p. 208; the triolet "When first we met," p. 114)—is typical of his unspectacular yet sometimes profound originality, which owes a good deal to the clarity with which he distinguishes one shade of feeling from another at a level much below the surface.

His meters are highly original but as unspectacular as his themes. Sometimes he employed a modified form of Hopkins's sprung rhythm; in his later years he experimented with syllabic verse. For the most part, however, he wrote in standard meters so subtly varied from the normal that they produce a haunting, almost unidentifiable music. Like many of the best poets, Bridges is a great borrower from his predecessors. Bits of Milton, Wordsworth, Keats, and Hopkins are noticeable in the selections printed here; but as with all good poetic borrowers, the echoes are always absorbed into the fabric of the new work.

P. 359.   "A Passer-By"

In theme and language, this poem should be compared with the two sonnets of Wordsworth on a similar theme (p. 203).

The common belief that sailing vessels are more beautiful than steamships may not be valid, but is founded on more than mere sentimental attachment to the past. One can *see* the balance of weights that holds up a suspension bridge, and it is almost as if a sailing vessel makes the wind itself visible. Such man-made structures seem to make natural law visible to the eye and in this lies their profound appeal.

Study the meter and listen with particular care to the sound of this and all the other poems of Bridges.

P. 360. "London Snow"
What sounds are especially prominent and what effect have they on the poem as a whole?
What saves this descriptive poem from being static?

P. 361. "Nightingales"
It has long been disputed—a highly subjective question—whether the song of the nightingale represents to the human listener sadness or joy. Association with the legend of Philomela (see p. 454) suggests the former, and Milton called the bird "most musical, most melancholy"; yet others have called its notes "merry" or happy. This is the background of Bridges' double view.

The poem is often interpreted as a symbolic statement of the idea that the greatest art originates in suffering, not joy; and certainly the poem lends itself easily to such an interpretation. Whether Bridges meant it so or not is questionable, for at nearly the time when this poem was written his belief seems to have been, in his words,

> For howsoe'er man hug his care
> The best of his art is gay.

The poem might also be interpreted as Bridges' reply to Keats: what the nightingale meant to Keats, represented in the first stanza, is rejected by the birds in the second. Under this interpretation the theme has to do with life, not art. Or the poem may not be a symbolic—really, allegorical—statement of either of these ideas; it may be only loosely and generally suggestive of a contrast that does not require abstract, logical formulation.

Whether what the *poet* meant or did not mean has any bearing upon what the *poem* means no doubt depends on what we mean by "meaning," a question much in dispute at the present time. The answer depends on one's basic aesthetic assumptions.

The subtle relations between sound and meaning in Bridges are illustrated by the first two lines in which the opening key word, "beautiful," is carried into the second line by the redistribution of all its sounds into other key words, "*bright in the fruitful*," with the addition of *r* sounds, which have been absent from the first line but are prominent afterwards. Read the lines again, listening to the effect on both sound and meaning.

P. 362. "November"

21 amorets: probably a local name for some kind of bird. No such meaning of the word appears in standard reference works, but *amore* in Anglo-Saxon was a name for a kind of bird, and Bridges' word may be a local survival of this.

Consider the interplay of loneliness and busy life and the effect of these on tone and mood.

P. 364. "Narcissus"

The meaning of this poem is much easier to feel than to formulate. The legend of Narcissus, the beautiful youth who fell in love with his own image reflected in a pool, is employed as a symbol for the Christian doctrine that God created man in His own image. But the God of this poem, in spite of the human figure of Narcissus, is conceived not anthropomorphically but rather as some unbodied creative urge toward beauty which, through evolutionary ages, forced its way through undifferentiated matter from the core of earth to "embroider" earth's thin crust with the life and beauty of nature and man.

All the best of man's wisdom, art, and religions derives from this creative source. But in the end the poet sees the result of this creation as not so fine after all; it is a shadow and not the self of the "beauteous everlasting." The thought, however, is not the Platonic idea that the material phenomenon because of intrinsic inferiority cannot achieve the perfection of the Ideal; Bridges traces the imperfection ultimately to the "beauteous everlasting" itself. "Hast thou mistaken?/ Or dost forget?" he says. This is but a crude formulation of the cosmic thought of the poem, but perhaps it is enough to relieve the reader of initial puzzlement and permit him to enter into the spirit of the work as a whole.

WILLIAM BUTLER YEATS

Regarded by most critics as the greatest modern poet writing in English, Yeats was an Irishman, though in youth and early manhood he lived much in England. Returning to Dublin, he took an active part in the Irish Nationalist literary movement, was a prime mover in the founding and conduct of the Abbey Theater, and when Ireland gained independence became a senator in its parliament. Though not by temperament a mystic himself, mystical cults—theosophy, Rosicrucianism, the Society of the Golden Dawn, astrology—as well as Irish legend and modern folk beliefs in the supernatural, attracted and influenced him. Old age preoccupied him even before he himself grew old; and—not least—he was haunted for many years by love for Maud Gonne, a well-known, beautiful Irishwoman who devoted her life to the Irish revolutionary struggle against England, whose violent activities and opinions Yeats frequently disliked, and whom he could not forget. All these preoccupations were reflected directly in his poetry, much of which seems almost a series of crystallized moments in a continuous, subjective autobiography. The individual poems, however, are entirely crystallized—that is, are self-contained wholes in themselves.

The poetic style of Yeats changed considerably over the years. His early work is characterized by the romantic, even sentimental melancholy of waning loves, falling leaves, and fading roses, all excellent of their kind though now somewhat dated—"of museum quality," as Marianne Moore said in another connection—and even then graced with distinction of language. Gaining in strength and boldness, his work came increasingly to be marked by the imagery and language of everyday life and by the presence of strange, grotesque, sometimes coarse words and images, often side by side with highly wrought poetic ones. This fusion of the grotesque and the poetically grand became at last one of the hallmarks of his style.

Many of the later poems are founded on an elaborate symbolic system representing all history and human psychology in terms variously conceived as phases of the moon, intersecting cones, cycles, antithetical constructs, and spiral forms which he called "gyres." The prose exposition of these required a book from Yeats (*A Vision*, 1925) and would require scarcely less here. A few clues will have to suffice for partial light on certain poems.

P. 366. "The Lake Isle of Innisfree"
This is an early poem. Cf. Pound's "The Lake Isle" (p. 260).

P. 366. "Cuchulain's Fight with the Sea"
The first version of this poem was written early; the present text is a much-altered later version.

Cuchulain (pronounced Cu-hŏo-lin) is the great hero of the Red Branch (Ulster) cycle of Irish legend. According to Yeats's version of the hero's death, his wife, Emer, learns from her swineherd that he is returning from the wars with a young concubine. In revenge, she sends their son out to fight his father under conditions that will prevent their recognizing each other till too late.

Originally the poem concluded with the lines:

> For four days warred he with the bitter tide,
> And the waves flowed above him, and he died.

The later version condenses everything into the long, abstract word "invulnerable," with, in this context, its concrete etymological association of wounds in battle (from Latin *vulnerare*, to wound), so that it sums up for the imagination the old battles won, the recent battle that cannot be undone, and the final battle that cannot be won against the inevitable.

P. 370. "The Cold Heaven"

Like the two preceding poems in the text, this refers to Maud Gonne. Its implications are much broader, however, for it represents any moment when the cold light of truth suddenly breaks into a man's consciousness to shatter an illusion upon which his life has been built. The climax of the poem, the words "riddled with light" (line 9), strongly marked by their metrical inversion, is developed in subsequent lines through the newly introduced image of the naked soul scourged along the road after death by the light of the skies. The poem is extremely subjective. Consider how the effect of violence is produced in a poem in which all that happens is purely internal.

P. 370. "The Magi"

Consider particularly in this poem the sound pattern of rhyme and assonance, the metrical variations, the unusual thought and use of language toward the end, and the tension produced by constant slight delay in the resolution of grammatical constructions. Then read the poem aloud, very deliberately.

P. 371. "The Hawk"

The presiding image is derived from the art of falconry. Elsewhere Yeats uses the hawk as a symbol for the argumentative, logical part of the mind, and he disliked people in whom that was dominant. Here the bird, having soared out of control, no longer brings down its catch; and so the larder and spit are bare and the kitchen in turmoil. The key to the meaning of the whole lies in the last stanza, where the speaker turns upon himself with self-contempt. The hawk of his mind (in the second stanza) has "learnt to be proud" and refuses to descend. It is brought down with a question. What kind of pride was it, the poet asks, that led the hawk of his mind last evening to sit "dumfounded [when he should have spoken up] before a knave," and then, stung by his own weakness, to show off with cheap wit afterwards to his friend. The poem is an expression of self-contempt for a momentary failure of integrity.

P. 372. "Under the Round Tower"

This poem exhibits Yeats's particular kind of grotesquerie, his special blending of incongruous elements. The beggar, trying to sleep on his once-rich ancestor's tomb, is plagued by cosmic dreams and in the morning says he must find a way to sleep indoors tonight. The dream itself, represented absurdly and with some tinge on the poet's part, apparently, of self-mockery, is nevertheless made up of ornate symbols that Yeats elsewhere employed seriously: golden king and silver lady (sun and moon), the dance with its spiral form, the round tower, all are symbols in Yeats's composite theory of historical cycles, of types of human beings and changing phases of the nature of all men, of "objective" and "subjective" mind, and much else of which a full explanation is impracticable here. (The incongruities of the poem are not diminished by the fact that the O'Byrnes were an actual, once wealthy local family who had run into bad luck and had fallen under the spell of bad fairies, so it was said.)

P. 373. "The Second Coming"

Early in life Yeats rejected Christian belief. Later he elaborated his theory (or myth) of historical cycles, each lasting some two thousand years, each in character antithetical to the preceding cycle, and each beginning with a supernatural birth sprung from the mating of human and divine beings. The birth of Helen, daughter of the mortal Leda and Zeus in the form of a swan, caused the Trojan War and opened the Graeco-Roman cycle of history; Jesus, son of Mary but also of God, began the Christian era; and another, perhaps brutish, cycle is approaching: "After us the Savage God," Yeats once prophesied. This mythical theory underlies both "The Second Coming" and "Leda and the Swan."

The first stanza describes the state of the world as Yeats viewed it shortly after the close of World War I. A century earlier, in *Prometheus Unbound,* Shelley had expressed the same thought in very similar terms:

> The good want power, but to weep barren tears.
> The powerful goodness want; worse need for them.
> The wise want love; and those who love want wisdom;
> And all best things are thus confused to ill.

P. 375. "Among School Children"

While he was writing this poem, Yeats referred to it in a letter as his "curse upon old age." In the end, it became much more than that.

The shape of the poem may be described by Yeats's own image of a "gyre." It begins with a small commonplace event and spirals out in theme until at the end it raises questions almost too vast to be expressed clearly in language: What is reality or what is value? The emotional energy that starts the widening spiral movement is sparked, once more, by the thought of Maud Gonne. Because of this, an experience that begins as a cursory visit of inspection by Yeats, in his official capacity as an Irish senator, to a convent school, comes to engage all his power of feeling and thought, makes him wonder what he has given his life to, what others give their lives to—ultimately, what is worth giving one's life to.

Stanza II. Seeing the little girls in school, the poet is reminded of an occasion when "she" had sat by the fire telling him a story of her childhood. He remembers it as a rare moment when he and she had felt united.

26–28   Usually quattrocento would mean the fifteenth century. Yeats, however, may have meant the fourteenth and may have been thinking of pictures of Dante, whose "hollow face," he said, was "more plain to the mind's eye than any face but that of Christ." Maud Gonne's portraits show exaggeratedly hollow cheeks and eyes in her later years. "Mess" merely means a quantity of food for a meal (confusion is not implied).

33–35   honey of generation. Yeats explained this as a legendary drug that destroys the recollection of prenatal freedom. It therefore makes life tolerable while its effect lasts.

The connection of Stanza VI with the preceding is made clear by Yeats's explanation of its meaning, "that even the greatest men are old scarecrows by the time their fame has come."

Stanza VII. The images worshiped by nuns are unchanging, those worshiped by mothers (their children) change; but both break the hearts of worshipers, Yeats says. Here he breaks off and addresses the images themselves as "Presences," bringing together the three devotions from the earlier stanzas: "passion" (Yeats's for his love), "piety" (the nuns' to religion), "affection" (mothers' for children). To the worshiper, these Presences symbolize "all heavenly glory." But in the end they only mock him, for in a sense they are not real but are "self-born," self-created: the value that man worships in them, imagining it to be an objective value outside of himself, is only the value that he has subjectively created.

In the last stanza, the specific materials of the earlier part of the poem are still recognizable: the nun's asceticism (line 58), Maud Gonne's hollow beauty (line 59), his own wisdom that is not worth what it cost him (line 60); but these have grown far beyond their individual meaning and have become part of the universal question of values. The thought of the final stanza can be paraphrased only very crudely. It concerns ends and means: that the end cannot be separated from the means, that labor *brings* reward (blossoming, dancing) only when it *is* in itself reward. Or of the chestnut tree, the question is asked: Which is means—leaf, blossom, or bole—and which end? Which is the real, the essence? Does the dancer exist except through the dance? The implied answer may be phrased even more abstractly: that there is no *being* except *becoming*.

We shall not attempt to explain or describe the final poetic character and quality of "Among School Children" further than to call attention once more to the gyre-like structure of the poem and to the extraordinary style of Yeats, who can combine the most colloquial language and undignified imagery with the most dignified and remote in such a way as to create something quite different from either alone. Consider the homely and grotesque "comfortable kind of scarecrow," for example, and the "old clothes upon old sticks," in which the mere repetition of "old" before "sticks" helps transform the phrase from commonplace into poetry. The pattern of contrast between such phrases as these and very different ones like "a marble or a bronze repose" or the abstract apostrophe "O Presences," a contrast that runs through the poem almost to the end, contributes to produce the combined feeling of reality and importance in the poem. The dropping away of commonplace material toward the end is part of the gyre-like movement of the whole.

P. 377. "Sailing to Byzantium"

More clearly than the preceding, this is a poem about old age. It is also an assertion of the value of the artificial, that which has been constructed by the intellect of man. Byzantium was chosen as a symbol partly because in his historical system Yeats regarded medieval Byzantium as perhaps the only time in history when "religious, aesthetic, and practical life were one," when a unity of being and of culture existed in which the artist was not set apart but spoke to all the people. As a subsidiary theme, Yeats introduces the eastern doctrine of reincarnation, which he often talked about elsewhere. Here he expresses a wish for reincarnation not as a living being subject to physical deterioration but as a work of art.

13–14 but studying . . . magnificence: except the study of arts created by the soul of man.

Stanza IV. Yeats said he had read that in the Byzantine emperor's palace there was a tree made of gold and silver, with an artificial bird that sang an artificial song. This at the close of the poem becomes the antithetical counterpart to the living, perishable birds who sing in the trees in "that [other] country," the natural world, where the young dwell.

P. 378. "Byzantium"

In "Sailing to Byzantium" were interwoven the two themes of youth-and-age and the permanence of art. In "Byzantium" the main strands are life-and-death and, again, the permanence of art. The poet is no longer sailing toward Byzantium; he is in imagination there, as if he were a spirit looking on. The scene has the immediacy of a vision, in contrast with the more indirect and fragmented metaphorical imagery in the earlier poem. But the symbolic city comes into being only when its everyday imperfect realities—the "unpurged images of day," "drunken soldiery," "night-walkers"—have disappeared after the hour of midnight has struck. Then one of those monuments of the soul's magnificence, the great dome of St. Sophia's (it has been called one of the "greatest architectural achievements of all time") dominates the scene: the permanent in art "disdains" the blood and mire of sensual life.

In Stanza II an image (of the dead) "floats" before him, for the dead, Hades' bobbins, may partly retrace the winding path by which they came (the image of the winding path redoubles that of the spiral "bobbin's" mummy cloth unwinding), and so may approach and summon those (i.e., himself) who are little more than dead themselves ("breathless mouths," but in an earlier draft of the poem "breathing mouths"). In the third stanza, the superiority of art over sensual life is asserted again through the golden bird, which knows and can speak what the dead, the "cocks of Hades," know. The fourth stanza presents the vision of spirits of the recent dead who are not yet freed of all the fury and complexity of life, dancing on the mosaic pavement of Constantine the ritual dance of purification in supernatural flames which will transform them into the "artifice of eternity." And in the final stanza the poet sees more and more spirits arriving for this purification. The sea symbolizes the sensual world to which the dolphin belongs, but the dolphin also traditionally serves to carry the dead to Paradise (cf. *Lycidas,* line 164) or, in this poem, to Byzantium. The sea of the sensual is broken by the seawall of the artificial—that is, by the marble mosaic pavement of the Forum and the golden birds, created by the smithies.

This brief sketch provides only the bare outline of meaning and does not touch on the really poetical aspects of the poem, the "sound of meaning" which haunts it whether one understands the details or not, and the magnificence of its language. Consider, as a single instance of the latter, the sound and the connotations of the final line.

A most interesting study of the process of poetic creation may be found in an article by Curtis Bradford ("Yeats's Byzantium Poems," *PMLA,* LXXV, March 1960), where the successive drafts of these two poems are printed.

P. 380. "The Circus Animals' Desertion"
This is a late poem in which Yeats sums up his life's achievement with bitter irony.

ROBERT FROST

One of the most "native" of American poets, Frost needs no introduction to any reader. Though his longer narrative poems, for the most part founded on farm life in New England, gained popularity for some years, he will perhaps be remembered best for some of the shorter lyric and reflective poems.

WALLACE STEVENS

Though now regarded as among the best of the twentieth century, the poetry of Wallace Stevens is difficult and for a long time failed to attract more than a very small audience. Its obscurities were not often so spectacular as to gain for it the success of notoriety, and though Stevens had published many separate poems earlier, he delayed assembling his first volume until 1923, when he was past forty.

His writing is that of a man familiar with the work of his contemporaries, and particularly with French Symbolist poetry and modern philosophical thought. It is not, however, literary or learned in the usual sense: it does not bristle with literary and mythological allusions or with obscure historical references. Its obscurity is owing to the character of Stevens' own mind, which is both philosophical and concrete. The ultimate effect of his poetry is that of philosophical abstraction, however vividly his concrete scenes and images may cling in the memory, as they almost always do because of their extremely specific and unexpected character and their bright color. He writes of such subjects as the aim and art of poetry, of humanist philosophy as opposed to doctrinaire Christianity, of man's "blessed rage for order" which impels his imagination to creative activity. Yet he may present such abstractions merely by saying, for example, that he placed a round, man-made jar on a hill in Tennessee ("Anecdote of the Jar"). The titles of his poems—titles typical of much of their imagery—can be particular to the point of oddity: "The Revolutionists Stop for Orangeade," "Mud Master," "Dance of the Macabre Mice," "A Rabbit as King of the Ghosts," or those three more celebrated titles, "Le Monocle de Mon Oncle," "The Emperor of Ice Cream" (the subject of which is death), and "The Comedian as the Letter C." Possibly a very little but certainly not much of this oddity is mischievous in intention; a little of it seems to spring from Stevens' antipathy to the pompous and the self-important; none seems to spring from a mere desire to dazzle the reader. His poems represent a view of the world that is completely serious without being solemn or didactic, one that is ironic and occasionally comic without being trivial. Controlled by self-discipline yet unfettered by convention, Stevens' highly original imagination creates a world in which the cosmic and the minute, great art and the "roller of big cigars" exist side by side, illuminating each other.

Technically, much of Stevens' verse may be classified as free verse, since little of it quite scans by conventional rules and it employs conventional end rhyme only sporadically. One scarcely notices that it is free verse, however, because there is always a recognizable rhythm founded on similarities of length, cadence, and often accent between phrase and phrase, line and line. Some poems are written in a very free, flexible blank verse. Assonance, alliteration, repetition of words or phrases, and parallel structure all contribute to its highly wrought texture.

P. 385. "Domination of Black"

Study the symbolism of this poem, not forgetting the title.

10   The cry of the peacock, in contrast with the beauty of its plumage, is a harsh, frightening scream.

P. 386. "Disillusionment of Ten O'Clock"

Though it should be quite clear, this poem is often misinterpreted from unfamiliarity with one or two simple facts of the past. When the poem was written (in 1915 or earlier), women's underwear and nightgowns were plain white and nothing else. A gossip columnist might report a rumor that some fashionable Parisian courtesan had a black nightgown, but respectable people, and all the people one really knew, wore white; that was what the stores sold. And ten o'clock was an average middle-class bedtime. The disillusion, then, is the poet's as he sits thinking of all the people doing the same thing at the same time in the same clothes. Even in dreams, original imaginative life has vanished except here and there among the unrespectable. (As usual, the summary is crude; the thought dwells in, not apart from, the images.)

P. 387. "Sunday Morning"
A Sunday morning, bright, lazy, and comfortable, becomes the background of a deeply felt debate between Christian and humanist values. "She" in the midst of this brightness is haunted by the dark thought of Christ's ancient sacrifice in Palestine. He asks why divinity should reside only there; why not here in one's living self, in the comfort, beauty—and sufferings too—of natural, not supernatural life. The Greek religion (Stanza III) began with supernaturalism, but it brought Jove to earth to become a somewhat human god. This so satisfied man's desires that the Christian imagination also—shepherds seeing the star of Bethlehem—brought God down to earth. Should heaven not, then, be a part of natural life instead of "this dividing and indifferent blue" of a supernatural religion?

Though "she" takes pleasure in natural life, in the birds (Stanza IV) while they are present, she still longs for the absolute, the permanent (when the birds are gone, where is Paradise?). Nothing, he answers, is as permanent as nature itself is, through the change and recurrence of life and season: no heaven, no religion "has endured / As April's green endures." "Death is the mother of beauty," he says. If there is no change, how can there be life and beauty? If the apple is eternally ripe on the tree and never falls, how can buds and blossoms come; and how can blossoms grow into fruit without themselves dying? Through a vision of sun worshipers, he foresees a natural religion for the future, a belief which will accept the transitory as the permanent; and in the end this message seems to reach "her." A voice says that the tomb in Palestine is not the entrance into eternal life; it is the simple grave of the human Jesus. We live in the natural, changing world; and this is as it should be.

P. 390.   "The Death of a Soldier"
Death in battle is reduced to two terms, stillness and motion: the poem progresses to this end. Consider the language and imagery, and the movement of the verse, with this in mind.

P. 391.   "The Idea of Order at Key West"
Irrelevant associations of a Florida resort town should not be allowed to creep into the mind, for when the poem was written Key West retained some of its earlier character of a lonely outpost of sand, sea, sky, fishing boats, an occasional freighter, a sparse town. The poem is quiet and solitary.

"She" in this poem is of course not an actual woman and probably not even a feminine symbolic figure; "she" is the Idea of Order itself.

P. 394.   "Asides on the Oboe"
The title defines the mood and spirit of the poem. The tone color of the oboe is not a clear, round, smooth tone like that of the flute but a trifle nasal and perhaps gritty, rather (though lower in key and more whining) as if a flute had sand or grit in it—a complex, not a simple tone. The poem appeared during World War II, in December, 1940, a time when the humanist had to re-examine his faith in the potentialities of man. This is the theme.

EDITH SITWELL

Dame Edith Sitwell is descended from an ancient aristocratic English family, and her poetry often reflects this background. Much of her earlier work consists of experiments in elaborate patterns of rhythm, rhyme, assonance, and movement. She calls them "abstract" poems, though their titles are concrete enough: "Clowns' Houses" and "Trio for Two Cats and a Trombone," for example. The first two selections here belong to this period. In introductory notes to her *Collected Poems* she explains her patterns of sound and the meaning—or sometimes deliberate meaninglessness—of her images. The subject of "Said King Pompey," she says, is "the triumphant dust." "Dark Song" is "about the beginning of things and their relationship"; hence the "long, harsh, animal-purring 'r's'." Though perhaps few readers find in these poems precisely what she says is there, most will find them an entertaining and witty kind of verbal music. Over the years, her writing has become increasingly serious.

T. S. ELIOT

T. S. Eliot, as even the uninitiated reader knows, is one of the major poets of our time. A few critics still dispute the greatness of his poetry itself; none disputes the importance of his influence on other poets, on modern criticism, or on the taste of modern readers. His earlier poetry, published for the most part in the decade between 1915 and 1925, shocked readers by its unconventional view of modern civilization and by its startling imagery and bold juxtapositions of material that could not be connected by logical but only by psychological modes of thought. The most important works of this period are "The Love Song of J. Alfred Prufrock," which is discussed below, and *The Waste Land*, which it has been found impracticable to include in the present volume because of restrictions of copyright. Fortunately, a recording of Mr. Eliot's own reading of this poem is easily available for those who wish to hear it as he presents it. In this and several other poems of the period, Eliot presents the modern world as a corrupt civilization in need of spiritual rebirth.

Subsequently he became convinced that Christianity, and more specifically the high-church party of the Church of England, represents the hope for modern man's salvation. Most of his later poetry is directly or indirectly founded on this belief, but it is never didactic and rarely sectarian.

Eliot's early style is characterized by its conversational inflections, its frequent literary allusions and borrowings, and its use of unpoetic modern urban imagery. His later work is less noticeably intellectual, though not necessarily easier to interpret. Its style owes more to the poetic books of the Bible and to the English Church service; it is less conversational, more musical and lyrical.

P. 399. "The Love Song of J. Alfred Prufrock"

Although interpretations of "Prufrock" vary in emphasis, the main outlines are familiar enough to be fairly well agreed upon. There will continue to be differences of opinion about details because, to a greater degree than most earlier poets, Eliot excludes mere explanation, and omits transitions, just as the mind itself, in associating ideas, often seems to do.

The epigraph comes from Dante's *Inferno*, Canto 27. Guido da Montefeltro, one of the damned, has been asked about himself and speaks from out of a flame: "If I believed that my answer were to one who ever could return to the world, this flame should shake no more. But since, if what I hear is true, no one ever returned alive from this depth, without fear of infamy I answer you." The poet perhaps implies that what Prufrock (or the poem) says will be understood only by those who share his hell. What that hell is, appears gradually in the poem.

In outline, the poem resembles a dramatic monologue of Browning in which the speaker, placed in a specific situation, talks about the situation and in so doing reveals his own character. Prufrock, however, does not speak to another character in the poem. He speaks as if to himself—his other or split self—but also possibly to the other Prufrocks of the world, who will understand him. The "you and I" of the opening and the "we," who share the same fate at the close, are appropriate to either or both of these interpretations.

The moment chosen for Prufrock's self-revelation is that of a decision. Shall he, can he, dare he propose to a woman (marriage probably, possibly an affair)? The answer is no, and so the "love song" of the title is ironic, for Prufrock is incapable of breaking through the barrier of his reserve, incapable of any genuine relationships with other human beings. The rise and fall of the merest possibility of action provides the structure or "plot" of his soliloquy. At the beginning he is irresolute: "Let us go (line 1) . . . and make our visit (line 12) . . . there will be time (line 23) . . . And indeed there will be time . . . to turn back (lines 37–40) . . . Do I dare disturb the universe? (lines 45–46) . . . should I then presume? And how should I begin?" (lines 68–69).

This see-saw of the will brings Prufrock to the point —almost—of thinking he really will make his proposal. The turning point of decision is not explicitly stated. It is reflected as if unconsciously in the imagery and even in the grammar, particularly the shifting between indicative and subjunctive moods of the verbs. At his most hopeful moment, thinking in the regular future tense, he asks himself how he "shall" do it. Shall he say he does not want to be lonely all his life (lines 70–72)? He thinks of those streets of "one-night cheap hotels" (lines 4–6), where "lonely men in shirt-sleeves," with no home and nothing to do but look on at other people's lives, lean out of windows smoking pipes. Shall he say he does not wish to be one of these?

In this moment he comes closest to an affirmative decision; but the very contemplation of an action as something he may in real life carry out brings an extreme revulsion. Retreating, he flees in spirit to the bottom of the sea; his real self is a subhuman "pair of ragged claws," a lobster that avoids impingement of the external world by wearing its skeleton on the outside. It is an image of the essentially cold solitary spirit. Prufrock's decision is crystallized in this instant. After his flight to the bottom of the sea he ceases to think of his choice in affirmative or future indicative verbs. He thinks in subjunctive and then in "contrary to fact" constructions: "Should I . . . have the strength (lines 79–80) . . . in short, I was afraid. And *would it have been worth it,* after all?" (lines 89–90). So the reader knows by the tenses and moods of verbs that the possible moment has gone by. The several-times-repeated question "Would it have been worth while?" is the dying fall of Prufrock's subsided will. It leads presently to his clear recognition: "No! I am not Prince Hamlet, nor was meant to be." Even Hamlet, without much will to act, acted finally. But not Prufrock. And he is not even the center of the piece, he reminds himself. He is no hero, no prophet, but "an attendant lord"— cautious, well-intentioned, at best an adviser, at worst almost a buffoon, but in either case a man on the fringe of life. So he will accept his fate and continue as he was, keeping up appearances and taking care of himself. But love is not for him. He knows its lure, at a distance only and with its back turned: the mermaids are "riding seaward" (lines 124–125).

At the end (as occasionally earlier) Prufrock speaks again in the plural. He has been talking of himself as "I." Now he returns to the "you and I" of the opening, since his plight is not unique. He has spoken as an individual, but the world contains others like him, and most people have a touch of Prufrock. His conclusion is therefore appropriately inclusive, though still framed in the light of his own experience. In our solitude "in the chambers of the sea," he says, "we" are capable of love ("by sea-girls wreathed"), but it is only a dream love. The approach of reality wakes us from the dream ("*human voices wake us*"), and at the touch of the real "we drown."

This is the outline of Prufrock's monologue, and through it his hell is defined. The imagery that runs through his mind completes the picture and makes vivid for the reader both his outer and his inner life. Possibly "hell" is too strong a word. Certainly it is strong for the elements of Prufrock's outer life: the social boredom, the women who chatter about art, the current novels, the innumerable teas, the measuring of one's life by that least of units the after-dinner coffee spoon. The word "hell" is appropriate, however, for the more significant internal imagery that presents him as a man paralyzed by self-distrust and agonizing self-consciousness.

These last terms are not those in which a psychologist would explain Prufrock's malaise. Eliot, however, is not psychoanalyzing Prufrock. What he presents is *what it feels like* to be Prufrock, not what is wrong with him or why it is wrong. Much of the excellence of the poem derives from the vividness with which the imagery conveys that feeling.

Most of what might be called the "subjective" images are concerned with stagnation or inaction, varying degrees of ill health, and the feeling of being split in two. The tone is set immediately by the apparently outrageous image of the evening sky as "a patient etherized upon a table"—pale, stagnant, and scarcely alive. The pools in drains, the catlike fog, and the smoke are stagnant; the evening itself "malingers," psychological malaise disguising itself as physical.

Images revealing his self-consciousness ("self-consciousness," of course, is a surface term for deeper things) range from petty anxieties of everyday life—thin hair, thin arms, thin legs that "they" will notice—to the greater, when the petty fear of servants who may snicker behind his back is magnified to the universal, the "eternal Footman" (line 88). More violent images express the extremes of his self-shattering consciousness. "The eyes that fix you," pin you to the wall like an insect specimen to be stared at as it dies, ejecting its insides at both ends in its death agony: this is rather a horrible image (lines 55–60). And scarcely less so is Prufrock's feeling as if his whole nervous system were exposed, projected "in patterns on a screen" to be examined (line 105). There is the split-self in the image of John the Baptist: Prufrock has *seen his own head* brought in upon a platter (lines 82–83). Finally, there is the image that brings back the initial quotation from Dante. Supposing he did try to make a human contact, did tell her he was "Lazarus, come from the dead" to tell her "all" (lines 94–98). She would not understand. What have those in hell to say that those outside could understand?

Eliot has presented a dramatic picture of a man who from the outside is correct, well dressed, over-self-conscious, perhaps a trifle pathetic and a trifle absurd. But Prufrock knows he is all this, and the acceptance of this knowledge dignifies him. Moreover, his sufferings are real and in some degree universal. Eliot presents him, sufferings and all, in a dry tone; the man himself is a dry man.

The poem is a complex one, and therefore many other meanings can be extracted from it or read into it. More could be said of the superficial society in which Prufrock lives. What we have given here, however, is the main thread that holds it all together.

29 and 33   works and days, visions and revisions: phrases borrowed from titles that span the entire history of Western thought, the first being one of the earliest Greek works, by Hesiod, the second a book by John Cowper Powys, published in 1915, the year in which "Prufrock" appeared.

94–95   There are Biblical accounts of two different men named Lazarus who died. One was raised from the dead. The other was not, but Abraham was asked to let him return from the dead to testify. See Luke 16 and John 11–12.

97–98   Cf. Kipling's "The Vampire" (p. 36).

117   high sentence: high thoughts. The phrase is borrowed from Chaucer's description of a scholar as thin as Prufrock.

121   trousers rolled. Robert H. Llewellyn furnished the key to this often misunderstood detail; he noted that trousers with cuffs had recently come into fashion and that the word "rolled" was used for this. Here (as in lines 42–43, 123) Prufrock is concerned with wearing precisely the right clothes.

122   Peaches used to be considered indigestible.

P. 404.   From "Landscapes"

Rannoch is a bleak, desolate Scottish moor, "a featureless tract of bog bordered by dark bare mountains"; Glencoe is a wild glen nearby, passing between the steep bare mountainsides. In 1692 certain lowland Scots treacherously attacked Macdonald of Glencoe and his highland clan. The slaughter of this Massacre of Glencoe aroused bitter feeling. Eventually there was an official investigation, but the issues of right and wrong remained confused, and the bitterness also remained long after the battle. Eliot's poem fuses the bleak emptiness of the present scene with the memory of this ancient violence.

P. 404. "Journey of the Magi"

The quotation marks at the beginning have no significance except as an acknowledgement that Eliot is using almost word for word the language of a sermon on the Nativity by the seventeenth-century bishop Lancelot Andrewes. Eliot quoted the passage elsewhere in an essay on Andrewes, commenting on the older writer's remarkable "sentences in which, before extracting all the spiritual meaning of a text, Andrewes forces a concrete presence upon us." Perhaps this is what Eliot too does in the apparently irrelevant concrete details he gives.

The specific subject is the journey of the Magi, and the ostensible theme, of course, the birth of Christ. Yet the poem says at least as much about Death. The underlying theme is the painful difficulty of changing oneself fundamentally, a difficulty so great as to make the birth of a new self seem more like a death.

24–27 The "three trees" and the "dicing for pieces of silver" foreshadow the scene of the Crucifixion and the dicing at the foot of the Cross; thus on the historical as well as the symbolic level, death is here implicit in birth.

31 The climax of the difficult journey, the seeing and worshiping of the Christ-child, is recorded in this colorless understatement which some readers have condemned as wholly inadequate. Perhaps the flatness of the language is a way of implying that language itself is inadequate for the event.

P. 405. *Marina*

Toward the end of the play *Pericles* occurs what Eliot described as the finest of all the "recognition scenes" in Shakespeare. Pericles of Tyre, having left his kingdom, sails the seas in desolate mourning for his beloved wife, whom he had long before buried at sea, and for his infant daughter Marina, born at sea and now believed dead. He speaks to no one; nothing can rouse him. In a foreign port, an unknown girl—Marina, now grown up and escaped from murderer, pirates, and brothel—is brought by chance to the ship in one last effort to rouse him. She sings, and then speaks of her past. Pericles' recognition of her is gradual and at moments half unwilling. He can scarcely bear to return to life only to be hurt, perhaps, once more. The poem distills the experience of this recognition, with its wavering advances and retreats. In lines 23–30, his oscillation between the will to live and the will to remain unalive, between recognition and fear to recognize, is expressed through the alternating imagery of the old ship—the dead past—with "bowsprit cracked," "canvas rotten," "garboard leaking," and the recovered daughter—"I made this . . . ," "Made this unknowing . . . ," "This form, this face, this life" that will live beyond him—until the past is transformed in "the awakened . . . , the hope, the new ships."

The poem has a symbolic meaning beyond its connection with *Pericles*, however, for, like "Journey of the Magi," it was published originally as one of an annual series of Christmas poems. Even apart from this circumstance of its publication, the poem itself suggests another kind of recognition and rebirth, a spiritual one.

The Latin epigraph, from Seneca's *Hercules Furens*, "What place [is] this, what country, what region of the world?" is spoken by Hercules when he awakens from a supernatural sleep, asks where he is, and gradually learns that in a fit of madness he has killed all his family. Within Eliot's poem, the "Death" (lines 6–13) from which the speaker awakens is the death of the deadly sins, four of which are represented (lines 6–13) in symbolic images—gluttony (or perhaps envy), pride (the humming-bird of the final version replaces "peacock" in an early text of the poem), sloth, and lust.

The verse form of *Marina* will repay study.

P. 407. "Burnt Norton"

This is the first of four poems later published under the title of *Four Quartets*. A detailed discussion of the poem is beyond the scope of the present volume, and in any case it is probably best read at first as a piece of "mood music," though it is much superior to what generally goes by that name and it is by no means devoid of meaning. The reader who wishes to study the poem more fully should consult Helen Gardner's *The Art of T. S. Eliot* (New York, Dutton, 1950), a book-length study chiefly of the *Four Quartets*, or her earlier and shorter essay in *T. S. Eliot: A Study of His Writings by Several Hands* (ed. B. Rajan, New York, Funk, 1948).

The poem is preceded by two quotations from Heraclitus, both of which have a bearing on the meaning: "Although the Word is common to all, most people live as if they had each a private wisdom of his own"; and "The way up and the way down are the same."

The structure suggests that of a string quartet (in particular, Beethoven's Opus 132, in five movements, has been suggested). Poetically it is a meditation in a garden, with garden imagery recurring throughout except in the contrasting third movement, where the scene shifts in imagination to the London Tube, that gray, soulless region where "the world moves in appetency, on its metalled ways," in contrast both with the supreme, still moment of serenity in the rose garden and with the "dark night of the soul" of St. John of the Cross, in which the soul meets itself honestly and from which it may rise again toward the moment in the rose garden.

The abstract theme of time present, past, and future (change and not-change, being and becoming) is stated in the opening lines of the poem and then becomes concrete, first through the "echoes" in the garden—presences from the past, faces reflected in the moment's hallucinatory brightness of the empty pool—and later in the symbol of the wheel and the dance, which unite the stillness of the center with movement of the circumference. The short lyrical opening of the second movement introduces these images of wheel and dance (as well as "the way up" of Heraclitus, and of Dante, St. John of the Cross, and other Christian mystics) as part of the imagery describing the renewal of life and elation of spirit in spring. "Garlic and sapphires in the mud" has been traced to lines in two poems of Mallarmé, one of which brings together in a nonrational sequence rubies and chariot-wheel, the other rubies and mud. In Eliot, however, the images are primarily those of New England spring: wild garlic, green and blue of trees and sky reflected in the mud puddles of the spring thaw, in which wagon wheels sink to the hub.

These few clues should be enough to enable the reader to make his way into the finely patterned structure of image, symbol, and theme. Musically the poem is one of the most distinguished pieces of modern versification. Its meter tends toward a four-stress or four-measure line, though much of it can be read as three-stressed verse; it has some affinities with Hopkins's sprung rhythm and some with the old English "strong stress" verse. It is one of the limited number of modern poems which have successfully broken away from conventional verse forms, not into formlessness but into genuinely new forms.

Glossary of Terms Commonly Employed in Versification

alliteration. Correspondence of sounds at the beginning of syllables (usually accented syllables) that are close together: "The *p*lowman homeward *p*lods his *w*eary *w*ay." Some writers confine the use of the term to consonant sounds and include initial repetition of vowels under *assonance.*

anapest. A foot of three syllables with accent on the third.

anaphora. Repetition of one or more words at the beginning of successive clauses or phrases.

assonance. Repetition of a vowel sound in consecutive or nearby words. Also, in a broad sense, any repetition of sound in nearby words: "As w*i*thereth the Pr*i*mrose by the r*i*ver."

ballad meter or *ballad stanza.* These terms commonly designate a quatrain of alternating four- and three-stress lines, with the second and fourth rhyming (*abcb*). This is sometimes printed as a couplet of seven-foot lines. The term is also used for the same quatrain with alternate rhyme (*abab*).

blank verse. Unrhymed iambic pentameter. Nominally, any unrhymed metrical verse, but in English practice the term is regularly confined to pentameter lines.

caesura. An internal pause in a line of verse, usually a pause required by the meaning.

consonance. Repetition of consonant sounds elsewhere than at the beginning of syllables: "Pa*rch*ed, he lu*rch*ed to the bar." This kind of repetition, however, is most often included under the general term *assonance.*

couplet. A unit of two lines rhyming with each other; they are usually of the same length.

dactyl. A foot of three syllables with accent on the first.

dimeter. A line consisting of two feet.

elegy. See the introduction and notes to Chapter VII.

enjambment. See *run-on line.*

feminine ending. An extra, unstressed syllable at the end of an iambic or anapestic line.

feminine rhyme. See *rhyme.*

foot. The unit of conventional English verse. It usually consists of either two or three syllables.

free verse. Verse that follows no regular metrical scheme.

heroic couplet. Iambic pentameter rhyming in couplets. Some writers confine the use of the term to the "closed" couplet, in which the two rhyming lines form an independent unit of thought or a complete sentence.

hexameter. A line consisting of six feet.

iamb (noun), *iambic* (adj.). (The adjectival form is commoner than the noun). A foot of two syllables with accent on the second.

lyric. See the introduction to Chapter IV.

masculine rhyme. See *rhyme.*

metaphor. In its narrow sense, a metaphor is an implied (not expressed) comparison between unlike things. "A shower of leaves" is a metaphor: leaves are essentially unlike rain, but one resemblance is seized upon. A metaphor may imply the comparison by taking for granted the identity of two things, as in this example where, by the mere use of the word *shower,* the identity of leaves and rain is implied. Or the identity of unlike things may be stated outright as if it were a fact, as in saying "Joe is a pig," in order to express vividly his greed. See *simile.*

In recent years the term *metaphor* has come to be used in a much broader sense for almost all nonliteral statement. It is even applied to language itself because, unlike such things as pictures, which can represent objects by imitating them, language is by nature symbolic. The word *hat,* for example, does not resemble a hat; it is an arbitrary sign, quite unlike the object, yet representing it. See also the "Introduction."

ode. See the introduction to Chapter VII.

onomatopoeia. The use of sounds that by imitation suggest the meaning, as in the words *buzz, hiss, bubble.* This is a device more commonly discussed in the classroom than actually used by poets, for there are very few genuinely onomatopoetic words.

ottava rima. An eight-line stanza of iambic pentameter, rhyming *abababcc.*

pentameter. A line consisting of five feet.

pyrrhic. A foot made up of two unaccented syllables.

quatrain. Any four-line stanza.

rhyme (or *rime*). See the introduction to Chapter II. In its broadest sense (rarely used) the term may refer to any repetition of the sounds of words. Commonly it means *end-rhyme,* repetition at the ends of lines. It consists usually in the matching of sounds beginning with an accented vowel and continuing to the end of the word: *blow, go; haul, maul; dart, apart; destroy, joy.* These are masculine, or one-syllable rhymes, by far the most common in English verse. *Feminine* or *double* rhyme occurs in lines with feminine endings, when the last two syllables rhyme (*reeling, peeling*). Triple, or three-syllable rhyme (*bearable, wearable*) is uncommon except in comic verse. *Internal rhyme* occurs when one or both rhymes are within the line instead of at the end:

> We were the *first* that ever *burst*
> Into that silent sea.

rhyme royal. A stanza consisting of seven lines of iambic pentameter, rhyming *ababbcc.*

run-on line (enjambment). A line in which the sense runs on to the following line without a noticeable pause, as in

> Dust to the dust! but the pure spirit shall flow
> Back to the burning fountain whence it came.

simile. An expressed comparison between unlike things. A simile differs from a metaphor in being introduced by "like" or "as." For one of the most famous similes in modern poetry, see the opening lines of Eliot's "Prufrock."

sonnet. See the introduction to Chapter V.

Spenserian stanza. A stanza of nine lines. The first eight are iambic pentameter, the ninth is hexameter. The rhyme is *ababbcbcc.*

spondee (noun), *spondaic* (adj.). A foot of two syllables, both accented.

synecdoche. A figure of speech in which a part stands for the whole or the whole for a part (or any similar substitution): e.g., the "pair of ragged claws" in "Prufrock."

tercet. A stanza of three lines.

terza rima. A three-line stanza or group of lines in which the middle one is linked by rhyme to the following group. *aba/bcb/cdc,* and so on. For an example, see Shelley's "Ode to the West Wind."

tetrameter. A line consisting of four feet.

trimeter. A line consisting of three feet.

trochee (noun), *trochaic* (adj.). A foot of two syllables with an accent on the first.

Index of Authors and Titles

A slumber did my spirit seal 101
After Apple-Picking 382
After great pain, a formal feeling
  comes 155
After the Funeral 311
Ah Sun-flower! 340
Alas, how soon 252
ALDINGTON, HILDA DOOLITTLE
  ("H. D.") (1886–1961) 129
Among School Children 375
Ancient Music 258
Anniversary, The 323
ARNOLD, MATTHEW (1822–1888)
  299, 300
Asides on the Oboe 394
At the Keyhole 164
At the round earth's imagin'd
  corners 331
AUDEN, W. H. (1907–   )
  177–178, 309–310
From Auguries of Innocence 342
Autumn Refrain 393

Back and side go bare, go bare 135
Bagpipe Music 263
Bait, The 316
Balloon of the Mind, The 128
Being your slave, what should I do
  but tend 190
Bellman's Song, The 95
BENTLEY, EDMUND CLERIHEW
  (1875–1956) 256
Birds at Winter Nightfall 110
Bishop Orders His Tomb at Saint
  Praxed's Church, The 47
BLAKE, WILLIAM (1757–1827)
  104, 238, 337–344
Blossom, The 327
Bonny Barbara Allan 53
Bredon Hill 159
BRIDGES, ROBERT (1844–1930)
  114, 208, 359–365
Brown is my Love 139

BROWNING, ROBERT (1812–1889)
  46–51
BURNS, ROBERT (1759–1796) 239
Burnt Norton 407
BYRON, LORD (1788–1824) 154
  252–253
Byzantium 378

CAMPION, THOMAS (?1567–1620)
  120–121
Candle a Saint, The 393
Canonization, The 324
"CARROLL, LEWIS" (Charles
  Lutwidge Dodgson)
  (1832–1898) 257
Castaway, The 66
Cherry-Tree Carol, The 63
Chimney Sweeper, The 104
Circus Animals' Desertion, The 380
Cold Heaven, The 370
COLERIDGE, SAMUEL TAYLOR
  (1772–1834) 68, 124, 284
Collar, The 333
Come away, come away, death 145
Composed upon Westminster
  Bridge 201
Convergence of the Twain, The 156
Conversion 129
Corinna's Going a-Maying 122
COWPER, WILLIAM (1731–1800)
  66
Cuchulain's Fight With the Sea 366
CUMMINGS, E. E. (1894–1962) 40
Cupid and my Campaspe played 119

Dark Song 396
Darkness 253
DAVIES, WILLIAM H. (1870–1940)
  161
Death, be not proud 332
Death of a Soldier, The 390
Dejection: An Ode 284
DE LA MARE, WALTER
  (1873–1956) 27, 107, 164–168, 255

Denial 335
Desert Places 384
Devouring Time, blunt thou the lion's paw 188
DICKINSON, EMILY (1830–1886) 155–156
Disillusionment of Ten O'Clock 386
Domination of Black 385
DONNE, JOHN (?1572–1631) 314–332
Dover Beach 299
DRAYTON, MICHAEL (1563–1631) 185
Dust of Snow 103

Easter Hymn 128
Ecclesiastes (from Chapter 12) 121
Ecstasy, The 318
ELIOT, T. S. (1888–   ) 399–407
Embankment, The 128
England 176
Engraved on the Collar of a Dog... 237
Epitaph on King Charles II 238
Euroclydon 171
EVANS, ABBIE HUSTON (1881–   ) 171, 209

Fact of Crystal 171
Farewell! thou art too dear for my possessing 193
Father William 257
Fear no more 102
Felix Randal 355
Fern Hill 131
Finding is the first Act 156
Fire and Ice 383
Fish, The 174
Flea, The 317
Follow thy fair sun 120
Fragment: A Wanderer 103
From you have I been absent in the spring 195
FROST, ROBERT (1874–1963) 103, 382–384
Full fathom five 102
Full many a glorious morning have I seen 189
Funeral, The 327

Gallows, The 162
Garden of Love, The 341

George III 256
Ghost, The 167
Good-Morrow, The 321
Great Day, The 256

HARDY, THOMAS (1840–1928) 110, 156–158
HARINGTON, SIR JOHN (1561–1612) 237
Hawk, The 371
"H. D." (see Aldington)
Heart and Mind 398
Heaven-Haven 352
Her whole life is an Epigram 238
HERBERT, GEORGE (1593–1633) 333–336
Hermit, The 161
HERRICK, ROBERT (1591–1674) 110, 122, 149
HOOD, THOMAS (1799–1845) 42
HOPKINS, GERARD MANLEY (1844–1889) 126, 352–359
Host of the Air, The 88
House, The 27
HOUSMAN, A. E. (1859–1936) 106, 126–128, 158–160
How like a winter hath my absence been 194
HOWELL, THOMAS (Sixteenth century) 138
HULME, T. E. (1883–1917) 128–129
Human Abstract, The 342

I hear the cries of evening 179
I must hunt down the prize 352
I wake and feel the fell of dark 356
Idea of Order at Key West, The 391
If by dull rhymes our English must be chain'd 207
If poisonous minerals 332
Imitation of Pope: A Compliment to the Ladies 238
In der Fremde 363
In Memory of W. B. Yeats, Part I 310
Indifferent, The 315
Inquisitors, The 261

JEFFERS, ROBINSON (1887–1962) 261
JONSON, BEN (?1573–1637) 146
Journey of the Magi 404

INDEX

KEATS, JOHN (1795–1821)
  205–207, 344–351
*Keen, fitful gusts are whisp'ring here
  and there* 205
KIPLING, RUDYARD (1865–1936)
  34–36
Kubla Khan 124

La Belle Dame sans Merci 344
Lake Isle, The 260
Lake Isle of Innisfree, The 366
*Lament for Our Lady's Shrine at
  Walsingham, A* 108
Lament of the Frontier Guard 170
Lancer 106
LANDOR, WALTER SAVAGE
  (1775–1864) 252
*Leave me, O Love, which reachest but
  to dust* 185
Leda and the Swan 374
*Let me not to the marriage of true
  minds* 196
Lethe 129
*Like as the waves make towards the
  pebbled shore* 191
*Lines Composed . . . Above Tintern
  Abbey . . .* 273
Lines: When the lamp is shattered 105
Listeners, The 107
*Little Ghost Who Died for Love,
  The* 397
London 341
London Snow 360
Look, stranger, on this island now 177
Lotos-Eaters, The 293
*Love Song of J. Alfred Prufrock,
  The* 399
LOVELACE, RICHARD (1618–1658)
  148
*Lover Compareth His State to a Ship in
  Perilous Storm Tossed on the Sea,
  The* 184
*Lover Showeth how He Is Forsaken of
  Such as He Sometime Enjoyed* 137
Low Barometer 365
Lucifer in Starlight 208
Lycidas 267
*Lyke as a ship that through the Ocean
  wyde* 186
Lyke-Wake Dirge, A 118
LYLY, JOHN (?1554–1606) 119

From Macbeth 246
MacLEISH, ARCHIBALD
  (1892–   ) 173
MacNEICE, LOUIS (1907–1963)
  209, 263
Mad Song 338
Madman's Song, The 251
Maerchen 168
Magi, The 370
Marie Hamilton 55
Marina 405
MARLOWE, CHRISTOPHER
  (1564–1593) 139
MARVELL, ANDREW (1621–1678)
  151–153
MEREDITH, GEORGE (1828–1909)
  208
Meru 380
From Milton 343
MILTON, JOHN (1608–1674) 150,
  199–200, 267
Miniver Cheevy 39
Mock on, mock on, Voltaire, Rousseau
  343
Mocking Fairy, The 165
MOORE, MARIANNE (1887–   )
  174–176
Motive for Metaphor, The 395
Mower against Gardens, The 153
Mower to the Glo-Worms, The 152
Mr. Flood's Party 37
Musée des Beaux Arts 309
Museums 263
Mutability 204
My Last Duchess 46
My love is as a fever, longing still 199
*My mistress' eyes are nothing like the
  sun* 197
*My own heart let me more have
  pity on* 356

Narcissus 364
NASHE, THOMAS (1567–1601) 141
New House, The 163
Nightingales 361
*No longer mourn for me when
  I am dead* 192
No Second Troy 369
No worst, there is none 355
nobody loses all the time 40
Nocturnal upon St. Lucy's Day, A 330
*Not marble, nor the gilded
  monuments* 190

Nothing Gold Can Stay 383
November 362
Nuns fret not at their convent's narrow
  room 201
Nymph's Reply to the Shepherd,
  The 140

O'CONNELL, RICHARD
  (1928–   ) 181
O weary pilgrims, chanting of your
  woe 208
Ode: Intimations of
  Immortality . . . 278
Ode on a Grecian Urn 348
Ode on Melancholy 351
Ode to a Nightingale 346
Ode to the West Wind 288
Of Jeoffry, His Cat 42
Of Treason 237
Old Man's Comforts, The 256
Old Men, The 166
Old Shellover 165
On First Looking into Chapman's
  Homer 205
On His Disceased Wife 200
On the Grasshopper and Cricket 206
On the Late Massacre in Piedmont 199
On the Sea 206
On Time 150
One day I wrote her name upon the
  strand 186
Out in the Dark 163
Out upon it! I have lov'd 148
Ozymandias 204

Passer-By, A 359
Passionate Shepherd to His Love,
  The 139
Peace 336
Peak and Puke 166
PEELE, GEORGE (?1558–?1597)
  141
Philomela 300
Pied Beauty 354
Poison Tree, A 339
Poor soul, the centre of my sinful
  earth 198
POPE, ALEXANDER (1688–1744)
  213, 237
POUND, EZRA (1885–   )
  169–170, 258–260
Proud Maisie 65

Pulley, The 334
Pur 178

Question 130

RALEGH, SIR WALTER
  (?1552–1618) 140
Rannoch, by Glencoe 404
Rape of the Lock, The 213
Remember now thy Creator
  (from Ecclesiastes) 121
Renouncing of Love, A 183
Rime of the Ancient Mariner, The 68
River-Merchant's Wife: A Letter,
  The 169
ROBINSON, EDWIN ARLINGTON
  (1869–1935) 37–39
ROCHESTER, JOHN WILMOT,
  SECOND EARL OF
  (1647–1680) 238
Rose-cheekt Laura, come 121

Said King Pompey 396
Sailing to Byzantium 377
Salutation the Second 259
SCOTT, SIR WALTER
  (1771–1832) 65
Sea and the Skylark, The 353
Sea Turtle 181
Second Coming, The 373
SHAKESPEARE, WILLIAM
  (1564–1616) 17, 102,
  143–145, 187–199, 246
Shall I compare thee to a summer's
  day? 187
Shall I, wasting in despair 146
She dwelt among the untrodden
  ways 101
SHELLEY, PERCY BYSSHE
  (1792–1822) 103, 105, 204, 288
Sick Rose, The 340
SIDNEY, SIR PHILIP (1554–1586)
  15, 185
Sin of self-love possesseth all mine
  eye 191
Since brass, nor stone, nor earth, nor
  boundless sea 192
Since there's no help, come let us kiss
  and part 185
Sir Patrick Spence 59
SITWELL, DAME EDITH
  (1887–   ) 396–398
Sluggard, The 103

SMART, CHRISTOPHER
  (1722–1771) 42
Snow Man, The 386
Soliloquy of the Spanish Cloister 51
Song (Adieu, farewell earth's bliss) 141
Song (Go and catch a falling star) 314
Song of Finis, The 255
From Song of Myself 110
Song (Whenas the rye . . .) 141
Sonnet: On Mistress Nicely, a Pattern
  for Housekeepers 42
SOUTHEY, ROBERT (1774–1843)
  256
SPENDER, STEPHEN (1909–   )
  179–180
SPENSER, EDMUND (?1552–1559)
  186
Spring 143
Stanzas for Music 154
STEVENS, WALLACE (1879–1955)
  385–395
Still to be neat, still to be drest 146
Stopping by Woods on a Snowy
  Evening 383
Strike, churl [Fragment] 126
SUCKLING, SIR JOHN (1609–1642)
  12, 148
Sumer is icumen in 134
Sun Rising, The 322
Sunday Morning (MacNeice) 209
Sunday Morning (Stevens) 387
SWENSON, MAY (1927–   ) 130

Take, O take those lips away 145
Tam O'Shanter 239
Tell me where is fancy bred 144
TENNYSON, ALFRED, LORD
  (1809–1892) 291–293
That Nature Is a Heraclitean
  Fire . . . 357
That the Night Come 370
That time of year thou mayst in me
  behold 193
Th' expense of spirit in a waste
  of shame 197
The rain, it streams on stone and
  hillock 160
The Soul selects her own Society 155
The world is a bundle of hay 252
The world is too much with us 202
Then hate me when thou wilt;
  if ever, now 194

THOMAS, DYLAN (1914–1953)
  131, 311
THOMAS, EDWARD (1878–1917)
  162–163
Thomas Rymer 61
Thou art indeed just, Lord 358
Three Beggars, The 90
Three Ravens, The 57
'Tis better to be vile than vile
  esteemed 196
To a Lady to Answer Directly with
  Yea or Nay 137
To a Steam Roller 175
To an Athlete Dying Young 126
To Autumn 350
To Daffodils 149
To His Coy Mistress 151
To Lucasta, on Going to the Wars 148
To R. B. 359
To the Accuser who is The God of
  This World 344
To the Muses 337
To the Virgins, to Make Much
  of Time 149
Tom O'Bedlam's Song 249
Tommy 34
Triolet (When first we met) 114
Triple Fool, The 318
Twa Corbies, The 58
Twickenham Garden 329
Tyger, The 339

Ulysses 291
Under Cover 209
Under the Round Tower 372
Upon Julia's Clothes 110

Valediction: Forbidding
  Mourning, A 325
Vampire, The 36

Waiting Both 158
Was it the proud full sail of his
  great verse 193
WATTS, ISAAC (1674–1748) 103
WEBSTER, JOHN (?1580–?1625)
  251
We'll to the woods no more 127
Westron winde, when will
  thou blow 135
What I expected 180
When I consider how my light
  is spent 200

When I have fears that I may
    cease to be 207
When I have seen by Time's fell
    hand defaced 17
When I peruse the conquer'd
    fame 111
When in disgrace with fortune and
    men's eyes 188
When in the chronicle of wasted
    time 195
When lilics last in the dooryard
    bloom'd 301
When my love swears that she is
    made of truth 198
When smoke stood up from
    Ludlow 158
When to the sessions of sweet silent
    thought 189
Where lies the Land 203
WHITMAN, WALT (1819–1892)
    110–111, 301
Who killed John Keats? 252

Who will believe my verse in time
    to come 187
Who would have thought that face
    of thine 138
Why so pale and wan, fond lover? 12
Wild Swans at Coole, The 371
Windhover, The 354
Winter 143
With how sad steps, O Moon, thou
    climb'st the skies 15
With Ships the sea was sprinkled 203
WITHER, GEORGE (1588–1667)
    146
WORDSWORTH, WILLIAM
    (1770–1850) 101, 201–204,
    273–278
WYATT, SIR THOMAS (?1503–1542)
    137, 183–184

YEATS, WILLIAM BUTLER
    (1865–1939) 88–90, 128,
    256, 366–380
You, Andrew Marvell 173